TURN UP THE RADIO!

ROCK, POP, AND ROLL IN LOS ANGELES 1956–1972

HARVEY KUBERNIK

Foreword by **TOM PETTY**
Afterword by **ROGER STEFFENS**

SANTA
MONICA
PRESS

Published by: Santa Monica Press LLC
P.O. Box 850
Solana Beach, CA 92075
1-800-784-9553
www.santamonicapress.com
books@santamonicapress.com

Printed in Canada

Santa Monica Press books are available at special quantity discounts when purchased in bulk by corporations, organizations, or groups. Please call our Special Sales department at 1-800-784-9553.

ISBN-13 978-1-59580-079-4

Library of Congress Cataloging-in-Publication Data

Kubernik, Harvey, 1951-
 Turn up the radio! : rock, pop, and roll in Los Angeles 1956/1972 / by Harvey Kubernik ; foreword by Tom Petty.
    pages cm
 ISBN 978-1-59580-079-4
 1. Popular music—California—Los Angeles—1961-1970—History and criticism. 2. Popular music—California—Los Angeles—1951-1960—History and criticism. I. Title.
 ML3477.8.L67K83 2013
 781.6309794'94—dc23
                                   2013002642

Cover and interior design and production by Future Studio

For **RAYMOND DANIEL MANZAREK**

"What do you mean the Doors have to go onstage now?
There's a UCLA Bruins basketball game on the TV, and our team is on a big run."

CONTENTS

FOREWORD

BY TOM PETTY

Here in a stream of consciousness are some random thoughts on Los Angeles.

Before I even held an instrument, I knew I had to get to L.A. I lived in a small college town in north central Florida called Gainesville. Quite a nice place in the '50s, but something inside told me that the road I was on was going somewhere else.

I was born in 1950. At the age of 10, I entered the much-explored decade of the '60s. I wouldn't trade coming of age in those years for another 10 lifetimes. But anyway, as I was saying, age 10 was a big year because for some reason the radio began speaking directly to me. Rides in the car were becoming magical, the music on the AM pop station was intoxicating. The other kids my age weren't much interested in records or the radio, confirming my belief that this music was being played for me alone. I didn't realize until years later, I had memorized the words to a hundred or so pop treasures.

Historically, rock and roll was in the doldrums in the early '60s and even the late '50s. Years later, with a greater education and broader overview, I agree the flame was somewhat turned down. But, I tell you, there was still a lot to love. Roy Orbison's voice came from another world. Ricky Nelson's was vibrant and cut through the bullshit with the most badass electric guitar. Brenda Lee's voice was pure and smoky teenage lust. Many say Elvis was already dead after the army but to me "His Latest Flame" or "Return to Sender" were feel good pills. "The Twist"? Bring it on! Check out Chubby's Cameo-Parkway single or Joey Dee's "Peppermint Twist," and tell me those don't rock! However, in those days "rock" was considered far too juvenile to be analyzed in print.

None of the artists had books written about them. I

Tom Petty at Mudcrutch Farm, 1970.

went mad trying to dig up any information on Elvis Presley. However, my radar began to pick up some big time info when I was forced to spend the day at my older cousin's house. Looking around his room, to my huge surprise, he owned rock and roll records! He told me simply that all the kids his age dug this music. TEENAGERS! I needed to find some. The 16-year-old girl at the end of my block had always been kind and tolerant of me. So I began to drop by and she turned me on to her record collection and some important info like "there are no girls singing on the Everly Brothers' records."

When I finally became a teen in '63, the Beach Boys were my favorites and guess where they came from? The shows on television ended with the announcer saying, "From Television City in Hollywood." The call of the West began for me very early. In '64 the penny dropped. Like thousands of musicians my age, the Beatles' *Ed Sullivan Show* appearance was a blueprint for building the rest of my life. English bands became the rage and that was fine with me. Rock and roll's flame had been turned up . . . way up. The U.S. artists at first seemed to have no real answer until the day I heard the transcendent guitar intro to "Mr. Tambourine Man" on the radio, coming through that tiny dashboard speaker. It was bigger than life itself. The intro spilled into lush harmonies and intriguing lyrics by some songwriter by the name of Bob Dylan. But for me, more than anything, it was the guitar intro that gave the record a profound credibility.

To be specific, a twelve-string Rickenbacker guitar played by Roger McGuinn, who had first seen the instrument in the Beatles' film *A Hard Day's Night* in the hands of George Harrison. If you, like me, were a teen at this time, you know the Beatles' impact on music and culture could never truly be covered in any amount of literary volumes. But the Byrds' music came across as totally original. This record would later be viewed by many as maybe the most important cross-pollination in the history of rock. The deejay identified the group as the Byrds from Los Angeles. By the way, so were Rickenbacker guitars. The floodgates had opened. The music business would grow leaps and bounds in L.A. The music hit new highs with the Buffalo Springfield, Love and many more you will soon read about.

I was playing the bass in a band called Mudcrutch with my longtime friend Tommy Leadon. Tommy's brother Bernie had a group with a guy from my neighborhood named Don Felder. When their group split up Bernie made the bold move of moving to L.A. In what seemed like no time, he had joined a group called the Flying Burrito Brothers. Tommy left our group for L.A. not long after, and quickly secured a gig with Linda Ronstadt.

My mind was made up around the time Bernie started a group called the Eagles that Don later joined. I was on my way west. L.A. was everything I wanted it to be, history around every corner. Mudcrutch landed a record deal after a whole two days in town. After one failed single we broke up. Later we ran into two musician friends from Gainesville and formed the Heartbreakers. Every record we have made since has been in L.A. and I have been a happy resident of the city since 1974.

The musical contributions of the City of Angels follow in fascinating detail on the next pages. I hope I've warmed you up for taking in the magic of the city and the power of its radio on innocent bystanders and rock and roll junkies alike. Harvey has done a great job on L.A. and its musical jar of lightning. Enjoy.

TOM PETTY
Malibu, California '13

PROLOGUE

I remember a late summer day in 1966. There was a company picnic at the Columbia Pictures Ranch in the San Fernando Valley. My mother, Hilda, worked as a secretary and was a fixture in the steno pool for Screen Gems and Raybert Productions, part of their television division. My brother, Kenny, and I scarfed hot dogs and Cokes, making dyspeptic noises at the parade of "hot" young talent being offered up by the studio flacks. I can't recall if we were equally scornful of the four guys introduced as the next big thing—the Monkees—whose show was about to premier on NBC. We dug Micky Dolenz, because he had starred in *Circus Boy,* so how bad could it be? But I was suspicious; another Hollywood hustle wasn't going to claim my ear the way the Rolling Stones and the Kinks already had. Then I heard a Monkees acetate, and I was a believer. Still am.

On April 29, 1967, KHJ was hosting its second annual Fan Appreciation Concert at the Hollywood Bowl. All tickets were ninety-three cents each, just like KHJ's number on the dial. What did you get for that princely sum? How about the Supremes, Johnny Rivers, the Seeds, Buffalo Springfield, Brenda Holloway, and the 5th Dimension?

I danced on Dick Clark's *American Bandstand,* cross-stepping through the Slauson Line, when the show was first relocated to Hollywood. The Mamas and the Papas and Bob Lind were the in-studio guests one afternoon. That same week, I met J. W. Alexander and Bobby Womack at the Frigate record shop on Third Street.

I first saw the Beach Boys perform at a Culver City record store appearance in 1962. It was a time for Brylcreem and A&W Root Beer. I saw them next in December 1971. Brian Wilson surfaced like a great white whale from some unfathomable depth at the Long Beach Arena to join the group onstage for the first time in who knows how long. Brian, seemingly compos mentis, was hoisted behind a Hammond organ, his

Johnny Rivers at KHJ's Appreciation Concert for the United Negro College Fund at the Hollywood Bowl, 1967.

The Frigate record store logo on a shopping bag, 1968.

Michael Nesmith, Micky Dolenz, Peter Tork, and Davy Jones on the Columbia Ranch set of "Hillbilly Honeymoon," an episode of *The Monkees*, Burbank, 1967.

pitch perfect. Pop's missing link, right there in person. The crowd was beside itself. The group was on a creative high—"Surf's Up" had just dropped—and we sat there, rapt, as a decade-long run of hits and wipeouts finally coalesced around their transcendent reading of "Long Promised Road." It was just like Elvis's *'68 Comeback Special*, a magic Hollywood moment wherein the stars finally delivered on their promise. The King held court with guitarist Scotty Moore and drummer D. J. Fontana, transposing the two Jews blues of Leiber and Stoller into a howling reverie.

It was one thing to read about your favorite bands in the *KRLA Beat*. It was quite another to swing up La Cienega to Sunset, turn left, and cruise through their world. "Hey, there's Ray Manzarek of the Doors at Norm's Restaurant, next to the Elektra Records office. Whoa, there's Mama Cass and Michelle having a nosh at Ben Frank's. Think they'll mind posing for an Instamatic, or just, y'know, hanging for a while? There's McGuinn and Hillman in matching Porsches, so cool . . . probably heading to Gower to cut some tracks. RCA is right on the way, where Jack Nitzsche is sure to be conjuring spells. Can you believe he knows Brian Jones?"

The story of the Los Angeles music scene is a tale of celebrities and unknowns, creative artists and ambitious businessmen, fast-talking DJs and patient engineers, money and love, death and immortality. It's the odyssey

KCBS DJ Hunter Hancock with Fats Domino at a taping of *Rhythm and Bluesville*, **Los Angeles, 1956.**

of how American cultural and social life changed, profoundly and permanently, and how music accompanied, or even initiated, that change. It's a part of American history. It is also my life.

One afternoon in 1992, at the California African American Museum in downtown Los Angeles, poet and activist Amiri Baraka concluded his fiery speech by exclaiming, "If anyone ever asks you to run it down, you tell them to run it all the way back." In this book, I run the history of popular music in Los Angeles—including its players, writers, producers, engineers, and broadcasters—all the way back.

In 1956, when I was a young child in Crenshaw Village, I discovered the television show *Rhythm and Bluesville* on Channel 2, hosted by DJ Hunter Hancock. Hancock was also the voice of the radio show *Huntin' with Hunter* on KGFJ. I was only in kindergarten at Coliseum Street Elementary School at the time, but it set a pattern for the rest of my life. Radio would become my soul salvation. I heard a never-ending parade of hit-making rabble-rousers, deftly spun and back-announced by a nexus of four AM radio stations the likes of which we shall never hear again. It was a universe where 93 KHJ, 1110 KRLA, KFWB 980, and 1500 KBLA offered me hope, validation, and possibilities—or, at the very least, a three-minute musical escape from the hurly-burly of adolescent angst. The revolution wasn't televised; no, it was transistorized. It was personal in the deepest way. I could listen to the revolution in my bed, through my pillow, before I slept.

In 1957, when I was a kid, I learned to swim in the new pool built at Dorsey High School, which was pretty close to our apartment. Right around the same time, my parents took me to the L.A. County Fair

KHJ Boss Radio billboard, Hollywood, 1966.

Left: KFWB DJ Gene Norman, Hollywood, circa 1950.
Right: KFWB DJ Ted Quillin and DJ Huggy Boy at a radio broadcasters event, Los Angeles, 1959.

in Pomona, and we saw Spike Jones with Helen Grayco.

In 1958, the "Seven Swingin' Gentlemen" of KFWB moved to Hollywood Boulevard, and along with the move came a shift from the *Make-Believe Ballroom* programming of DJs Al Jarvis, Jim Hawthorne, and Gene Norman to a playlist that radically deviated from their previous jazz, vocal, and instrumental sounds. Program director Chuck Blore instigated a Color Radio lineup that championed local pop and rock 'n' roll talent touted by Quillin. Joe Smith was briefly a DJ on the station in 1962.

DJs Gene Weed, Larry McCormick, and Wink Martindale introduced us to the Beach Boys, then crossed the Mersey to bring us the Beatles. B. Mitchell Reed (Burton Mitchell Goldberg) started playing LP cuts in 1965, showcasing other English imports like the Moody Blues, the Who, the Hollies, and the Kinks, previewed the latest from the Byrds, and brought the community together through the Yoda-like wisdom implicit in his vocal delivery. Lord Tim Hudson, actually from Britain, followed BMR at the station microphone.

Another DJ, Jimmy O'Neill, hosted the *Shindig!* television series from September 1964 to January '66. I went to live tapings at the ABC-TV studio on the appropriately named Prospect Avenue.

For six years, KFWB beat KRLA in the Southland ratings. Then KHJ relegated KFWB to a third-place slot in the heated L.A. rock 'n' roll radio market. In 1966,

KFWB Fabulous Forty survey.

Left: Sam Riddle inside the KHJ studio booth, Los Angeles, 1968. ♪ *Middle:* Ian Whitcomb with *Shebang!* host Casey Kasem
at a promotional appearance for Whitcomb's hit single, "You Turn Me On," 1965.
Right: Los Angeles Free Press advertisement for Peter Bergman's KMET radio program *Radio Free Oz,* 1968.

Westinghouse purchased KFWB, and in March 1968, the station was relaunched as an all-news radio outlet.

KRLA, formerly country music station KXLA, gave us information with a beat, more important than anything we were gleaning from tenth-grade algebra class. This station had changed formats in September 1959 to become *The Big 11-10,* competing against KFWB and KHJ for the Top 40 listenership in Southern California. Its DJ roster included Bruce "Frosty" Harris, Jimmy O'Neill, Sam Riddle, Casey Kasem, Charlie O'Donnell, Johnny Hayes, Dick Moreland, Bob "Emperor" Hudson, Gary Mack, Bobby Dale, Dick Biondi, Bob Eubanks, Reb Foster, Sie Holliday, Russ O'Hara, Richard Beebe (hired in '59 as the first news anchor), and Dave Hull, the *Hullabaloo*-er who opened his own club to force the playlist to expand and expose fresh talent. Kasem, as durable and empathetic a voice as has ever graced the airwaves, brought drama and desire to dedications, consolation to the lovelorn, and an inexhaustible sunniness to his afternoon television show, *Shebang!* I slow-danced with a girl from my Fairfax High School homeroom while Beau Brummels serenaded us.

Peter Bergman and *Radio Free Oz* also landed at the station. Bergman would later become (in)famous as a member of the Firesign Theatre; on KRLA, he was already tweaking convention, spinning Ray Charles's "Ruby (It's You)," Donovan's "Epistle to Dippy," and "Another Time," by Sagittarius, along with the Cyrus Faryar-narrated "Cancer" selection from the *Zodiac* astrology LP. These were fitting choices for the man who birthed the term "love-in." In the late sixties, Lew Irwin was the KRLA news director and created *The Credibility Gap,* a fifteen-minute program that incorporated music and satire along with Irwin's views and news. KRLA's expansive programming included Johnny Hayes hosting a specialty hour called *Collage,* John Gilliland's *Pop Chronicles, Sunday Night* with Derek Taylor, and the inspired spin-doctoring of Jimmy Rabbitt.

Meanwhile, in April 1965, Bill Drake and his business partner, Gene Chenault, were brought in as radio consultants to design KHJ's new Top 40 playlist. Originally owned by the *Los Angeles Times,* KHJ was long a fixture in the Southland, going on the air in 1922 and introducing Bing Crosby on a broadcast in 1931. Drake hired program director Ron Jacobs, who had been a vital figure in the radio world in Hawaii, and kept him until July 1969. KHJ had a wide open playlist philosophy and successfully competed against the three already-established and influential R & B radio stations: KGFJ, KDAY, and the immortal border radio station XERB, where Wolfman Jack howled from Del Rio, Texas. Drake and Jacobs restricted the KHJ music playlist and limited what announcers could say on-air, although Robert W. Morgan, Johnny Williams, Frank Terry, Sam Riddle, Humble Harve, Charlie Tuna, and the Real Don Steele carved out their own unique personalities. Thanks to its DJs, KHJ was fizzy and frenetic, the home of the irrepressible Steele and his "Tina Delgado is alive, *alive!*" sign-off, the companionable Sam Riddle, the inviting Roger Christian, the Brit Tommy Vance, and those incessant station IDs featuring the Johnny Mann Singers.

The "Boss Radio" format installed by Drake and Chenault soon governed other stations, like KFRC in San Francisco and KGB in San Diego, and spread throughout the United States. I heard the first airplay of the Merry-Go-Round's "Live" in 1967, and was interviewed inside their studio a dozen years later. In 1969, Jacobs produced the forty-eight-hour *History of Rock & Roll,* which aired for a full weekend on KHJ and then on other stations in the RKO chain. The Library of Congress dubbed it "the first aural history of rock and roll music." It was the radio event of the year. But in 1970, Jacobs left KHJ and teamed up with Casey Kasem and veteran radio executive Tom Rounds to co-create the syndicated radio program *American Top 40.* Jacobs had joined Watermark Inc., formed by Tom Driscoll and Rounds, who was president of the company.

Promotional supplement for soul radio station XERB, 1967.

Ron Jacobs with two of the albums from the *CRUISIN'* series he produced, Los Angeles, 1970.

Kasem pitched Ron on an idea for a nationally syndicated weekly show, based on the *Billboard* chart. Then Jacobs and Rounds worked out the details of the production, including building a studio. Rounds came up with a name—*American Top 40*—while Jacobs commissioned the construction of a studio at the Watermark offices on La Cienega. The first *AT40* show was aired on July 4, 1970.

It is KBLA, the impertinent Burbank upstart, however, which remains for me the station that best captured those vibrant times. It valiantly clung to its puny operating signal at the far end of the spectrum, and started, in February 1965, with the most iconoclastic programming on AM radio. The KBLA "Entertainers" were William F. Williams, Harvey Miller, Bob Dayton, Roger Christian, Tom Clay, Vic Gee, Don Elliot, and Dave Diamond, a refugee from KHJ who changed the tenor of commercial radio with his watershed report, *The Diamond Mine* (an oasis of sanity where my life was truly measured in mono moments). Diamond's narratives were laced

Below left: KHJ DJs Frank Terry and Humble Harve Miller at Santa Monica Beach, 1968.
Below right: KHJ DJ Johnny Williams at home in Los Angeles, 1969.

Left: **Casey Kasem at the radio syndication company Watermark Inc. in West Hollywood, 1971.**
Middle: **KHJ DJ Robert W. Morgan, Los Angeles, 1969.** ♪ *Right:* **KHJ DJ the Real Don Steele at home in Hollywood, 1969.**

with free-form beatific musings and psychedelic ravings pitched to the underground refrains of Love, the Doors, the Rainy Daze, Paul Revere and the Raiders, Music Machine, Palace Guard, the Mamas and the Papas, Strawberry Alarm Clock, Sonny and Cher, the Electric Prunes, Buffalo Springfield, the Knickerbockers, the Sloths, the Sons of Adam, the Mandala, and the Seeds.

Most memorably, Diamond hosted *Stones City,* a three-hour Sunday evening tribute to those rascally midnight ramblers. Sprung by Humble Harve, the baritone purveyor of all that was hip, *Stones City* was a shot across the bow of radio's increasingly constricted formatting, and pointed the way toward the Tomorrowland stage of the FM world.

KBLA aired its last record, *The End* by the Doors, on June 16, 1967—the same day the Monterey International Pop Festival began. In its wake, FM radio arrived in Southern California, plunging headlong into the uncharted sonic underground from the "Summer of Love" through 1972.

KPFK, the subversive Pacifica station in North Hollywood, didn't rely on advertising or corporate funding.

Operating since 1959, this radical outpost spread new sounds mixed with musical-guest-themed interview shows like *Looking In,* hosted by Elliot Mintz. Peter Bergman continued the mad laughs with his Firesign Theatre cofounders, Phil Proctor, David Ossman, and Phil Austin.

From 1967 to 1971, there was KPPC, established in the basement of a Presbyterian church in Pasadena. Program director Les Carter, a former DJ on the jazz station KBCA, oversaw the likes of Outrageous Nevada (his wife, Susan Carter), Don Hall, B. Mitchell Reed, Dr. Demento, Charles Pierce and his family, the Obscene Steven Clean (Steven Segal), Barbara Birdfeather, Jeff Gonzer, Ted Alvy (aka Cosmos Topper), Elliot Mintz, Johnny Otis, the Firesign Theatre (what channel didn't they get booted from), and the Credibility Gap (Harry Shearer, Richard Beebe, David L. Lander, and Michael McKean). The station promo spots were sung by the Persuasions. The station's powerful signal—the product of two transmitters used simultaneously—allowed them to provide some groundbreaking programming; they broadcast, for example, the stereo simulcast for the one-hour program *Leon Russell*

Left: **KBLA bumper sticker, 1966.** ♪ *Middle left:* **KFWB button, 1958.** ♪ *Middle right and right:* **KRLA buttons, 1964.**

Left: KPFK button for *Looking In* with DJ Elliot Mintz, 1965. **Right:** KPFK DJ Elliot Mintz, North Hollywood, 1966.

and Friends with the PBS station KCET. George Harrison also visited the station on November 4, 1968. In August 1970, KPPC helped sponsor Elton John's career-altering Troubadour debut.

Alas, the good times didn't keep rolling. In late October 1971, the entire on-air staff was fired. Rookies and robots were brought in that decimated the station's freewheeling spirit and legacy.

In June 1968, Metromedia in Los Angeles had debuted KMET on 94.7 FM. Nicknamed "the Mighty Met," KMET furthered the "underground" progressive rock format in Los Angeles. Initially, it was an automated format, but B. Mitchell Reed, then on KPPC in Pasadena, joined forces with San Francisco legend Tom Donahue to convince Metromedia to use KPPC's basic format at KMET. Reed, Elliot Mintz, Steven Clean, Tom Gamache, Jimmy Rabbitt, Tom Reed, Jim Pewter, Warren Duffy, Dr. Demento, Mary Turner, Jim Ladd, and Raechel Donahue, carved out a new identity for the station.

The KMET DJs played Steppenwolf, the Doors, Frank Zappa, the Byrds, the Rolling Stones, Canned Heat, Delaney and Bonnie, the Jimi Hendrix Experience, Led Zeppelin, the Chambers Brothers, John Mayall, Lee Michaels, Eric Burdon and War, Pacific Gas and Electric, Crosby, Stills and Nash, and singer-songwriters like Todd Rundgren, Tim Buckley, Leonard Cohen, Neil Young, Joni Mitchell, Harry Nilsson, Emitt Rhodes, Leon Russell, Carole King, and Dave Mason, as well as *Dylan's Gospel* by the Brothers and Sisters.

The birth of KLOS can be partially traced to a January 1968 Federal Communications Commission rule that required all FM stations to have separate programming from their counterparts in the AM bandwidth. Still in operation, KLOS (formerly KABC) first began in 1971 with a taped format that announced the term "Love Radio" with a voice track by DJ Brother John

Rydgren. Later that year, the ABC-owned station hired program director Tom Yates and launched the first album-rock format, announcing "Rock 'N' Stereo," shepherded by broadcasters like Jim Ladd and, later, J. J. Jackson.

Also on my AM dial during the 1969–1972 period was the re-vamped 1580 KDAY, which was, at the time, adopting a playlist guided by the familiar voices of Jimmy O'Neill, Johnny Hayes, Wolfman Jack, and Sam Riddle.

KPPC poster featuring the Jimi Hendrix Experience, 1968.

By 1972, KRTH, a station molded after KHJ, began programming "golden oldies," thereby creating an adult contemporary format that spotlighted proven listener favorites in regular rotation, culled from the 1956–1972 library. Robert W. Morgan was on the air that year, and gas was fifty-five cents a gallon.

These AM and FM radio stations were dimensions without borders, blessings from a church I subscribed to. They accompanied me through those "sweet sixteen" years—1956 to 1972—that have defined me and refined me throughout my entire life. Their inspiration went with me to countless concerts, through the front (and back) doors of legendary record labels great and small, and through the electric charge of interviewing a rising young talent or sharing a confidence with a musical hero.

Believe me, this was no land of make-believe; the pop and rock sounds pouring out of the dashboard of your car were dispatches from my front yard. From Watts to West Hollywood, Los Angeles was thrumming with the good vibrations of a music industry about to burst at its seams.

I heard and felt the Wall of Sound like a smack to the face, and I'm still shaking. It's become part of my DNA, and this book is my fervent attempt to unravel its mystical code. Perhaps it will help uncover yours as well.

Look back in pleasure.

Harvey Kubernik
Los Angeles, California

CHAPTER 1

THE SOUTH CENTRAL SHUFFLE

JOHNNY OTIS: What is this thing called rhythm and blues? Where did it start? How did it come about? I'm gonna try to trace it right now for you briefly. First of all, to understand the history of rhythm and blues, let's get one thing straight. It started here in Los Angeles. Now, I know other cities played a great part, but we predate them by ten or fifteen years. The music really was incubating in the late thirties and the early forties right here in Los Angeles. I feel privileged to have been here and been part of it, and I saw it come to life.

What happened was, many, many folk—black folk, because remember, this is a black art form—this music was invented, created by black artists. Black men and women from the community who had come, for the most part, from the south into Los Angeles. It was the war years, and there was a lot of work here. There was employment in the aircraft industry, and as the people came, the artists came, too. Pretty soon, we had a wild scene of blues and jazz and gospel music here in Los Angeles. Good-time music. Pretty soon, you know, they called it blues and rhythm. Then it wasn't long before they turned that around and called it rhythm and blues.

JIM DAWSON: The Flash Records store goes all the way back to around 1938. One was on Western Avenue, and the other on East Vernon. It was owned by Charlie "Flash" Reynolds. The older brother of Charlie Reynolds, Pat, was the first one to come out here from Georgia and open a camera and radio shop—the original Flash. There were a few Flash Records stores over the years. Charlie started his on Western Avenue, near the Adams section of town. Pat was teamed up with Leroy Hurte, who started a label called Bronze after he left Pat. He was the first one who recorded the Soul Stirrers in 1938, and Joe Liggins and his Honeydrippers. [Private] Cecil Gant, once hailed as "the G.I. Sing-sation," had a hit with "I Wonder." They would walk into his place first. There was a label named Black and White in Beverly Hills, owned by Paul Reiner, which had hits with Jack McVea's "Open the Door, Richard" and T-Bone Walker's "Stormy Monday."

The Jayhawks, in 1956, with "Stranded in the Jungle," happened right after Elvis Presley signed in November of 1955 to RCA, but didn't really hit until early 1956. The Jayhawks' [album] was cut in L.A. [They were] local guys, four high school kids and a slightly older guy from Brooklyn named James Johnson, and they were rehearsing in a church down around Western when their manager first heard them. Flash had just started. A later group called the Cubans was made up of singers from other groups, and one of the guys, David Johnson, went on to help form Little Caesar and the Romans, who hit later with "Those Oldies But Goodies Remind Me of You."

At that time, you had

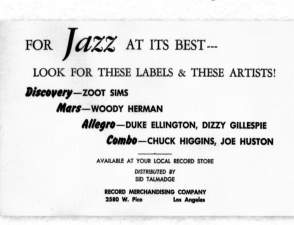

FOR *Jazz* AT ITS BEST---

LOOK FOR THESE LABELS & THESE ARTISTS!

Discovery—ZOOT SIMS

Mars—WOODY HERMAN

Allegro—DUKE ELLINGTON, DIZZY GILLESPIE

Combo—CHUCK HIGGINS, JOE HUSTON

AVAILABLE AT YOUR LOCAL RECORD STORE

DISTRIBUTED BY
SID TALMADGE

RECORD MERCHANDISING COMPANY
2580 W. Pico   Los Angeles

Opposite: Flash Records, Los Angeles, 1950. ♪ *Above:* Advertisement for jazz combo albums.

several black entrepreneurs who had record stores, and they all were operating record labels out of the back room. There was another black-owned label, Combo, from "Pachuco Hop" trumpeter and arranger Jake Porter. At that point, Charlie Reynolds was following the footsteps of John Dolphin. "Pachuco Hop" was by Chuck Higgins on Combo.

In 1948, John Dolphin, a former Detroit car dealer, opened Dolphin's of Hollywood, a record store at 4015 South Central Avenue in the Watts area of Los Angeles. Dolphin provided space just inside his store window for a remote show on KRKD featuring DJ Ray Robinson, who held live, on-air interviews and autograph signings. Youths of all colors came to his church of vinyl. Dolphin moved the store onto the corner of Vernon and Central in 1950.

The location was mandated by the fact that, in the forties, Hollywood landlords and property owners would not rent space to "Negroes" or let them own or operate any sort of business in the district. Dolphin, who came from a black township in Oklahoma, was very aggressive and not intimidated by racism. Two months later, Robinson relocated to another store and another radio station. Dolphin replaced him in the window with Jack Low and Robin

Bruin. Then came Charles Trammel, whom Dick "Huggy Boy" Hug replaced in 1953.

The entrepreneurial Dolphin formed the Recorded in Hollywood record label that same year and had a hit with Percy Mayfield's "Two Years of Torture" and Jimmy Grissom's "Once There Lived a Fool." He also released records from Jesse Belvin and the Hollywood Flames. Like the René brothers, Dolphin was a pioneer and one of the leaders of West Coast black independent record label owners, going on to establish three other labels: Cash, Money, and Lucky. In 1956, Money had a big local hit, "All Night Long," from Joe Houston.

A well-respected marketer, Dolphin went so far as to keep his shop open twenty-four hours a day, seven days a week. White teenagers discovered the mecca when Huggy Boy broke "Gee" by the Crows in 1953 and "Earth Angel" by the Penguins in 1954. In 1964, Dolphin's Money label hit pay dirt with the Larks' "The Jerk," which sold over two million copies.

JIM DAWSON: Dick "Huggy Boy" Hugg was the first white guy in the window around 1953, on a radio remote from the Dolphin's of Hollywood record store. Along with the other DJs, it was suddenly hot. It's like anything

HISTORY LESSON FROM A U.S. CITIZEN

In his book, *The Beckoning Fairground,* Ian Whitcomb plunged deeper into the socio-economic roots of the bourgeoning black music phenomenon that started in Los Angeles in the thirties:

The basics of R & B had been formed in the East and the Southwest, and now the new audience was moving from Texas and Oklahoma and Kansas into California. In 1880 there were but 188 blacks in Los Angeles County; by 1935 there were a few thousand; in 1940 the census reported more than 75,000, but most of these had come from the poorest areas of Mississippi and Alabama. It was only in the Second World War, when the war industries needed more skilled workers, that blacks (and whites) from Texas and Oklahoma were

attracted into Los Angeles. The whites, the "Okies," staked out their territory, like Southgate and Bellflower, and the blacks moved into the traditional Watts—once known as "Mud Town." And it was possible to be a successful black businessman; since the teen years, there had been black wealth in such businesses as real estate and hog farming—and music. There had been Sunshine Records in Culver City in the twenties, releasing such records as Kid Ory's "Ory's Creole Trombone"; in the thirties, Leon and Otis René started Exclusive Records with money from their hits "When It's Sleepy Time Down South" and "When the Swallows Come Back to Capistrano." By 1950 there were 200,000 blacks in L.A.

else with teenagers. They suddenly grab on to something, and it becomes viral. Even though Hollywood was here, it lagged behind everything back in the fifties. This country was still New York-centric. L.A. didn't have a major league professional baseball team until the Dodgers relocated from Brooklyn for the 1958 season. There were two popular minor Pacific Coast League teams: the Hollywood Stars and the Los Angeles Angels. All these songs were hits in town, but didn't reach a lot of people until later.

In L.A., there was a real solid scene. Take it back to Dolphin's of Hollywood, when all the white kids went down there—the L.A. cops would come down and roust the white kids, because it was threatening to the status quo.

LITTLE WILLIE G.: When I was ten years old, I went to the Strand Theater on Vernon and Main and watched the movie *Blackboard Jungle*. I heard Bill Haley and the Comets, and I was never the same.

I grew up in South Central. R & B is on the radio. Hunter Hancock is yelling about Gonzales Park. He's throwing these gigs in Watts at baseball diamonds like Wrigley

DJ Hunter Hancock hosting KGFJ's Huntin' with Hunter, Los Angeles, 1956.

Field. Tom Fears was a football player for the L.A. Rams, and he had Taco Tom's on the corner of 41st and Central. We would walk by and talk to him. He would sign an autographed picture of himself, and then we'd sell it for a nickel.

I went to school on Thirty-Fourth and Central. St. Patrick's, a few steps from the Elks Ballroom on Jefferson and Central—this is where I first heard Duke Ellington, Ella Fitzgerald, and Sarah Vaughan rehearsing for a show they were going to be doing at the Lincoln Theater. We made the trip every day to Flash Records and Dolphin's of Hollywood.

John Dolphin was shot to death in February of 1958 by Percy Ivy, a store clerk and would-be songwriter. Dolphin's assistant, emerging comic monologist Rudy Ray Moore ("Dolemite"), then helped widow Ruth Dolphin run the shop. Moore was working the little night spots on the once-glorious Central Avenue, like the now-forgotten Cotton Club.

BILL GARDNER: My mother, Althea Gardner, worked at Flash Records from 1944 to 1947. It was real close to our house on Thirty-Fifth Street.

The Cotton Club, Los Angeles, 1953.

BLUES BLOODHOUND

ELLIOT INGBER: It was located "on the magic corner of Vernon and Central." Having to take a Red Car from Hollywood [felt] like I was landing on another planet. Discovering a place where this music was available was wonderful. They carried LPs, and not just 45s. To see the music of Jimmy Reed and Bo Diddley so available . . . I heard Lafayette Thomas, who did "The Walk" with Jimmy McCracklin, and guitarist Lowman Pauling with the "5" Royales. Jody Williams, who played on Bo Diddley's "Mona," and Hubert Sumlin were on Howlin' Wolf's "Evil" and "I'll Be Around," amongst other records. Pat Hare was on the live Muddy Waters album from Newport and played with Junior Parker. I also found and heard "Big Boy" by Bill Doggett, that featured Bill Jennings on guitar. For me, it was all about 1954 to 1958, and after that, the music and the cars turned to crap.

The Flash Records shop was on Western, between Thirty-Fifth and Thirty-Sixth.

My mother worked for Daisy, one of the owners' wives. This is a world that pre-dates Elvis and rock 'n' roll in town. Black people would dance to it at parties, but for white people, it was very sexual and it was just hip to listen to it. It was like a rebellion. Elvis Presley and James Dean . . . you were not listening to the same stuff your parents were listening to. My mother loved Elvis. I liked him, but I was buying the Penguins, the Five Satins, and the Drifters—the vocal groups. Hunter Hancock would spin the Robins' "I Must Be Dreaming" and their "Cherry Lips" on the GNP record label. We loved "Smokey Joe's Café" by the Robins, who later became the Coasters.

There was a DJ named Zeke Manners with a show around 1956 on KFWB, a white dude who would play vocal groups. Huggy Boy, Art Laboe, and Hunter Hancock—plus Johnny Otis, although he was a musician, bandleader, songwriter, and activist—had the music on the radio before rock 'n' roll really hit. They were playing music primarily for Mexicans and blacks in Los Angeles. But what happened, all of a sudden—there is a complete explosion of this music. Music starting in 1946 set up the 1956 world.

Blacks were encouraged to become entrepreneurs in town, although you still weren't welcome all over and you just had your section of town, and that was it. Black people were not allowed in certain areas after dark.

The record shops were just an extension of black culture. You had the theaters on Central Avenue, and they were named after black artists, [like] the Bill Robinson Theater that was real close to Dolphin's of Hollywood on Vernon and Central.

I don't know if Brian Wilson ever made the pilgrimage to Dolphin's of Hollywood, because what happens is that once a white dude takes that pilgrimage and starts listening, they're hooked, man.

Vallejo-born and Berkeley-raised, Johnny Otis was a central figure in the development of R & B and rock 'n' roll in Southern California. He was a drummer, pianist, vibraphonist, bandleader, songwriter, and talent scout. He was also the drummer on the Charles Brown-penned

8:00

TONIGHT

KTTV 11

Now you fans of rock 'n roll rhythms can have a full hour of solid entertainment on the **JOHNNY OTIS SHOW.** See it Thursday from 8 to 9 p.m. (Co-sponsored by B r e w 102 and Maywood-Bell Ford)

Advertisement for *The Johnny Otis Show.*

"Drifting Blues" for Johnny Moore's Three Blazers.

After Nat King Cole and Jimmy Witherspoon encouraged him to relocate to Los Angeles, Otis joined Harlan Leonard's Kansas City Rockets at the Club Alabam on Central Avenue. After the Leonard band left the Alabam, Otis formed his first orchestra, which became the house band in 1944. They scored big with a saxophone-driven instrumental, "Harlem Nocturne" (which became a national anthem for strippers), later cut by the Viscounts. In 1945, Otis and his orchestra accompanied Jimmy Rushing on "My Baby's Business" on their No. 142 Billboard entity for the Gramercy Place-based Excelsior label.

In 1948, Otis joined Johnny Miller and Bardu and Tila Ali to open the Barrelhouse in Watts. It was here that Otis discovered Little Esther Phillips, Mel Walker, and the Robins. He also spotted saxophonist Big Jay McNeely, who appeared on his "Barrelhouse Stomp" in the late forties. Otis played drums on Big Mama Thornton's "Hound Dog," written and produced by Jerry Leiber and Mike Stoller.

Otis was a DJ around town, heard on KFOX as early as 1954, and a talent scout for Savoy and Dig Records. As an A&R man for King Records, Otis produced Johnny Ace's "Pledging My Love," a number-one Billboard R & B chart hit in 1955, and also played the vibraphone on the track. That same year, the Sheiks recorded the Otis composition

"So Fine," later a national hit for the Fiestas. Otis also had a stint as a talent scout for King Records, where he discovered Jackie Wilson, Hank Ballard, and Little Willie John.

Otis cut sides at Radio Recorders, a facility on Santa Monica Boulevard that was the first studio to feature an acoustic echo chamber, which introduced a "sonic signature" done there. In 1958, Otis garnered a Top 10 national hit single with "Willie and the Hand Jive," produced by Tom Morgan of Capitol Records at Master Recorders. The Otis songbook also contains additional copyrights that have gained worldwide acclaim, including "Every Beat of My Heart," done originally for Jackie Wilson and later popularized by Gladys Knight and the Pips, and "Roll with Me Henry," an answer song to "Work with Me Annie" that was written by Otis and recorded by Etta James, featuring uncredited vocal responses by Richard Berry. It was an R & B smash, but Georgia Gibbs bleached out James's song with "Dance with Me Henry." Otis had discovered James, a native Angeleno born Jamesetta Hawkins; it was her manager who rechristened her.

In November 1958, rock 'n' roll devotees tuned in to The Johnny Otis Show, *Tuesday nights on KTTV. The premiere episode kicked off with Mel Williams and the Sheiks, Jeannie Barns, Don Julian and the Meadowlarks, Marie Adams, and Little Arthur Mathews. KTLA later broadcast the* Otis *program.*

Etta James at the World Wide Concert at Long Beach Auditorium, 1968.

JIM DAWSON: Jules Bihari started Modern Records, an R & B label, in 1945. He and his brother, Joe, later started the RPM, Flair, and Kent subsidiaries. Kent eventually became their soul label in the sixties.

Hadda Brooks, who was raised in Boyle Heights, was the one who got Modern off the ground with "Out of the Blue," which went back to the forties. Jules Bihari, who began as a scrappy jukebox man, started the label mostly to record her, as well as to provide himself with a product for his jukeboxes. He sold a lot of Hadda Brooks records. Though she was billed as "the Queen of the Boogie," she was primarily a white club performer, more at home with the classics and the American songbook. Her biggest hit

VOICE YOUR CHOICE

No one in the history of L.A. radio has done more to promote the music throughout Southern California—and indeed, the world—than Art Laboe.

He was the very first DJ to spin West Coast rock 'n' roll, to merge race music under one broadcast. When Elvis Presley came to town in 1956 with manager Colonel Parker, their only interview granted was to Laboe. Art had been the first person to play the Sun records of Elvis Presley and Jerry Lee Lewis. He introduced Ricky Nelson to the radio airwaves. Laboe hosted dances at the El Monte Legion Stadium; in 1960, he teamed with Dick Clark to stage an unprecedented rock 'n' roll show at the Hollywood Bowl that sold 18,000 tickets.

Born Arthur Egnoian in 1925, Laboe graduated from George Washington High School in Los Angeles in the thirties. He began locally at radio station KXLA in 1950, which later became KRLA in Pasadena. He soon moved on to KPOP, hosting a shift at Scrivener's Drive-In that started at midnight and went to 4:00 AM. From there, it was on to co-hosting duties with KFWB's DJ Larry Finley at Ciro's nightclub on Sunset Boulevard. Laboe interviewed band leaders like Lawrence Welk, and such Hollywood stars as Frank Sinatra, Clark Gable, Lana Turner, Sammy Davis Jr., Susan Hayward, Janet Leigh, and Tony Curtis on his program *Show People*.

came after she started singing, with "That's My Desire." Frankie Laine had the pop hit. She appeared in at least three classic film noirs: *In a Lonely Place, Out of the Blue,* and *The Bad and the Beautiful.* In 1957, she had her own television show on KCOP.

Leroy Hurte was an electronics guy who built the first record presses for the Biharis at Modern. Leroy went to Jefferson High in the early thirties, where he put together a vocal group that got signed to Decca and made a couple of records. That group sort of got tied in with the Jones Boys, which in turn got involved with Leon René of Exclusive. There was a very influential music teacher at Jefferson High named Samuel Brown.

The Leiber and Stoller team had been working with the Bihari brothers since 1951, when they wrote "That's What the Good Book Says" for the Robins. So even though they were Jewish kids from the Fairfax

Advertisement for a Lowell Fulson concert, 1970.

District, they were really part of the rhythm and blues scene, and grew up in it. Maxwell Davis, an arranger at the label, was their mentor. B.B. King had been on Modern since about 1950. Lowell Fulson wrote "Everyday I Have The Blues," B.B. King's theme song, and later, on Chess, wrote and recorded "Reconsider Baby."

MARSHALL CHESS: I loved Modern Records. The Bihari brothers! I loved Jules Bihari. He'd have me over for breakfast. They were my fuckin' family. We weren't in competition. There was a great sense of camaraderie. We were all in it together, man.

I was attending the University of Southern California; I wanted to be in L.A. after going to the University of Denver. Chess had an office with Paul Gayten. He ran the West Coast operation. He was part of our family. A bandleader, songwriter, and producer. In L.A. there was this record shop, Flash Records. I used to go there all the time with Paul Gayten. I knew the DJs in L.A. on KGFJ and KDAY, including Larry McCormick and Hunter Hancock with his sidekick, Margie Williams.

JIM DAWSON: The Mesner Brothers (Eddie, Ira, and Leo) ran Aladdin, which began as Philo back in the forties, with artists like Illinois Jacquet and Lester Young. After the mid-forties, Amos Milburn and Johnny Moore's Three Blazers, featuring Charles Brown, were big hit-makers for Aladdin. The Blazers' big hit was "Drifting Blues."

There was a huge R & B scene out here. People and the media don't give L.A. credit. As early as 1950 and '51, Joe Houston and Big Jay McNeely were doing these battles of the saxophones at theaters and clubs around town. There are photos of Hunter Hancock's midnight matinees at the Olympic Auditorium. You see a lot of white kids, Mexican American kids, black kids, too. So you had this mixed crowd, as early as 1951.

BILL GARDNER: In 1951, Dootsie Williams had the Dootone Records label. In 1954, he recorded the Penguins, who later hit big with "Earth Angel." He had the Dootone Center, a little ballroom. Dootsie Williams owned some property in Compton, a combination bowling alley and a place where you could have people perform or give parties. Besides "Earth Angel," he had Don Julian's "Heaven and Paradise."

Dootsie basically made money from Redd Foxx comedy albums. He was an entrepreneur.

ART LABOE: In 1955, I resigned from KFWB. I remember on my earlier radio show that there was a lot of rhythm and blues. The kids liked it, but I wasn't allowed to play anything like that on KFWB, who wanted me to play more of the new music than interviewing movie stars.

They thought I was nuts, going back to Scrivener's. I had to package the show with Paul Scrivener, who paid KPOP for the airtime.

My show followed Hunter Hancock. He was a friend

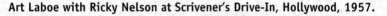

Art Laboe with Ricky Nelson at Scrivener's Drive-In, Hollywood, 1957.

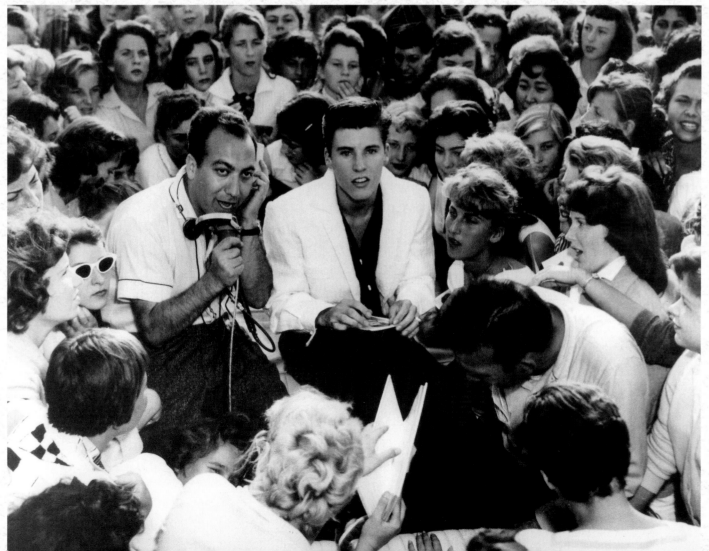

DJ and concert promoter Art Laboe with Jerry Lee Lewis at El Monte Legion Stadium, 1957.

of mine and played only black artists. Then this thing got hot and I knew all the artists to play—Ruth Brown, Big Joe Turner. The other stations had no idea of what the hell was going on.

Laboe was on the air from 3:00 AM until sunrise. After his stint at KPOP from 1955 to '59, he moved to KDAY for 1960 through '61.

ART LABOE: Hite Morgan, who ran a label and Studio Masters—which did the first Beach Boys recordings—brought me over "Confidential" by Sonny Knight. I put it on the air, and off it went. He told me I had a great ear, and said I should get into the music business.

I started Original Sound in 1957 and put out Preston Epps's "Bongo Rock." The song got on the charts, and here I was making a hundred dollars a week. ABC Paramount [Records] calls me and offers $20,000 in advance and royalties for this master of "Bongo Rock." Sam Clark, the president of ABC. He was cool. Sam said, "We could cover your record, plaster the country, and your record would die." The actress Jayne Mansfield also was on my label.

At the time, I was making money with Hal Zeiger, who was my partner. He had this place called World Wide Attractions. He came out to Hollywood one afternoon and told me that he did all these dances with Huggy Boy and Johnny Otis. Hal asked if I wanted to be involved. Johnny "Guitar" Watson was on my shows quite often. But the Latinos were heavy at that time at El Monte Legion Stadium—that's where they all lived, that's where the Latino thing came in with Art Laboe and that connection. I would play "A Casual Look" from Trudy Williams and the Sixteens, "Earth Angel" by the Penguins (which Dootsie Williams gave me), and Rosie and the Originals' "Angel Baby." Original Sound would later release the Penguins' "Memories of El Monte." I never took any money when I was on the radio, 'cause I was making a couple of thousand dollars a week at my dances.

We started doing shows at the Legion Stadium. We did them there because there was a city ordinance in L.A. that if you were under the age of eighteen, you could not attend a public dance unless it was sanctioned by the school board. There were dress codes at some places. The phrase on the radio ads was, "No Levi's, jeans, or capris, please." In El Monte, because it was an incorporated city, we played there.

Rock 'n' roll was regularly scheduled at the El Monte Legion Stadium. The room had been the site of Cliffie Stone's *Hometown Jamboree* radio broadcasts over KLAC (with Merle Travis, Joe Maphis, and others) in 1949. Hal Zeiger presented the inaugural show with Johnny Otis in the spring of 1955.

KIM FOWLEY: Local promoter Hal Zeiger booked shows for Mickey Katz, Dick Dale, some Ray Charles

U.S. tours, and Johnny Otis.

It was eons before MTV and the Internet. If a record came out and nobody knew who the band was, you could form a schoolboy version of it, and then show up and be that band and get ten dollars apiece to sing their song or lip sync it in front of a couple thousand teenagers, gang members, high school girls, drunken service men, sailors, marines. It was an audience of Mexicans, blacks, and some whites. Then you'd go home.

If you weren't good, you'd get stabbed in the parking lot, or beat up with a brick or a pipe, or shot. I came in there one time with the phony Jayhawks and did "Stranded in the Jungle" around 1957.

LITTLE WILLIE G.: I was sixteen or seventeen on my first trip to El Monte Legion Stadium. You needed a permit from the school district to go to the place. That always

Art Laboe with actress Jayne Mansfield, 1957.

used to blow my mind. Don Julian and the Meadowlarks with the Penguins were on the show, along with Tony Allen, who had "Night Owl." He was actually my neighbor. Richard Berry, Don Julian and the Meadowlarks, Jesse Belvin, and Tony Allen used to rehearse at Tony's grandmother's house. I would hear them and shine their shoes. When Jesse died in 1960, they had his funeral at the Angelus Funeral Home on Jefferson. My first singing quartet I was in, we went over there and paid our respects to Jesse, who is overlooked in history.

WHO ARE THESE PEOPLE?

FRANK ZAPPA: Don and Dewey really worked hard to put their act together. They played a lot at El Monte Legion Stadium, thrilling the audience with their zany antics. One of them would play an electric violin and double on guitar and the other one would play organ and sometimes bass, and they had this special type

of vocal harmony that was very individualistic. They had these gala costumes which were sort of Dayglo nylon with bolero balls hanging over their chest, and phenomenally huge processed pompadours going up about two and a half feet from the top of their heads, and they really had it together.

CHAPTER 2

THE BIRTH OF THE COOL CATS

n November 21, 1955, Elvis Presley, under the advice of his manager, Colonel Tom Parker, signed a recording contract with RCA Records. He had left Sam Phillips's Sun Record Company label, where his performance of "Baby, Let's Play House" had entered the national country charts. Having just been voted "Most Promising New Male Vocalist of 1955" by Cash Box magazine, Presley was on the cusp of a generational turn of events.

On January 27, 1956, RCA released its first official Elvis Presley recording, "Heartbreak Hotel." By April 28, it had reached number one on the Billboard singles chart. Two months later, Elvis and his group performed at the Municipal Auditorium in Long Beach and the Shrine Auditorium in Los Angeles.

In September, Presley entered the Radio Recorders studio on Santa Monica Boulevard with engineer Thorne Nogar. On his first night, Presley recorded four songs, including "Love Me," written by Jerry Leiber and Mike Stoller. Presley had recorded their tune "Hound Dog," first made popular by Big Mama Thornton, after he heard a novelty arrangement of it performed by Freddie Bell and the Bellboys in Las Vegas, Nevada.

Jerry Leiber was born in Baltimore, Maryland, in 1933; Mike Stoller, also born in 1933, hailed from Belle Harbor, New York. At age twelve, Leiber moved with his mother to the Larchmont area of Los Angeles and went on to graduate from Fairfax High, becoming a resident of the city's Jewish "Borscht Belt" District. Meanwhile, Stoller relocated to Los Angeles with his family and graduated from Belmont High School, near East L.A.

MIKE STOLLER: I had moved to Los Angeles with my parents in 1949. Before then, all I wanted in the world was to know, from James P. Johnson or anyone else, how to play boogie-woogie piano. I lived in Sunnyside, which was part of Long Island City.

But first what happened—there was a guy in the neighborhood who was a cartoonist, who loved jazz. He heard me when I was eight or nine playing boogie-woogie piano, and he said, "That's amazing. You should study." He's the one who set me up with James P. Johnson. I also listened to Albert Ammons, Meade Lux Lewis . . . more the boogie-woogie players, not stride players like Johnson and Willie "the Lion" Smith. I can't put my finger on the kind of influence they all had on my piano playing, but I knew what blues singing and blues accompaniment was, because I bought boogie-woogie piano records.

Above: Mike Stoller playing his piano at home, Los Angeles, 1950.
Opposite: Jerry Leiber, Lester Sill, Lou Krevetz, and Mike Stoller, Los Angeles, mid-1950s.

While attending Fairfax, Leiber started writing lyrics, filling one notebook after another. He worked at Norty's record shop on Fairfax Avenue. He heard Amos Milburn's "Bad, Bad Whiskey," and thought he could do it himself.

In 1949, Leiber and Stoller finally met. A mutual friend put Leiber in touch with Stoller, a classically trained pianist whose tastes leaned toward jazz and the challenging dictates of bebop. He was reluctant to collaborate at first, being largely indifferent to the shake, rattle, and roll of teenage dilemmas. With a shrug of stoic resignation, he sat down with Leiber and began to craft a series of hit singles that shook up lip-smacking, hip-shaking listeners around the world.

JERRY LEIBER: I went down to the Orpheum Theater [in downtown Los Angeles] to see Mike a couple of times where he worked as an usher. I started writing songs in high school with a drummer, Jerry Horowitz. He was a carrot-red, kinky-haired guy, a really nice guy. He had written a couple of songs, and he wasn't able to make two or three sessions. I hadn't seen him for a while. I ran into him at the school hall at Fairfax. I said, "Hey man, are you gonna write songs, or what?" He said he had to contribute to the family's economic situation. So he said, "You know what? I've been saving this for you. I got a gig last Saturday night in East L.A., and the piano player was real good and struck me as somebody who might want to write songs. I got his name. Mike Stoller."

I was brought up on the perimeter of a black neighborhood in Baltimore, so it wasn't new to me; it was renewed. In downtown L.A., I was a busboy at Clifton's Cafeteria, and there was this Filipino short-order chef who was stoned constantly. I didn't know what he was doing until later on, when I found out he was smoking joints. He used to chop food as fast as a latter-day sushi chef. He kept the radio going, listening to a Hunter Hancock-type rhythm and blues station constantly, and I loved it. I heard songs by Amos Milburn and Jimmy Witherspoon, like "Ain't Nobody's Business," and knew I could do that.

MIKE STOLLER: We learned from watching Johnny Otis, who was a major talent scout. We learned a lot from watching guys like Maxwell Davis, who was wonderful. I learned about arrangements from Johnny Otis just like I learned from Maxwell Davis, an unsung hero.

Johnny would yell out, he'd give you half a title or something: "That style in the third verse. Go into that lick." We had the same kind if shorthand. If we wanted a certain pattern, we'd say, "Yancey" or "Long Gone." [*Note: "Yancey" is undoubtedly a rhythm pattern played by barrelhouse blues pianist Jimmy Yancey.*]

JERRY LEIBER: After a while, we learned styles of songs that led to styles of arrangements. It was shorthand.

Leiber and Stoller's earliest songs were recorded by Bull Moose Jackson, Linda Hopkins, Amos Milburn, and Jimmy Witherspoon, who sang their "Real Ugly Woman" live on-stage one evening at a Gene Norman-produced blues event at the Shrine Auditorium. The performance was taped and commercially released as a record.

JERRY LEIBER: I did a one-day shift at the May Company department store in L.A., on the corner of Wilshire and Fairfax in 1951. I was living with my mother on Cloverdale and Pico. She handed me the mail the next day, and inside was a royalty check for $600. Man, I never had to have one of those gigs again.

In 1953, Leiber and Stoller's production of Big Mama Thornton's recording of their "Hound Dog" song brought them to the attention of Ahmet Ertegun and Jerry Wexler, executives at Atlantic Records. Leiber and Stoller were considered the first truly independent record producers in 1955, when they signed a multi-tiered production deal

Jerry Leiber, Carl Gardner, Mike Stoller, King Curtis, and Bobby Nunn at a Coasters recording session at Atlantic Studios in New York City, mid-1950s.

(songwriting, publishing, and talent scouting), along with then partner Lester Sill, under the Spark Associates umbrella label pact with Atlantic Records.

JERRY LEIBER: I took a job at Norty's record shop. Lester Sill came to Norty's one day. I looked at him and said to myself, "I've never seen a better-looking suit." He was wearing a brown suit and was head of promotion for Modern Records. Lester was the source of my confidence.

Lester took us around, and we met the little independent record labels. That was a *secret world.* Modern Records and Aladdin Records, they were in Beverly Hills. We [were] waiting for a meeting with the Bihari brothers at Modern Records. They were late, and Mike said, "Let's get out of here." We walked up the street to Aladdin Records and sold them four songs. Lester took us to the right music people, the places where they made rhythm and blues. Capitol wasn't. If we went to other labels with anyone else instead of Lester Sill, it would have been all over. But he knew. He knew the difference between songs for Eddie Fisher and songs for Memphis Slim.

You know who else knew the difference? Harry Goodman, Benny's brother. He took us later, and was great. He was not the monolithic support system that Lester Sill was, but he was a good publisher and a lot of fun, and he knew what he was doing. Harry ran Arc Music. He had Eddie Boyd and Willie Mabon. They had everything. Lester, and later, Harry Goodman, reinforced our blues vision.

Harry was lethal. We'd go into his office on Selma in Hollywood, and he'd be in a three-piece suit that cost more than the buildings on the block. He was so elegant. He was loaded sometimes, but he could function. He'd sit there with his feet on the desk. Cary Grant didn't dress better than Harry Goodman. He'd say, "Play me some shit, boys. Mike would go to the piano, and I'd rip off a song from my legal pad and start singing. "Wait a minute, that's a piece of shit," he'd say. "Throw it away. Play me something else." I'd sing another. "Throw it away in the wastepaper basket." He'd then lean over and smooth the wrinkled paper with the lyrics that were tossed. I'd ask, "What are you doin' Harry? You just said that was another piece of shit." He'd answer, "Yeah, baby, but that's the kind of shit I can use."

We formed Spark Records later with Lester Sill.

Lester introduced us to Gene Norman, a DJ who also had a record label and put on jazz and blues shows. We worked with the Robins on his [Gene Norman Presents] label.

LESTER SILL: I worked for a company called Modern Records in 1948. We had artists like B.B. King and Hadda Brooks. I went from there into a publishing and record company deal with two young songwriters by the name of Leiber and Stoller. I found the Coasters and put them together with Mike and Jerry. We had an enormous amount of success with them, and Mike and Jerry moved to New York.

Leiber and Stoller wrote (or co-wrote) virtually every record by the Coasters and their predecessors, the Robins, including "Charlie Brown," "Three Cool Cats," "Framed," "Poison Ivy," "Down in Mexico," "Along Came Jones," "Young Blood," "Yakety Yak," and "Smokey Joe's Café."

JERRY LEIBER: I must say, I really didn't think about the songs I was writing. They were the natural sort of evolution of a state of mind. I'd be walking down the street and start singing a line. I didn't think of it. It would happen. These things happened. The multiple-narrative voice I had heard before. Jimmy Ricks and the Ravens— he'd come in with a bass line. The only time I started actively thinking was when I started to edit the work and make it fit [singer Carl Gardner] better. Then you got the hysterical woman voice [of Cornell Gunter].

Jerry Leiber and Mike Stoller did not simply command the airwaves with their legions of hits. Rather, they empowered a youth culture never previously addressed in song—not by Tin Pan Alley, Broadway, or even Hollywood. Their words and music articulated the hopes and dreams of the post-war generation, which would lay the bedrock for the modern music industry in its emerging affluence. Leiber and Stoller penned, and produced in many cases, the following songs: "Jailhouse Rock," "(You're So Square) Baby, I Don't Care," "Trouble," "Treat Me Nice," "Little Egypt," "Love Me," and "Loving You" for Elvis Presley; "Ruby Baby," "Dance with Me, " "There Goes My Baby," and "On Broadway" for the Drifters; "Only in America" for

CHRONICLERS IN MOTION

DAVID RITZ: I think Mike and Jerry are an example of East Coast Jews who had an East Coast experience with African Americans and translated that experience into the culture of L.A. They went to high school in L.A. and did their first work out here. At the time, there were a lot of people taking the train back and forth from L.A. to New York. They were among the first bicoastal music people, probably the most deeply bicoastal in that they forged their style here. Jerry, the crazy genius lyricist. The idea of taking these kinds of radio shows and turning them into little playlets and having African American singer-actors do 'em, like the Coasters, was certainly developed in L.A., and they were all L.A. groups.

L.A. was a place away from New York. There wasn't the kind of "hierarchy of hip" in L.A. the way there was in New York. I'm not sure that Leiber would have been as free in New York [or] as inclined to be that kind of whimsical. Then Neshui Ertegun introduces them to Ahmet [Ertegun] and [Jerry] Wexler at Atlantic, and they go to the East Coast and become kings of the Brill Building. They are ten years older than Carole King and all the other guys and gals. So they kind of plant their flag at the Brill Building, where they become gurus.

Jay and the Americans; "Saved" for LaVern Baker; "Drip Drop" for Dion; "I (Who Have Nothing)" for Ben E. King; "Love Potion #9" for the Coasters; "Black Denim Trousers and Motorcycle Boots" for the Cheers; and "Riot in Cell Block #9" for Wanda Jackson.

CHRIS DARROW: Their ability to be white and write for the black sensibility was phenomenal. Only a handful of writers have had as much luck with that approach. Johnny Mercer, Hoagy Carmichael, Gerry Goffin and Carole King, and Barry Mann and Cynthia Weil were all able to bridge that gap, but it was Jerry Leiber and Mike Stoller who really changed the heat of rock 'n' roll.

When Leiber and Stoller entered into the writing world of early rock 'n' roll, the singing group was one of the most popular ways that a song was presented on record. It was mostly coming from the Ink Spots model. Usually there was a lead singer, with other singers who basically sang backup harmonies. Jerry Leiber wrote lyrics for the whole group. Thus, his ensembles, like the Robins and the Coasters, created characters within the group structure and gave the group a dialogue, as well as a song to sing. There was a call and response consciousness that certainly came from early Negro gospel singing. But there was also a more sophisticated storytelling interaction, where the various characters took on the roles of actors within the story. It became more like a musical on Broadway than a song from the rock 'n' roll idiom. That's what set their partnership apart from other songwriters and producers. Like Duke Ellington, who wrote for a set of musical personalities, so too did Leiber and Stoller. The Coasters were a cast of singing actors playing little vignettes of everyday life.

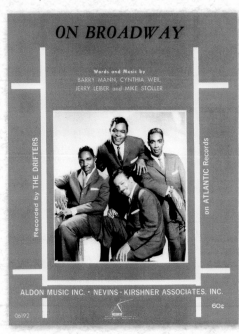

Sheet music for Leiber and Stoller's "On Broadway," recorded by the Drifters.

PETER PIPER: Ike Turner, Chuck Berry, Bo Diddley, and Little Richard might be the architects of rock 'n' roll, but Leiber and Stoller really helped create the blueprint.

The world changed when I heard the Robins and, later, the Coasters. At ages seven and eight, your mind is like a sponge. At the time, it was Gogi Grant, Kay Starr, Perry Como, and Patti Page on the dial. My father, Ralph Piper, was a jazz pianist who played with Jack and Cubby Teagarden and the Dorsey Brothers. Then the Coasters hit. This was L.A. music I had never heard before. My babysitter from L.A. High School, who was age seventeen at the time, heard them on the soul radio station KGFJ. It was a sound that liberated us. The white radio stations started playing the black music. The Coasters' "Down in Mexico" combined several sounds, and yet there was a novelty part of it. We then wanted to surf in Mexico instead of just Long Beach. At the time, I didn't know some of Jerry Leiber's lyrics were so regional. I met him years ago, and he told me the Coasters' "Shopping for Clothes" was partially based on a visit to a Robert Hall clothing shop in town.

GARY STEWART: Listening to Leiber and Stoller, their non-Coaster records often get missed. Their records had this great sense of humor, but clearly were about teenage identity. They even worked in politics and race. If you hear their song "What About Us," it can work as an Occupy Wall Street song. There are bits of that in "Riot in Cell Block #9" and "Shopping for Clothes."

The Best of the Robins album, 1956.

Elvis Presley covered twenty Leiber and Stoller compositions. "Hound Dog" was initially written at the request of Johnny Otis, the bandleader and A&R man for Big Mama Thornton who wanted Leiber and Stoller to write some songs for his acts.

MIKE STOLLER: Elvis knew the Big Mama record because he was a student, and, in addition, his first records were on Sun Records. They did the answer version, "Bear Cat" with Rufus Thomas. It was a big record on Sun. It was a woman's song. Jerry wrote the lyrics for Big Mama, and I think we recorded it in 1952, and it was released in early '53. It was a big R & B hit. Segregated radio, segregated charts, etc. But Elvis heard a lounge act doing it in Las Vegas and they corrupted it so they could sing it because they were guys. They put this rabbit thing in there that

wasn't in the original. Jerry's lyric has a woman singing to a gigolo. Elvis heard them sing it. I think the group was Freddie Bell and the Bell Boys, so he recorded it the way they had done it, lyrically.

Jerry and I actually produced, without credit, the songs that were in the film *Jailhouse Rock*. Elvis asked for us to be there. We had never met him before. He was a very good-looking young man, very energetic. I mean, he just kept going and going in the studio. He'd say, "Let's do another one!" And it would go on and on until he felt he had it. The studio was booked for the day, and we were used to three-hour sessions.

JERRY LEIBER: He loved doing it. Elvis had more fun in the studio than he did at home. He was very cooperative, and a workhorse. I thought he was the greatest ballad singer since Bing Crosby. I loved to hear him really do a ballad, 'cause there weren't too many people who could do our ballads to our satisfaction. We didn't have people like Tony Bennett or Frank Sinatra, because we were writing rhythm and blues—torch ballads—and they didn't do those things, you see. They did Sammy Cahn songs, Sammy Fain, they did those other kinds of structures that we, by the way, admired very much and love—still do. We wrote a couple, and Frank finally did one. It's unreleased. The thing is, that was what we were writing, and that's what he sang better than anybody. As far as I'm concerned, nobody cuts Little Richard on rhythm tunes. You have to go far and wide. But Presley was the ultimate in the ballad.

BONES HOWE: The first time I saw Elvis was at the Florida Theater in Sarasota, Florida, when I was in high school. He was a young country singer. He performed between movies.

I did some sessions with Thorne Nogar. He was a mastering engineer and was just beginning to get opportunities to mix when I came to Radio Recorders in 1956. In those days, RCA didn't have a recording studio of their own. So it was really the West Coast home for RCA

Records. Studio B at Radio Recorders was a big room at 7000 Santa Monica Boulevard. Radio Recorders had the wonderful echo chamber in Studio B. A live chamber in those days, not tape reverb. Thorne was very good to me and took me under his arm. I was a recordist and he asked me to do some sessions with Elvis.

I first did some work with Elvis in September of 1956, in Hollywood at Radio Recorders. Elvis drove out from Tennessee in a stretch Cadillac with drummer D. J. Fontana and guitarist Scotty Moore, with all their gear in the back seat. They came out to record with Steve Sholes, the A&R guy who was responsible for signing Elvis to RCA Victor Records in 1955. RCA was doing all their recording in those days at Radio Recorders. Elvis and the guys stayed in Hollywood at the Roosevelt Hotel or the Plaza, and later, the Knickerbocker.

In Hollywood, I saw Elvis with his buddies. It was the first time anyone ever heard of block-booking a studio for a month. We never had to tear it down. We could leave the studio at night. I worked on "Love Me" and "Old Shep." I was around the session for "Return to Sender." Elvis never stopped moving in the studio. He recorded everything live. In those days, you didn't separate people, so everyone was in the same room. Direct to mono when we started. The two-track that we did on Elvis had his voice on one track and everybody else on the other track. When we started with Elvis, there was no stereo.

As an engineer, and having played in a rhythm section, I knew the rhythm section was piano, bass, and drums. So the other guys besides Elvis were important, too. A good rhythm section is three guys joined at the hip.

Elvis would come in with Hill & Range music publishers, and he would record only their songs at Studio B. They would show up with a box of acetate dubs, and my job on those sessions, aside from running the tape machines, was that I had a turntable there which was hooked up to the playback system. I would take these dubs out, one at a time, and put them on a turntable and play it outside to him. He would signal to me, like running his finger across his throat, if he didn't like the song and I would toss it to another box. Or he would pat the top of his head, meaning play from the top again. The guys would learn the song off the demo. It was all there for me—demo, artist, song, record. The Colonel never showed up or came to the studio. Maybe once, to get some papers signed. Elvis ran the session, and Steve

Mike Stoller, Elvis Presley, and Jerry Leiber on the set of *Jailhouse Rock* at MGM Studios, Culver City, 1957.

Sholes ran the clock. "Okay, Elvis. That's 2:14. Sounded good in here. Want to listen?"

By the end of 1956, Elvis Presley had sold over ten million singles, three million EPs, and eight hundred thousand albums in the United States alone.

MALCOLM LEO: I performed chores to get my mother to let me go to see Elvis at the Pan-Pacific Auditorium. I got permission to go out on a school night. I went to the first Elvis show. He had the gold suit on, and he rolled on the floor with Nipper, the RCA Victor dog. I sat off to the side, like on county fair seats—hardback seats, like in a school auditorium.

The moment he came onstage, my heart skipped a beat and I lost my breath. Okay, the guy could sing. But there was an aura about him that was so commanding. I was staring at him and locked in. It was almost overwhelming for me because, you know, you see this guy and you see his movies, but when you see him onstage live . . . it just brought me to my knees. Elvis was it for me. He was the mountain.

The appearance of Elvis in Los Angeles not only changed the culture, but it catalyzed the whole record industry. R & B was mom-and-pop. Elvis was corporate.

I glommed onto him because I think he taught America how to fuck, first of all. But more importantly, as a kid, there was no visual identity to these groups we had heard on the radio. I had seen Elvis on television. The first Dorsey show [*Stage Show*]. I saw all of his *Ed Sullivan Show* appearances, as well as *Milton Berle* and *Steve Allen*.

The world before Elvis was the 5/4 Ballroom at Fifty-Fourth and Broadway. I had an older friend, Leland States, who could drive and he took me to see Eddie Cochran. I also saw Richard Berry. That world, for me, was West Coast R & B—it seared my brain in terms of that old 6/8 beat, and it had a style. Part of it was pachuco, but it had seeped into the white areas in and around Hollywood, North Hollywood, and Studio City.

There was another record store on Lankershim Boulevard—Dennels, near Magnolia. It had listening booths. The first three records I bought on 78 rpm were the Penguins' "Earth Angel," "Pachuco Hop" by Chuck Higgins, and "Let Me Go Lover" by Joannie Weber.

The flash point was Jefferson High School. My mind was blown by the Coasters' records, like "Down in Mexico." It catalyzed me so that when Elvis hit, I was ready. I had already gotten R & B and what that whole attitude was. The fashion, the girls, the close dancing, and the cars. The freedom.

BILL GARDNER: Black music evolved and continued to evolve every year. It was like a timeline, from the swing of Louis Jordan and then the electric guitar of B.B. King. All of a sudden, there was this explosion of vocal groups before 1954; it was now kids singing kids' music. You know, you just hear something you like, and that's it. You really didn't think of the labels on the 45s, or what went on. All this comes about later, and you notice trends or the impact of this music on things after 1956. All you are doing as a teenager is buying 45s and getting some girls over to your home and dancing.

JIM DAWSON: By 1956, the old scene was pretty much ending and going into the next phase. The whole business was sort of [the] Wild West. Everybody was a hustler, and hustling was really the name of the game. You just tried to find a record that kids were latching on to, 'cause back then, the DJs had the power to play what they wanted to play. Hunter Hancock would do record hops and find out if a certain group was hot, and he would play their record.

Back then, radio was more in touch as feedback for the kids. Request lines and song dedications. Dances originated out of L.A. in the late 1950s. One of the first popular dances where the kids sort of stood apart from each other was a thing called the Bop. There were people on Capitol like Gene Vincent and Wanda Jackson singing about the Bop. It was a hoppity kind of thing. A dance where the kids were not touching each other.

A NEW DISCOVERY AT EL MARINO ELEMENTARY SCHOOL

"The Beatles opened our minds and hearts, but Elvis opened our legs. Of course, the pill helped."
—ANDREW LOOG OLDHAM

In 1957, on October 28 and 29, Elvis Presley did two personal appearances at the Pan-Pacific Auditorium in Los Angeles. He closed the thunderous show with "Hound Dog." The Los Angeles Vice Squad filmed the second show as evidence for a possible legal action, contacting Colonel Parker about his protégé's stage behavior and graphic dance moves. The authorities caught a toned-down show with Elvis telling his ecstatic audience, "You should have been here last night!"

Ricky Nelson, Tommy Sands, Nick Adams, Carol Channing, and Sammy Davis Jr. were among the "celebrities" present. An inspiring young songwriter and record producer named Lou Adler was there, as was future music documentary filmmaker Malcolm Leo.

CHAPTER 3

THE DOTTED LINE

L os Angeles and Hollywood had many independent record labels formed in the mid-1940s and 1950s that
eventually had to deal with rock 'n' roll records when
1956 began.

KIM FOWLEY: Rock 'n' roll was brand new in 1956 and '57.
The landscape had changed a decade earlier, going back
to post-World War II and the collision and combination
of different music communities. From 1957 to 1963, you
could walk in the door at a record company, and they
would either say, "Leave" or "Sit down and play it." So you
had access. In those days, any teenage schmuck could be
the next *American Bandstand* one-hit wonder.

In 1957, I went to Beverly Hills and the Norman
Granz Verve Records office. I parked my bicycle and
[told] the receptionist that I wanted to see Norman
Granz. His label had just put out Ricky Nelson's "I'm
Walkin'." I told them I was doing "garage doo-wop," and
was instructed to "get out of our office!"

Then I pedaled my bicycle to Specialty Records, on
the corner of La Cienega and Sunset. I walked in with
the bike and demanded to see the A&R guy. "I'll see
you." It was Sonny Bono, and he gave me an hour of his
time. He played me a demo by Randy Jackson—"She
Said Yeah," a song he co-wrote under another name. The
Rolling Stones later did it. Sonny encouraged me to be
a producer one day. The first guy to give me a meeting.

Capitol Records went back to 1942. It was Capitol
Records Distribution Company. Glenn Wallichs, songwriter Johnny Mercer, and Buddy DeSylva. Mercer had
hits already in '42—"Skylark" and "I Remember You."

DeSylva was a songwriter and a production chief at Paramount Pictures, and Wallichs was the founder of Wallichs Music City in 1940, on Sunset and Vine in Hollywood. It was run by Glenn's brother, Clyde, and was
entirely separate from Capitol. Wallichs got the new-
ly-formed label distribution hustle together. Bandleader
Freddie Slack and his orchestra, featuring vocalist Ella
Mae Morse, recorded "Cow Cow Boogie" in May of
1942 and was the label's first million seller.

Capitol had the ongoing success of the King Cole
Trio. In 1956, Ken Nelson produced Gene Vincent
and the Blue Caps' "Be-Bop-A-Lula" for the compa-
ny. Throughout the 1950s and into the early seventies,
Wallichs Music City was the destination record store in
Southern California.

Art Rupe owned Specialty Records from 1949. Roy
Milton and His Solid Senders hit with "RM Blues" in
1945, and Joe Liggins and his Honeydrippers charted
with "The Honeydripper." Percy Mayfield recorded
in town, and later was a staff writer for Ray Charles.
Rupe signed Lloyd Price out of New Orleans. Rupe then
found Little Richard in 1955, off a demo audition tape.
"Tutti Frutti" happened. Larry Williams was also on
the label in the late fifties. He wrote songs the Beatles
covered—"Slow Down, Bad Boy" and "Dizzy Miss Lizzy." The Soul Stirrers, featuring Sam Cooke, were on
the label.

JIM DAWSON: The climate changed after Elvis hit
on RCA. There were some record label owners with
open-minded attitudes, like Lew Bedell at Dore. He had

Opposite: **Nat King Cole and engineer Bill Putnam at Putnam's Western Recorders studio, Hollywood, 1962.**

Larry Williams (*right*) and his associate, Johnny "Guitar" Watson, at a recording session with Kaleidoscope for their version of "Nobody," 1967.

the Superbs, early Jan and Dean, the Teddy Bears. Lew was a kind of song and dance comic. By the early fifties, he was doing radio. He got into music publishing and recording through his cousin, Herb Newman. Lew put up the money to help Herb start Era Records and become a partner. It was Herb who had the music chops, but Lew had the commercial savvy from all those years on the nightclub circuit.

The whole point of that is they were concentrating on the publishing, I think, even more than the recordings. To the bigger labels, everything these little labels put out was like a demo. If you could have the publishing on that, you could give your singles and masters to RCA or Capitol and hope the stuff got covered.

KIM FOWLEY: Simon Waronker started Liberty Records in 1955. Al Bennett was the vice president. They had a big hit record with Julie London's "Cry Me a River." Henry Mancini was on the label around then. Margie Rayburn had a hit record with "I'm Available" in 1957.

Billy Ward and his Dominoes were on Liberty in 1957. One time, I saw them rehearse in Gene Mumford's garage in Watts. Nik Venet took me. David Seville [Ross Bagdasarian Sr.] scored with "Witch Doctor" in 1958, and again had "The Chipmunk Song" later in '58. Then Bobby Vee, Johnny Burnette, Timi Yuro, and Gene McDaniels worked with staff arranger and producer Ernie Freeman.

Rock 'n' roll and the new music was now in motion and started getting taken a bit more seriously in town. We weren't New York. We were L.A., and in Hollywood, there was a sense of freedom in outlets, venues, record

AN OBSERVATION ABOUT SPECIALTY RECORDS

by Chris Darrow

Little Richard sang as though there was no tomorrow, at the top of his lungs, and played piano like no one else. His songs were so blatant that there was no doubt as to what they were about. Of all his records, "The Girl Can't Help It" is my favorite. It's the title song to a rock 'n' roll movie of the same name. The 1956 film features a number of rock 'n' roll stars of the time. Besides Little Richard, there was Gene Vincent, Eddie Cochran, Fats Domino, and the Platters, to name but a few. Little Richard's entrance in the film is unforgettable, and the song, written by Bobby Troup, is perfect for him.

The thing I don't understand is why Don and Dewey, basically two screaming Little Richards, never became a household name. They recorded a number of songs for Specialty in 1957 and 1958. Don was Don

"Sugarcane" Harris and Dewey was Dewey Terry. They were both born and raised in Pasadena, California, the home of the Rose Bowl and Rose Parade. After becoming Don and Dewey, they recorded two singles comprised of two vocals and two instrumentals for another small label. Their tune "I'm Leavin' It All Up to You," a ballad, didn't fare well, either, but became a number-one hit for Dale and Grace in 1963. Many songs that they wrote, or recorded, were covered by other artists and made the charts. But somehow, the great Don and Dewey just couldn't make it click. The Righteous Brothers were the most obvious, as they pretty much copped Don and Dewey's deal and included "Koko Joe," written by Sonny Bono, "Justine," and "Big Boy Pete" in their repertoire.

RHYTHM & NEWS DIG - 1959

Recordsville

by KIM FOWLEY

bbb **NOW THAT THE SHOCK** has passed, all of us here at DIG still feel a deep sense of sadness at the tragic loss of Ritchie Valens, The Big Bopper, and Buddy Holly. I never met Buddy or the Big Bopper, but I knew Ritchie and I honestly felt he was headed straight for the top. I'll miss them all, as will every one of their fans and admirers.

IT'S A FUNNY THING about this new trend to folk music. Before very long, the sound begins to get monotonous. The Kingston Trio started the trend with TOM-YOU-KNOW-WHO. Then Johnny Cash cashed in with DON'T TAKE YOUR GUNS TO TOWN, and the Glaser Brothers followed up with LAY DOWN THE GUN. Me, I've just about had it with these things. I'm looking for something new.

bbb **SO I GOOFED AGAIN.** I said the Five Blobs (from the record of the same name) were all brothers. Now they tell me that the Blobs are actually only one voice belonging to a "singer" named Bernie Nee. Oh well, we'll probably never hear of him . . . er, them . . . again.

ḥḥḥ **AS GREAT AS EARL GRANT** is, it's really too bad that he'll never reach his potential. Why? Because his style is just too close to Nat King Cole. Some parts of EVENING RAIN sounded so much like the King that I couldn't believe it. But what a fantastic sound E.G. has.

THE PLATTERS DID IT with their fabulous waxing of SMOKE GETS IN YOUR EYES. They started everyone off on a race to re-do the old standards. Best of the whole lot are two pressings of the same goodie, NOLA, by Billy Williams on Coral and the Morgan Brothers on MGM. Personally, I just can't go Tab Hunter's APPLE BLOSSOM TIME. Either my turntable needs oiling, or there are a lot of squeaks coming from the "Young Lover's" voice.

Bobby Darin and Buddy Bregman

bbb **I'LL SAY THIS FOR BUDDY BREGMAN.** His new show on NBC-TV may not be as "lively" as Dick Clark's ABC-TV spectacular, and Buddy may not have the ease and warmth that Dick has, but there's something about Bregman, call it charm or sex-appeal or anything you like, but there's something about him that just cries out "success"!

A NEW DANCE is being introduced on King Records. It's the "Twist", and they're hoping that it'll follow in the footsteps of the Stroll and the Bunny Hop. Naturally they've got a record (THE TWIST, what else?) to go with it. But it's not really very unusual, and it'll need a lot of luck to ever get off the ground.

labels, and distribution of product. We made the music and some of the new rules. This was the Wild, Wild, West. It also applied to the freedom that existed in town at the time. The music and sports world further emerged, and we were no longer viewed and reported on as a cow town.

The city didn't have a major league baseball team until the Los Angeles Dodgers left Brooklyn and came to town for the 1958 season. When they arrived, I put on my University High School baseball uniform with cleats and marched into the first ever game the Dodgers played at the Los Angeles Memorial Coliseum. Everyone thought I was with the team. I'm six feet five inches. I watched that baseball game in the dugout with Harold "Pee Wee" Reese, Gil Hodges, Duke Snider—he was from Compton—Don Drysdale, and Sandy Koufax. I still have the ticket. There weren't record label executives networking yet at the stadium. Just some movie stars like Danny Kaye and Kirk Douglas. At the time, the L.A. Rams football team still owned the city, along with boxer Art Aragon. It was a new frontier, on some level.

In 1959, I started at Ardmore-Beechwood, the music publishing division of Arwin Records in Beverly Hills, run by Marty Melcher, Doris Day's husband. I got future Beach Boy Bruce Johnston signed as a writer there.

Eddie Cochran was a real rock 'n' roller on Liberty. "Sittin' in the Balcony." He then hit with "Summertime Blues" and "Come On, Everybody." In 1960, I was throwing shows on Sunset Boulevard for teenagers at Jimmy Maddin's place, the Summit—later the Red Velvet, and eventually Club Lingerie. It was a jazz room with Gerry Mulligan and Terry Gibbs in the daytime. At night, DJs Frosty Harris and Jimmy O'Neill, who were on KRLA, would come down. I was the last guy to book Eddie

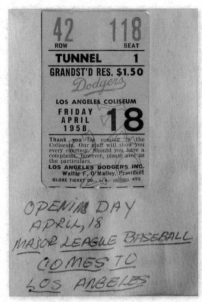

Ticket stub for the first major league baseball game at the Los Angeles Memorial Coliseum, 1958.

Dig magazine column by Kim Fowley, 1959.

Cochran before he died. He came out and did "Three Steps to Heaven." He died three weeks later in England.

In 1960, DJ Alan Freed came to L.A. and took over the market, immediately broadcasting on KDAY. He was a friend of the kids. Alan would say, "Put one hand on your heart and one

Ticket stub for the 1959 Hollywood opening of *Gidget,* one of the first surf culture movies shown on the silver screen.

hand on the radio, facing the one you love." Stuff like that. He had record hops. Alan said, "Even tough guys need music to dry hump at the CYO dances."

Chess Records had an office in Hollywood. Alan took me out to eat with the co-owner, Leonard Chess, one

CHRIS DARROW REMEMBERS DOT RECORDS

CHRIS DARROW: Randy Wood, the founder of Dot Records, started out having a mail order business and record shop called Randy's Record Shop in Gallatin, Tennessee, a town just outside Nashville. As business grew, Randy founded Dot Records to add to the increased interest that was being shown in his merchandising of music. Dot Records had regional success with "Gene Nobles' Boogie" from Richard Armstrong.

In 1955, five of the Top 10 on the *Billboard* charts were Dot Records. Colonel Parker visited the Wood house, looking for a national distributor for his Elvis record on Sun. On July 4, 1956, Randy Wood moved his offices to Hollywood and Vine in Los Angeles, next to Wallichs Music City. His love of southern music led him to Arthur Alexander, an Alabama native and one of the greats who pioneered the sound of Muscle Shoals. Dot released a song by Alexander called "You Better Move On" in 1961, produced by Noel Ball. This song was a hallmark recording of the Muscle Shoals sound, and was done by everyone from the Rolling Stones and the Hollies to George Jones and Mink DeVille. This song started the foundation for the ultimate success of FAME Studios in Muscle Shoals.

Several Dot singles were huge in Los Angeles. I discovered "(The) Green Door" by Jim Lowe and "The Fool," by Sanford Clark. Lee Hazlewood wrote it, and I heard it all the time on the radio. Ted Quillin was a DJ on KFWB from 1958 to 1961, and one of the original "Seven Swingin' Gentlemen" when the

Chris Darrow's Claremont High School graduation photo, 1962.

station first really went rock 'n' roll in the L.A. market.

In 1957, I heard "Only You" by the Platters, and then Tommy Dorsey's "So Rare." Then, like, overnight, by '58 there was Robin Luke, another Dot label guy, with "Susie Darlin'."

The vibe changed immediately. There was a television show, *Jukebox Jury*, hosted by Peter Potter in the 1956–1959 period. It started earlier in 1953 as a radio program. On the TV series, the celebs would vote "hit" or "miss." Johnny Mercer, Natalie Wood, Steve McQueen, Walter Brennan, Stan Kenton, Dean Martin, Raymond Burr, and Zsa Zsa Gabor appeared on the show.

The biggest seller for Dot for 45 rpm was Pat Boone, who practically invented the cover record as a concept. Since many records from country or black audiences were not being played on mainstream radio, guys like Pat Boone, who were white, could bring these types of songs to a larger audience. Boone did a number of covers, from Little Richard to Fats Domino, and had a very successful reign at Dot. He also had songs written specifically for him by Johnny Mercer, Dimitri Tiomkin, and Sammy Fain.

Due to the advent of the Top 40 format, songs from different genres began to appear more often on mainstream radio. In 1959, Wink Martindale had a big hit with "Deck of Cards." He then went to work for Dot as a talent scout before he was a DJ on KHJ, KFWB, and KRLA.

time after I told him I knew the Jewish dietary laws— even though I was a goy who liked to put mayonnaise on my hot dog and drink milk with it. It was a restaurant at the corner of Sunset and Gower. I was allowed one record business question at our nosh: "Leonard. Who do you pay first at your label?" They laughed, and Alan said, "You're good, kid."

JOHN WOOD: Chase Webster wrote the song "Moody River." He came out to our house. In 1961, Pat Boone was recording at the Annex on Melrose Avenue. I was running the clock. It was the first song on the 6:00–9:00 PM session. When they got the take on "Moody River," and while they were running down the second tune, my dad was excited about it and went upstairs and cut a ref [reference disc]. He had it messengered over to radio station KFWB on Hollywood Boulevard. So, when the session was over and Pat was on his way back to his home in Beverly Hills, he turned on the radio and heard the first notes of something that sounded familiar. And he said, "That's the first song we did tonight on the date." The DJ might have been Joe Yoakum. "This is the world premiere of Pat Boone's 'Moody River!'" Two weeks later, it was number six in the country, then number one on *Billboard,* and went on to sell a million copies.

It's what made the record business great. It was like sports. There was no re-mixing. There was no overdubbing. You had a three-hour session with four finished songs. One of the reasons American popular music was at a height then was that it was like sports—still is. It was real. What you heard really happened.

The Dot label had thirty-seven gold and platinum records, starting in 1950 with "P.S. I Love You," backed with "Trying" by Billy Vaughn until Jimmy Gilmer and the Fireballs' "Sugar Shack" in 1963. Randy Wood sold Dot Records to Paramount Pictures in 1958 for $3 million, but remained as the president of the label for another ten years, until 1968.

When studio owner and sound innovator Bill Putnam came to Hollywood from Chicago in 1957, his initial competition in town was Radio Recorders, which he had attempted to purchase. As United Recording was being developed and built, Putnam and producers in Hollywood often did early rock 'n' roll bookings for labels like Dot, Mercury, Liberty, Imperial, and Colpix at Master Recorders, the Bunny Robyn-owned studio at 535 North Fairfax. By 1958, Studio B at United was complete, with two reverb chambers, a mix-down room, and mastering rooms, one of which had stereo. By 1960, the Ventures were recording in Hollywood, and their instrumental sounds were enhanced by the echo chamber as well.

In 1961, Putnam bought Don Blake's Western Recorders, located next door on Sunset Boulevard. Engineers Bones Howe and Wally Heider came to the newly christened United Western, followed by Chuck Britz, Lanky Lindstrot, and Lee Hirschberg.

BONES HOWE: In 1960, Universal Studios in Chicago was an extremely successful business. I was the hot young engineer then, and [they] tried to hire me away from Radio Recorders. I resisted until 1961; then Putnam offered me so much money that I moved over to United and became one of *his* hot young engineers. Meanwhile, Al Schmitt had also left Radio Recorders and gone over to RCA.

When Bill bought Western, he walked me down the street to see the building, where Studio 3 was. Chuck Britz was an engineer there and remained there after Bill

Engineer and studio owner Bill Putnam (*right*) in session at United Western Recorders in Hollywood, 1961.

Recording session for Sammy Davis Jr. at Western Recorders in Hollywood, 1961, including: (*left to right*) William Green, Davis, Bones Howe, Larry Bunker, Red Callender (*seated*), and Buddy Collette (*seated*).

bought the building. When Putnam opened his studio, the first thing he did was that he got a new Grampian cutting head that you could pump a lot of volume into. You could really pump a lot of voltage and signal into it, and it would cut a much hotter 45 than the Altec head that everybody else used for cutting LPs and 45s. UREI was the development company, and a different division of United Recording. They developed a 1176 limiter, which I ran and did all the test runs on. He had a prototype, and gave it to me in the studio to use. United just became the place to record.

Randy Wood of Dot Records worked exclusively at Studio B at Radio. His first call engineer was on staff, and his name was Ben Jordan. The mixers at Radio were Jordan, Val Valentin, Ralph Valentin, Thorne Nogar, Don Thompson, and myself. I did sessions with Pat Boone, Tab Hunter, and Billy Vaughn in Studio B at Radio. I did the *Sinatra Swings* album, and it was fine. All the musicians knew me, and I was out in the room with them when Frank walked in. So it was very easy. On the second night of the session, Frank came in with Marilyn Monroe. That was somethin' else. She was amazing. It

was lots of fun to do. I also engineered Sammy Davis Jr. sessions. Larry Bunker, a drummer and percussionist, was one of my favorite guys.

Bunny Robyn had his tiny studio at that time, and did some sessions with Ricky Nelson, Larry Williams, the Coasters, and others; but it was best known for his mastering of "extra hot" 45s. He cut the hottest 45s in town. I mean, his 45s were a couple of 3 dB hotter than anybody else's. When they got on the radio, they shouted out. In those days, the radio was the outlet. I went over there a couple of times when he was recording Ricky [Nelson]. That was kind of his big star.

BILL GARDNER: In about 1958 or '59, the record labels, locally and nationally, they started to have black crooners who could look a woman in the eye and sing love songs. Mercury Records had Brook Benton. RCA Victor had Sam Cooke, and Jesse Belvin made "Guess Who" for the label. Then he died suddenly in a car accident. We were quite aware of Richard Berry and the Dreamers' "Bye Bye." Richard went to Jefferson High School like we did, and he wrote "Louie Louie" and "Have Love Will Travel."

KIM FOWLEY: There was the SAR Records label that started around 1957. In 1961, they were on Hollywood Boulevard [and] run by Sam Cooke, J. W. Alexander, and Roy Crain. René Hall, Johnnie Morisette, Zelda Samuels and producer Bumps Blackwell were in the office. The Soul Stirrers, Mel Carter, Johnnie Taylor and Billy Preston were on the roster as well.

Bobby Womack came out to L.A. in 1962 from the Cleveland area with his brothers Cecil, Harris, Friendly, and Curtis to join SAR. They were the Valentinos who cut "Lookin' for a Love" and, later, "It's All Over Now," which Bobby co-wrote. He had been a guitarist in Cooke's band. I met Sam Cooke a few times. We shared the same lawyer, Walter E. Hurst, who started the first music business class at UCLA beginning in 1956. Bobby Womack kept his pit bull in one of Walter's offices.

The Olympics, from the late fifties and early sixties, were fantastic. I was friends with their producers and songwriters, Fred Smith and Cliff Goldsmith, two musical geniuses who worked as promotion and sales men on the floor by day, at California Record Distributor down on Pico Boulevard. They put out records like "Western Movies" and "(Baby) Hully Gully" on the Demon and Arvee labels.

Robert Kuhn, later to be known as Bob Keane, started Keen Records in 1955. Keane then formed the Del-Fi label. An early release was the Nite Hawks' "Chicken Grabber." In 1958, Keane discovered Ritchie Valens playing in a movie theater in Pacoima. That year, Keane took Valens to Gold Star Studios in East Hollywood and recorded "Come On, Let's Go," soon followed by "Donna" and "La Bamba." Del-Fi also issued several important recordings over the next few years, including Chan Romero's "Hippy Hippy Shake," and early tracks from Frank Zappa, Johnny Crawford, Ron Holden, Brenda Holloway, and Little Caesar and the Romans.

Herb Alpert, the "A" of A&M Records, began his fabled music career studying the trumpet at Melrose Elementary School in Los Angeles. He was eight years old. "They had a room with a bunch of different instruments on a table, and I picked up the trumpet," Alpert recalled. "It took a long time before I made any sense out of it. I was very fortunate that I stuck with it."

At Fairfax High School, Alpert formed a band called the

Colonial Trio, booked for weddings, parties, and bar mitzvahs. Still, Alpert never thought he would have a vocation in music. "I was playing weekends and making a moderate sum of money, but I still wasn't sure where it was going to lead," he said. "I liked playing the horn, but I wasn't looking for music as a career when I was growing up."

After graduating from Fairfax, Alpert enrolled at USC, but the army took him in 1955. "I was in the army band for two years," he said. "I went to music school for about a year at the Westlake School of Music, and I studied classical trumpet. I went through a period of wanting to be a jazz musician, still not wanting to be a professional musician." After his military discharge, Alpert was playing trumpet around L.A. and Beverly Hills when he composed "Pick Up the Papers Even Before They Fall" for a contest staged by the Los Angeles County Parks Department in their anti-littering campaign. While waiting for an answer, Alpert met Lou Adler, a product of East L.A.'s Boyle Heights. Adler was a prize-winning essayist and a student sports writer for the Los Angeles Herald-Express.

LOU ADLER: I met Herbie just after he got out of the army. His girlfriend introduced me to my girlfriend, and that's when Herb and I started hanging out together. We started talking about what he did and what I did, and we started writing songs. I had written one song before that. I wrote school songs, lyrics to existing songs. Then I had one attempt of writing songs with another lyricist.

We cut four demos we wrote that Herbie sang on. We started going around to companies on Sunset and Vine, because the three major labels were RCA, Columbia, and Capitol, and you couldn't get into those. They didn't let us in. A&R men at the time were dealing with established songwriters. There was a music publisher, Sherman Music—before we met Bumps Blackwell—that published the four songs. We actually got covers off those demos. One was "Circle Rock" for the Salmas Brothers on Keen Records, and Louie Prima's band with Sam Butera recorded "Bim Bam."

Herb was recording as the Herbie Alpert Sextet for Andex Records—"Hully Gully" and "Summer School." Andex was a part of the Bumps Blackwell scene. Bumps was then head of A&R at Keen Records, and Herb and I apprenticed under him at the label.

I first met Sam Cooke at the Orpheum Theater in

Herb Alpert and the Tijuana Brass: (*left to right*)
Lou Pagani, Pat Sanatore, John Pisano, Bob Edmonson, Nick Ceroli, Herb Alpert, and Tonni Kalash.

downtown L.A., where LaVern Baker was performing. Sam said, "So, you're the new kid in town . . . "

BONES HOWE: Bumps Blackwell hired Lou and Herb to listen to demos as apprentice A&R men and tell him what young people would want to buy. That was the beginning of that whole Sam Cooke thing. Herb Alpert and Lou Adler would arrive, sitting in the hallway at Radio Recorders. Herbie had his horn in a brown paper bag.

Bob Keane first heard Sam Cooke singing in the Soul Stirrers in 1957. Cooke then notched a hit pop single, "You Send Me," under the name Dale Cook on the Keen label. The nom de disque was an attempt to keep Sam's voice and identity from the sanctified music community. No one was fooled. By the end of December '57, the record had sold close to two million copies.

In 1960, Cooke moved to RCA Records, and Adler and Alpert wrote their first song for him, "All of My Life." After that, they collaborated with him to compose "(What) a Wonderful World."

LOU ADLER: Herbie and I started writing "(What a) Wonderful World," and then I finished it with Sam at the Knickerbocker Hotel in Hollywood. Sam taught me how to communicate with musicians when you're not a musician. He gave me a body language for working in the studio. I went out with him as kind of a road manager with the Soul Stirrers—that included Lou Rawls. Herbie and I produced Rawls's first pop record.

Sam also introduced me to a black world in Los Angeles, because I roomed with him for about eight months, including the Knickerbocker. I learned more about the music and the people than I'd ever known, and I never experienced one bit of racial intolerance. People took me in because I was with Sam. We would go to the 5/4 Ballroom. Sam sang at my wedding [to Shelley Fabares in 1964].

No one really looks at Sam as a singer-songwriter. His songs were not always personal experiences. Like "Twistin' the Night Away." At Keen, I also produced a recording session with Johnny "Guitar" Watson on "Deana Baby." First of all—Sam's instrument. As a vocalist, he influenced Jackie Wilson and Otis Redding. He was the voice of that era. A tremendous vocalist. Also, he had a tremendous charisma that just spewed out of him in the recording studio, the stage, wherever he was. One time we went to the California Club to see Ed Townsend, who had a hit with "For Your Love." He was up there singing that song, and, of course, getting a response. [He] tried to get Sam to come up onstage. We were just going for a night out. Finally, Sam came up and went into some gospel spiritual number. It was the first time that I saw the entire female audience get out of their seats and on top of their chairs. That was amazing. Charisma, I think, explains Sam in the right way. He had it walking into a recording studio, and he had it onstage. There was just something about him that was so beautiful.

BONES HOWE: When Sam went to RCA, Radio Record-ers was the de facto studio in Hollywood. I worked with Sam and ran the tape machines on one of his RCA al-bums. He was a sweetheart of a guy. He was a singer and a songwriter. He brought in a lot of his stuff. In the beginning, RCA was throwing stuff at him. Sam did so many of the things he wrote, and they started to be hits. At that point, you don't mess with success.

Sam Cooke, 1962.

BOBBY WOMACK: Sam Cooke was the first guy who introduced me to Nat King Cole at RCA on Sunset. Nat was coming down the stairway, and Sam was a very likeable guy and he knew everybody. "Hey Nat, I want you to meet Bobby Wom-ack. He's gonna be big one day. He sings with a group called the Val-entinos." They were talking like they knew each other for a hun-dred years. "Pleasure meeting you, man." Then I walked away, thinking about it.

"Man, I just met Nat King Cole . . . "

To me, nobody sounded like Lou Rawls. He had his own style. Totally different and very comfortable in that. Lou and Sam were very close, and he and Sam went to school together.

Earl Palmer was always on the Sam Cooke sessions. He was a hell of a drummer. I knew René Hall; he was a hell of a soulful arranger. We worked with Sam together. Sam had a big influence on anybody. I mean, to me, can-cer would be good if Sam gave it out. I'm serious.

I bought a lot of equipment at Wallichs Music City in Hollywood and met a lot of people. Like this guitar player, a hell of a player. He did "Moonlight in Vermont." Kenny Burrell! I would follow him around. "Who is this guy?" Damn, that cat was so bad. This guy is a one-man band, and could sit onstage with a drummer and bass and kill them. I liked Barney Kessel, but Kenny was my hero.

KIM FOWLEY: I met Sam Cooke a few times. Walter E. Hurst was our lawyer, and he handled Sam, J. W. Al-exander, Bobby Womack, Eddie Cochran, Sharon Shee-ley, Jimmy O'Neill, Eden Ahbez, and Roger Corman. In 1960 or '61, Sam and I did separate panel discussions at UCLA in the first-ever music business class Walter taught on campus. Sam would cruise around on Friday nights in Hollywood, in a green Maserati or Ferrari with the top down so everyone could see him.

After Sam moved over to RCA Records, I remember there was all this frustration that René Hall wasn't as involved in the RCA records as he'd been previously in the Keen records. René's wife, Sugar, worked for me and ran my office. Around the same time, my secretary was Lois Duncan, married to Cleve Duncan, the lead singer of the Penguins.

Sam was probably hustled in the way they used to hustle you in the very early sixties, which was to say, "If you stay in L.A., perceived by New Yorkers as a sec-ond-class music city, you'll be a piece of shit forever." When I first went to New York City with Gary Paxton off our hit single of "Alley-Oop," we heard that same rap. Mike Stoller wanted to write and produce the follow-up Hollywood Argyles record. We had a meeting with him in his New York office. We passed on his suggestion. Gary and I thought that, because we had a hit single, we could do it ourselves again. We failed.

CHAPTER 4

THE NEW KIDS ON THE BLOCK

Harvey Phillip Spector was born in the Bronx in 1941. His father, Ben, was an ironworker in Brooklyn who had taken his own life when Phil was nine years old. By the mid-fifties, Spector had relocated to the Fairfax District in Los Angeles with his family, residing in a Hayworth Avenue apartment he shared with his widowed mother, Bertha, and sister, Shirley.

As a teenager, Spector was glued to the sounds of the AM radio dial. He loved Patti Page singing "I Went to Your Wedding," and the Chordettes' "Born to Be with You." He worshiped songs like "60 Minute Man" and "Treasure of Love."

Spector had begun to play the guitar as a student at John Burroughs Junior High in L.A.'s Wilshire District. He then attended Fairfax High School beginning in 1954. Phil never liked the name Harvey, which he went by throughout his childhood in New York. He dropped it in favor of his middle name, thereby demonstrating a willfulness that would come to define his career.

In 1955, Spector's mother and sister took him to see Ella Fitzgerald at a local nightclub, with noted jazz guitarist Barney Kessel in the backing group. Shortly afterward, Shirley tracked down Barney at a studio and pressed him for career advice over pie at Du-pars Restaurant on Hollywood and Vine.

DAN KESSEL: When Phil Spector was fourteen, he wanted to become a jazz guitarist. My dad advised him to become a songwriter and producer instead. He further helped Phil by playing on his earliest Gold Star Studios demos for free. My dad had already played on "Cry Me a River" with Julie London, "Return to Sender" and "Can't Help Falling in Love with You" [by Elvis], "Rockin' Robin" by Bobby Day, and various hits with Leiber and Stoller and the Coasters.

Barney was head of A&R for Verve Records in Beverly Hills from 1956 to 1960. Mo Ostin was the controller/accountant. Verve president Norman Granz asked Barney to find some "rock 'n' roll product," because his distributors were asking for it when Elvis Presley hit. Barney, years earlier, had played in a band with Ozzie Nelson.

Barney saw Ricky on *The Adventures of Ozzie and Harriet* one evening when Ricky was playing drums on the show. Barney called Ozzie, Ricky's father/manager, and put Ricky Nelson's recording deal together. He suggested they have the kid out front, and put a guitar in his hand. He helped engineer the child star as a TV attraction into the national hit parade, setting the table for numerous TV kids to cut records. Barney then set about producing Ricky's first three major hits, contained

barney Kessel
HI-FI

His First Recording for
CONTEMPORARY RECORDS

C2508 Just Squeeze Me, Tenderly, Bernardo, Vicky's Dream, Salute To Charlie Christian, I Let A Song Go Out Of My Heart, What Is There To Say?, Lullaby Of Birdland.

10" LONG PLAY, AND DOUBLE EXTENDED PLAY CEP 2-08.

A TRUE HI-FI RECORDING · + 1 db from 20 to 15,000 CYCLES · AES CURVE

OTHER GREAT CONTEMPORARY ARTISTS

C2501 HOWARD RUMSEY'S LIGHTHOUSE ALL-STARS, VOL. 2
C2502 HENRI RENAUD'S ALL STARS—MODERN SOUNDS: FRANCE
C2503 SHELLY MANNE & HIS MEN
C2504 DIZZY GILLESPIE—DIZZY IN PARIS
C2505 LARS GULLIN—MODERN SOUNDS: SWEDEN
C2506 HOWARD RUMSEY'S LIGHTHOUSE ALL-STARS, VOL. 3
C2507 MARY LOU WILLIAMS—PIANO '53
C3501 HOWARD RUMSEY'S LIGHTHOUSE ALL-STARS, VOL. 1 (12" Long Play)

Write for free catalog.

CONTEMPORARY RECORDS 8481 MELROSE PLACE
LOS ANGELES 46, CALIFORNIA

Above: Contemporary Records promotional supplement for Barney Kessel, 1959.
Opposite: Phil Spector at a Marvin Gaye concert at the Trip, Hollywood, 1965.

on two singles, when Nelson was still sixteen.

The initial release in April 1957 ended up being a double A-side. The first A-side, "I'm Walkin'," was written by Fats Domino and Dave Bartholomew and was originally a hit for Fats on Imperial Records. Barney recorded it against the protests of Ozzie Nelson and Verve Records owner Norman Granz, who thought Ricky shouldn't cover a recent hit. But Barney had already determined that Ricky gave his best performance on it, and Barney liked the combination of Ricky with the R & B/rock 'n' roll/Fats Domino-inspired sound. BK decided that, not only would they record it, but it would also be Ricky's debut release. Barney wrote the arrangements, assembled the musicians—including himself on guitar—and produced all the sessions. It hit the Top 40 and went to number four.

In 1957, Spector, along with his future Teddy Bears bandmate Marshall Lieb, appeared on the local KTLA-TV program Rocket to Stardom, *sponsored by salesman Bob Yaekel, who used to hawk Oldsmobiles during the broadcast from his showroom. The duo sang "In the Still of the Night." Spector then formed and recorded with the Phil Harvey Band.*

Lead Teddy Bears singer Annette Kleinbard,
Los Angeles, 1965.

CAROL CONNERS (formerly Annette Kleinbard): I was at Louis Pasteur Junior High School, and Phil was dating my best friend at the time, Donna Kass. I was always singing, even if the ice cream truck drove by, or in algebra class. Phil was going out of high school when I was coming in. The bottom line is that he fell in love with my voice. He said to me one day, "I love your voice. Do you have ten dollars?" "Ten dollars? I don't have ten cents." He wanted me to help out for a recording session. So Phil says to me, "I'm gonna write a song for your voice, but you have to come up with ten dollars."

I go to my mom and dad. "Can I have ten dollars?"

My mom suggested I do my homework, but my father wanted to hear what I had to say. "If you give me the ten dollars, we're gonna be famous with a song. We're gonna be rich, and I'm gonna buy you a beautiful home. Daddy, I'll buy you a racehorse." So, finally, they gave me the ten dollars.

Me, Marshall Lieb, Harvey Goldstein, and Phil paid for the two-hour, forty-dollar recording session. I remember rehearsing at the house of Marshall's parents. That song was "Don't You Worry My Little Pet."

Two weeks go by. All of a sudden, middle of the night, the phone rings. I answer it. "Annette. Listen to this." He starts to sing with his guitar, "To Know Him Is to Love Him," [which] was inspired by Phil's father's tombstone that read, "To Know Him Was to Love Him." "What do you think?" I went, "It's fine." I didn't know. And he said, "Be at my house. We have a rehearsal." I thought the song was pretty. I couldn't judge my own voice. I didn't even know I had a voice. But Phil did. That was the key. He totally knew, and instilled belief.

Phil then went to Lew Bedell and Herb Newman at Era Records. My favorite song in the world at that time was Gogi Grant's "The Wayward Wind" on the label. I was beside myself. They had just set up another label aimed for the rock 'n' roll market called Dore Records.

In July of 1958, Marshall, Phil, and I then schlep over to their office to sign a contract. Phil talked them into letting us go back in to cut "To Know Him Is to Love Him" and "Wonderful Lovable You." This was after we did the first recording. Phil then called Sandy Nelson to play drums, and we did "To Know Him Is to Love Him" in two takes at Gold Star. One was for balance, and [on] the second one, Phil suggested, "Sing this like you are in love with him." "I'm too young to have a boyfriend!" And Phil says to me, "Then sing it to your father."

I was done in twenty minutes. Two-track machine. Stan Ross was the engineer. We never spliced. I sang it all the way through. I tried to be sexy, 'cause I always wanted to be sexy—which I became. But naturally, I wasn't. Marshall and Phil were very much part of the dynamic. They did the background chorus. Phil played guitar on the session. Nobody cared about that song. It was going to be the B-side of "Don't You Worry My Little Pet."

RUSS TITELMAN: In 1958, I'd come home from John Burroughs Junior High, and the Teddy Bears would be rehearsing in our living room on Fourth Street. My sister, Susan, was at Fairfax High. Her best friend, Donna Kass, was Phil's girlfriend, and Marshall Lieb in the Teddy Bears was my sister's boyfriend. I'd come home from school, and they'd be rehearsing those songs in the living room. "Wonderful Lovable You," "Don't You Worry My Little Pet," "To Know Him Is to Love Him." So I got to stand around and be there.

They all sounded like hits to me. I thought this was the greatest thing in the world. It was quite obvious that "To Know Him Is to Love Him" was a hit song. I listened to Johnny Otis and Hunter Hancock at night on the radio, and I went to Norty's Records on Fairfax Avenue.

Phil was studying to be a court reporter at Los Angeles City College. He recommended I take lessons from his guitar teacher, Burdell Mathis, who had a place right across the street from Wallichs Music City on Sunset Boulevard.

ANNETTE KLEINBARD: The record came out, and I helped orchestrate my friends to call local DJs. We became the number-one record in L.A. They were supposed to play "Don't You Worry My Little Pet," and spun "To Know Him Is to Love Him" instead. But nothing happened for about a month. Nobody cared about it.

Then a disc jockey in Minneapolis at KDWB, Lou Riegert, turned "Don't You Worry My Little Pet" over. He fell in love with my voice, and the lights on his request line went crazy. They went nuts. They got an order out of Minneapolis for a hundred records, and then another hundred, then five hundred, a thousand, and then I think ten thousand. Lew Bedell said, "Oh my God, I think we have a number-one record!" Nobody believed in the record except Phil and this DJ, Lou Riegert.

RUSS TITELMAN: Then the Teddy Bears record went to number one, and they're on *American Bandstand*. When I saw that . . . this was the place where the Everly Brothers appeared with all of the other greats. It was a thrill to see them.

I idolized Phil and thought he was the greatest thing in the world. I kind of wanted to be Phil. Music was a huge part of one's existence, at that time.

Phil was so smart, and so funny, and so charming, and so incredibly charismatic, and so you were sort of charmed by it all. Then there was the other side of him, which was this dark, murky, scary person, you know, who made shit up. Some tall tales.

The Teddy Bears made an album for Imperial, and Phil would come over with the master tapes. "What do you think of this drum sound?" That was my education.

DON PEAKE: Phil studied guitar with Howard Roberts. I knew Phil in the late fifties, with his friend, Michael Spencer. We used to meet at a house on Highland Avenue, and they would play "Wonderful," the two of them in unison, and Phil would take a solo. Phil was a pretty good jazz guitarist. May I point out to you that, if you listen to his recording with the Teddy Bears on "To Know Him Is to Love Him," when that bridge goes off to the planet Mars and changes key, that's the stamp of a jazz musician.

ANDREW LOOG OLDHAM: I heard the record in the UK. It made an impact because of the use of room. The usage of tape delay. You knew something was going on, even if you didn't know what it was. Later, I recorded the Rolling Stones' "Not Fade Away"—or let's say "Little Red Rooster." You realized, by recording in similar mono circumstances, in London's Regent Sounds as opposed to Gold Star, or wherever Phil did "To Know Him," what the room brought to the game.

There is a lot of magic to "To Know Him Is to Love Him." Basically, how can anybody resist those backgrounds? It's a great part for the public to sing along with and be at one with the song. Maybe one of the things that drew me to the record was that there was a subliminal audio text from Eddie Cochran records. Eddie had already recorded "Summertime Blues" at Gold Star. So we didn't know, but you do know, man. That's my memory of it.

DANIEL WEIZMANN: Phil was born on Christmas Day in 1940. But I see him as the first truly post-Holocaust American Jew. He refused to grovel and play the Borscht Belt guy, the entertainment guy. Yet he had one foot in that old world grandiosity. His music was for the new utopian, free-spirited teenagers, but it also contained the secret mania of having grown up with the shadow of genocide and the bomb. He meant business. In a way, he is the link between Lenny Bruce and Bob Dylan. Once Phil planted the seed, the sixties just had to happen.

As far removed from Spector's urban Jewish upbringing as corned beef on rye is from taquitos, singer-songwriter Ritchie Valenzuela earned his stripes on the hard-scrabble streets of Pacoima, a Mexican American enclave in Los Angeles's San Fernando Valley. He grew up steeped in a musical marinade of mariachi, R & B, and the nascent beat of rock 'n' roll. Though left-handed, Valenzuela mastered the commonplace right-handed guitar, encouraged by his father, who recognized Ritchie's talent and ambition.

In May of 1958, the seventeen-year-old signed a recording agreement with Bob Keane and Del-Fi Records under his real name, Richard Steven Valenzuela. Keane

subsequently suggested a name change to Ritchie Valens for the debut release of "Come On, Let's Go," backed with "Framed," a Leiber and Stoller composition. It was released in July. Gene Weed at KFWB was the first person in town to spin the platter.

In July, Valens met Phil Spector during the recording session of the Teddy Bears' "To Know Him Is to Love Him" at Gold Star's Studio B.

PETER PIPER: In very late 1958, I saw Ritchie Valens at an Art Laboe show on Melrose and Van Ness in the KTLA-TV station. The thing was, the studio was so small, we were almost right onstage with him, and that made it really great. There he was, singing "Donna," sitting on an amp, along with the Kaylin Twins and Skip and Flip. It was just nice to see this music growing in front of me. Everybody is taking a little bit from somebody else and making it their own. It was a real experimental time, like when surfing went from longboards and somebody came in with a short board.

By November 29, 1958, Ritchie Valens's recording of "Donna" was number one on the KFWB Fabulous Forty Survey. In early January of 1959, the disc was number

Ritchie Valens with producer Bob Keane on the set of *Pik-A-Platter,* circa 1958.

CHRIS DARROW ON RITCHIE VALENS

CHRIS DARROW: I saw Ritchie Valens a month before his death at the Rainbow Gardens, an all-wooden building with a low ceiling that was just south of the YMCA in Pomona, California. I was from a mixed race white and Hispanic neighborhood in Claremont called Arbol Verde. My best friend, Roger Palos, was Mexican. He and I were both learning to play guitar, and we would sing together a lot. The songs that we learned that were not from the folk music genre were popular songs mainly by Elvis Presley, the Everly Brothers, Buddy Holly, and Ritchie Valens. For some reason, our favorite song of Ritchie's was not "La Bamba" or "Donna," but "Hi-Tone." We just loved that song.

I was fifteen and in the ninth grade and was not allowed to go out many places by myself at night. I was attending a private school in Claremont called Webb. Since I wasn't driving yet, it took a lot for my folks to let me go into the dark part of Pomona to see a rock 'n' roll show in late 1958 or early '59. My parents weren't square, but my mom always worried about me.

I went with Roger to the concert, as it was a kind of pilgrimage for us. Since I really identified with the Mexican culture and wasn't afraid, I couldn't wait to see one of my main men, Ritchie Valens. After all, he was only seventeen and not much older than me and Roger. I wore my bright red corduroy coat with silver buttons that my Grandma Darrow had made for me that Christmas. I also wore white bucks, white pants, and red argyle socks. I looked sharp! I'm not sure who the house band was, but it could have been Manuel and the Renegades, or the Mixtures, for they both used to be regulars at the Rainbow Gardens. I was very excited and hadn't been to too many concerts before this.

I was really into dancing at the time and had a chance to dance a few numbers with some strangers before the show. The opening act for Ritchie was Jan and Dean; possibly really Jan and Arnie. In those days, no one had their own bands, and acts would use house bands as their own. Either the band didn't like Jan and Dean, or they just didn't care. Before they could get through the first song, which sounded awful,

Jan stopped, ran off the stage followed by Dean, and plowed through the locked stage door and out into the night. Jan just kicked it open like some thug in a movie. I was so shocked and dumbstruck by this. They never came back.

After the commotion died down, it was time for Ritchie to come on. He whirled in, probably from some other gig earlier that night, and I went right up next to the edge of the stage. He was a pretty big guy and loomed onstage with a graceful power. He was not overtly hardcore in his presentation, but was very soulful, and I ate it up. There was a tenderness and sweetness about him, even as he rocked. The house band knew his stuff and did a great job on the songs. He did "La Bamba" and "Donna," and even played my favorite song, "Hi-Tone."

I liken Ritchie to another L.A. guy, Eddie Cochran. Both had the soul and drive of the Sun label and Clovis, New Mexico records, but they were from our own backyard. As soon as Ritchie finished, he was whisked off in a flash. There was no chance to say hello or offer a handshake, but I was ecstatic over the event.

The house band played on, after the set, to people doing the Stomp, and I was awarded a prize for being one of the five best-dressed guys of the night. A perfect end to a perfect evening.

I read somewhere that Frank Zappa saw Ritchie in Pomona, so he was probably there, too. I got to know Frank later on. A month after the gig, I was at school and heard about the deaths of Ritchie, Buddy, and the Big Bopper. I was crushed, and went off by myself and cried like a baby. It was the first time I remember crying for someone who had died. Ritchie Valens and Buddy Holly were like gods to me at the time and could do no wrong. It was one of the great losses in rock 'n' roll history. It wasn't too long before we lost Eddie Cochran in a car accident. That event also caused bodily injury to another unsung hero, the great Gene Vincent. Later in my life, I had a chance to meet Gene and had the honor of playing on one of his last albums.

two in the nation, and a flipside of the same 45 rpm, "La Bamba," was in the Top 30. Valens then made his big-screen debut in the Alan Freed-hosted Go, Johnny Go! alongside Eddie Cochran, Jackie Wilson, the Flamingos, and Chuck Berry.

In late January, Valens and his band embarked on the 1959 Winter Dance Party tour, which also included Buddy Holly and the Crickets, the Big Bopper (J. P. Richardson), and Dion and the Belmonts. After their February 2 show at the Surf Ballroom in Clear Lake, Iowa, Ritchie Valens, Buddy Holly, the Big Bopper, and airplane pilot Roger Peterson perished shortly upon departing in a snow storm on their way to their next stop in Fargo, North Dakota. At age seventeen, Valens was buried at the San Fernando Mission Cemetery.

Spector and Valens had discussed the possibility of the Teddy Bears joining the tour. The trauma of the plane crash further convinced Spector that a life on the road played no part in the future tycoon of teen dreams.

Ritchie Valens, circa 1958.

HERE WE COME

DAVID RITZ: The Texas migration to Los Angeles is tremendously important. Like Charles Brown and T-Bone Walker from Texas. They come not only because there is a large African American population and work, but they come here with the dream of crossover. Johnny "Guitar" Watson comes to L.A. It's huge. Then David "Fathead" Newman. Nat Cole moving from Chicago. They know this is Hollywood, and it's movies and TV. It's enormously important.

Then there is Ray Charles. When he was on Atlantic Records in the fifties, he'd go into a little studio in New York. Ray would be off the road, uptight, and go in. In November 1959, he signs with ABC-Paramount Records. So when Ray comes to L.A. and then lives here, he now has all the time in the world. He said, "I think I'll do a country album. I think I'll do an album with the names of chicks for every song."

"Ruby"; "Georgia on My Mind," which Sid Feller arranged and produced. In 1961, Ray cut "Hit the Road Jack," written by the R & B great, Percy Mayfield. In 1962, his album, *Modern Sounds in Country and Western Music* [came out]. Then "I Can't Stop Loving You," followed by "Busted" and "Take These Chains From My Heart." Ray Charles was positively an L.A. guy.

Ray Charles at the Moulin Rouge during a taping of
***The Big T.N.T. Show*, Hollywood, 1965.**

Lobby card for *Go, Johnny Go!* (1959) starring Ritchie Valens, Alan Freed, Jimmy Clanton, Sandy Stewart, Chuck Berry, Jackie Wilson, Eddie Cochran, Harvey Fuqua of the Moonglows, Jo-Ann Campbell, the Cadillacs, and the Flamingos.

MARK GUERRERO: In 1959, when Ritchie Valens died, I was aware of it. I was ten. But what was so cool about "La Bamba" was that it was the first time you could listen to KFWB radio and hear something in Spanish. Something we knew [was] that he was a Chicano. It meant a lot to the community and inspired a lot of people to get guitars. I got my first guitar when I was twelve. My dad bought it for me in Tijuana for eight dollars.

TOM WALDMAN: Valens did die very young, and he didn't, unfortunately, leave behind a huge body of work. Ritchie didn't have the chance to have the career of a Little Richard, Buddy Holly, Fats Domino, or Jerry Lee Lewis—the gods of the fifties. But he certainly contributed more

than the one-hit wonders, or the people with a single or two. Here is what I will tell you: Ritchie Valens was the biggest name in Los Angeles rock until the Byrds. The only competition was Ricky Nelson. He was great for what he did, but he had a world-class team behind him and a television series. Ritchie Valens was just Ritchie Valens, his band, Del-Fi Records, and Bob Keane.

Ritchie was a songwriter, which already puts him in a different category than most of the Chicano artists that came after him until the seventies. Valens was a songwriter and performer, and he had major hits. I think that he was such an L.A. phenomenon, and because he's Mexican American, it's just the same old story that he gets overlooked.

CHAPTER 5

TAPE IS ROLLING

There it sat, another anonymous cinder block facade in the working class section of Hollywood, far off the map of celebrity homes. But discerning eyes and ears knew that, behind this unprepossessing veneer, there lurked an authentic powerhouse of star-making capacity. This was Gold Star Studios, ground zero for transforming the fervid imaginings of pop music's visionaries into three intoxicating minutes of backbeat and hum.

Like Merlin's apprentices, engineers Stan Ross, Dave Gold, and Larry Levine presided over this exercise in alchemy, where inspiration and perspiration produced hit after hit. Their clients included Eddie Cochran, Herb Alpert and the Tijuana Brass, Sonny and Cher, Cher as a solo artist, Buffalo Springfield, Brian Wilson with the Beach Boys, Iron Butterfly, the Cake, the Chipmunks, Dick Dale, Bobby Darin, Johnny Burnette, Dorsey Burnette, Thee Midniters, Donna Loren, the Sunrays, Mark and the Escorts, the Murmaids, Jackie DeShannon, Led Zeppelin, Duane Eddy, Kim Fowley, Marlon Brando, the Band, the Seeds, the Monkees, MFQ, and the Turtles.

Stan Herbert Ross was born in Brooklyn in 1929. At age fifteen, he moved with his parents to Los Angeles, where his father worked as an electrician in Hollywood. He enrolled at Fairfax High in 1946 and began writing a music column in the Fairfax Colonial Gazette called "Musical Downbeat."

As a teenager, Ross worked at Electro-Vox for four years and studied recording from a pioneer of modern disc recording, Bert B. Gottschalk. Ross made one hit record there: "The Deck of Cards" by T. Texas Tyler. Following this apprenticeship, Ross was ready to set up his own shop.

In a 2000 interview with me for Goldmine magazine,

Ross described the history and mystery of the Gold Star atmosphere. "Gold Star used to be a dentist's office," he said. "We started pulling teeth a different way." Built in 1950, Gold Star endured at 6252 Santa Monica Boulevard until a fire destroyed the property in 1984. Upon closing that year, the property became a mini-mall.

"Gold Star was built for the songwriters," Ross said. "They were fun, wonderful people to be around—Jimmy Van Heusen, Jimmy McHugh, Frank Loesser, Don Robertson, Sonny Burke."

Ross, Gold, and Levine integrated the concept of phase-shifting, or "phasing," a sweeping effect that they incorporated on their hit record, The Big Hurt by vocalist Toni Fisher. Larry cut the basic track and Stan infused the phasing, introducing a revolutionary technique with producer Wayne Shanklin.

Dave Gold (*left*) and Stan Ross in Studio B at Gold Star Studios, Hollywood, 1975.

Opposite: Gold Star Studios in the 1950s, 6252 Hollywood Blvd., Hollywood.

THE REASON WHY

DAVID KESSEL: Stan Ross and Dave Gold designed the studio. They knew what they were doing. They really had their acoustics down very early in the game. Of course the echo chambers, and of course the board. It was a heavy metal board. I mean, the quality of the metal inside the board, and the wiring . . . it was very thick, and very powerful. Not like today, where you have all the digital stuff and then you have to bring in all the boxes and try to beef it up. At Gold Star, that was the real deal.

The metals made after World War II had degraded considerably from the metal made before the war. It was much weaker metal, because they had to use so much during the war. It became thinner, got into aluminum, transistors. Stuff like that. When they have the real deal metal, the real deal magnets, and the real deal wiring, that really enhances the sound.

When you bring in brilliant acoustics with a powerful board, and then you have Phil and his genius working the musicians and hearing those sounds in his head and being able to articulate it with the help of Larry Levine, Stan Ross, and Dave Gold, who were outstanding . . . they were called engineers, and didn't have aspirations of being record producers and running record labels. They were sound engineers and business owners of a studio.

Johnny Crawford's "Cindy's Birthday," Dobie Gray's "The In Crowd," and Chris Montez's "Call Me" were Gold Star creations. Global music cult hero Scott Engel (later Scott Walker) first cut his teeth at Gold Star doing a variety of menial tasks while attending Los Angeles High School and playing bass with the favorite band on campus, the Routers. Brian Wilson was a regular Gold Star visitor and client for many years. In that room, he produced the Beach Boys' "Do You Wanna Dance," "Wouldn't It Be Nice," the original version of "Heroes and Villains," and "I Just Wasn't Made for These Times," which featured the first usage of a theremin on a pop recording. A tiny portion of the first session of "Good Vibrations" was also tracked at the studio.

STAN ROSS: We used Studio A. Eddie Cochran used our Studio B, down the stairs by the parking lot. I cut "Tequila" there, by the Champs. I did a whole lot of Eddie Cochran's records, including "Summertime Blues," "Twenty Flight Rock," and "C'mon Everybody." The vocal of Ritchie Valens's "Donna" was recorded at Gold Star. The backing track was done up the street at Bob Keane's studio. He owned Del-Fi Records.

[The studio's echo chamber] gave it the Wall of Sound feel. Dave [Gold] built the equipment and the echo chamber. We had so much fun with that echo chamber; it never sounded the same way twice.

Eddie Cochran playing his 1955 Gretsch 6120 Chet Atkins G-brand Western model.

Gold Star brought a feeling, an emotional feeling. Gold Star was not a dead studio, but a live studio. The room was thirty by forty feet. It was all tube microphones. We kept tubes on longer than anyone else, because we understood that when a kick drum kicks into a tube, it's not going to distort. A tube can expand. The microphones with tubes were better than the ones without the tubes, because if you don't have a tube and you hit it heavy, suddenly it breaks up. But when you have a tube, it's warm and emotional. It gets bigger and it expands. It allows for impulse.

"Back to Mono" button, 1972.

When it came to multi-track, you could put everything on mono—the bass drum, the guitars—and keep it. Once you have it on mono, it never changes. It will be the same on Wednesday as it was the previous Tuesday. So when you do transfer from one track to four tracks, it's okay. And to that, you can add voices, never losing the quality of the bass drum track, because it's been transferred, it hasn't been disturbed. You took the mono and transferred it to track one of a four-track; tracks two, three, and four are for voices and guitar fills. You follow? Everything is a fresh generation. It saves you from having to overdub four generations. You have less highs and less sibilance. We didn't use pop filters and wind screens—we got mouth noises. Isn't that life?

Stan Ross died in March 2011 in Burbank, California, of complications following surgery for an abdominal aneurysm. He was best described by partner Dave Gold in his Los Angeles Times *obituary: "Stan was born with a musical ear. He was extremely likeable and very outgoing. When 'young,' inexperienced producers found themselves hopelessly out of their depth, Ross rescued them."*

No story on Gold Star would be complete without citing resident recording engineer Larry Levine, who passed away in 2008 on his eightieth birthday. Levine joined Gold Star in 1952 and engineered albums for Eddie Cochran, the Beach Boys, and Sonny and Cher, and was behind the dials for Jerry Wallace's "Primrose Lane."

Levine won a Grammy in 1965 for his work on "A Taste of Honey" by Herb Alpert and the Tijuana Brass. Alpert later recruited Levine as chief engineer to design A&M Records' Studio B, modeled after Dave Gold's "compact" studio blueprints, developed and first installed at Gold Star, and to oversee the first recording there. He later worked on the Spector production of the Checkmates' "Black Pearl."

LARRY LEVINE: I used to have a theory [that] part of the reason we took so long in actually recording the songs was that Phil needed to tire out the musicians, [until] they weren't playing as individuals, but would meld into the sound that Phil had in his head.

Good musicians start out and play as individuals and strive to play what Phil wants. As far as the room sound and the drum sound went, because the rooms were small with low ceilings, unlike other studios with isolation, your drums sounded the way you wanted them to sound. They would change accordingly to whatever leakage was involved. As a matter of fact, Phil once said to me that the bane of his recording existence was the drum sound. A lot of people attribute to echo what Phil was doing. The echo enhanced the melding of the Wall of Sound, but it didn't create it. Within the room itself, all of this was happening, and the echo was glue that kept it together.

I kind of categorize producers into three broad spectrums. The toughest one to work with, from my standpoint, is the one who doesn't know what he wants and can't communicate it to me or the musicians, so it's futile. Then there is the producer who doesn't know what he wants, but will sit back and wait for something to happen. Of course, the best producers are people who know what they want and know how to communicate so that all of us can strive towards their goal, while the producer is still amenable to something else that may happen along the way. In my career, I've worked with three great producers—Phil Spector, Herb Alpert, and Brian Wilson.

KIM FOWLEY: I went to Gold Star my first day in Hollywood, on February 3, 1959. It was the day Buddy Holly, Ritchie Valens, and the Big Bopper died in an airplane crash in Iowa. I took it upon myself to take their place. I thought that they had passed the baton on to me from beyond. I thought it was my turn to take over.

I met the legendary rockabilly cats Johnny and Dorsey Burnette in 1959. It was during that day in Hollywood at Gold Star, around a Champs recording session I was covering for *Dig* magazine. I was their campus correspondent and was invited to have lunch with Dorsey and Johnny, who were in to play on a long-forgotten B-side of a Champs single. Dave Burgess was the producer, who later produced Jerry Fuller. The Burnette Trio were a band. In those days, pre-Beatles, you didn't sing and play at the same time and write. There was a songwriter, the musicians, and there were the singers. Three different components who performed on the record.

That was in Studio B. I went into Studio A and met arranger Danny Gould, who was passing out charts for a soon-to-be held Gogi Grant recording. I said, "What do you do?" He replied, "I'm an arranger. And you must be a producer." "Why?" "Because you're arrogant like one and you're asking the right questions. What do you do?" I said, "I make guys like you look good, because I musicalize your ideas."

Little did I realize, I was looking at a forerunner of Jack Nitzsche, who was also an arranger later on, as was Perry Botkin Jr., who turned into a producer for "Wonderful Summer" by Robin Ward. At any rate, I learned what an arranger did.

I slept in my dad's car and then met Nik Venet on Selma Avenue, after spending my last twenty-two cents on French fries at the Hollywood Ranch Market, along with ketchup. So I made tomato soup, and had the two cents tax. I found Nik Venet, who got a pile of money from Billy Sherman of Sherman De Verzon, for a $300 song. I got $500 for two songs, and I made $200 for myself to produce the demo at Gold Star. After, Billy Sherman said, "Does anybody know who you are in the industry?" I said, "Call up Gold Star." And Dave Gold and Stan Ross told him, "Oh yes. Smart kid. He was here all day yesterday with the Champs and later that night with Danny Gould." So Gold Star got me going. A year later, I was number one in the world.

I produced "Nut Rocker" in 1960 under the name B. Bumble and the Stingers on Transworld Records. I wasn't allowed to be in the room at the session, so I took a walk.

Top: "Nut Rocker" by B. Bumble and the Stingers, 1962. **Bottom:** "Alley-Oop" by the Hollywood Argyles, 1960.

René Hall was on guitar and bass, Al Hazan on piano, and Jesse Sailes was the drummer. I was just the publisher and the writer. I was twenty-two years old. I didn't care about going to music business parties. I was going to Tijuana every weekend.

I had a partnership with Gary Paxton. He was a hillbilly genius who worked with a Hollywood child. One hustler and conceptualist. One musical and vocal guy. We did well, did work together, and we quit. We were both damaged goods, but interesting people in terms of what our product was.

I studied the country musicians Speedy West and Joe Maphis on the 1959 and '60 local television shows. [They] appeared weekly on *The Spade Cooley Show* and *Cal's Corral,* that car salesman Cal Worthington hosted. Everyone would go on *Town Hall Party.* I saw Eddie Cochran, Gene Vincent, and Johnny Cash on that show. We all got hot over Molly Bee. I then met Eddie Cochran and songwriters Sharon Sheeley and Jackie DeShannon.

I scored in 1960 with the Hollywood Argyles' "Alley-Oop" on Lute Records. [They] were the white Coasters, with a black backing group that no one ever saw. Gary Paxton did the lead vocal, Sandy Nelson did the caveman yell, and a girl who was tall with red hair, who was dating Gary, was the high voice on the record. I was co-publisher and co-producer. Bill Parr was the engineer.

We did "Alley-Oop" at American Recording Studio. The session recording had keyboardist Gaynel Hodge, a member of the Hollywood Flames who sang with the Platters and co-wrote "Earth Angel" for the Penguins, as well as Harper Cosby, who was on Johnny Otis's "Willie and the Hand Jive," [and] drummers Sandy Nelson and Ronnie Selico, who worked with the Olympics and is heard on "Big Boy Pete." Ronnie was also on the Marathons' "Peanut Butter." He later went with Ray Charles and Shuggie Otis, and is on Frank Zappa's *Hot Rats* album.

I learned that you had to have black people with white people on my sessions to get the groove. We then marched into Gold Star, which had mastering facilities, and Stan Ross mastered the record. Stan proclaimed it was going to be a number-one record. He was right.

Gold Star was the epicenter of teenage rock 'n' roll recording culture in 1959. If you were in Memphis, Tennessee, you would knock on the door of Sun Records. If you were in Detroit, Michigan, you would knock on the door at Motown. But in 1959, I went to Gold Star. "Here I am. Let's see if I get accepted." If you got accepted, you were off and running. You start at the top, and I did. So I will always be grateful.

It was possibly a double-edged sword for Larry Levine, Stan Ross, and Dave Gold, because they figured they would service the emerging rock 'n' roll community. At that point, the other studios in town had a suit-and-tie vibration. So if some kid had a hundred dollars, he couldn't even get in there. If a kid had a hundred dollars, he could cut a hit record at Gold Star if he saved it or got his friends and family to pitch in with band members. I later worked with their engineer, Doc Siegel, as well. You could go in there and not get intimidated, and you had equal footing with the legendary guys. I saw Eddie Cochran work at Gold Star. He invited me in to watch, listen, and learn.

RUSS TITELMAN: In 1959 or '60, Lou Adler and Herb Alpert produced a television pilot for a dance show that they shot at the Renaissance Club on Sunset Boulevard. Eddie Cochran was the guest, and I was on as one of the dancers. He had magic. Man, I'll tell you. "Summertime Blues." "C'mon Everybody." The sound that he got with his guitar and bass was so completely compelling.

LOU ADLER: I was hired by Aldon Music in 1960 to run their publishing office, after Herb and I had a hit record with our version of "Alley-Oop" by Dante and the Evergreens. I got a phone call from Donnie Kirshner. "I like the record a lot. If you need any follow-ups or if you ever want to work in New York, call me." That's where I first met Carole King.

Lou Adler subsequently oversaw the West Coast Aldon office from 1960 to 1963, guiding over three dozen Top 10 records.

RUSS TITELMAN: Back then, you could get meetings with music publishers and could hang out at their offices. The door was open. Once you were in the studios, if you came, you were welcome to come in and look around and see who was there.

I started studying guitar with Ray Pohlman and met Ed Cobb, who was the bass singer with the Four Preps. I did some sessions. I later met Jack Nitzsche through Phil Spector. I met Lester Sill through Phil. I made my demo, which had "Just a Little Touch of Your Love" and some others, and brought it to Lester, 'cause I used to hang out at Lester and Lee Hazlewood's Gregmark label. I stayed over at Lester's house, so I was kind of family, you know. But I took my demo, and he listened to it. "I think this is good. Let's go upstairs and see Lou Adler at Screen Gems-Columbia Music"—formerly Aldon Music. He played it for Lou, who thought it was great. Lou then played it for Donnie [Kirshner], and I got signed as a writer.

I wanted to be where Barry [Mann] and Cynthia [Weil] were, and Carole [King] and Gerry [Goffin]. I went to meet Donnie at the Columbia Pictures lot in some big office, and Julie Stein was there. I signed. Fifty dollars a week. I'm rolling in dough. My mother was thrilled. She was thrilled when I coughed. She thought I was a genius when I coughed. I was going to Los Angeles City College, and then to New York to write. Gerry Goffin and I wrote "I Never Dreamed" for the Cookies.

I met Brian Wilson around Screen Gems, because Brian knew Lou Adler and used to visit him all the time at the office in Hollywood on Sunset and Vine. Leiber and Stoller's Trio Music was also in the same building. Brian had a large office with a piano, and I saw him a lot by hanging out at the Screen Gems office. I watched him write "Fun, Fun, Fun" but the lyric at the time was "run, run, run." He had just starting writing it in his office, at the southeast corner of Sunset and Vine, across from Wallichs Music City. It had different lyrics to it. My first impression of Brian was that he was a genius.

CHAPTER 6

LEGENDS IN THEIR SPARE TIME

As the studios themselves were developing a signature sound, so too were the players cultivating an equally recognizable voice. It was striking how much this centered around the unassuming electric bass guitar. It was happening at Motown with James "the Hook" Jamerson, and at Muscle Shoals with David Hood.

Los Angeles had an empress holding down the bottom—Ms. Carol Kaye. Along with Joe Osborn and the odd jazz refugee (Chuck Berghofer thumping upright on "These Boots Were Made for Walkin'"), Carol provided the pivot for a motley ensemble of big-band vets, country pickers, classical cast-offs, and anyone who could unravel the mysteries of the theremin. Like Dodger pitchers Sandy Koufax and Don

Drysdale, the "Wrecking Crew" had a dazzling command of whatever pitch was required—taffeta pop, folk rock, or alpaca schmaltz (double-scale for Gregorian chants)—and could spin it into gold or any other precious gem (yes, that was Leon Russell playing keys on Gary Lewis's "This Diamond Ring"). Sure, a lot of the time it was just a union gig—paying off a mortgage or sending a kid to college—but it was also a wonderful showcase to slip in a lick worthy of their heroes: Bird, Kenton, Atkins, Christian. When the tape was rolling, there was no time for squares.

The Wrecking Crew membership began in the 1950s, with the slow demise of the studio system at the big movie companies in Hollywood. Large orchestras started getting replaced by smaller session calls for movie and television soundtracks, in addition to rock 'n' roll dates that were now getting booked by record producers and music supervision executives.

The studio musicians determined the pop and rock sound, as the record companies and producers simply didn't trust their incorrigible young charges to play on the instrumental tracks themselves. No one epitomized that unique Wrecking Crew hauteur more than Bernard Alfred "Jack" Nitzsche. Born in Chicago on April 22, 1937, he moved to Los Angeles at age eighteen after seeing an advertisement in Downbeat magazine for the L.A.-based Westlake School of Music. Nitzsche's passions were jazz—the Kenton big band—and cinema. Seeing Rebel Without a Cause drew him westward as surely as his desire to break into the music business.

Sonny Bono, who was handling A&R duties for Specialty Records at the time, gave Nitzsche his start when

Jack Nitzsche and his wife, Gracia,
at home during the holidays, Hollywood, 1965.

Opposite: Bob Eubanks and Barney Kessel (*holding guitar*) during a taping of
Pickwick Dance Party to promote Kessel's record, "Diamonds," Burbank, 1962.

Jack Nitzsche relaxing at home in Hollywood, 1965.

he hired him as a copyist. They soon teamed up to write "Needles and Pins" for Jackie DeShannon. In 1962, he hooked up with Phil Spector after holding a variety of arranging gigs, including one at Capitol Records, where he met his first wife, singer Gracia Ann May, an original member of the Blossoms.

In a 1988 interview with me published in Goldmine, *Nitzsche provided the backstory of his melodic bond with Spector and the Hollywood session players he created charts and arrangements for.*

JACK NITZSCHE: I had heard about Phil for a long time. In 1962, I used to hang out at Lester Sill's on Sunset Boulevard, when Lester and Lee Hazlewood were partners. One day, Lester came downstairs and said that Phil Spector was in town and needed an arranger. He played me the demo of "He's a Rebel." We went to a rehearsal with the Blossoms. I introduced Phil to the Blossoms. I had been working with them for years. It started on "He's a Rebel." Remember the horns on "Duke of Earl"? Phil wanted something like that. The musicians played at once. Before that, I was working with compact rhythm sections and three or four players. This was groundbreaking for me.

I put the band together for the session, a lot of the same guys I had been working with for years. Phil didn't know a lot of these people; he had been in New York from 1960 to 1962. Leon Russell, Harold Battiste, Earl Palmer, Don Randi, Hal Blaine, Glen Campbell . . . a lot of the players came out of my phone book. Phil knew Barney Kessel. He had taken guitar lessons from him. [Drummer] Hal Blaine . . . I liked his work, but sometimes felt he overplayed. That's just the way he plays. A lot of fills. As it turned out, Phil and the people loved the breaks Hal took, especially at the end of the tunes, the fades. Hal had a big kit. I liked the fills.

Earl Palmer was the other drummer on the records. He's the best—like a rock. A real good New Orleans drummer. Harold Battiste, Mac Rebennack. New Orleans guys were on the dates, so you had a good mixture of jazz guys, West Coast studio cats, and New Orleans players.

Leon Russell. I met him with Jackie DeShannon; she

Sonny Bono at a Gold Star Studios session for *A Christmas Gift for You from Phil Spector*, on which he played percussion and sang background vocals, Hollywood, 1963.

Left: Leon Russell performing at the University of California, San Diego, 1970.
Middle: Hal Blaine at a recording session, 1969. ♪ **Right:** Larry Knechtel at a recording session, 1969.

introduced me. Leon, at the time, was playing piano in a bar in Covina. He was an innovative piano player. In those days, it was real hard to find rock 'n' roll piano players who didn't play too much. Leon talked the same language.

During the Spector sessions, a lot of the time we had two or three piano players going at once. I played piano as well. Phil knew the way he wanted the keyboards played. It wasn't much of a problem who played. Leon was there for the solos and the fancy stuff, rolling pianos. The pianos would interlock and things would sound cohesive. I knew Leon would emerge as a bandleader.

I had met Don Randi a long time ago. He was a pianist at a jazz club on La Cienega. He was cool; he looked like a beatnik, and his hair was right. He had the attitude. He didn't smile when he played. Al De Lory was on keyboards, too.

The horn players: Steve Douglas on tenor, Jay Migliori on baritone, and other horn players as well. I had met Steven through Lester Sill. We were friends for a long time. Phil had an idea about horns.

Sonny Bono played percussion. Julius Wechter, later of the Baja Marimba Band, was on a lot of the sessions. Frank Kapp was on a lot of sessions. He was a jazz drummer who used to play with Stan Kenton. Phil would dream these percussion parts up at the session. They were his ideas. There were no formulas. I played percussion, chimes, orchestra bells.

Bass players. Jimmy Bond and Red Callender were on most of the dates. Ray Pohlman, Ray Brown, and Carol Kaye. The bass parts were written out, and the players had to stick right with them. They were mixed way low in the back—almost a suggestive element to the song. No one really had a lot of room with those sessions. Really, only the drummer had any sort of freedom. They weren't R & B records.

A lot of the guitarists were jazz players and weren't rock 'n' roll players, like Howard Roberts, Joe Pass, Herb Ellis, Tommy Tedesco, Barney Kessel, and Dennis Budimir. A lot of the guitarists were good and well-known session players: Glen Campbell, Bill Pittman, Don Peake, Al Casey. There was a lot of acoustic guitar on the songs. It was hard for any of the guitarists to breathe or stretch out on the records.

I was amazed how big Glen Campbell made it as a total entertainer. I knew he was a great guitarist. I never knew he would show up as a singer later. Billy Strange was good, too. I became aware of the twelve-string guitar during the last Phil years. It was a new sound, and a new toy to play with.

Recording session at the Annex with Ian Whitcomb (*standing, far right*)
and members of what would later be known as the Wrecking Crew, Hollywood, 1965.

FOREIGN EXCHANGE STUDENT

IAN WHITCOMB: Ray [Pohlman] and lot of these guys probably came up through the 1950s in jazz bands. By the time I met them in 1965, they had already had a long run of playing really good professional rock 'n' roll sessions. Ray Pohlman and his wife, Barbara, befriended me; I actually stayed at their house. That's where I wrote several of my arcane songs. Carol Kaye played bass on "Groovy Day." Ray arranged some of my ragtime stuff.

The guitarist James Burton recorded with me long before he went to Elvis. Practically all my Hollywood records were with Burton and Arthur Wright, who played bass, drummer Micky Conway, Jim Horn, Larry Knechtel, and Ray Pohlman on Fender bass.

The thing that struck me most about the session players—I was amazed that grown men, smartly dressed in beach costumes, would be playing good rock 'n' roll. Because, in England, there was nobody who specialized in that. A mixed group in age and color. But what impressed me was here were adults playing rock 'n' roll, and playing it well. It was like their first language. They were good musicians who could read music, but they could also play freely.

I got in there as a neophyte, and there was this array of really smartly dressed, really slick men with fabulous haircuts and sideburns, all wearing velour and had tight trousers that were tapered down. Nothing like I had seen in England or the East Coast. Now it turned out, these were the members of what would later be called the Wrecking Crew.

Barney Kessel Guitar Strings

Since 1944, Barney Kessel has been recognized as one of the world's leading figures in Jazz, and today is accepted in every corner of the globe as the world's finest exponent of the electric guitar. He has always been as demanding in his choice of strings as he has for his instruments and music. As a result he has got together with Darco Strings to produce a range of strings that would be superior to anything previously marketed. And so you now have available this outstanding new range of electric guitar strings. *The Barney Kessel String by Darco—* *Unconditionally guaranteed.*

CSL SUMMERFIELD BROTHERS
GATESHEAD • NE8 3AJ • GREAT BRITAIN

Barney Kessel Strings

E-1st ACOUSTIC/ELECTRIC

Left: **Dan Kessel recording with Phil Spector and Dion at A&M Records, Hollywood, 1975.**
Right: **Barney Kessel guitar strings, 1972.**

DAN KESSEL: When my father was being Barney Kessel, jazz artist, he stuck exclusively to his 1947 Gibson ES-350, which he'd modified with a 1939 Charlie Christian pickup. But in his role as studio gun-for-hire in Hollywood, he used a large arsenal of equipment in order to accommodate a wide variety of artists and producers, including Elvis, Sinatra, Sam Cooke, Phil Spector, and Brian Wilson and the Beach Boys.

My dad was signed by Frank Sinatra to his Reprise label in 1962. The attorneys did the real paperwork later, but my dad and Frank originally signed something on a napkin at Martoni's restaurant on Cahuenga. Frank's other signings to Reprise included Dean Martin, Sammy Davis Jr., Rosemary Clooney, Duke Ellington, Count Basie, Errol Garner, and Ella Fitzgerald. My dad recorded three albums for Reprise and also played on records with all of the above. Jack Nitzsche told me that my dad's record, "Diamonds," which came out on Reprise in '62, was an influence on him regarding his instrumental record, "The Lonely Surfer" in '63. Of course "The Lonely Surfer" is phenomenal in its own right. The other side of my dad's Reprise 45, "TV Commercials," featured vocals by Darlene Love and Jack's wife, Gracia Nitzsche.

I was riding with my dad to a *Pet Sounds* session for Brian. His Chevy station wagon was filled with all kinds of guitars and other instruments, including some basses, a banjo, mandolin, ukulele, etc. He stopped at a gas station to fill up. This was back when they used to pump your gas, check your oil, and all that. The young attendant was cleaning the windshield. Seeing all the instruments, he was intrigued and asked my dad what he was doing with all those guitars. My dad said, "I'm a guitar player." The kid said, "Hey, that's great. I'm a guitar player, too!" He seemed lost in thought for a second, and then said, "So, what do you do for a living?"

DON PEAKE: I studied with Barney Kessel and Howard Roberts. I took lessons from Ray Pohlman. Then I end up being on Phil's session dates with Ray and Barney, sitting next to them.

I first started studying with Barney Kessel privately. He taught me how to play with conviction, no matter what. Even if you were looking at the music and you didn't know where to go next, your right hand had to keep going. You never stopped playing. Barney would say, "Don. There's a rod which connects to your right forearm to your toe and you tap your toe. You tap your toe, and that wrist keeps going no matter what, even if you don't get to the chord on time. You keep playing."

KIM FOWLEY: I did various recordings with the session musicians and the players later to be heralded as "the Wrecking Crew."

Early on, when I was attempting to get into the record business, there was a "fuck you" mentality according to age. Especially the arrangers. If you were too young, they

Brian Wilson and Hal Blaine (*right*) at Western Recorders, Hollywood, circa 1966/1967.

were hoping you would go back to school. Pre-Beatles. Jack Nitzsche, when he first started arranging, used to do my lead sheets for ten dollars on onion skin paper. Arrangers were mean people. They were all very talented. Billy and Gene Page were a bit overpriced. Ernie Freeman was elitist. It's never been easy.

Al Casey was the real Duane Eddy. Tommy Tedesco. Aggressive on a Lee J. Cobb level during the filming of *On the Waterfront*. Carol Kaye was everybody's favorite schoolteacher and big sister. Cher was everybody's fantasy. Don Randi did not look down at you playing on rock 'n' roll recordings, even though he was a jazz genius. Earl Palmer was a gentleman and very helpful to young producers. Glen Campbell wore alpaca sweaters and was very efficient. Hal Blaine would always come an hour early to set up, so no time would be wasted. Joe Osborn was a genius bassist from the Dale Hawkins band. Plas Johnson and Jackie Kelso were supportive to young musicians and new producers. And arranger H. B. Barnum. Extremely talented. He played piano on a Robins record

SPECTOR ON SPECTOR

One evening in 1975, Phil Spector appeared at the Sherwood Oaks Experimental College on Hollywood Boulevard. He spoke as though his every word resonated in an echo chamber of his own imagining. Phil commanded your attention with the authoritative swagger of General Patton landing in Sicily. You didn't converse; you took dictation. Here is the world according to Phil Spector, which I dutifully notated over the many years I spent in his company—at his Beverly Hills mansion, the studio, and the bowling alley.

PHIL SPECTOR: I was a young aspiring guitar player. I played on some of Big Mama Thornton's records. I always wanted to be a producer. There's an old story I've told before: "Okay. Let's play baseball. You be the pitcher, you're the catcher, and you're the batter. Spector, you be the producer." I was always into that.

Dave Bartholomew, Sam Phillips—I wanted to know about the people behind the scenes. The guy who played the solo on "Rock Around the Clock." The tape echo sound. These things interested me. They were exciting. I played on records before I made 'em. I worked with Leiber and Stoller.

We made a lot of records, played on sessions by the Drifters, the guitar on "On Broadway," "Lavender Blue," and "To Know Him Is to Love Him," the first one. That was the one I was gonna kick ass with. I was part of the group the Teddy Bears. We did *The Perry Como Show*.

I like to have all the musicians there at once. I get everything on one track that I need. I put everything on twenty-four tracks just to see if it's plugged in. The finished track never ends up on more than one track. I don't wear a "Back to Mono" button for no reason at all. I believe in it. I can make quad, it's easy.

I record in a strange way. I haven't changed. I go from the basic track and put it onto twenty-four. Then I have one track and twenty-three open. That's the difference between having twenty-four filled or nineteen filled, which means I can get twenty-three string players and overdub them ten times and have two hundred strings, then I put them on one track.

My engineer was scared to death to work with me. When I record, I put everything on tape echo—everything. My engineer said, "You're out of your mind." Do you know Ray Conniff uses more tape echo than I ever used in my life? That's a fact. I record basic tracks and then put it all onto one track, or maybe two. Then I condense. I put my voices on.

I've used Barney Kessel all the time for the last ten years. Terry Gibbs on vibes . . . everybody. The better the talent is around you, the better the people you have working with you. The more concerned, the better you're gonna come off as a producer, like a teacher in a class.

The musicians I have never outdo me. I'm not in competition with them. I'm in complete accord with them. You need the ability, so you hire the best. I have the creativity. I know what I want.

Stan Ross (*top left*), Kim Fowley (*top center*), and Ruth Conte, president of Chattahoochee Records (*top right*), with the Murmaids (*bottom*) at Gold Star Studios, Hollywood, 1964.

and worked with singer Oma Heard, who I cut in my West Coast doo-wop period.

In 1963, I was hitchhiking and a budding songwriter. Before he was with Screen Gems Music, David Gates picked me up and gave me a ride. We talked; he mentioned he was a songwriter. He had a bass guitar in the back seat. "Are you a musician or a songwriter?" He wrote songs. I told him who I was. He knew about "Alley-Oop" and "Nut Rocker." We went into my house and he played me "Popsicles and Icicles," and I said, "Hit record!" I found a group to do it—the Murmaids. Stan Ross was the engineer. In 1964, the Beatles knocked it out of the number-one slot in *Cash Box* with "I Want to Hold Your Hand."

One day, at Gold Star Studios, I ran into Brian Wilson and he asked me who the Murmaids were. I asked

Brian Wilson and Don Randi (*left*) at Western Recorders, Hollywood, circa 1966/1967.

him, "What is the basis of your songwriting?" And he said, "Well, school is nine months a year and the summer holidays are three months, and you write about that and getting in trouble with your parents."

Like the catcher on a baseball team, the session keyboardist serves as the fulcrum through which the tracks cohere. Charts are arranged, parts are assigned, songs are transcribed, and the key is transposed—all of these critical roles take place at the piano. Phil Spector and Brian Wilson's go-to keyboardist was Don Randi, a New York City transplant who brought his jazz chops to bear on some of the most iconic pop songs of the sixties. Randi was never afraid to call time out.

DON RANDI: Everybody would play parts with a lot of time duplication. Like on the pianos, you would have one guy doing a thing on the high end of the piano, somebody in the middle, and Phil would want the different sounds of a concert grand, an upright, or a Wurlitzer electric piano. So he liked to have the spread of the different tonality. That was Phil. He understood tonality very well. At Gold Star, it was magic because all those harmonics rising were part of the Wall of Sound.

Phil's songs were always great, and they told a story. The songs in themselves were films, and, especially in Phil's case, he knew how to write them and how to produce them. In Brian Wilson's case, Brian always knew where he was going with it. He may not have known at the beginning, but after a while, he had an idea and he developed it. We were there to help him develop it.

STUDIO MASTER

MIKE MELVOIN: We created a lot of music that became renewable copyrights just by what we played. Sometimes they'd put a lead sheet in front of you that just had a few basic chords, and we brought that stuff to life and made music out of it. Many times, people booked sessions and they didn't have the faintest idea of what they wanted. The L.A. studios had the reputation of being able to interpret and create any kind of music and sounds that you wanted.

CHAPTER 7

A SANDBOX AS BIG AS AN OCEAN

In 1961, Hawthorne, California was a sleepy South Bay bedroom community serving the growing aerospace industry. However, it would soon come to rival England's Liverpool as the birthplace of a pop music phenomenon: the Beach Boys. The three teenaged Wilson brothers, Brian, Carl, and Dennis—along with their cousin, Mike Love, and a school friend, Al Jardine—formed the band. In 1962, neighbor David Marks joined the group for its first wave of hits on Capitol Records before leaving in late 1963. In 1965, Bruce Johnston was asked to join when Brian Wilson retired from touring to focus on writing and producing records for the group.

Those are some basic facts, but the sound and saga of the Beach Boys is mythic; Homer himself would have been hard-pressed to catalog the travails of the Wilson family—the father-son torment, the musical gifts fulfilled and squandered, the heartbreaking deaths and improbable rebirths. Their music was the hymnal to an age of luminous innocence, affording America, and indeed the world, a glimmer of what it meant to catch a wave and sit on top of the world. Too much time and energy has been devoted to the lurid legend. For once, we'll just stick to the facts.

It began inauspiciously. On December 23, 1961, the Beach Boys made their first public appearance at the Rendezvous Ballroom Balboa in Newport Beach. There they played two songs at the intermission of a show featuring Dick Dale and the Del-Tones, the Challengers, and the Surfaris. They were paid ten dollars. On New Year's Eve, 1961, the band performed at a memorial dance dedicated to Ritchie Valens at the Long Beach Auditorium. Donations were a dollar.

Alan Jardine was born in Lima, Ohio, on September 3, 1942. He relocated with his family to Hawthorne, California, when he was a child. Jardine and future Beach Boy Brian Wilson attended school together at Hawthorne High, and both played on the football team. Jardine later attended El Camino Junior College. Jardine and Brian were the first two in the lineup when the Beach Boys were formed. Jardine's mom helped pay for the musical instruments and equipment when the group recorded "Surfin'," on which Jardine played bass. The song was released on the Candix Records label in November 1961 and landed on the Billboard *Top 100* chart.

MIKE LOVE: We all stood around one microphone while Brian hit a

Top: "Surfin'" by the Beach Boys, 1961.
Bottom: Ticket to Surf Nite, featuring the Beach Boys, 1962.

Opposite: Beach Boys concert flier, 1962.

snare drum and Carl played the stand up bass. We sang "Surfin'," and it was done in two takes. We've been going ever since.

There was also an extremely rare limited edition version of the "Surfin'" hit single, available on the X Records label in December '61. It was allegedly either manufactured by Candix at another pressing plant to satisfy sales demand and to settle an outstanding product payment, or the pirated disc was initiated by someone affiliated with the group to capitalize on their instant popularity.

In 1962, Jardine quit the band to return to his college studies. At the time, a musical career was hardly encouraged by anyone, and for nearly a year he pursued dentistry. Then Brian invited Al to rejoin the Beach Boys after guitarist-vocalist David Marks left the outfit.

Russ Regan came to Los Angeles in 1957 from the Modesto, California, area to become a singer and songwriter. In 1959, he was signed by Capitol Records. Regan did four songs as a Capitol Records recording artist produced by Ernie Freeman, including "Joan of Love" and "Calling All Cars."

During 1960, Regan, disenchanted with performing, switched from being an artist to promoting them. He was recruited by Motown Records and became integral in establishing what we know today as the "Motown Sound."

RUSS REGAN: I met record promoter George Matola when I came to town. He was working for the Bihari brothers at Kent Records. The first record I promoted was "Please Mr. Postman" by the Marvelettes in 1961. I also worked with the Supremes, Smokey Robinson and the Miracles, and Marvin Gaye. Believe it or not, Marvin Gaye had moments of greatness onstage, or he could be lousy. I'll tell you why. He really didn't like performing. It was a job to him. It can't be a job for a performer. People don't realize this. You can't be up there thinking you are working.

MARSHALL BERLE DISCOVERS THE BEACH BOYS

MARSHALL BERLE: I went to Fairfax High School with Phil Spector. We both attended Laurel Elementary. I had a friend, Barry Martin, who played the trumpet, and he invited me to a music rehearsal he was doing in Hollywood with Phil inside promoter Hal Zeiger's office, next to the Hollywood Palace.

I met Eddie Cochran at Gold Star just before he died. In those days, instead of using a drum, he sometimes utilized a cardboard box or suitcase. I had met Elvis Presley once in San Diego in 1956 around a TV show with Milton Berle, who was my uncle. I later met Elvis at NBC Studios in Burbank at a taping, and he did "Blue Suede Shoes."

In the fall of 1960, Milton then got me a job in the mailroom at the William Morris Agency. After a few months, I became an agent trainee for Fred Moch, head of the variety department. I wanted to be in the variety and music department, while everyone else wanted to be in TV and motion pictures.

In 1962, there was a guy named Bill Lee. He was the responsible agent for the act Dick and Dee Dee. One night, he had a date and asked me to cover for him at a Dick and Dee Dee headline show at the Hollywood Palladium. "Can you go backstage and just tell 'em you're an agent from William Morris and service them?"

I go to the gig and I walk in, and the opening act is the Beach Boys. Holy shit! I had never heard anything like them before. The radio had been playing "Surfin'," and it was on KFWB. The show ends, and there are Murry and Audree Wilson standing there. I'm in a suit and tie. I walk up to them and they say, "Who are you?" "I'm Marshall Berle from the William Morris Agency." "The William Morris Agency! [The Wilson brothers] are our sons." "I'd love to sign them to the company. Do they have an agent?" "No." "Then come on over on Monday."

Fred knew that I knew music, and gave me his office for the meeting and removed his name from the slide on the front door. Murry, his wife, and the whole

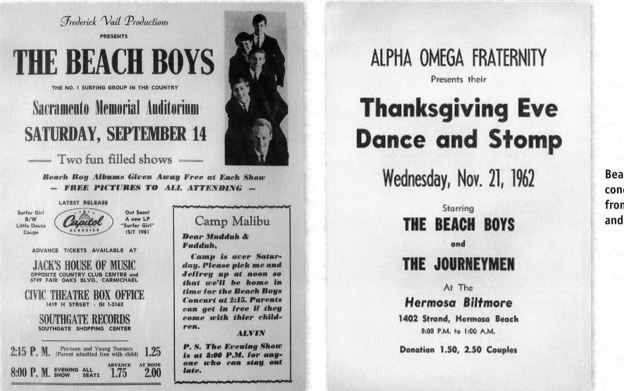

Beach Boys concert fliers from 1963 (*left*) and 1962.

group. He had papers drawn up, and we signed them for three years. Ten percent fee. I went on the road and settled up at the box office at the shows.

The Beach Boys weren't very good musicians live, but their voices were just phenomenal. Their double and triple harmonies. Every girl in the place was going nuts. I was, too. When I signed them [everyone said,] "Oh, Marshall, Milton's nephew," and no one paid much attention.

Murry was at my office all the time—at least two or three times a week about bookings. He was a total control freak. Then "Fun, Fun, Fun" broke on the radio, and then there were twenty phone calls a day. Then when the Beach Boys started getting $5,000 and $10,000 a show, William Morris gave me an office and made me an agent. I met and knew Nik Venet, who produced their early Capitol albums, and really liked him. I also met DJ Roger Christian, who wrote "Don't Worry Baby" with Brian, and a few other songs.

On New Years Eve 1962, my uncle Milton had a party at his home on Alpine Drive, just north of Sunset in Beverly Hills. I'm sitting with Natalie Wood, Frank Sinatra, and the Hollywood A-list. The Beach Boys performed. It was incredible. Milton always invited me everywhere, and I got there early. I was very shy. Frank came into the den and looked at me, came over, and stuck out his hand. "Hi. I'm Frank Sinatra." He was a gentleman.

In 2012, I saw David Marks—who is in the Beach Boys again, recording and touring—backstage in Tampa at their concert. He remembered me giving each guy in the band twenty dollars for doing the show at Milton's home. Almost overnight, the Beach Boys became so huge. I went to every show, went on the road with them, from Pandora's Box to the Hollywood Bowl in 1963. I drove to Monterey in 1963 to a gig with Dennis in his new XKE. I booked a lot of dates with Fred Vail, who worked closely with them and did shows. Even the live album, they recorded in Sacramento.

When I saw the Beach Boys in 1962, it was the same feeling I got later, when I saw Van Halen for the first time in Pasadena. It was after Kim Fowley gave me David Lee Roth's phone number and said, "There's a band in Pasadena that's incredible." I signed them to Warner Bros. and managed them for their first two albums. They had three-part harmonies, like the Beach Boys.

Berry Gordy Jr. used to come to town. He taught me about hooks in songs, and that people buy records because they have to love them, not like them. There used to be record hops at high schools. One time, at Jefferson High School, I took Marvin Gaye to Watts. He had never been out there before. The girls attacked him. He lost one shoe of his penny loafers. We went to Fairfax High School. Groups played in the auditorium. I was working at Buck Eye, a record distributor.

I hung around Candix Records in 1961. The Dix brothers were from California. My good friend, Joe Saraceno, worked there as an A&R guy. Joe called me at Buck Eye. "I want you to hear a record on the telephone." He played me this record that sounded like a Jan and Dean

rip-off. "It's a new group I got called the Pendletons [with a song called] 'Surfin',' and I'm changing the name to the Surfers." "Joe, there is already a group on Hi-Fi Records called the Surfers. You are not going to be able to get that name." So Joe says, "Well, give me a name." "How 'bout the Woodys, after the Woody Wagon." "I don't like that." "Call them the Hang Tens." "No." "Then call them the Beach Boys, because that's it." That's how they got their name. I was a body surfer, spending all my free time at the beach. About a month after we put the record out, it started breaking out.

Here's a true Hollywood story. Buck Eye promoted Dot Records, and I got to know the owner, Randy Wood. I loved his label, and I really liked Randy, who

BRIAN WILSON AND HARVEY KUBERNIK: A CONVERSATION

HK: The Beach Boys signed with Capitol Records in July 1962. Do you have a memory of the first day you went into the label's offices?

BW: I remember walking into the Capitol Records building with my father and Gary Usher in 1962. We met the A&R man, Nik Venet. He listened to our demos, and he signed us right on the spot. We played him "409" and "Surfin' Safari." "I want to sign you guys right now." I just wanted to make records. I didn't know how big it would get. I didn't think it would.

HK: Nik Venet, besides producing the early Beach Boys for Capitol, also produced the Lettermen and Bobby Darin. He told me that around 1958, you went to see the Four Freshmen at a show.

BW: I was fourteen years old. It was at the Coconut Grove (at the Ambassador Hotel) in Los Angeles, and I was shaking. I was so scared to meet them after seeing the show. My dad said, "Hi. I'm Murry Wilson. This is my son, Brian." I was so afraid. I was a big-time fan and shaking so hard I could hardly talk. It was my first live music. They could reproduce their album sound onstage. Absolutely.

HK: Wink Martindale on KFWB was the first DJ to spin "Surfin'."

BW: I couldn't believe I was actually on the radio. Could not believe it.

HK: Your record, "409"?

BW: My buddy Gary Usher had a red [Chevy] 409. After we wrote the song and recorded it, we took a tape recorder and he revved up his 409, and we took the tape to the studio and overdubbed it on the record. How 'bout that for a story?

HK: "Catch a Wave?"

BW: Was my attempt to create a group style that mixed falsetto, mid-range, bass, and backup singers all at once.

HK: Some reflections on a few records. "Wendy"?

BW: It was not written about my daughter, Wendy. This was way before she was born. You know, it starts with a bass, slowed down with a guitar. It was an attempt to flatter the Four Seasons. I wanted to try and imitate the Four Seasons in a way they would like to hear it. 'Cause I like Bob Crewe and the way they do their vocals.

HK: "The Little Girl I Once Knew"?

BW: Is my very favorite introduction to a song in my whole life. It kills me every time. It might have been the first time the music stopped and started again on a

Engineer Chuck Britz (*left*) and Brian Wilson at Western Recorders, Hollywood, circa 1966/1967.

record. I wrote the intro at the studio before we cut the thing. It was Larry Knechtel's idea to keep the music rolling. We tried one, and then I put a second guitar overdub on top of the other guitar. And the rest of it was history. We were doing stereo, but I could only hear mono. I always put the vocals up front in the mix. Mixing in mono.

HK: You recorded all over Hollywood.

BW: I didn't like recording at Capitol, and not because it was too close to the label. I liked the Capitol rooms, and I liked the instrumental sound, but I didn't like the vocal sound. I didn't like that kind of echo chamber. Tell me I'm an idiot! I just didn't like the vocal sound, so we switched over to Western and Gold Star. Western had a big room, and Phil Spector was over at Gold Star. I like the bass sound of Western, and I like the echo at Gold Star. I like the tack piano at Sunset Sound, and I like the vocal sound at Columbia. Each studio has its own kind of thing.

HK: Phil Spector's work influenced your productions and the way you recorded bass.

BW: I asked engineer Larry Levine what Phil Spector did with his basses, and Larry said that Phil used a stand-up and a Fender at the same time, and the Fender guy used a pick. So I tried it out at my session, and it worked great! You also get a thicker sound, putting the two basses together. I start with drums, bass, guitar, and

keyboards. Then we overdub the horns and the background voices.

HK: Tell me about "Please Let Me Wonder."

BW: That was cut at 4:30 in the morning. I went to the studio in the middle of the night. I called my engineer, Chuck Britz, at Western, and my wife and I went to the studio. We were there from 5:00 to 8:00 AM. One of my favorite recording sessions I ever had in my life.

HK: "Let Him Run Wild." I know you never really liked your super high lead vocal on it.

BW: I was just a little too effeminate on it. If I played it right at this moment with my wife or friends around, I just push the stop button.

HK: "The Warmth of the Sun"?

BW: Is probably Mike Love's most beautiful lyrics, and one of the prettiest songs I ever wrote. I think it's because JFK had died the day before. We dedicated it to him and I tried to sing it sweetly, you know, trying to capture the sound of an angel.

HK: "All Summer Long."

BW: That was inspired by my wife, Marilyn, when I spilled Coke all over her at the Pandora's Box club in Hollywood.

was a true gentleman. He was a legendary music man. Murry Wilson brought me "Surfin' Safari," and he said, "Russ, we've gone from Candix to Era Records." Herb Newman's label. He and Murry did not hit if off. Murry came to me one day and said he was looking for another label. I said fine, and I would take it over to Randy Wood at Dot. I called Mr. Wood, and he passed. Wink Martindale was working for him at the time, and he liked the record. When I took the Beach Boys around Los Angeles, A&R people said, "Surf music is a dying fad, and it will be over in a couple of months."

I then called Nik Venet at Capitol Records, who was in A&R. Nik was a damn good record man. "I want you to know what's going on—I have this record by the Beach Boys." "Why me?" "Well, number one, you're my friend, and I think this can be a hit record." Kim Fowley had also mentioned the Beach Boys and surf music to Nik Venet.

So I sent Murry over there. Venet then called me at Buck Eye. "You're right! This is a hit, and I'm gonna buy it." And Murry gets on the phone and says thank you. Murry asked me to promote "Surfin' USA" for $300. I said, "Tell you what, Murry. I think it's a number-one hit. Let me get $200 now, and when it goes to number one, make it $400."

I took it to number one. I would go to radio stations, bring coffee and donuts to DJs at KFWB and KRLA. Dick Moreland at KRLA was one of the great program directors, and he had great ears. He recognized a hit, and a lot of radio guys didn't use the word "hit."

The Beach Boys signed with Capitol Records in July 1962, and released their debut album, Surfin' Safari, *produced by Nik Venet, later that year. The LP spent*

EAST MEETS WEST IN HOLLYWOOD

MARK GUERRERO: In 1964, my dad, who was a singer and songwriter [Lalo Guerrero, the father of Chicano music], received a phone call from producer Don Costa asking him to come to Western Recorders on Sunset, where he was working with Trini Lopez. They wanted him to write a Spanish lyric to a song Trini was recording, that my dad titled "Chamaka."

Dad invited me to come with him to the session to help Trini with the lyric. I invited Richard Rosas from my band, Mark and the Escorts, to come along. We arrived at Western Recorders and were led into a big studio, where Trini was about to sing with a large orchestra. Strings and the whole deal. There might have been some Wrecking Crew guys in the band, but I didn't notice them at that age. We met Trini and Don, which was pretty exciting for me and Richard. We were only fourteen years old and in some pretty impressive company.

We watched the session for a while, and then Richard and I went wandering through the hallways when I see these two blonde guys. "Are you Jan and Dean?" And they said, "No. We're the Beach Boys." It was Al Jardine and Mike Love. They said, "Come on

in." They didn't know who the hell we were.

We walk in, and lo and behold, there was Brian Wilson at the board and all the other members. Nobody else. They were recording the song "All Summer Long," and about to overdub some vocals. They were all around the mike, and we're just sitting there in the control room, in front of the mixing board with Brian Wilson.

On a break, Dennis Wilson came over and handed us a couple of singles with picture sleeves of their soon-to-be-released "I Get Around." I asked him to sign it, and Mike as well, on the back of the picture sleeves. We were thrilled to get the records signed. Then "I Get Around" went to number one on June 6, 1964.

Richard and I were sort of East L.A. music kids from the scene that had Cannibal and the Headhunters, the Premiers, and Thee Midniters, and here we are meeting the Beach Boys, purely by chance. And they couldn't be nicer. We went back to the Trini Lopez session, which came out great. It was quite a night for a couple of teenage Chicanos from East L.A. Mark and the Escorts and the Beach Boys both played the Rainbow Gardens in Pomona.

**Dennis Wilson (*left*) and Brian Wilson (*standing, center*) visiting Joey Paige (*third from left*)
and Phil and Don Everly backstage at the Hollywood Bowl, with KRLA DJ Dave Hull (*right*), 1967.**

thirty-seven weeks on the Billboard *chart. The surf was
definitely up.*

*Al Jardine's first lead vocal with the Beach Boys was
on "Christmas Day," a selection from* The Beach Boys'
Christmas Album. *His memorable reading on "Help Me,
Rhonda" came a year later.*

AL JARDINE: I remember every time walking down the
hallway at Capitol's Studio A. Pictures of Frank Sinatra,
Judy Garland, Bobby Darin, and Gene Vincent and the

Blue Caps were on the wall. "Am I really here?" There
would be a microphone with Frank Sinatra's name on it.
A special Neumann 47 in a box. We used a 67 vocal mic.
A C 12 AKG was also something that worked for us a
lot. I had to stand on a box to sing vocals with the guys.
I had my own box!

With Brian, everything is, "What key is it in?" How
does it sound the best to him in his head? He chose
"Rhonda" for me. I sound best on my leads in D and
C-sharp, and C, or E, maybe. But this C-sharp key was

Brian Wilson and the Honeys (Diane Rovell, Ginger Blake, and Marilyn Wilson) at Western Recorders, Hollywood, 1967.

perfect for me. Mike's range is in a different key than mine. Carl or Brian could have done it, but Brian was thinking ahead. In 1965, he was thinking, "I've got to get these guys leads that they can sing on the road." We did the vocals en masse at RCA one day. I think Brian might have cut the track there as well. You get attached to a particular environment.

The initial bass line on "Rhonda" was entirely different, and Brian thought, "I've got to make this more musical." That's Brian's genius working with bass lines. He put this beautiful dancing bass line around my vocal. The first "Rhonda" track, with the early harmonica, was a shuffle, and the tempo was designed around a more laid-back style with a ukulele and harmonicas on it. It initially didn't have the backbeat you were accustomed to on a rock record. So Brian redesigned it as more of a performance tune, with a good backbeat.

We did it again. Two different sessions. I went back and did the vocal. That great bass line is more uptempo. The ukulele is gone. The guy experimented with everything. It was a totally different direction for us. I was going in there to do the best performance I could, and the other guys were also maybe more aware than I was. I just wanted to get it done and finish it.

CHRIS DARROW: Randy Wood at Dot Records understood surf music as a commercial genre in the early sixties. He acquired the regional hit single "Boss" by the Rumblers, who were from Norwalk and cut in Downey. Then another Downey studio band, the Chantays, who hailed from Santa Ana in the nearby Orange County area, did "Pipeline." Wood also picked up "Wipe Out" by the Surfaris from Glendora.

Liberty Records was sort of into the surf music. They released the instrumentals of the Ventures. A lot of their recordings were connected with the surfing. Initially, it was their great "Walk, Don't Run" single, and then the really popular "Play Guitar with the Ventures" albums that helped make kids pick up the electric guitar and further exposed both instrumental and surf music. They covered "Wipe Out."

DON WILSON: The Ventures signed to Dalton, who was distributed by Liberty Records. We were in Tacoma, Washington. I happened to meet the Champs, when we went to see them at the Tacoma Armory in Washington. That was the first time we knew "Walk, Don't Run" was doing something nationally. They were very good and had charted with "Tequila." When they got offstage, we went back and said, "We play guitar and have a song out, too, 'Walk, Don't Run.'" And they said, "'Walk, Don't

Carl Wilson (*left*) and Bill Pittman at Western Recorders, circa 1966/1967.

Run.' Are you the Ventures?" "Yes." "I don't know how many times we heard that coming up from Los Angeles. Fifty times. They are playing the hell out of that."

We mostly went on the road. Played Pandora's Box in Hollywood, probably in 1963, and did one or two shows later on with Chuck Berry. Jan and Dean at the Santa Monica Civic Auditorium. Initially, we were never booked with surf packages, and I've always wondered how, later, we got grouped with surf music. One of our biggest albums was a surfing album, and we got stuck with that label. It's worked out okay. We got stamped with a relationship to water and surf music. It continues to this day.

If you play "Walk, Don't Run" all the time, it's just not gonna happen. We were looking for anything we could do, and those TV themes were mostly instrumental songs, nine out of ten. *Batman* and *James Bond*. That was a natural for us to go on, instrumentally. The songs could work without the visual. They were cinematic in nature, and minor keys we love. That's one of the reasons we got so popular in Japan. Minor keys are very prominent in Japanese music.

I think that our early learning and our musical appreciation, even before we picked up guitars, were quite different from somebody who picks up a guitar and has only heard and appreciates rock 'n' roll. We go back to Frank Sinatra, Bing Crosby, Jerry Vale—so many of these people that we really respected—and we learned those kinds of songs. We learned tunes like "Stardust" after we really started playing, and probably playing not the most perfect chords, but good enough. We were very conscious of playing something that sounded not right. There could have been better chords, no doubt about it, but they weren't bad chords. I've heard a lot of that. And we'd modulate—change keys—in our records. Modulating; we've done that a lot of times. You don't want the damn thing to get boring.

For many followers of the band, *Ventures in Space*, done in 1964, is their favorite album. I don't know if it has anything to do with not using anything electronic. We had a steel guitar player, Red Rhodes, he was absolutely great, and he put the first fuzz tone together. He owned a couple of equipment patents, and he could play anything. Using his steel guitar and all the things he could come up with sounds, and all the sounds that we could come up with . . . we tried—we accomplished—using no electronics at all. I think that impressed a lot of players.

We then did a psychedelic album. A local L.A. DJ, the Real Don Steele on KHJ radio, came to us and said, "There's something coming up called psychedelic, and you guys should get on that right away because it's really gonna be something." So we did an album of it. We stretched out on that album, and I really like it.

PETER PIPER: In the late fifties and early sixties, my dad and I got exposed to rock 'n' roll when it was used as theme songs for TV shows or some movies. Like the *Rebel* series with Nick Adams, where Johnny Cash did the theme. Johnny was around Los Angeles then, from 1958 to 1964, when he lived in Ventura County, and always would be on TV shows in town like *Town Hall Party*, that I think was done in Compton. We were all looking and searching for something in what I call the "Eisenhower Years." I also found escape in surfing, which I started in 1957. My name was "Water Baby." It was also a world when people lived in L.A. and didn't lock their doors or cars.

Surf music was Dick Dale and the Del-Tones. He showed up and delivered instrumental music with a good beat, and it was loud. It worked. I saw him many times at the Rendezvous Ballroom with the Righteous Brothers.

It was kind of an accepted thing that groups performing didn't have all original material. Surf and soul music were played in the same room together. The electric guitars made you dance and move to it. In the summer of 1962, '63, we would go to the Rendezvous to see the surf bands, including the Rhythm Rockers. These people and bands, a lot of them surfed. Not like the Beach Boys, where only Dennis Wilson, the drummer, went in the water and surfed. The early surf movies of the late fifties had jazz soundtracks, like *Slippery When Wet* with Bud Shank, Gary Peacock, and Larry Bunker. Henry Mancini with the *Peter Gunn* theme. In the early sixties, the Sandals did the music for *The Endless Summer*.

In Los Angeles, there was a deep connection between rock 'n' roll and surfing, since both had shows on television—*Lloyd Thaxton,* and later, *Walt Phillips' Surfing World*. I mean, half-hour or hour programs. Eventually, surf film director Hal Jepson, in his *Cosmic Children* and *A Sea for Yourself* movies, used the groups Love and the Dragons in his soundtracks.

DENNIS DRAGON: There was usually a relationship between jazz and surf music, and the message we put on-screen with the visuals was via our music. I was influenced by KBCA, the local jazz channel. The Dragons in 1960 or '61 actually did some gigs and recording with Natalie Cole at that time. Both my dad, Carmen Dragon, and Nat King Cole were then Capitol Records mainstays. I seem to remember that they actually had a band title for their collective kids and friends: the Malibu Music Men Plus One. Later on, the Dragons had a single on Capitol Records in 1964—"Elephant Stomp," an instrumental released in limited distribution.

CAROL CONNORS (formerly Annette Kleinbard): One day I went to visit [automotive designer] Caroll Shelby. I got an appointment. I was wearing hip-huggers. He loved the Teddy Bears' "To Know Him Is to Love Him," and he remembered it. Carroll said in a Texas accent, "If you write a song about my car and it goes to number one, I'll give you one." I went home and wrote "Hey Little Cobra" with my brother Marshall. It was done at our mother's house. I had always been writing songs. I knew Terry Melcher at Columbia Records. I had previously recorded in their studio. I played Terry the song in a room with a piano, and he responded, "This is fabulous!" I didn't

go to the recording session done with the Rip Chords. I went to Mexico.

I was the only girl to ever really write a hot rod song. The Rip Chords had a big hit with it, and at one point it became a number-one record produced by Bruce [Johnston] and Terry [Melcher]. They also sang on the session. Then Terry started producing Paul Revere and the Raiders and the Byrds. In 1964, Bruce would join the Beach Boys.

I loved Brian Wilson and the Beach Boys. I just thought their music was free, exciting, and West Coast. I was never a surfer, but I was a water baby—a scuba diver and water skier.

They hated the fact that "Hey Little Cobra" was written by a girl. Remember—it was a car song, and I was a girl who wrote a car song. Unheard of. It did go number one in *Cash Box*. Brian Wilson later came up to me and said, "We knew it was written by a girl." He spit the word "girl" out. [*Laughs.*] I asked him, "How did you know?" "Well, you can't take your car out of gear and let it coast to the line." I said, "Yes you can, Brian, if it's that far out in front." I remember that.

Of all the things, then Brian moved on to my street on Ferrari Drive. Caroll Shelby, to this day, says, "You know, Carol, you're really a traitor." "Why?" "You live on Ferrari Drive."

"The story of Jan and Dean begins under the showers at Emerson Junior High in Los Angeles, with [Jan] Berry leading his football teammates in after-game doo-wop sessions," music historian Gary Pig Gold explained. "Soon, these sing-alongs moved into Berry's garage, where, with friends Dean Torrence and Arnie Ginsburg [accompanied by drummer Sandy Nelson and future Beach Boy Bruce Johnston], songs were written and painstakingly recorded. They first performed as the Barons at a University High School dance."

"Jennie Lee," an ode to the Hollywood burlesque queen, was recorded by Berry and Ginsburg in 1958 and climbed to the Top 10. Their second single, "Gas Money," also climbed the Billboard *charts, but their third, "The Beat That Can't Be Beat," failed to chart. As 1958 drew to a close, Dean Torrence returned from an army reserves obligation and reclaimed his partnership with Berry.*

Annette Kleinbard in Los Angeles, 1964.

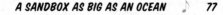

Jan and Dean at Western Recorders, Hollywood, 1965.

Kim Fowley then introduced Berry and Torrence to Lou Adler, who signed and managed them. Aided by Adler and Herb Alpert, Jan and Dean achieved a Top 10 hit with a remake of the Laurels' "Baby Talk" on Dore Records. They went on to record for Gene Autry's Challenge label in 1961 before signing with Liberty in '62.

Jan and Dean recorded over two dozen hits, all arranged and produced by Berry. "Surf City," "Drag City," "Dead Man's Curve," and "The Little Old Lady from Pasadena" stood firm against the tsunami of the British Invasion. Following their wonderfully wacky surf and car craze ditties, they turned to more emotionally-centered material; "You Really Know How to Hurt a Guy" and "I Found a Girl" went Top 30 in 1965.

ELLIOT KENDALL: Dean Torrence was the perfect comic foil to Jan Berry's animated antics throughout their career. He injected such warmth and spontaneity into the live performances, and always appeared to be keeping his sense of self throughout the success of the duo. Jan was incredibly ambitious, and their friendship very likely went through any number of tests, as would be commonplace for the sudden attention they achieved.

If Jan was the classic example of a driven, Type A personality, Dean was a Type H, for humor. They both shared a love of the comedic abilities of Laurel and Hardy, and while the influence of that duo on the "Clown Princes of Surf Rock" was apparent, J and D seemed to inject their own West Coast sensibility into everything they did.

Bones Howe and Jan Berry at Western Recorders, mixing the Jan and Dean recording of "Surf City," Hollywood, 1963.

From the outside, Dean always seemed to be a truly cool-headed, carefree spirit, and that came through big time in their live performances and especially in their recorded skits, such as "Schlock Rod" or "Submarine Races." Even if the spoils of success were in abundance during that era, Dean had an air of ease, as if to say to the world, "This is a cake walk," like he could have been just as happy in Southern California without the accolades. There's a certain grace to that, especially in retrospect.

P. F. Sloan once told me that Brian Wilson was checking out Jan's sessions to pick up on techniques and ideas—just as much as Jan was checking out Brian's sessions. Exciting to think about those times, when crack session cats all recorded in one room with tube equalizers and fat-sounding microphones, [with] the warmth of analog tape and a minimum of overdubs—coupled with a maximum of ideas—to create the California sound.

GARY PIG GOLD: It continues to astound me how Jan Berry is never credited with being one of the first and foremost architects of California rock. From his practically pre-Spector garage, reel-to-reel experimentations as a teen through his, in many ways, beyond-Brian Wilson, mid-sixties studio creations, Jan was just as energetically at home handing out complex scores to the Wrecking Crew as he was yukking it up on weekends onstage with Dean.

Had he not taken that one last ride in the spring of '66, there's absolutely no telling where Jan's multitude of talents, good looks, spirit, and all-American drive would have taken him—with the rest of the California sound in his back pocket.

DON PEAKE: I was with Jan at his house after his car crash. He was in a coma for six months. His father invited me up, and the Corvette was sitting there—smashed, like

Jan's head was smashed. Hal Blaine and I sat together for almost three months, waiting for Jan to come out of the coma at UCLA. Now Jan wakes up and looks at us. He can't remember a thing about medical school (he'd been studying pre-med), but he remembered the music—because it's right-brain, and his left brain was smashed. And he says to me, "Don. Don. French horn."

Later, I was at my house in Laurel Canyon, and the doorbell rings at 2:00 AM. I go downstairs, and it's Jan. He walked from Mulholland Drive and the 405 Freeway all the way to Laurel Canyon to my house. He was covered in sweat, he had a music score clutched in his hand, and wanted to talk about the score. We had him sleep on the couch, and the next morning we drove him home.

Jan Berry was an amazing musician. He could write scores. After the crash, the only thing that was left was the music. We did some sessions, but it was never the same.

By the end of 1961, Herb Alpert had been producing and writing songs, gigging around, surfacing in over twenty movies as a musician, including playing the kettledrums in director Cecil B. DeMille's The Ten Commandments. *But activity was no substitute for achievement, and Alpert struggled to find his "voice."*

WINK MARTINDALE: Herb Alpert recorded "Tell It to the Birds" as Dore Alpert for Dot Records. I was the A&R man at Dot and signed Dore [Herb], who took his $750 record advance monies and quickly plowed it into his next record ["Love Is Back in Style," on the Carnival label]. Afterwards, Herb started A&M Records with Jerry Moss. Their first hit single was 1962's "The Lonely Bull" by Herb Alpert and the Tijuana Brass.

It all came together in Tijuana, Mexico, when Alpert and Moss attended a bullfight. The drama and pageantry of the regal sport inspired "The Lonely Bull," Alpert's breakthrough 1962 hit that launched A&M Records out of his garage and into the big time.

HERB ALPERT: That's where it all started, back in the garage in 1962. We were watching a bullfight. The great Carlos Arruza. "We" being my partner, Jerry Moss, and myself. We were sort of intrigued by the sound of the mariachi band in the stands, which is the traditional music of Mexico. We got this idea of trying to fuse the two forms of music together—the mariachi sound with sort of an American jazz pulsation underneath. That's basically the sound of the group.

On the first record, "The Lonely Bull," we also tried to capture the "*olés*." We tried to get a sort of audio and video effect on record. It opened up with a fanfare, and I had an engineer friend of mine go down to Tijuana and actually tape the crowd's reaction to the bullfight, which we overdubbed on the recording.

I wanted to find my own identity. I don't really think of my music as a sound. I think of it as a pulse, and there's quite a difference between a sound and a pulse.

In 1964, the Clark Chewing Gum Company took one of Alpert's 1964 recordings, "The Mexican Shuffle," written by his friend, Sol Lake, and retitled it "The Teaberry Shuffle" for a popular television ad campaign.

In 1964, Alpert formed a live Tijuana Brass unit for touring that formally debuted in 1965. The group recorded the most popular instrumental version of "A Taste of Honey," included on their 1965 album, Whipped Cream and Other Delights. *Their rendition ruled the easy listening charts for weeks, and* Whipped Cream *won Record of the Year at the Grammy Awards in 1966.*

The critical and retail success of Alpert and his band encouraged A&M to sign additional acts, including South Bay's Chris Montez, the Sandpipers, Burt Bacharach, Tommy Boyce and Bobby Hart, Sergio Mendes and Brazil '66, and the Baja Marimba Band with Julius Wechter, the marimba player with the Tijuana Brass.

JULIUS WECHTER: I think, because it's right down the middle, it appeals to people in our generation, and it appeals to older people because they can understand that the melody is there. Yet it has a fantastic beat to it, which the kids certainly understand.

SERGIO MENDES: I think it's happy music. Very happy. The rhythm is very strong. It is the kind of music that reaches a lot of people, you know. He communicates with the mass—a lot of people.

CHAPTER 8

GO EAST, YOUNG MAN

GENE AGUILERA: The East L.A. music scene was a sleeping giant, as far as I am concerned. The media, especially rock history books and documentaries, have ignored or rarely acknowledged our vast contributions to popular culture and music.

The Phil Spector Wall of Sound hit records of the early sixties certainly influenced people like Eddie Davis and Billy Cardenas, who were key architects of the East L.A. sound. Eddie Davis was a Jewish kid who grew up in Boyle Heights, started out as a child actor, went on to flipping burgers, and then started Rampart Records. He unearthed local talent in the East Side, and became our answer to Motown Records.

EDDIE DAVIS: In 1949, I had a restaurant that was called the Pancake Twins on First and La Brea. I had it for three years. This was at the time they were building the Hollywood Freeway. Then I had the Eddie Davis Steakhouse, which at the time was a club on Cahuenga and Hollywood Boulevard.

I was always involved with music back then. I had this hankering to sing and I had money, so I tried to get somebody to take me out as a singer, and nobody would. So I got a hold of a music director, Ralph Hallenbeck, and asked him to help me do a session for myself. This was in 1956. I believe he was on the A&R staff at Capitol Records. I needed background singers, so I called the choir and got Tony Butala, who was part of the group the Lettermen, and a girl named Constance. They came in and did the background vocals, and we did the first "custom" session after they built the Capitol Tower.

Non-Capitol, meaning the first outside entry to be done there—the first custom job.

I did four sides and could never get anybody to do anything with them. It was disheartening. Incidentally, the girl named Constance was Constance Ingoglia, who later became known as the actress Connie Stevens. It was her singing on my record of "Between the Devil and the Deep Blue Sea" that got her the job of singing with Edd Byrnes on "Kookie, Kookie (Lend Me Your Comb)."

DJ Dick Moreland came to KRLA in 1962 from KACY in Oxnard, [and] really helped me. We put our heads together with the idea that we could promote KRLA, and they could promote our bands. Dick and I met Bob Eubanks, who was the all-night disc jockey. I met Bob and DJ Wink Martindale through Dick, and we initiated the KRLA Friday Night Dance at Rainbow Gardens in Pomona, featuring the Mixtures. We got them on local television shows, Saturday afternoons on Channel 13 with White Front appliance stores paying the television time. The show was called *Parade of Hits*. Live performances were at Pomona on Friday nights, and on Saturdays we moved all around—El Monte, Compton, San Bernardino, Burbank, everywhere.

In 1962, we did an album with the Mixtures. We were at Rainbow Gardens, and because of KRLA, in those days the stars were going around doing promotions, and KRLA used to get us our feature acts. They would come out and do a show. We had everybody—Frankie Avalon, Roy Orbison, and Herb Alpert, when he was known as Dore Alpert. The Beach Boys did their very first job there. They'd all come for nothing, only

Opposite: **Thee Midniters on Olvera Street in Los Angeles, 1968:** (*left to right*) **Larry Rendon, Roy Marquez, George Dominguez, Danny LaMont, Romeo Prado, Little Willie G., and Jimmy Espinoza.**

Memory Dance flier, 1965.

as a promotion and a favor for the radio station. Most of the acts lip-synced their records. Roy Orbison would play live.

So then we tried another Mexican American band of Billy Cardenas's, the Premiers. I then heard "Farmer John," by Don and Dewey. I told him that I wanted to record it, and we did. The Premiers were the greatest groove band in the world, but they couldn't sing for shit! The vocal on the record was so bad, I just didn't know what to do.

When I recorded my Rainbow Gardens album, I used Wally Heider, who became a famous technician. At that time, he had just gotten his first remote three-track, and he did my first album "live" from the Rainbow Gardens in Pomona. I was interested in live sounds, trying to develop that, so I suggested that we record "Farmer John" live. We got a crowd, and we took them over to the studio and just over-dubbed the music with the party going on. That's how that happened. It was on my Faro label, then licensed to Warner Bros. It's a very groovy single, and

we made it live. All those voices screaming . . . nobody had ever done that. They were a girls' car club called the Chevelles that used to follow the Premiers. They were cholitas. They would scream and holler for the Premiers.

The Blendells were another of Billy Cardenas's groups. They had "La La La La," a number-one record in Hawaii and the number two-record in L.A. I released it on Rampart, but it went to Reprise. They were the backup band on the recording of "Land of a Thousand Dances" by Cannibal and the Headhunters. They had a backup band called the Rhythm Playboys.

All the bands I recorded were Hispanic. I never really planned to do it. I just happen to like the sound of that ethnic thing. I don't think they knew they had it—it kind of caught me. It was inbred. It turned me on, and that's what I was trying to develop. A couple of times, it captured great public acceptance. That's what I was always trying to record, and then they started calling it "the East Side Sound."

TOM WALDMAN: DJs like Art Laboe, Huggy Boy, and later, Godfrey, were vital in exposing doo-wop, early rock 'n' roll, and R & B to the East L.A. community. They had an audience there, and they were accessible. Like, Billy Cardenas might not have known how to put a record of his in front of the head of Capitol Records, but what he did know was to go see Huggy Boy at the Dolphin's of Hollywood record store and ask him to put a record on. And Huggy Boy would. That was their way of promoting the record, and maybe getting a deal out of it. Their recognition early on of the Mexican American audience enabled Mexican American producers and groups to, in a certain sense, do an end run around the music establishment and get their stuff played on shows that could be heard by tens of thousands of Mexican American listeners. So it became part of the whole marketing plan for that area and those groups. Without them, this music stays really buried underground. They recognized the Mexican American audience before America did. They recognized it as a distinct audience.

MARK GUERRERO: I was an East L.A. kid from the scene that had Cannibal and the Headhunters, the Blendells, the Premiers, Thee Midniters. We loved the Blendells. We had the same manager, Billy Cardenas, so Mark and

```
The GODFREY Show          SOUL of TODAY           The GODFREY Show
4:30 - 5:30 PM           SOUL of TOMORROW          4:30 - 5:30 PM
    K T Y M              SOUL of YESTERDAY             K T Y M
      A M                                                A M
. Radio  1460            Week ending May 15, 1971     Radio  1460

 TW  LW               S O U L   of   T O D A Y

  1   4   BRIDGE OVER TROUBLE WATERS     ARETHA FRANKLIN        ATLANTIC
  2   1   WANT ADS                       HONEY CONE             HOT WAX
  3   2   NEVER CAN SAY GOODBYE          JACKSON FIVE           MOTOWN
  4   5   I LOVE YOU FOR ALL SEASONS     THE FUZZ               CALLA
  5  10   RIGHT ON THE TIP OF MY TONGUE  BRENDA/THE TABULATIONS TOP & BOTTOM
  6   8   BOOTY BUTT                     RAY CHARLES ORCHESTRA  TANGERINE
  7  22   FUNKY MUSIC SHO-NUFF TURN ME ON EDWIN STARR           GORDY
  8  19   SHE'S NOT JUST ANOTHER WOMAN   THE 8TH DAY            INVICTUS
  9  13   DON'T KNOCK MY LOVE            WILSON PICKETT         ATLANTIC
 10  15   I NEED SOMEONE                 Z.Z. HILL              KENT
 11  20   IT'S TOO LATE                  CAROLE KING            ODE
 12  16   I NEED YOU BABY                JESSE JAMES            ZEA
 13  12   I'M SORRY                      BOBBY BLAND            DUKE
 14   9   MELTING POT                    BOOKER T. & THE MG'S   STAX
 15  21   REACH OUT, I'LL BE THERE       DIANA ROSS             MOTOWN
 16  17   BABY SHOW IT                   THE FESTIVALS          COLOSSUS
 17  24   I CRIED                        JAMES BROWN            KING
 18  28   SUNSHINE                       FLAMING EMBER          HOT WAX
 19  29   THE SWEETEST THING             THE PRESIDENTS         SUSSEX
 20  DB   YOUR LOVE                      WATTS 103RD STREET BAND WARNER BROS.
 21  DB   THERE'S SO MUCH LOVE           THREE DEGREES          ROULETTE
 22  DB   I'LL ERASE THE PAIN            THE WHATNAUTS          STANG
 23  DB   WHOLESALE LOVE                 BUDDY MILES            MERCURY
 24  25   AIN'T NOTHING GOING TO CHANGE ME BETTY EVERETT        FANTASY
 25  DB   NEVER CAN SAY GOODBYE          ISAAC HAYES            ENTERPRISE
 26  DB   NATHAN JONES                   THE SUPREMES           MOTOWN
 27  27   YOU MAKE ME WANT TO LOVE YOU   THE EMOTIONS           VOLT
 28  DB   TREAT HER LIKE A LADY          CORNELIUS BROS.        U. A.
 29  30   LONELY FEELIN'                 WAR                    U. A.
 30  DB   I KNOW - I'M IN LOVE           CHEE CHEE & PEPE       BUDDAH
  S       CUBANO CHANT                   EL CHICANO             KAPP
  O       LONG NIGHTS                    B. B. KING             KENT
  U       LILA, LOVE ME TONIGHT          MARK GUERRERO          ODE
  L       MANDRILL                       MANDRILL               POLYDOR
     of   EVERY DOG'S GOT HIS DAY        JOHNNY COPELAND        KENT
  T       IT AIN'T NO ACHIEVEMENT        THE MILLIONAIRES       SPECIALTY
  O       I MADE MY OWN WORLD            VERNON GARRETT         WATTS USA
  M       IF I SHOULD WIN YOUR LOVE      THE SOUL GENTS         FROS-RAY
  O       EVIL WAYS                      CAL TJADER             FANTASY
  R       HEY DOES SOMEBODY CARE         GOD'S CHILDREN         UNI
  R       TROUBLE                        FOXY                   DOUBLE SHOT
  O       YOU'RE GONNA MAKE ME CRY       STAPLE SINGERS(LP CUT) STAX
  W       COME BACK FINISH WHAT YOU STARTED FAITH, HOPE, CHARITY SUSSEX
      Y   LOVERS                         THE BLENDTONES         FLASHBACK
  S   E   OUR DAY WILL COME              RUBY & ROMANTICS       KAPP
  O   S   PLEASE PLEASE PLEASE           JAMES BROWN            KING
  U   T   25 MILES                       EDWIN STARR            GORDY
  L   E   B-A-B-Y                        CARLA THOMAS           STAX
      R   LEAVIN' IT ALL UP TO YOU       DON & DEWEY            SPECIALTY
  o   D   OH HAPPY DAY                   EDWIN HAWKINS          BUDDAH
  f   A   SOMEBODY PLEASE                THE VANGUARDS          WHIZ
      Y   DREAM A LITTLE DREAM           PEREZ BROS.            OFIES
```

Playlist for *The Godfrey Show* on KTYM, 1971.

the Escorts were on the bill with them several times.

We did "Get Your Baby" for the Rampart label. We played with Cannibal and the Headhunters. I was proud of them, and they had a hit record, "Land of a Thousand Dances." I saw them open for the Beatles at the Hollywood Bowl. And they were the only act that got any response at all. They were a dancing vocal group, like the Temptations.

Thee Midniters were probably the most popular group in East L.A. at that time, even with these other groups having hits. They got screams. They had the look; they were polished and smooth. Little Willie G., I always looked at like a Frank Sinatra—a skinny guy who sang ballads. That was his strong suit, and still is. The girls screaming. We liked them. "Whittier Boulevard" was a local and national hit.

Billy Cardenas describes himself as a *vato* from East

L.A., this street kid. He just loved music. He took a lot of guys—for example, the Premiers, these lowrider kind of guys. Pachuco kind of guys. They were playing in the backyard, [and Billy] polished them up, got them in suits—sort of like what Brian Epstein did to the Beatles, but Chicano style. He managed so many bands. He was a record company owner and kind of a record producer sometimes, but more the manager. But Billy also was in the studio producing.

I'm just saying, if it weren't for Eddie Davis, none of that would have happened. We needed his record labels, and getting the stuff out . . . his record savvy that created the Blendells and Cannibal and the Headhunters, it was essential. And we needed Billy because he was out there in the trenches, finding these groups and grooming them.

Mark and the Escorts, 1964: (*left to right*) Ricky Almaraz, Trini Basulto, Rick Rosas, Mark Guerrero (*seated*), Ernie Hernandez, and Robert Warren.

BORN TO SING AND PERFORM

LITTLE WILLIE G.: In 1960, when I started going to high school, I met Raul, Benny, and Richard Ceballos, and they had a band. The drummer was Jerry Ainsworth, who was an Orthodox Russian Jew who lived in Boyle Heights. As a dig to his dad, we called the band "the Gentiles," 'cause every Wednesday, when we would pick up Jerry for rehearsal, we could hear his dad yelling, "Jerry! Jerry! What's the matter with you, hanging around with those unclean Gentiles!" Every Wednesday, the same spiel. What a way to get back at his dad, by seeing our names on posters all over East L.A.

We were just a garage band. After a while, the name "the Gentiles" didn't look as glamorous on posters as "the Romancers" and "Richard and the Emeralds." So we felt we had to change our name and image. So we kicked it around, and Hank Ballard and the Midnighters were one of our favorite groups.

Little Willie G. (*left*) and Bobby Cochran in a photo taken by Cochran's mother, performing at the first "Battle of the Bands" show in St. Alphonsus Hall at East L.A. College, 1962.

We all were throwing names into the hat that day. "Thee" was Eddie Torres's idea to set us apart, and thus started a wave of "Thee" bands all over the East Side. We talked a lot about who were our favorite bands, and Hank Ballard and the Midnighters was high on everyone's list!

First we changed the spelling of "Midnighters." It could have been our manager, or someone in the band who suggested "Thee" at the front. Perhaps Bobby Cochran, Eddie Cochran's nephew, who was one of our guitar players in that early band. We said, "Let's be 'Thee Midniters!'" In 1961, it was Benny and Thee Midniters, and we did a battle of the bands at St. Alphonsus Hall [at East L.A. College]. We employed "Thee" in front of our band name because we wanted to emphasize who we were.

The group recorded in Hollywood on Melrose Avenue, at Studio Masters with Bruce Morgan, who was a godsend. He had worked with the Beach Boys there and was just an incredible guy. "What do you guys want to sound like?" We told him, "We want to sound the way we sound live, when we are playing on a stage or in a backyard." There's an energy, vibe, and cohesion with a unity that comes across.

We recorded over twenty-five singles. It was right across the street from Paramount Pictures. Studio Masters was right next door to Lucy's El Adobe Café. It was not unusual to go into Lucy's El Adobe and see Leonard Nimoy and William Shatner come in wearing full makeup during their lunch break from filming the *Star Trek* television series.

After "Land of a Thousand Dances," the British Invasion happened in 1964 and 1965. At rehearsal, one of our warm-up songs was "2120 South Michigan Avenue" by the Rolling Stones, from their *12 X 5* LP. We needed a follow-up record for Chattahoochee Records. Samy Phillip [later known as Hirth Martinez] wrote a song, "Evil Love." We went in and did it. Then Bruce Morgan said, "Okay, what's the B-side?" And we looked at each other. We didn't even think of that.

I suggested that we cut "2120" as a cover. Then Romeo Prado, the trombone player in the group, said we had to change it, you know. "Let's put some horns on it." Romeo is the architect of Thee Midniters' sound. We also knew the value of instrumentals. Like, there were surf music instrumentals. The instrumental is not a novelty in East L.A. We were following James Brown. "Night Train," those type of things. "Harlem Nocturne."

The street Whittier Boulevard became a cruising

mecca. They started coming from Orange County and the San Fernando Valley, and from the beach cities. Our audience was everybody. They'd come from San Pedro, Hermosa, Manhattan Beach, Van Nuys, Pacoima. They would come to Whittier Boulevard partly because of our song, but we also had three things in common: music, cars, and girls. You could find all that on Whittier Boulevard.

We weren't throwing beer bottles at each other as the highway patrol and the sheriffs tried to make it out to be when they started to shut Whittier Boulevard down. There was actually an article in the *L.A. Times* where they blamed it on Thee Midniters' "Whittier Boulevard" song. There was always white fear. Before Mayor Sam Yorty, it was Chief Parker. This goes back many years.

Thee Midniters had strong support from the local DJs. Art Laboe, Huggy Boy, and Godfrey, as well as Sam Riddle on KHJ and Casey Kasem and Dave Hull from KRLA, took us to the air force bases. We were Casey's favorite band to book. He was an advocate of what we did, and then Dave Hull, and then Sam Riddle. They hired us for their private events and the dances they sponsored.

We were not stuck in a doo-wop bag, either. We were total entertainers. We played a lot of backyard, family-oriented parties. The older folks wanted to hear *boleros*; they wanted to hear *corridos*. Then you had the second generation that wanted to hear Duke Ellington and big band stuff—Frank Sinatra and Bing Crosby stuff. We learned all that stuff. Because music really transcends borders and colors. I think our band was indicative of that. If you saw the band, you left as a fan.

We were a very versatile band. We added percussion and a horn section, before Chicago and Blood, Sweat and Tears. Johnny and the Crowns had a full horn section, but they never got recognized. If the audience was predominantly black, we could knock out some R & B like anybody else, like "Sad Girl" and "The Town I Live In."

We played everywhere. We were able to go to Thousand Oaks and to Hawthorne for the Drop. We performed at the Rendezvous Ballroom on Balboa Island with Dick Dale. We toured a short season with

Paul Revere and the Raiders in Idaho, Oregon, and Washington.

Thee Midniters played with the Turtles at the Rose Bowl. We used to hang out with the Lovin' Spoonful whenever they came to town to play the Trip. Also, Them with Van Morrison. We actually took Them and Steppenwolf to East L.A. and the Big Union Hall in Vernon. Bought them a quart of vodka. We hung with the Young Rascals every time they were in town. Eddie Brigati of the group would come to East L.A.

We auditioned at most of the clubs on the Sunset Strip. But, at the time, they didn't know what to do with an eight-piece band. That was not common. They were used to trios and four pieces, or four pieces with a singer. We were with the William Morris Agency for a little bit. RCA Records was checking us out when we opened up for Jose Feliciano. When we did our songs then, they were popular music and not oldies.

We did the Teenage Fair in Hollywood on Sunset Boulevard, and the audiences were all white kids. They were looking at us like we were aliens from outer space, some of them making really derogatory comments. "Where are your burritos?" We would hear stuff like that and ignore it, because we knew that as soon as we started playing, they would change their minds about us. That was our attitude. As soon as the music hit, they gravitated towards us. Sometimes they couldn't get us off the stage. They kept calling us back.

Going to Hollywood was utopia for us. We grew up color-blind. Okay, even when the Chicano movement started, and the Brown Berets and those political factions would come and tell us that we were being exploited by the white man and whatnot, we never felt that. We were working. We were recording. We were sitting with record company executives. What they were saying to us didn't register. We weren't experiencing that, man—their whole concept and portrayal of what was going on in the world. We would hear them out and then have discussions about it. We didn't get political with it. We took it someplace else after guitarist George Dominguez said, "I never knew we had it so bad." George, drummer Danny LaMont, and I even wrote a tongue-in-cheek song, "I Never Knew I Had It So Bad," for our third LP, *Unlimited*, on Whittier Records.

I was at all the classic recording studios: Gold Star, RCA, one time at Columbia with Little Ray [Jimenez]. He's very important, and did "I (Who Have Nothing)" on Donna Records, later distributed by ATCO. Arthur Lee, before Love, wrote the B-side "I've Been Trying." Lee [and Johnny Echols] also wrote and worked with Ronnie and the Pomona Casuals on a recording.

East L.A. was always part of the music world. The Byrds played East L.A. College in 1965. I later saw Linda Ronstadt do a show there. Sonny and Cher, when they were Caesar and Cleo, performed all around the area.

RICK ROSAS: Back then, people didn't look at a racial or geographical divide between East L.A. and West L.A. See, people didn't look at your color back in those days. I remember being in Garfield High School, and there were maybe three or four black guys in the school, and you treated them like brothers. They were all very good friends of mine.

I went with my parents to St. Alphonsus Catholic Church. That hall had teen dances. I saw Thee Midniters and the Mixtures, another great band. That was the first time I saw an electric bass onstage. "I gotta get a Fender bass." I got one at Phillips Music Store in Boyle Heights on Brooklyn Avenue. I still have the bass—a '64 jazz bass. My mom bought it for me. I still have the receipt.

There was always Thee Midniters. The records did them justice. Little Willie G.—oh man. He was an entertainer. And the bass player, Jimmy Espinosa—I took lessons from him. He taught me how to read music. Thee Midniters were big mentors to Mark and the Escorts, at the time.

Eddie Davis and Billy Cardenas were very important. They would release stuff on their little private labels, like Rampart, and it would get picked up by a major label because it was making noise in L.A., not just East L.A. Then it became national, like Cannibal and the Headhunters' "Land of a Thousand Dances." Cannibal and the Headhunters and the Blendells were very good. They were mentors, also. We opened up a lot of shows for them, and they showed us the ropes. We listened to all the same radio stations. Even KHJ played our first single on GNP Crescendo.

East Side Revue flier, 1965.

RUSS REGAN: During 1964, '65, and, really, '66, I was the hottest record promotion man in Southern California. I knew Eddie Davis really well and helped spread his records, from the Premiers and Cannibal and the Headhunters. I would go out with him—Topanga Plaza, Johnny Magnus's Sight and Sound store—for an event, and Casey Kasem from KRLA would host.

In 1962, Al Burton started producing the yearly Teen Fair at the Hollywood Palladium on Sunset Boulevard. He also produced TV teenage music shows like *Hollywood a Go Go*. The Teenage Fair was a very important weekend for many years to promote acts and connect with the teenage culture and fashion.

The Teen Fair was not heavily radio-sponsored. The vendors would advertise on KFWB, KHJ, or KRLA. Dick Biondi, a jock on the station, would be around. Sam Riddle, a DJ, was on TV and would introduce acts like the Challengers, who were an instrumental surf group. Knudsen had a yogurt booth. Bands and musical equipment were all part of it. There would be Fender and Vox instrument booths right next to advance label products or promotional items. There were exhibits and dance contests.

Groups from both the East Side and the West Side would all be there. Dick Dale and the Del-Tones played there in 1964, then Sonny and Cher and Captain Beefheart and His Magic Band. The Bobby Fuller Four. The Challengers. Donovan. Jimi Hendrix. The Ventures. They had a battle of the bands.

Top: Thee Midniters performing "Land of a Thousand Dances" during a taping of
9th Street West, their first television appearance, Hollywood, 1964.
Bottom left: St. Alphonsus Youth Club Teen Dance and Show flier, 1965. ♪ *Bottom right:* KRLA "Survey of Hits," 1965.

ST. ALPHONSUS
YOUTH CLUB
Presents: TEEN DANCE & SHOW
★★★
THEE MIDNITERS BAND
☆ ★ ☆
with their New Release "WHITTIER BLVD. & EVIL LOVE"

★ LI'L WILLIE G. (EVIL LOVE)
Singing

★ THE 4 QUEENS ALL GIRLS BAND
Don't miss this

★ RICKY SHADE with his new release
Everybody do THE FILLIE

THE SLAUSON Bros. To do All your favorite songs
Mark & The Escorts with (The Return of Farmer John)
The Impalas Band To do your favorite songs

Plus the Ever popular Group:

★ The Sisters (with Gee Baby Gee)

SAT. MAY 8 ☆ ST. ALPHONSUS HALL
8 p.m. to 12 Mid. 552 S. Amalia Ave. 1 Block E. of Atlantic, E.L.A.

Sporty Dress - Donation $2.00. Midniters fan Club $1.75
Midniters New Release Available this week - Come Early

'THE SURVEY OF HITS'

KRLA TUNE-DEX FEB. 7 - FEB. 13, 1965

THIS WEEK	LAST WEEK			
1	1	YOU'VE LOST THAT LOVIN' FEELIN'	RIGHTEOUS BROS.	PHILLES
2	3	DOWNTOWN	PETULA CLARK	WARNERS
3	2	THE NAME GAME	SHIRLEY ELLIS	CONGRESS
4	6	LAND OF 1000 DANCES	HEADHUNTERS	RAMPART
5	4	MY GIRL	THE TEMPTATIONS	GORDY
6	5	LAUGH LAUGH	THE BEAU BRUMMELS	AUTUMN
7	7	THIS DIAMOND RING	GARY LEWIS	LIBERTY
8	12	LAND OF 1000 DANCES	THE MIDNITERS	CHATTA.
9	10	TELL HER NO	THE ZOMBIES	PARROT
10	13	JOLLY GREEN GIANT	THE KINGSMEN	WAND
11	8	LOVE POTION NO. 9	THE SEARCHERS	KAPP
12	9	ALL DAY & ALL OF THE NIGHT	THE KINKS	REPRISE
13	11	KEEP SEARCHIN'	DEL SHANNON	AMY
14	16	I GO TO PIECES	PETER & GORDON	CAPITOL
15	17	RICHEST MAN ALIVE	MEL CARTER	IMPERIAL
16	31	TWINE TIME	A. CASH & CRAWLERS	MAR-V-LUS
17	14	HOLD WHAT YOU'VE GOT	JOE TEX	DIAL
18	21	KING OF THE ROAD	ROGER MILLER	SMASH
19	23	PAPER TIGER	SUE THOMPSON	HICKORY
20	39	THE BOY FROM NEW YORK CITY	THE AD-LIBS	BLUE CAT
21	35	THE BIRDS & THE BEES	JEWEL AKINS	ERA
22	15	THE "IN" CROWD	DOBIE GREY	CHARGER
23	53	HEART OF STONE	ROLLING STONES	LONDON
24	26	WHERE LOVERS GO	THE JAGUARS	FARO
25	20	GOING OUT OF MY HEAD	ANTHONY & IMPERIALS	DCP
26	19	I FEEL FINE / SHE'S A WOMAN	THE BEATLES	CAPITOL
27	34	LOOK OF LOVE	LESLEY GORE	MERCURY
28	46	NEW YORK'S A LONELY TOWN	THE TRADE WINDS	RED BIRD
29	45	VOICE YOUR CHOICE	THE RADIANTS	CHESS
30	28	WALK AWAY	MATT MONRO	LIBERTY
31	36	FANNIE MAE	RIGHTEOUS BROS.	MOONGLOW
32	47	FERRY ACROSS THE MERSEY	GERRY & PACEMAKERS	LAURIE
33	42	NO ARMS CAN EVER HOLD YOU	THE BACHELORS	LONDON
34	38	RED ROSES FOR A BLUE LADY	BERT KAEMPFERT	DECCA
35	44	CAN'T YOU HEAR MY HEART BEAT	HERMAN'S HERMITS	MGM
36	37	BYE BYE BABY	FOUR SEASONS	PHILIPS
37	41	SHAKE / CHANGE IS GONNA' COME	SAM COOKE	RCA
38	18	COME SEE ABOUT ME	THE SUPREMES	MOTOWN
39	32	THE BOY NEXT DOOR	STANDELLS	VEE JAY
40	50	BORN TO BE TOGETHER	THE RONETTES	PHILLES
41	48	DON'T FORGET I STILL LOVE YOU	BOBBI MARTIN	CORAL
42	43	AT THE CLUB	THE DRIFTERS	ATLANTIC
43	49	THANKS A LOT	BRENDA LEE	DECCA
44	DEBUT	RED ROSES FOR A BLUE LADY	VIC DANA	DOLTON
45	DEBUT	LEMON TREE	TRINI LOPEZ	REPRISE
46	DEBUT	FOR LOVIN' ME	PETER, PAUL & MARY	WARNERS
47	DEBUT	ASK THE LONELY	FOUR TOPS	MOTOWN
48	DEBUT	HE WAS REALLY SAYIN' SOMETHING	THE VELVELETTES	V.I.P.
49	DEBUT	I GOT A TIGER BY THE TAIL	BUCK OWENS	CAPITOL
50	DEBUT	LITTLE THINGS	BOBBY GOLDSBORO	UNITED ART.

KRLA SMASH PREVIEW OF THE WEEK!

8 DAYS A WEEK / DON'T WANT TO SPOIL THE PARTY   THE BEATLES   CAPITOL

DISPATCHES FROM DAVE HULL, THE HULLABALOOER

DAVE HULL: I attended Alhambra High School starting in 1948. In the late forties and early fifties, my favorite radio station was KLAC-AM. The disc jockeys were Dick Haynes, Gene Norman, Al Jarvis and his *Make Believe Ballroom*, Peter Potter, and Jim Hawthorne, who had an instrument on the air called the "hogan-twanger."

After I graduated, I enlisted in the air force and did Armed Forces Radio in North Africa. My national radio career began in 1955, at KGFL in Roswell, New Mexico. I played Elvis Presley, Pat Boone, and Fats Domino. Then, stops at stations in Ohio, WQTE in Detroit, Michigan, and Florida.

My name, "the Hullabalooer," came from my shift in Dayton, Ohio, honking horns and tinkling bells. A woman sent a postcard from a hotel, complaining about me in the afternoons. She wrote, "I can't stand all this hullabaloo." I went to the dictionary, like my dad always told me to do, and looked up the word "hullabaloo." It said, "A tumultuous uproar. A noise." I said, "Jesus. That's me!" So I just put an "-er" at the end of it.

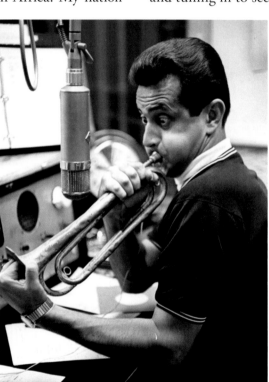

Dave Hull at KRLA in Pasadena, 1965.

I came to Pasadena and KRLA in June of 1963, and stayed until 1969. KFWB was just far and away number one, and beating the pants off KRLA. Then manager John Barrett and Reb Foster, the program director, hired me. John stuck out his hand, looked at me, and said, "We've hired you for Sundays, 6–9. Now go out there and prove us right."

L.A. was changing. In October of '63, the L.A. Dodgers beat the New York Yankees in the World Series. Back on the East Coast, in Ohio, I was already playing Ricky Nelson and Eddie Cochran. I knew when I got out here what the recording artists were like.

John Barrett had an idea that he wanted all of his disc jockeys to be like Jim Hawthorne. He wanted them to be personalities, and different—names and sound effects, horns. You had to do those things to get noticed, and noticing meant success. People talking about you and tuning in to see what the hell you were doing.

Reb told me that I needed a band if I was going to do record hops at schools and places. Because I'd go nuts just playing music, and the kids would go outside and not stick around. Reb said to me and Dick Moreland, "Why don't you and him go looking for a band." And in through the door comes a group called Thee Midniters. I said, "Do you guys have your instruments?" They played for me, without amplification, and they sounded great! I said to Moreland, "We better get this together, 'cause I've got dances on Friday and Saturday night."

I knew the DJ in this town had to wear many hats. Many of the DJs tried to manage bands or have clubs, because nobody at the radio stations wanted to pay us anything. The wages were so severely low at the time, we had to have other outside things to do. Like Reb Foster, who managed groups like the Turtles, and later Steppenwolf and Three Dog Night. And Casey [Kasem] had his TV show. We were making $18,000 a year. So myself and the KRLA DJs made local appearances all over the community, from record stores to shopping centers. When I got to KRLA and started doing it, they were paying $250 for an appearance. Boy, that was big money in 1964, '65, '66, and '67. That was better, sometimes, than working several days on the air.

I would attend the DJ meetings on Monday and hear about these different and new pieces of music, and play 'em. I was a lucky stiff. They did the hard work. KRLA had flexibility in their playlist. That was brought on by Reb Foster, John Barrett, and Dick Moreland. They insisted that we become totally different than everybody else. "If you find a record that has something to offer, especially by a local group, put it on the air. Or bring it to the DJ meeting so we can all hear it." We didn't view records as sections or cities. We didn't have all these people picking everything apart, like today. That's what helped us make decisions that we didn't realize were pretty profound at the time. We just threw it on air.

One aspect of KRLA, from 1964 to 1968, was the weekly *KRLA Beat.* The radio station had a house organ that went way beyond the "Tunedex" columns written by me and other Eleven-Ten Men. It spread the music—at first sixteen pages, and then twenty-four pages.

It came about since it was originally planned as a souvenir for the Beatles' 1964 Hollywood Bowl concert. A short fold-over. It was going to be devoted to the Beatles—KRLA Beatles. "What do you do when they leave town?" "Just drop the '-les' and you got the *KRLA Beat.* We'll make a newspaper out of it." Bingo! It was America's largest teen newspaper.

That's how it started. It went more in depth about the local and national bands, and it

DAVE HULL'S HULLABALOO

hosts

First Annual

**KRLA BEAT
POP MUSIC
AWARDS**

December 8, 1965

**First annual *KRLA Beat* Pop Music
Awards program cover, 1965.**

sent out some really interesting reporters, like Louise Criscone. It deepened the link to the community. And the Chuck Boyd photos . . . Brian Jones, Tom Jones, Bob Dylan, and the Byrds were on the cover. It revolutionized radio with the market, and no one could ever see that coming, even myself. I was one of those who didn't vote against it. The driving force was Dick Moreland. Cecil Tuck was the publisher. A year before *Tiger Beat*, and three years ahead of *Rolling Stone.*

Reb Foster and Bob Eubanks had nightclubs [Revelaire and Cinnamon Cinder, respectively]. I was approached by a company who wanted to do something with the Moulin Rouge. They came to me. I was enthralled. I had been to the Moulin Rouge before, but never inside. The Hullabaloo, on Sunset near Vine, became Hollywood's largest teenage nightclub. It accomplished a lot. It introduced a lot of new acts that people had not realized were that good. So the introduction was a real good thing. It was a showcase for the music of the day. It became [the Kaleidoscope] and then the Aquarius Theatre.

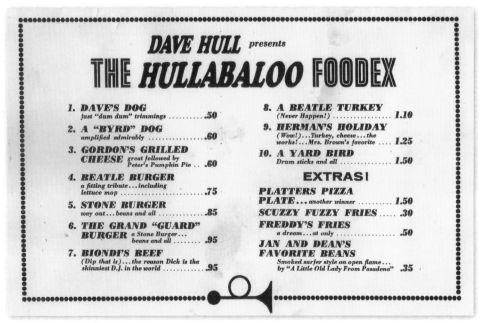

Hullabaloo menu, 1965.

CHAPTER 9

POWDERED SUGAR

BONES HOWE: So many recordings from the 1956–1972 period had background vocalists. They were more than than just coloring the recordings. Lead and background were really part of the records at the time. I mean, all the group records I made were a lead and background. The lead changed, and so the background changed.

I also worked with Gary Lewis and the Playboys with producer Snuff Garrett, and Leon Russell was on the dates. Jim Keltner came in on drums after "This Diamond Ring." Guys like Snuff were song guys. Lou Adler was a song guy. I learned from both of them. That's something I learned—you find great songs. You can't go wrong if you find great songs. There's interesting things going on in those Lewis records. Leon was very much a part of all of that. There was also a singer who sang along with Gary on those records, Ron Hicklin. Gary had someone to sing along with who helped on the phrasing. It was wonderful.

AL KOOPER: "This Diamond Ring" was a collaboration between Irwin Levine, Bob Brass, and myself. They wrote the words, and I wrote the music. They were older than me and grew up together, so they'd always gang up on me. I learned that you didn't have to write songs emotionally. You could write them capitalistically. I didn't know the difference at that time. I just wrote songs, because that's what I did for a living.

I heard "This Diamond Ring" when the publisher called and said, "We got a cover on it." So I said, "Oh, great. Who covered it?" And he replied, "Snuff Garrett produced it." And I said, "That is weird." I said to myself,

"He only does white records."

We wrote it with the Drifters in mind, but they turned it down. I mentioned that I'd be curious to hear it. So they played me the record, and I was horrified. Just horrified. But it was a white record. The song was a black song. There was no conception in my head, ever, of it being a white song. It never occurred to me that that would happen. I didn't even get it when he said Snuff Garrett produced it. I just . . . that was strange. So I said to him, "I don't even want to hear shit like this," and I just walked out. And, you know, three months later, it was a number-one record, and I was walking around goin', "I wrote that!"

GARY PIG GOLD: Snuff, with Leon's more-than-able assistance, was always first and best at riding up the charts on someone else's songtails—for example, "She's Just My Style," which *almost* beats "Help Me, Rhonda" at its own game. That particular hit's utterly ingenious flipside, "I Won't Make That Mistake Again"—and the gorgeous, octave-skirting, wholly pre-"You Still Believe In Me" piano line therein—remains one of the greatest seldom-heard classics from L.A.'s all-golden era.

DON PEAKE: The role of the background singer is very overlooked. One of the reasons these records sound so great is that they were like part of the orchestra. The arrangers knew how important the background singers were. It's a color, a texture. Look at Brother Ray [Charles] and his use of the background singers, besides the Raelettes. He had the whole Jack Halloran Singers in

Opposite: B. J. Baker singing background vocals for Sam Cooke's "You Send Me" at Radio Recorders, Hollywood, 1957.

the room. On "America the Beautiful," there were twenty singers standing around me.

The Ray Charles "Eleanor Rigby" session was so amazing! We did it at his studio in L.A. We all had heard the Beatles' version over and over, so when Brother Ray started singing ahead one bar, it was scary! I remember, when he came in and sang it, that it completely threw me and the singers off, because it was different than the

GIVE THE DRUMMER SOME

JIM KELTNER: Gary Lewis was studying acting at the Pasadena Playhouse, and on his lunch hours he would come into the music store I was working at, Berry and Grassmueck. One day, he asked me if I would give him drum lessons. After a few lessons, he told me he was going to go up front with the guitar, and said, "I want you to be my drummer." I went from $85 a week to $250 a week. A big jump—almost triple. One of the first things I did was go down to Felix Chevrolet on Figueroa, near the L.A. Coliseum, and buy a '65 Daytona blue Corvette Sting Ray.

I joined Gary Lewis and the Playboys after "This Diamond Ring" put them on the map. I played on the next single and album, and then did a couple of tours. We did the *Hullabaloo* TV show. We played Hawaii, we did *Shivaree.* We did a KRLA banquet on December 8, 1965. And we did Las Vegas, Oakland, *9th Street West* on KHJ. We did *American Bandstand* with Dick Clark, and a Coca-Cola commercial. We did *Where the Action Is,* and a couple of beach movies. Until Gary Lewis, I had pretty much been playing jazz. I was playing at Sherry's on the Strip, a nightclub on Sunset Boulevard with Don Randi.

Snuff Garrett from Liberty Records made me shave my mustache and get a professional haircut. Then he took me to meet Leon Russell at the studio. Leon was raised in Tulsa, and I loved that, because that's where I was born. I didn't realize I would be following in the footsteps of the great session studio drummers Earl Palmer, Hal Blaine, and Jim Gordon.

Leon was the first record producer and arranger I ever worked with. I was very fortunate to have him as the first producer I came in contact with, because Leon always had a slightly different musical angle that he came from. I think Leon was always looking for something a little bit out of the box. I didn't know

that at the time. Hal Blaine was there, by the way. I thought he was there to play tambourine, but in actual fact, Hal was there just in case I couldn't cut it [*laughs*]. I was coming from Don Randi, six nights a week playing at Sherry's. I thought I was on top of the world with that gig.

At the beginning of the Gary Lewis "She's Just My Style" recording session, Leon said, "Don't play any fills. Not even one fill." And I understood that instinctively. I thought, "This is the way rock 'n' roll singles are made." He asked for a fill just at the beginning, and I did. Then he said, "Can you do that backwards?" And I thought, "Oh yeah. I can do that. That's cool." So I played the fill backwards, and opened the hi-hat in the intro. He liked that a lot. So right away, we made a connection there. During the playback, he turned to me and said, "You're gonna be a great rock drummer."

I remember, at that moment, I felt a real confidence. Right around that time, I had begun to realize that playing rock 'n' roll was not just for morons. You really had to know what you were doing.

I always marveled at how Hal [Blaine] and Earl [Palmer] could do it so easily. It never occurred to me that I wouldn't be able to do that. Then when you are confronted with it, you realize it is not for the faint of heart.

I came from the jazz world. I came up at a time when, as Charles Lloyd says, "Giants roamed the earth." Bassist Albert Stinson, my best friend, was already one of those giants, barely out of his teens. I learned so many things from Albert—way too much to talk about, and how he affected my life. I used to hang on every word. The first of several geniuses who I was so fortunate to have in my lifetime.

Beatles. Sid Feller did the arrangement, and that was key. He and Ray worked so well together.

It took some musical muscles to keep playing the music chart after Ray sang. We all smiled and loved "The Genius." Billy Preston played organ on a lot of those sessions. On Ray's "Let's Go Get Stoned" recording date, I was next to Billy Preston at the organ. I played the guitar solo.

The role of the background singers was also very evident later, in Joe Cocker and Leon Russell's *Mad Dogs and Englishmen*. They even cut "Let's Go Get Stoned." Then Ray Charles did his version of Leon's "A Song for You."

DAVID KESSEL: Professional background vocalists are gunslingers for hire. They have to sight-read, adapt to on-the-spot arrangement changes, and blend in with the rest of the vocal group. They have to be on time and responsible for showing up to any gig they accept. If they can't make it for any reason, it is the singer's responsibility to get someone of like style and talent to sub.

The singers are hired by the vocal contractor. The vocal contractor is the "producer" of the vocal section. This is similar to the director of the second unit in filmmaking. The vocal contractor is responsible for filling out all

B. J. Baker backstage at a taping of
The Dean Martin Show at NBC Studios, Burbank, 1967.

AFTRA paperwork and assuring that everyone is paid proper fees. The vocal contractor is the go-between for the vocal group and the producers, arrangers, and engineers. The vocal contractor determines who to hire based on the producer's requirements. How many male and female voices? Who blends the best together? Who has the appropriate vocal range and quality, and availability?

BURT BACHARACH: Leiber and Stoller had me prep the background singers for [the Drifters'] "Mexican Divorce." Dionne Warwick came in with Cissy Houston, Dee Dee Warwick, and Myrna Smith. I'd spend three or four days rehearsing so that by the time tape was rolling, they nailed it. Dionne stood out—she had these high cheekbones, a lovely figure, and that star attitude. She called Hal [David] and me and asked to sing for us and we signed her.

We played her "What the World Needs Now Is Love," but she passed—thought it was too preachy. I put it in a drawer and forgot about it. A few years later, we're working with Jackie DeShannon, and it was Hal's idea to pull that one out. The rest is history.

For me, songwriting is about orchestration. I hear everything in my head—the strings, the horn parts, that special nuance that you have to sing to the players that you can't quite put in musical notation. When I was able

B. J. Baker and other singers at Radio Recorders, running
through the background vocals for Doris Day's hit record
"Everybody Loves a Lover," Hollywood, 1958.

**B. J. Baker and Burt Bacharach (*center*)
at a vocal overdubbing session for Dionne Warwick's
"I Say a Little Prayer," Hollywood, 1966.**

to get control in the studio—the right tempo, my rhythm section, cutting everything live—that's when something magical can happen. When I could take the most chances, that's when it happened.

Just about every Phil Spector recording would showcase the background vocalists to augment his production—none more than background singer and vocal contractor B. J. (Betty Jane) Baker. You may not know the name, but you've certainly heard B. J. Baker's voice for decades.

DAN KESSEL: My stepmother, B. J. Baker, worked among an elite corps of behind-the-scenes heroes in Hollywood. She was, in a manner of speaking, the Hal Blaine of the Wrecking Crew studio background vocalists. It was Hal Blaine who dubbed her "Diamond Lil." Before excelling as a Hollywood studio vocalist, she had been Miss Alabama and Mickey Rooney's second wife. Before that, at age fourteen, she'd fronted a big band and was featured on her own weekly radio show.

B. J. Baker was not only "Mom" to my stepbrothers

BOBBY SHEEN:
PRESENT AT THE CREATION OF THE WALL OF SOUND

by Kirk Silsbee

During the Korean War, aspiring jazz pianist Tony Sheen returned from an army hitch to his family home in the West Adams district, and noticed that his Little Jimmy Scott 78s were so worn that they were almost unplayable. It was years before his younger brother, Bobby, confessed to surreptitiously savoring the high-voiced singer, whom Tony and his friends called "Little Miss Scott," before he left in 1952. Bobby Sheen was part of the local doo-wop scene, and emerged as one of the greatest high tenors to follow in Clyde McPhatter's wake.

In 1962, Phil Spector took Bobby—as Bob B. Soxx and the Blue Jeans, at the time—to the Top 10 with "Zip-a-Dee-Doo-Dah," in an early entry into

the Wall of Sound fable. Sheen's semi-operatic tour de force on "The Bells of St. Mary's" in Spector's 1963 *A Christmas Gift for You* album (which inaugurated the rock holiday album genre) still thrills listeners each December.

As part of the fraternity of L.A. soul and R & B singers, Sheen always worked—he was most often employed by Dick Clark, and was in one of the many Coasters franchises (Sheen had the acumen to copyright the name). But it's a great-though-non-charting '66 single for Capitol Records that has given him year-round glory. Championed by British soul fans, Sheen's "Dr. Love" became the de facto national anthem of the northern soul movement, and flooded countless dance floors.

Mickey Rooney Jr. and Tim Rooney and my brother David and me—she was also the queen of the Hollywood session singers for several decades. There were other top girl singers, such as Vangie Carmichael, Jackie Ward, and Sally Stevens, but B. J. was the one who contracted for Elvis and Sinatra.

B. J. Baker sang on Dean Martin's TV show and his records, like "Everybody Loves Somebody Sometime," and on lots of records with Frank and Sammy. B. J. sang with the other background singers, such as Cher, the Blossoms [Darlene Love, Fanita James, and Jean King], Clydie King, and Gracia Ann Nitzsche.

I used to dig watching Snuff craft those hits and then hear them on KFWB and the jukebox at Bob's Big Boy on Van Nuys Boulevard. Standing in the booth, watching Snuff Garrett and Timi Yuro record "What's a Matter Baby," was exhilarating. B. J. sang on that. She was in the studio again, working on something else, when she walked past the room where Phil Spector was re-mixing "What's a Matter Baby" for Snuff. Recognizing the song, she stopped inside the room and told Phil, whom she didn't really know very well at the time, that it sounded incredible and would surely be a smash hit. Phil was very pleased to hear that from her. Timi was such a powerful vocalist, and Snuff had the genius of foresight to know that young Phil Spector's gigantic mix would be the perfect crowning touch of power for that particular record.

My stepbrothers, Mickey and Tim, and I would say hi to Timi when she was there sometimes at Mama Yuro's, her mother's pizza parlor on the Sunset Strip, usually after we'd been at the Whisky a Go Go or some other club on the strip. Timi and her mom would visit with us and talk to us.

B. J. Baker is present on "I'm Available" by Margie Rayburn, the mood-setting "Johnny Angel" by Shelley Fabares, and the haunting, echo-laden opening greeting on "Big John" by Jimmy Dean. That's her on Bobby Darin's "Dream Lover" and plenty of the classic Phil Spector productions, including "You've Lost That Lovin' Feelin'" and "Just Once in My Life" by the Righteous Brothers, and "River Deep—Mountain High," supporting Tina Turner. Baker is listed on Jackie Wilson's "Baby Workout," as well as Lloyd Price's "Personality," "Where Were You on Our Wedding Day?," and "Stagger Lee." She was also part

B. J. Baker's sheet music for "Ebb Tide," from her 1965 recording session with Phil Spector and the Righteous Brothers.

of many of the epic, Snuff Garrett-produced Liberty Records sides, including Gene McDaniels's "A Hundred Pounds of Clay," Bobby Vee's "Rubber Ball," and "I'm Hurt" and "What's a Matter Baby" by Tim Yuro.

Baker performed on "America the Beautiful" and "It's Cryin' Time Again" when she sang with the Ray Charles Singers. She's a voice on numerous Nat King Cole records, including "Those Lazy Hazy Crazy Days of Summer." Baker can also be heard on those gorgeous background vocals enhancing Frank Sinatra's "That's Life." She also guested on the Beach Boys' "Got to Know the Woman" for their Sunflower album. Baker ultimately earned a Grammy for her work with the Anita Kerr Singers.

PHIL SPECTOR: When you see a Kubrick movie, you tell me how many names you immediately remember in the cast. One? Two? It's the same with Fellini, and that's what I wanted to do when I directed a recording. Singers are instruments. They are tools to be worked with.

JACK NITZSCHE: The vocals would last all night—background groups doubling and tripling so it would sound

Ticket stub from an August 1966 concert at
Dodger Stadium featuring the Beatles, Bobby Hebb,
the Cyrkle, and the Ronettes.

like two or three dozen voices. Phil would spend a lot of time with the singers. I would split, and he'd still be working on lines with the singers. The rhythm section and the horns were done together. Vocals and string parts were overdubbed later.

I arranged the Christmas album. We had a lot of fun. Darlene Love singing "Christmas (Baby Please Come Home)" blew my mind. I got chills. Powerful. She could always sing. Sonny Bono always made everyone laugh. The album never really took off. I think some of that had to do with the world after the Kennedy assassination. It affected the public. No one wanted to celebrate Christmas in December 1963.

"Be My Baby." Ronnie Spector's voice—wow! I was amazed at her vibrato. It got bigger and bigger with each record. That was her strong point. When that tune was finished, the speakers were turned so high in the booth, people had to leave the room. It was loud.

GENE AGUILERA: Ronnie Spector's voice . . . it was quivering with teenage girl angst and pain. Like the first time you fall in love. You have a lot of emotion going on at the same time. To us, Ronnie looked Latina, but she was a half-breed of black/Cherokee and Irish. She looked like a chola. She had the beehive hairdo, which was big in East L.A. in the late fifties and early sixties. The bad girls used to hide switch blades in there and stick pins when they were fighting each other.

I actually thought the Ronettes were Latinas at first, because they weren't white and they weren't black. They were somewhere in-between. I could relate to them. In 1966, they opened up for the Beatles at Dodger Stadium, which I went to.

The Crystals were the first act signed to the Philles record label after forming in 1960. Dolores "LaLa" Brooks was the immortal singer of the Crystals and the lead vocalist on a slew of their hits with Spector, including "Da Doo Ron Ron" and "Then He Kissed Me." She is also featured on "Little Boy."

Brooks was born in Brooklyn in 1947. In 1962, the sixteen-year-old singer was invited to join the Crystals during a recording date for "Uptown," which became a Top 15 chart hit that year. Los Angeles-based Darlene Love, also a member of the Blossoms, was then introduced to Spector by arranger Jack Nitzsche, who subsequently handled the lead vocal chores on the Crystals' Gene Pitney-penned "He's a Rebel."

The Crystals' next single was "He's Sure the Boy I Love," spotlighting Love and the Blossoms. Phil then flew LaLa Brooks to L.A. for the lead vocal slot on the pulsating "Da Doo Ron Ron." Their teaming was followed by the seismic "Then He Kissed Me" and the poptastic "Little Boy."

LALA BROOKS: When I did "Da Doo Ron Ron" over and over, Phil was sort of like a perfectionist with that one. I remember being pooped in the studio [*laughs*]. I wanted to run out that door so fast, but he kept going over and over. Thirty, forty takes. I would say, "When are you gonna get it," you know?

I would initially sing with one headphone on. It was loud music, and I could not sing and keep both headphones on because it would blow my ears out [*laughs*].

I was singing on some monumental things. "Then He Kissed Me" sounded so beautiful as it was being played before I put the track down. I knew it was different. I knew it was a hit. I could feel it. I could hear the changes. I knew it was the type of song that could go all the way around. Pop, into movies, and all that.

I knew as a child how important the session guys were. I never took that for granted. In fact, I used to sit and watch them play. The strings, the movement, I really enjoyed. The kettledrums—they had a flow that was so captivating. So I never short-changed them for one moment. I knew they were definitely important.

I think Jack Nitzsche's roles were very much disrespected and not recognized [as] fully as they should have been. Even the artists on Phil's records were not recognized [as] fully as Phil Spector, which is totally crazy to

Phil Spector and Ronnie Spector at Gold Star Studios during a recording session for "Frosty the Snowman" for the album *A Christmas Gift for You from Phil Spector*, Hollywood, 1963.

me. For someone to focus on a producer that much—what he is doing, how does he live, all of this—the intimate part of his life—it's all nonsense and belittles the artist. That's what happened to Jack Nitzsche. I remember what Jack said to me before he died: "LaLa. If it wasn't for me, there'd be no Phil."

DAN KESSEL: For "On the Crystals" and "He's a Rebel," I performed handclaps. On early Phil Spector records with the Crystals, Barney played a Guild acoustic twelve-string which, at his request, had been modified with a pickup by repairman Milt Owen, whom he later hired to ply his trade at Barney Kessel's Music World on Vine Street. That early, electrified Guild got a slightly thicker, punchier sound than the Rickenbacker twelve-string.

When I was recording with John Lennon in the early seventies, he told me that my dad's twelve-string riff on "Then He Kissed Me" inspired the Beatles to get into the Rickenbacker twelve-string for their records. John smiled, commenting on the irony, when I told him that my dad had switched to the Rickenbacker twelve-string for record dates in '65, after the Beatles and Byrds started using them. The Ric's appealing, jangly sound was enhanced by the combination of the unique sound chamber of its body style, thinner gauge strings, and lower output toaster pickups.

As a session guitarist, no matter whom the artist was that you were backing, you could easily need to change instruments from song to song, let alone artist to artist. For a thick, full sound, he sometimes played his double-cutaway, hollow-body, Gibson Barney Kessel model with heavy gauge strings.

For a brighter, twangier sound, he often played a [blond] Fender Telecaster. Regardless of the ax, he always played through a Gibson amp with reverb and tremolo options. He sometimes played through a Gibson "fuzz tone" after those came out.

BROWN-EYED WOMAN: DARLENE LOVE BLOSSOMED THROUGH THE WALL OF SOUND

by KIRK SILSBEE

Phil Spector assembled a great team. His records melded together some of L.A.'s best session players, the canny Jack Nitzsche, and the brilliant Larry Levine. But the mortar in the Wall of Sound was the solid background vocals of the Blossoms.

They were led by the soaring Darlene Love. The daughter of a Louisiana-born minister, she was forbidden to listen to R & B as a teenager. But on Sundays, young Darlene Wright bathed in the roaring gospel caravan shows produced by Brother Henderson, L.A.'s premiere gospel impresario. Delois Barrett Campbell of the Barrett Sisters was a particular favorite of Darlene's.

With Fremont High classmates Fanita James and Jean King, Darlene formed a trio that quickly shaped up into the hardest-working background group in the studios. The indispensible Lester Sill, the promo man and creative enabler to countless local R & B figures, introduced the group to Spector in 1962. In Darlene's senior year, the Blossoms (as Capitol Records dubbed them) sang on Sam Cooke's "Everybody Likes to Cha Cha Cha." Big hits by Ray Charles, Ed Townsend, and Duane Eddy followed. Capitol frequently augmented white backup groups with the Blossoms, achieving a tangy, cross-ethnic sound.

Darlene Love's (Spector changed her name) career is filled with ironies. The Wall of Sound records were pop tunes that spoke of teen concerns. Yet she sang them in a woman's voice—a full-bodied alto that could arc effortlessly over the sonic din of those records. Although those songs were hugely influential, her solo career was hampered by the fact that she was often uncredited on the releases (put out under the names the Crystals, the Ronettes, and Bob B. Soxx and the Blue Jeans).

From 1964 to '66, the Blossoms became regulars on the television show *Shindig!* Their versatility made them ubiquitous, as they backed all kinds of acts. For a time, they were the most telegenically visible black Americans, when blacks were practically invisible on television. "The Blossoms were stars," Love said in 1995, "but we didn't realize it. The biggest stars in the world came on that show and were envious of us, because we were on every week."

Although she was one of the most important elements of Spector's success, Love never received much in the way of encouragement from the enigmatic, tight-lipped Spector. "I overheard him tell Jack Nitzsche, 'She's one of the greatest singers I ever heard in my life,' when I was in the control room and he didn't know I was there," she said. "I was really shocked. Then Jack once told me, 'He thinks you're the greatest singer in the world.'"

"Phil taught me all my songs; I never heard demos," she continued. "We'd either go to the piano in his office, or up to Jack's house. I think that had a lot to do with control: 'I taught her everything she knows.' But I have to say, he was the first record producer I ever worked with who knew exactly what he wanted. Other producers would mostly leave it up to the Blossoms—'You guys know what to do.'"

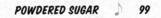

KFWB Fabulous Forty Survey

FOR WEEK ENDING MARCH 30, 1962

			LAST WEEK
1.	*JOHNNY ANGEL	Shelley Fabares—Col-Pix	15
2.	MIDNIGHT IN MOSCOW	Kenny Ball—Kapp	2
3.	*LOVER PLEASE	Clyde McPhatter—Mercury	12
4.	*GOOD LUCK CHARM	Elvis Presley—RCA Victor	10
5.	*SHE CRIED	Jay & The Americans—United Artists	4
6.	*LOVE LETTERS	Ketty Lester—Era	3
7.	*SLOW TWISTIN'	Chubby Checker—Parkway	6
8.	*MEMORIES OF MARIA	Jerry Byrd—Monument	9
9.	MASHED POTATO TIME	Dee Dee Sharp—Cameo	23
10.	TWISTIN' THE NIGHT AWAY	Sam Cooke—RCA Victor	5
11.	*COME BACK SILLY GIRL	The Lettermen—Capitol	8
12.	*I'VE GOT BONNIE	Bobby Rydell—Cameo	15
13.	ALL YOU HAD TO DO	Chris Montez—Monogram	7
14.	*YOUNG WORLD	Rick Nelson—Imperial	18
15.	NUT ROCKER B. Bumble & The Stingers—Rendezvous		37
16.	*LOVE ME WARM AND TENDER	Paul Anka—RCA Victor	24
17.	WHAT'S YOUR NAME	Don & Juan—Bigtop	14
18.	WHAT'S SO GOOD ABOUT GOODBYE	The Miracles—Tamla	22
19.	*HEY BABY	Bruce Channel—Smash	13
20.	*PLEASE DON'T ASK ABOUT BARBARA	Bobby Vee—Liberty	19

			LAST WEEK
21.	*DON'T BREAK THE HEART THAT LOVES YOU	Connie Francis—MGM	16
22.	NEED YOUR LOVE	The Metallics—Baronet	25
23.	LET ME IN	The Sensations—Argo	11
24.	*WHERE HAVE ALL THE FLOWERS GONE	The Kingston Trio—Capitol	21
25.	*JOHNNY JINGO	Hayley Mills—Vista	32
26.	CINDERELLA	Jack Ross—Dot	34
27.	*DREAM BABY	Roy Orbison—Monument	20
28.	TELL ME	Dick & Dee Dee—Liberty	30
29.	*TUFF	Ace Cannon—Hi	17
30.	*COTTON FIELDS	The Highwaymen—United Artists	26
31.	*HE KNOWS I LOVE HIM TOO MUCH	The Paris Sisters—Gregmark	35
32.	*OLD RIVERS	Walter Brennan—Liberty	Debut
33.	SMOKY PLACES	The Corsairs—Tuff	31
34.	DEAR ONE	Larry Finnegan—Old Town	40
35.	CRY BABY CRY	The Angels—Caprice	Debut
36.	SOMETHING'S GOT A HOLD ON ME	Etta James—Argo	Debut
37.	*SOLDIER BOY	The Shirelles—Scepter	Debut
38.	SHE CAN'T FIND HER KEYS	Paul Peterson—Col-Pix	Debut
39.	GINNY COME LATELY	Brian Hyland—ABC/Par	Debut
40.	STRANGER ON THE SHORE	Mr. Acker Bilk—Atco	Debut

*RECORDS FIRST HEARD ON KFWB

98 IS GREAT!

FAVORITE ALBUMS

1.	West Side Story	MST—Columbia
2.	For Teen Twisters Only	Chubby Checker—Parkway
3.	Sinatra and Strings	Frank Sinatra—Reprise
4.	The Astronaut	John Glenn Jr.—Reprise
5.	Breakfast at Tiffany's	Henry Mansini—RCA Victor

This survey is compiled each week by radio station KFWB, Los Angeles, California. It is a true, accurate and unbiased account of record popularity, based upon sales reports, distributor accounts and all information available to the music staff of KFWB.

Top: **Recording session at Hollywood's Gold Star Studios for "Paradise" by the Ronettes, including:** *(left to right)* **Phil Spector, Darlene Love, Sonny Bono, and Jack Nitzsche.**
Left: **KFWB Fabulous Forty survey, 1962.**

CHAPTER 10

WHEN SONNY MET CHER

He was a hustling song-plugger, songwriter, and aspiring producer who shadowed Phil Spector's every move, hoping to glean the wisdom of the master like a true acolyte. She was a young teenager, but savvy beyond her years; a long, cool drink of Armenian beauty with a voice imbued with more aspiration than range.

They partnered first as Caesar and Cleo, but that didn't fly; they soon recognized that their quirky chemistry demanded their authentic selves. So began the unlikely ascent of Sonny and Cher, tramp and gypsy, across the pop culture terrain, first as recording stars and then as television personalities. As their lives diverged—Sonny into politics and tragedy, Cher into a universe of her own design—it's worth knowing that, at their core, they drew from the very well that produced Spector and Wilson. And that is nothing to laugh about.

Cher, born Cherilyn Sarkisian, is now a global icon. It's hard to believe, but she was once a shy, demure presence, lurking in shadows. Her introduction to show business was at a Phil Spector session at Gold Star Studios. Sonny took her to the recording date, and she did some background singing work. Sonny produced "The Letter," a rendition of a Don and Dewey regional hit. Afterwards, Spector produced Cher's attempt at "Ringo, I Love You" under the moniker Bonnie Jo Mason.

Then, as Caesar and Cleo, Sonny and Cher cut "Baby Don't Go" in 1964. Sonny went on to produce Cher's "Dream Baby,"

arranged by Gene Page, and her version of Bob Dylan's "All I Really Want to Do," which became the title of her first LP. Sonny and Cher paired again on "I Got You Babe" for Atco Records, a song that landed on global record charts. Look at Us was their LP debut. For their work together for Atco and Cher's solo Imperial recordings, Sonny brought in the Wrecking Crew and arrangers like Page and Harold Battiste Jr. They topped the hit parade in both the U.S. and UK with "The Beat Goes On."

RUSS REGAN: Sonny was from Inglewood. I was with him when he met Cher. Sonny, myself, and DJ Gary Owens were having a beer at a restaurant. That was the beginning of Caesar and Cleo, who then cut "Baby Don't Go" that was on Reprise Records.

In 1965 and 1966, I was still good friends with Sonny Bono. He was a really good songwriter. I saw Sonny and Cher explode on Atlantic. Sonny worked at Record Merchandise, and then California Record Distributors, before he became the West Coast promo man for Spector's Philles Records.

I was going to the Sonny and Cher sessions all the time. I was at Gold Star when they did "I Got You Babe." At the playback, I said to Sonny, "This is it, Sonny. You're gone." That thing blew up right in front of me. I loved hearing them on the radio. Sonny was what we call a "commercial songwriter."

Above: Sonny and Cher with Don Peake (*center*) at a Hollywood Bowl sound check, 1966.
Opposite: Sonny and Cher at the eighth annual Grammy Awards, held in the Beverly Hills Hilton International Ballroom, 1966.

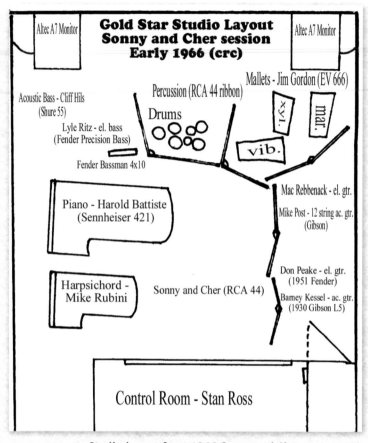

Studio layout for a 1966 Sonny and Cher
recording session at Gold Star Studios.

DON PEAKE: Sonny had a rock 'n' roll soul. He was underrated as a song guy. I think people never realized he was a writer. They were just interested because he was out in front.

He understood song construction, and he also understood musicians, because he'd hung around with Phil and had been on our sessions. He'd play maracas on occasion. He gave us a lot of respect. We dug him, and dug the songs he brought in. He brought in arranger Harold Battiste, which was a stroke of genius because he was so creative. The "I Got You Babe" session was just magic. Harold Battiste was genius, bringing that bassoon and the oboe in there.

Barney Kessel was also a great wit. He'd come in and greet us with, "Guys, I was so hungry on the way over here, I ate a whole octave and a half of ribs." On the "The Beat Goes On" session, we're sitting there, and Sonny is doing his six-hour Phil Spector thing at Gold Star. Finally, Barney yells, "Hey Sonny." "Yes, Barney," says Sonny, as he pushes the button. Barney replies with,

"Listen. If a doctor told me I only had two weeks to live, I'd rather spend them with you. Because each moment is like an eternity."

DAN KESSEL: I was a spectator on some of the Sonny and Cher sessions. My dad doubled the bass on "The Beat Goes On" for Sonny.

Sonny was a sweetheart, and Cher, too. When I freaked out over how cool Sonny's fur vest was, he let me feel it, and Cher would sometimes joke around with me. Sonny's song, "Laugh at Me"—that was pretty heavy, on a P. F. Sloan level.

Sonny and Cher would call my dad "the professor." He stood out from the mostly younger, California casual-dressed musicians. As a world-traveled jazz artist, with a hipster-jazz beard and suits from Boshard-Doughty and Carroll and Co., he could easily pass for a Zurich psychiatrist.

Many of the guys smoked a lot back then, but Sonny chain smoked to the degree that he always kept two cigarettes in his hand—the one he was smoking, and the next one he would soon be lighting with the one he was currently smoking. It was like one long, continuous cigarette throughout the session.

Sonny had a winning formula with his songwriting

**Dan Kessel, David Kessel, and Sonny Bono in the booth
at the Sonny and Cher recording session for
"I Got You Babe" at Gold Star Studios, Hollywood, 1965.**

FUNNY, KIND, AND CARING

Amidst all their success, there was always a playful tension between Sonny and Cher. For many, it was all part of a shtick that warmed them to audiences. Less forgiving observers thought it was the barely-veiled taunting of a controlling, Svengali relationship. Cher has always been generous in her feelings toward Sonny and the crucial role he played in making her career possible.

"First of all, I think it was very much hero worship," Cher mentioned to journalist Barney Hoskyns, "because I thought the sun rose and set on his ass. He was twenty-eight and seemed like he knew everything. And he was in the record business, which was really interesting to me even though that wasn't what I wanted to do. I can't tell you how unique a person he was. Crazy and nutty, but with the best sense of humor. I was studying acting. I didn't want to be a pop singer at all. And then I gave up acting because Sonny said it was a stupid profession.

"What I remember most is that I had to stand behind everybody, because my voice just cut through. Phillip would always say, 'Cher, can you just move back a couple of feet?' And then it became like a standard joke. For a background singer, my voice was too specific. Like it or not, you pretty much know it's me from the first note."

"There's an energy that Phillip would get," Cher told Denny Tedesco, director of the 2008 documentary *The Wrecking Crew.* "I remember Phillip would be so excited about every session. There was just a vitality

HEAR SONNY & CHER ON 93/KHJ

KHJ radio survey, 1965.

in the room that would lift you off of your feet. And also, there would be so many players, and that would be huge. It was definitely that Wall of Sound was really there.

"Phillip was walking in a different universe than everybody else. And so, in his mind it was all him, you know, and the guys were just some sort of an extension of what he couldn't do. They made fun of him all the time, but they really liked him. I think they really respected him. Thought he was nuts. Which of course he was, but I always think they looked forward, too, because there was always going to be something really cool. It was like a total friendship thing, too. Because they would come in and [be] talking about, 'What did you do on the golf course?' Or someone has this car. There was always a *Mad* magazine being passed around that somebody brought. They were session players and guys who were going from gig to gig, you know, playing on all the good music."

Cher also reflected on the Sonny Bono recording "Laugh at Me" to Hoskyns. "No, I didn't laugh because it was inspired by such a terrible experience," she said. "We were so tired of getting beaten up and having people call us faggots, and then our own friends kicked us out of their restaurant, Martoni's. This other guy had been the one to blame, but they said, 'We always have trouble when you come in here!'"

and song selection, often leaning toward a Dylan/Byrds folk-rock thing, mixed with his version of Phil's sound. Then, to top it all off, he had Cher, the grooviest of chicks. Those were some good-vibe sessions. Sonny was capable and cheerful. Everybody was professional and accomplished a lot. People weren't on drugs.

DICK CLARK: I think determination was Sonny's greatest asset. I've said for years . . . in a business that is a competitive one, young kids have said, "How do I get or make a break in the music business?" I've said, "Have bulldog determination." Artistic people very often wait for the lightning to hit. Sonny made the lightning come to him. There's something to learn from that. Put yourself in the right place at the right time. Be in the right city. Get to the right person. Hang in there. You have to be aggressive, otherwise it will be a miracle if someone walks into the nearest Holiday Inn and finds you in the lounge.

Stan Ross introduced Phil Spector to the Righteous Brothers at a Gold Star session. The duo had been using the studio with the owner of Moonglow Records, the label they were on at the time, and Ross engineered their stomper, "Little Latin Lupe Lu." Spector liked what he heard and consequently signed them to his Philles label. Then came "You've Lost That Lovin' Feelin'."

RUSS TITELMAN: I'm one of the rhythm guitar players on the Righteous Brothers' "Hung On You." I was an extra [*laughs*]. I conducted the choir for some of the overdubs on "Just Once in My Life." I loved those records.

BONES HOWE: I had to pull over on the side of the road on Barham Boulevard one night when I heard "You've Lost That Lovin' Feelin'" for the first time. That was the first record that kind of nailed me down. Oh Jesus . . .

PHIL SPECTOR: I would guess "You've Lost That Lovin' Feelin'" really captured something for me. It said the most to me, as far as a production was concerned at the time. It was made as an honest shocker, and was made as an experiment. It was really not made to necessarily become number one. That was not its goal. You see, the main force that I have that drives me is probably the same force of why Wagner wrote music: to make a forceful message, to have a forceful approach, to present his dynamic feelings through his music. This is the way I see a record. It takes me a few months to make a record, when I build a record.

I enjoyed all the records very much. I made them all from the heart. I made them all with art in mind, and all to reveal a picture of where I was when I made them, never to deceive or really to make people think I was putting them on or just to be commercial. I wanted the people to say, "Gee . . . you've really gone for a screwed-up time during that period, weren't you?" Or, "Jesus . . . you were

The Righteous Brothers at a recording session at Gold Star Studios, Hollywood, 1965.

really Wagner-crazy then, and you must have been loaded that time." I enjoyed that. It doesn't bother me at all. That's probably the only way I do reveal myself—on my records, through my art.

My high school graduation theme was "Daring to Be Different." The moment I dared to, they called me different. I always thought I knew what the kids wanted to hear. They were frustrated, uptight, I would say—no different from me when I was in school. I had a rebellious attitude. I was for the underdog. I was concerned that they were as misunderstood as I was.

TOSH BERMAN: My father, [assemblage artist and one of the figures on the cover of the Beatles' *Sgt. Pepper's Lonely Hearts Club Band*] Wallace Berman, went to Fairfax High, but was kicked out for gambling on the premises. He was very much a zoot-suit-wearing street guy at the time. School/jobs were not part of his personality whatsoever.

Phil Spector's personality really stood out on many levels. But I will always remember him coming to my dad's studio in Beverly Glen with a driven limo and Ronnie Spector by his side in 1964. He bought my dad's piece, "You've Lost That Lovin' Feelin'."

Phil was very brisk and hustler-like—not in a bad way—and I think that my dad bonded with him because maybe they're from the same part of the world. And yeah, my dad was obsessed with that song. He had the single, and he would play it over and over again till you [could] see the other side of the vinyl. From that, he made this "portrait" of Phil. It is one of his great works, for both artists.

We had a simple turntable that a teenager would own at the time. But it was an automatic, where the record

Success of Phil Spector Shows Creative Genius
By LARRY McCORMICK
(KFWB, Midnight 'Til Six A.M.)

Phil Spector is a millionaire in his early twenties. Phil Spector is considered a musical genius in his field.

Phil Spector is the man other record company executives wish they were. Phil Spector is liked by few, disliked by many, misunderstood by most, and envied by practically everybody.

The first Spector contribution of any importance to the music world was the song SPANISH HARLEM which he wrote. After that followed a series of successful records and record artists which he was instrumental in producing. The Crystals were first recorded by Spector, as were The Ro-

nettes and many others up to and including the fantastic Righteous Brothers.

The Righteous Brothers are two extremely talented guys who every disc couldn't make the transition from the minor hit status they were in to the super stars they are today . . . until they signed with Phil Spector.

His recent television appearances on panel shows have displayed to the world an honest, say it like it is, freak. I think he's "out of sight" . . . "fantastic" and remember . . . the "freak will inherit the earth".

Column by Larry McCormick in the
KFWB/98 Hitline newspaper, 1965.

can be played on repeat. My dad listened to songs in that manner—over and over again, where it became almost a minimal trance piece. Again, I can't underestimate my dad's love for that single. He was crazy for "You've Lost That Lovin' Feelin'."

Wallace rarely named his artwork—once for James Brown's "Papa's Got a Brand New Bag," and the other is the Spector song. They knew each other and spent some time together. Wallace liked Phil a lot.

There is a photo reproduction of the piece in one of my dad's books—I think, *Support the Revolution.*

The Beatles and the Stones had a symbiotic relationship with the exploding 1956–1966 world of the first burst of L.A.-sparked rock 'n' roll, provided by Leiber and Stoller, Nitzsche, Vincent, Cochran, Spector, and Wilson. This relationship extended to the mid-sixties, when they seemed to color the Sunset Strip, as it colored them.

The Rolling Stones, 1965: (*left to right*) Bill Wyman, Keith Richards, Charlie Watts, Mick Jagger, and Brian Jones.

DANIEL WEIZMANN: It's hard to imagine *Rubber Soul* and *Revolver* coming to fruition in a Byrds-free world, just as it's hard to imagine Arthur Lee and Love without *Aftermath* on the turntable. To dig the Beatles or the Stones in '65 is to dig that they were arrivistes, class-conscious Euros with work visas, thrown into this new world of spinning neon and Dodge Dart Swingers, Boss Radio, and go-go dancers. In a very real sense, they are American groups, as in immigrant Americans, and the rock 'n' roll melting pot was their Ellis Island.

Further evidence can be found on "What to Do," a selection on the Stones' Aftermath. *An homage to the Beach Boys, particularly their vocal harmonies. Mick Jagger initially remarked during that recording session to producer Andrew Loog Oldham, "What do you want me to do? Brian Wilson?"*

In 1958, Chan Romero wrote "'Hippy Hippy Shake" in East Los Angeles, and his 1959 record, discovered by Paul McCartney, formed a crucial part of most each and every Liverpool Beatles Cavern club and Star Club appearance in

Hamburg, Germany, as a set opener or closer.

"John, Paul, and George first developed their 'This Boy' and 'Yes It Is' three-part harmony to Phil Spector's 'To Know Him Is to Love Him' backstage in Hamburg," detailed Fab Four scholar Gary Pig Gold. "Meanwhile, Larry Williams was indeed the savage young Beatles' second-favorite Specialty recording artist, and Coasters songs featured prominently in the band's, albeit failed, January 1, 1962, Decca Records audition."

The Beatles' Live at the BBC *also reveals their fondness for Spector's "To Know Her Is to Love Her," Romero's "Hippy Hippy Shake," Little Richard's "Lucille" on Specialty, Leiber and Stoller's "Young Blood" and their "Kansas City / Hey, Hey, Hey, Hey" medley, and Williams's "Dizzy Miss Lizzy," "Bad Boy," and "Slow Down."*

Earlier in 1964, the first record Oldham produced in England was a cover of "Baja," written by Lee Hazlewood. It was the flip side of Nitzsche's "The Lonely Surfer" by solo recording artist John Baldwin, soon to be known as John Paul Jones—a name Oldham suggested to him from a poster he saw for an MGM Hollywood movie.

TWO WHO WERE THERE

ANDREW LOOG OLDHAM: It was Chess Records, the vinyl actuals, that re-united Mick Jagger and Keith Richards on Dartford Station in 1962. It was Chess Records, the company, the work, that drove Brian Jones to form the Rolling Stones. It was Chess Records—the wave that came over me in the Station Hotel in Richmond in April '63, when I first saw the Stones and we began our way of life together.

Chess was always the underbelly of the Stones beast, the fuel that charged the engine, even after they became their own brand. The first U.S. tour by the Stones was not the Beatles tour. We had a cult following in the cities, and were abandoned in the sticks. The boys needed cheering up. I could not have them de-planning in London, looking like the Brothers Glum.

I called Phil Spector from Texas, where the Stones had just supported a band of performing seals, and asked him to get us booked just as soon as possible into Chess Studios. Phil or Marshall Chess called back and said he'd set up two days of recording time, two days hence. Chicago was a piece of heaven on earth for the Stones. The earth had been scorched on most of our mid-American concert stopovers. We hadn't set any records; we didn't yet have the goods, apart from a trio of wonderful one-offs: "I Wanna Be Your Man," "You Better Move On," and "Not Fade Away." We had yet to find our vinyl legs.

In two days, the group put down some thirteen tracks, their most relaxed and inspired session to date—moved, no doubt, by our newfound ability to sell coals to Newcastle. Who would have thought a bunch of English kids could produce black R & B in the States? And here they were, in the sanctum sanctorum of Chicago blues, playing in the lap of their gods. The ground floor was a gem, as was Chess engineer Ron Malo. He treated them just like . . . musicians.

Nothing sensational happened at Chess, except the music. I was producing the sessions in the greatest sense of the word—I had provided the environment in which the work could get done. The Stones' job was to fill up the available space correctly, and this, they did. This was not the session for pop suggestions; this was the place to let them be. Oh, I may have insisted on a sordid amount of echo on the underbelly figure on "It's All Over Now," but that was only ear candy to a part that was already there.

I can remember being impressed with the order of things and how quietness and calm got things done. I remember meeting Leonard and/or perhaps Phil Chess, and being cognizant of the fact that there was no suppressive, limey stymying from the head office to the factory floor. There was just a factory floor and a very relaxed combo of artists, musicians, engineers, and salesmen all at one with each other and getting their jobs done, and royalty Cadillacs royally driven.

MARSHALL CHESS: Besides the band doing a song about our address, 2120 South Michigan Avenue, I was there during those sessions. We didn't know about the song title until the album came out. I used to fill out orders from England before I ever knew or realized some came from Mick Jagger after the Stones' sessions at Chess.

We had fabulous engineers. Ron Malo and Malcolm Chism. They were the two best engineers. Ron came from Detroit. He had worked on Motown studios, and he was a big part. Before Ron, we had Jack Weiner and his brother, who actually built the studio. It was a basic, classic studio design, with the echo chamber in the basement, and a very small control room.

Chess Records, for some reason, was a magnet for amazing artistry. All these magicians came to Chess, and we were able to capture it. It's something that can be experienced through audio. The music has stood up without a cinematic aspect like video. Because, when you recorded in mono and two-track with five or six players and a singer, there wasn't any correction possible.

I remember packing up some Chess LPs for the Stones as a gift, and taking them on a tour of the offices—introducing them to Phil and my father in the back office that they shared. I also remember driving Brian Jones back to the hotel. I had a '64 red Porsche convertible. I really hit it off with Brian. I don't know why. I drove him back to the Chicago Motel to party. He loved blues. He was in awe of Chess.

ANDREW LOOG OLDHAM: In '64, Keith [Richards] and I met Henry Mancini at a party in London, at the Dorchester Hotel. Mr. Peter Gunn was as smooth as breakfast at Tiffany's, and was very cordial to Keith and I. That was something that did not happen to us too often that year with the older generation in the music biz.

In 1964, the Rolling Stones' first stateside hit single was the Bobby Womack composition "It's All Over Now." They learned of it from a Valentino's disc handed to Oldham by DJ Murray the K (Kaufman) after a band interview at the WINS radio station in New York. Oldham then telephoned Phil Spector from the South, where the Stones had just appeared on a bill with some sea animals, and asked him to get them into Chicago's Chess Studios immediately. Andrew and his band waxed it ten days later, and cracked the Top 30 hit parade in America.

Before the Rolling Stones set foot inside RCA Studios, it had been home to Duke Ellington, Sam Cooke, Elvis Presley, Shorty Rogers, J. W. Alexander, Jesse Belvin, Alex North, Elmer Bernstein, Henry Mancini, the Beach Boys, Jack Nitzsche, and Nik Venet.

Venet produced Lou Rawls and had previously recorded Sam Cooke and the Pilgrim Travelers. He was also a close friend of Cooke's. When the singer was shot dead at the Motel Hacienda in downtown L.A. on December 11, 1964, he was wearing a jacket Venet had loaned him that same night, just after Cooke spent a portion of the evening eating and drinking at Martoni's Italian restaurant with music business friends, including Al Schmitt.

NIK VENET: I saw Sam later again at PJ's nightclub. I tried to talk him into taking my Cadillac convertible instead of his Ferrari, because he'd had a few drinks and mine was easier to drive. He was wearing my coat when he was shot. I took it out of my car because I thought I was going to take his car, but when I went to the parking lot he'd taken the Ferrari and gone and driven to downtown L.A., where he was shot. I had also left my own wallet in the coat that was on him. Three days later, I was called at my Capitol Records office by detectives from the West Hollywood police station on San Vincente, and questioned.

DAVID KESSEL: B. J. Baker is on all of Sam's records with female voices. She came home early from a session and was kind of shaken. BJB went on to [say] that the singers were all waiting at the studio for Sam to come in and record. Then one of the label guys comes in and says, "No session today. Sam has been shot and killed." They were all in disbelief, and the shock started sinking in. This was one of her eeriest moments in the studio. She really liked Sam's voice and enjoyed recording with him.

AL SCHMITT: I did a lot of work with Sam Cooke: "Bring It On Home to Me" with Lou Rawls; "Cupid"; "Another Saturday Night." I worked with Elvis Presley in 1960 and '61 on "G.I. Blues."

Studio A and B were both the same size. They were big rooms, and then there was also Studio C, a smaller room. You could mix in either room. The studios had very high ceilings and a nice parquet floor. One of the things that made them so unique was that we had all those great live echo chambers. I think there were seven of them.

Andrew Loog Oldham (*standing*) and Bill Wyman at a Rolling Stones recording session at RCA Studios for their *Aftermath* album, Hollywood, 1965.

RCA had a great microphone collection. Plus, they had the great, original Neve Console. They were just spectacular. There was a punch and a warmth, and [it was] still one of the best consoles ever made. There were no isolation booths. None whatsoever. But we had go-bos we would move around, like a separator where you could isolate things. We did have some small rugs that we would put down sometimes under the drums and things, but not too much.

There was very little overdubbing then. The nice thing about doing everything at one time was that you knew exactly what it was going to sound like. When you started layering things, you were never sure. Then a lot of experimenting came in, and it took longer and longer to make records, and the expenses went up.

Sonny Bono and Jack Nitzsche then brought Andrew Loog Oldham and the Rolling Stones in. The Stones also started a situation where songs weren't done in a standard four-hour session. They had the studio for weeks to do albums. That was new.

JACK NITZSCHE: I met the Stones in 1964. Andrew Loog Oldham called me up. He and the group had just met Phil Spector in England and wanted to meet me. Brian Jones was in a three-piece suit and tie. They saw me work with [singers] Merry Clayton and Edna Wright at RCA on a Hale and the Hushabyes date—"Yes Sir, That's My Baby." A little later, the Stones started working at RCA, and it had a big impact on me. A whole new way of approaching records. I was used to a three-hour record date, and they were block-booking twenty-four hours a day for two weeks, and doing what they wanted.

OH MY GOD THEY SHOT SAM COOKES

by Paul Body

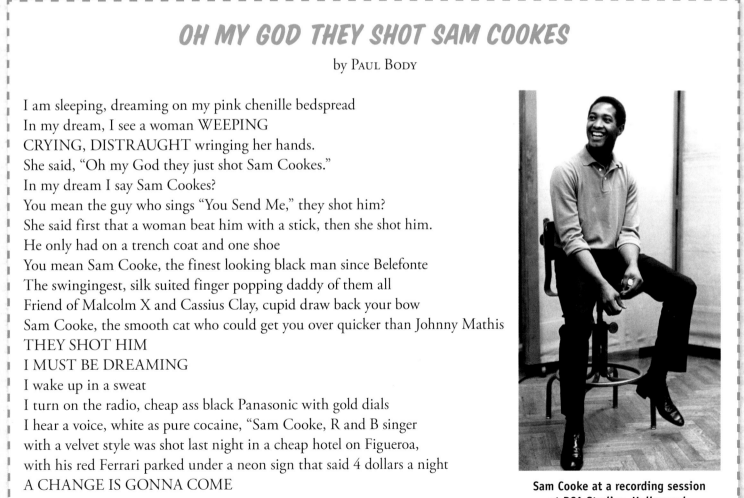

I am sleeping, dreaming on my pink chenille bedspread
In my dream, I see a woman WEEPING
CRYING, DISTRAUGHT wringing her hands.
She said, "Oh my God they just shot Sam Cookes."
In my dream I say Sam Cookes?
You mean the guy who sings "You Send Me," they shot him?
She said first that a woman beat him with a stick, then she shot him.
He only had on a trench coat and one shoe
You mean Sam Cooke, the finest looking black man since Belefonte
The swingingest, silk suited finger popping daddy of them all
Friend of Malcolm X and Cassius Clay, cupid draw back your bow
Sam Cooke, the smooth cat who could get you over quicker than Johnny Mathis
THEY SHOT HIM
I MUST BE DREAMING
I wake up in a sweat
I turn on the radio, cheap ass black Panasonic with gold dials
I hear a voice, white as pure cocaine, "Sam Cooke, R and B singer
with a velvet style was shot last night in a cheap hotel on Figueroa,
with his red Ferrari parked under a neon sign that said 4 dollars a night
A CHANGE IS GONNA COME

Sam Cooke at a recording session at RCA Studios, Hollywood, early 1960s.

Jack Nitzsche at a Rolling Stones recording session at RCA Studios for their *Aftermath* album, Hollywood, 1965.

BILL WYMAN: In 1964, the band had recorded at Chess for a couple of dates a few times. When we came into L.A., we went to RCA. At the time, we didn't know the R & B heritage of RCA Studios.

Hollywood and Los Angeles were very important. I used to go to [Teddy Bears vocalist] Marshall Lieb's house for breakfast with [Everly Brothers bassist] Joey Paige. They took us onto the beach for the first time.

We walked into the RCA studio, and it was too big. We were really worried. We were intimidated. We were used to recording in little places like Regent Sounds. The studio was like this hotel room, and Chess wasn't very big, either.

Suddenly, we're at RCA, and it's enormous. It was like [England's] Olympic, later. But we solved that same problem. We thought, "God, we can't record in here. We're gonna get the wrong sound." But Andrew had this brain wave, and he put us all in the corner of one room, turned all the lights down, and just tucked us all around in a little small circle. We forgot about the rest of the room and the height of the ceiling, and we just did it in this little corner.

Dave Hassinger, the engineer, got all the sounds we wanted. Brian [Jones] picked up all the instruments in the studio. The dulcimers, the glockenspiel, the marimbas. And I played some of that stuff, as well. The organ . . . I laid on the floor and pumped the rhythm for "Paint It, Black." We just experimented in there. Dave Hassinger helped us do those things. We never had one bad word with Dave. He was one of the pro-voters for

"Satisfaction" being a single. RCA was our first studio that had four tracks. We were on two and three tracks before that. We did all our albums with Andrew there.

Jack Nitzsche said it was the first time in his life he saw a band just come in with no thought or no preparation or anything. We'd just do it, and it sorta blew his mind [when he recorded with us], because we had no pre-plans and just did it in three takes. "Let's do that one." Jack Nitzsche was a sweet man.

ANDREW LOOG OLDHAM: That precious day in '64 was spent with Bob Krasnow and Tommy LiPuma and resulted in my leaving with Irma Thomas's take on the Jerry Ragavoy pearl "Time Is On My Side," a song that would mean so much to the Rolling Stones and their growth in the U.S. That song didn't mean dick in the UK; "You Better Move On" handled that pocket.

I had to listen to a lot of corn and molasses before I was played the Irma Thomas cut. Randy Newman was a Metric Music staff writer, so I was played a whole Metric yard before we got to what was on Imperial Records. Tommy LiPuma played me something by Randy that must have been written in a momentary Beatle panic for the writer. No fowl there; most of songwriting America went through it. Remember, the Beatles had only landed six months before. The song was awful. I'm surprised it was not on a Gary Lewis and the Playboys LP. There was no tin can being kicked down the street with this one! I told Tommy that he was looking for songs for the Rolling Stones, not a would-be Beatles. Ten minutes later, I had "Time Is On My Side," and my life changed again for the better.

Liberty Records, and Imperial and Metric Music, was an incredible place to be. I had met Al Bennett before in England—a sort of ethnic John Wayne and a force to be reckoned with. Al Bennett, Sy Waronker, the Skaff brothers, LiPuma, Snuff Garrett, Gene McDaniels, Eddie Cochran, Timi Yuro, the Fleetwoods, and the great Bob Krasnow, without doubt one of the primo record men in the game. Fire and guts with great heart, ears, and instinct.

The whole groove, the whole idea of being able to do your thing in this one-story piece of real, real estate heaven on Sunset Strip was inspiring. After all, this was the street of Jack Webb and Ben Alexander; Roger Smith, Efrem Zimbalist Jr., and Kookie; Dino's Lodge and Sy

Devore. Dreams did come true, and the little bastard called Immediate Records was born during these days.

Pretty good life, to end up in the sun on Sunset Strip.

CHARLIE WATTS: While we were recording in Hollywood, I went to Shelly's Manne-Hole twice—once to see Charles Lloyd, Albert Stinson [with Gabor Szabo and Pete LaRoca], and the Bill Evans Trio with Paul Motian on drums [and Chuck Israels]. I saw Shelly at his club.

RUSS TITELMAN: I went to the Rolling Stones' "Satisfaction" session at RCA. Jack invited me. He was playing the tambourine. Fantastic.

ANDREW LOOG OLDHAM: We liked J. W. Alexander. He hung in the studio. Used to wear a sailor's hat. He played percussion. Got a credit, as well, on *December's Children (And Everybody's).*

GUY WEBSTER: I watched the Stones record. First of all, I thought they were beautiful to look at. Visually beautiful. That's what happened in the sixties—when the long hair started coming in, men who were average-looking started to look beautiful. I'm talking about it as an artist. It was so much fun to photograph them because of that. They inspired me.

I loved the Stones, and couldn't believe their sound. As for the session, I took them up to a girlfriend's house in Hollywood, on private land by the reservoir. I knew the property. I didn't even ask. I didn't have to. I took the band out there with a limousine, up a dirt road, and we shot pictures. One was used as the front cover of the band's *Big Hits (High Tide and Green Grass)* LP.

ANDREW LOOG OLDHAM: Guy Webster did 'em. Great stuff, especially the picture of the Stones up in the Canyon. Now, that was opposites attracting . . . the leaves were brown, it was California, and the limo, natch, was black.

Aftermath and *Between the Buttons* and, in the U.S., *Flowers,* were some of my finest hours as Mick and Keith reached the ability to compose whole albums for the Stones. The songs were just brilliant, only eclipsed by the idea that the Beatles, Ray Davies, and, coming up

through the ranks, Pete Townshend, wrote better. The media and the BBC would just not accept what damn fine writers Mick and Keith had turned into. Wonderful social commentaries that had their roots somewhere between vaudeville and the BBC World Service. The laconic comments, the posed rancour . . . Mick and Keith's songs, at that time, cut right through the picket fence and into the very life of then. I'd better stop now, or Keith, if he reads this, might be reaching for the vomit bag.

I'm not just talking about the obvious—"Satisfaction," "Paint It, Black." I'm talking "She Smiled Sweetly," "Connection," "All Sold Out," "Back Street Girl."

"Back Street Girl" was influenced by the Phil Spector and Jerry Leiber tune for for Ben E. King, "Spanish Harlem." On "Back Street Girl," we must give a nod to Nick De Caro, who played accordion on that and was uncredited at the time, because I did not give credit to outsiders. Go figure! Anyway, Nick, sorry it took so long, and perhaps ABKCO could give him credit in future. That part had to be a real arranged part, like John and Paul on "We Love You"—a close shave would not have

Keith Richards and Charlie Watts onstage with the Rolling Stones at the Los Angeles Sports Arena, 1965.

worked. Nick did Cher's arrangements . . . maybe that's why we did not give him credit.

KEITH RICHARDS: In a way, maybe when you write songs without even knowing it, you're kinda saying, "Can I do this live?" And so, in a way, you add that in. You don't know if it's gonna work, but I guess [what] you keep in the back of your mind is, "We're making a record here. What happens if they all like it, and we gotta play it live?" So, in a way, that maybe in the back of the mind—it sets up the song to be playable onstage.

CHRIS HILLMAN: The record "Get Off of My Cloud" was recorded at RCA Studios in Hollywood. You know why I like "Get Off of My Cloud"? Brian Jones is on it. The unknown factor of what made the Stones great was Brian Jones, and nobody gives him credit. Yes, he was the pretty boy. However, as a musician . . . he was an unbelievably good musician.

I remember when the Byrds opened some shows for the Stones in May of 1965, and at a concert in San Diego when they were late arriving. We actually were doing a couple of their songs when they walked in the door, because we had run out of material. So we were doing our "club set" that included a couple of their tunes. We had done four of five shows with them.

I watched them from the wings. They were good. They were great. To me, I'm a kid coming out of bluegrass, where you didn't move onstage and had a glum look on your face, 'cause you had to keep concentrating and playing at breakneck speed on a musical thing. Chris Darrow can attest to the "bluegrass showmanship," which is nothing there. I'm watching these guys—at least, Mick and Keith—just going for it, and my mouth was open. Wow! I go back to Brian Jones, who was a real integral part of the band. He didn't do much onstage, either; he just looked great.

DAVE HULL: THE HONORARY FIFTH BEATLE

DAVE HULL: KRLA and I supported the Rolling Stones and the Beatles. In 1964 and '65, Bob Eubanks presented the Beatles at the Hollywood Bowl, and then at Dodger Stadium in 1966.

I was involved with the Rolling Stones. I was onstage as an emcee with Dick Moreland and Charlie O'Donnell at the Long Beach Auditorium in 1964. It was a great show. The kids received them better than I thought they would. The Stones, like the Beatles, would be on the cover of the *KRLA Beat.*

We played the Stones. We went heavy on "Satisfaction." It became number one worldwide, especially in this country. They blew everybody's mind, as far as disc jockeys like myself were concerned. We never thought that would happen, but if you go back and listen to "Satisfaction," you'll know why it was such a strong number one. When I first heard it, I didn't think it was gonna be as big as the Beatles. Well, it was bigger than the Beatles. Six weeks at number one.

There was the *KRLA Beat* Pop Music Awards dinner, in December of 1965 at the Hullabaloo, and Mick Jagger attended with the Stones' manager, producer, and press officer [Andrew Loog Oldham]. We were down the street from RCA on Sunset, where they did their recordings.

KRLA programmed the new English music, particularly embracing the Beatles and the Stones, as well as Sandie Shaw, Marianne Faithfull, the Animals, Petula Clark, and the Hollies. It made them giants. That was not us, but really, the power of KRLA.

It's important to note that earlier, back in 1961 and '62, KRLA played records from England that were local and national hits. Acker Bilk's "Stranger On the Shore," Kenny Ball's "Midnight in Moscow," and Haley Mills's "Let's Get Together" and "Cobbler, Cobbler" from the Disney movie *The Parent Trap.* I first heard the Beatles' "Love Me Do" as a promotional record in 1962 on WVKO in Ohio.

But we never forgot the Beach Boys, Jan and Dean, the Spector groups, Sonny and Cher, the Mamas and the Papas, Love, and the Byrds. At the time, we were just kicking everybody's tail in town. A fifty-thousand-watt

Left: Dave Hull interviewing George Harrison at the Cinnamon Cinder for KTLA, 1964.
Right: Derek Taylor, Dave Hull, Ringo Starr, and John Lennon at a Beatles press conference at the Cinnamon Cinder club in Studio City, 1964.

station. It reached to San Diego and up to San Jose.

I was close for a bit with Paul McCartney and Brian Epstein, through Derek Taylor. The relationship with them went beyond press conferences and show intros at the Hollywood Bowl and Dodger Stadium. My Indian horn went out on me onstage at their Bowl concert, just as I was gonna honk it for the Beatles.

I would see the Beatles at the places they rented in town. The closeness I had with the Beatles was owed to Louise Harrison, George's sister, who was the one that gave me inside information, because she wanted her brother George to be part of a famous group. Brian Epstein was the best, but Derek Taylor as his publicity man—he really knew how to advance anyone and go into a market, and press release stuff that would make people want to know the answers to questions before he'd leave town. He was brilliant. Derek and Tony Barrow wrote columns for the *KRLA Beat.* I went with Derek to Nassau as a guest of the Beatles, when they were filming *Help!* I did interviews for the *KRLA Beat.* In 1967, Derek handled PR for the Monterey International Pop Festival and the station broadcast reports from the event.

I came from a world that started with the 45 RPM.

The single. They didn't care about the B-side, just the A-side, and played the poop out of it. Then the LP, the long player, arrived, helped immensely by the Beatles. We are on AM radio. This is before FM rock. One thing about the Beatles—they brought one important thing to the American and worldwide music scene that nobody else did. Before them, like Frank Sinatra, one or two songs, maybe that were gonna be hits, the rest of it filler. When it came to the Beatles, everything they did was great. Therefore you were forced by the Beatles to play the albums, and cuts like "If I Fell" and "Girl." All of these things were not singles first, but taken out by KRLA and played on the air to become such hits that Capitol Records then had to release them as singles.

I later introduced the Beatles' "Strawberry Fields Forever" and "Penny Lane" as an exclusive. I got a copy from Capitol Records over the protest of KHJ and the Real Don Steele. This is what made me. I cared, and it was audience-building. It was before consultants and business people got involved. Record promo men like Russ Regan worked their butts off, and saw that we got what we needed. And they would run back to their record companies and bring it to us. Hardworking people that you cannot find in the business today.

CHAPTER 11

FOLK ROCKS

Few songs have come to define an era more than the Byrds' "Mr. Tambourine Man," the crystalline reverberation of a twelve-string Rickenbacker, a throbbing bass counterpoint, and layered vocals that didn't so much speak as shimmer. It was a sound nurtured in folk music, but it pulsed with a current that was electric to the ear. With one majestic thrum, the Byrds took flight as one of rock's most inventive and influential bands.

Through a lengthy series of artistic evolutions and personnel shifts, the Byrds remained vital, with founding visionary Jim McGuinn joined over the years by Gene Clark, David Crosby, Chris Hillman, and Michael Clarke. Their diverse talents combined to produce a body of work finely tuned to the moment, but timeless in terms of song craft and pure musicianship. They dabbled in Dylan and psychedelia, and laid the foundation for country rock, starting as a singles band and growing into album artists.

The Byrds began, like countless others, with a seed planted in New York's Greenwich Village, where a young folk guitarist named Jim McGuinn backed the Limeliters, the Chad Mitchell Trio, and Bobby Darin on guitar and banjo. Relocating to Los Angeles, he co-founded the Jet Set with Gene Clark and David Crosby, which hatched the Byrds, following the arrival of Chris Hillman and Michael Clarke.

JIM McGUINN: Our early manager, Jim Dickson, was a large part of the formation of the group and the attitude. It was his pick to do "Mr. Tambourine Man." He got a demo of it before Dylan released it. Jim loved the song. We didn't get it.

JIM DICKSON: When Dylan came to the Monterey Folk Festival [in] 1963 or '64, I went over to a room with his road manager, Victor Maymudes, and some other people. Dylan had a whole bunch of new songs, and he sat there and played them all. Just his voice and the guitar—that's what blew my mind. He had one great song after another. The songs became alive in front of me, and

Above: **Jim McGuinn with Billy James at a Columbia Records recording session, Hollywood, 1965.**
Opposite: **Bob Dylan jamming with the Byrds at Ciro's nightclub, Hollywood, 1965.**

they were all new songs that weren't on his first album. He sang about twenty songs, and I was just glued to them. I never heard anybody write like that. He was just playing one song right after another. They were amazing.

When I heard "Mr. Tambourine Man," I said, "That's the best. That could be a hit song." I put my head down and went after that one for the Byrds. They already had about a couple of dozen songs that Gene Clark wrote, and a couple by McGuinn. I didn't hear a hit in any of it, but there was a quality we were getting. I put "Mr. Tambourine Man" in there, and David [Crosby] got it kicked out for a while.

What happened was David campaigned against it. He talked Gene Clark out of singing it. Told him, "Your songs are better than that." So, when Gene said he wasn't gonna do it based on Crosby's influence, McGuinn volunteered. I said, "Okay. Let's give it a try." McGuinn created a voice I had never heard before. He tried to come down somewhere between Dylan and Lennon vocally, and it worked. I could hear it on the Byrds' *Preflyte* tape that I produced. He was getting the song, and it was working, and all I needed was the right music behind it and I would have a hit.

Jim Dickson at an Elysian Park love-in, Los Angeles, 1967.

Dylan showed up in town and wanted to come to World Pacific Studio. I told the band Dylan was coming, and [to] please do "Mr. Tambourine Man" again for him. He came to the studio more than once, one time with Bob Neuwirth, who played a key role. Dylan also played the piano with them, got to know them a little bit, and was charmed. Michael Clarke was still playing on cardboard boxes with a tambourine on top. He didn't have his drums. McGuinn had a twelve-string acoustic guitar with a pick up. Dylan walked around, listening to what each person was playing.

Then I sent the record to Dylan. We had to get his okay. That's where Bobby Neuwirth comes in. Dylan and Neuwirth sat on the floor, and they wore out the first acetate I sent 'em. They listened to it over and over, and that's when Neuwirth said, "You can dance to it." [Manager Albert] Grossman was trying to talk him out of it after we recorded it. Artie Mogull, who was involved in Dylan's publishing, just gave me the song. Dylan and Grossman had the finished product, but Neuwirth was able to persuade Dylan: "Hey, man, it's a rock 'n' roll band playing one of your songs." Going up against Albert was not comfortable for

Left: **Chris Hillman, Hollywood, 1965.** ♪ *Middle left:* **David Crosby, Hollywood, 1965.**
Middle right: **Gene Clark, Los Angeles, 1965.** ♪ *Right:* **Jim McGuinn, Hollywood, 1965.**

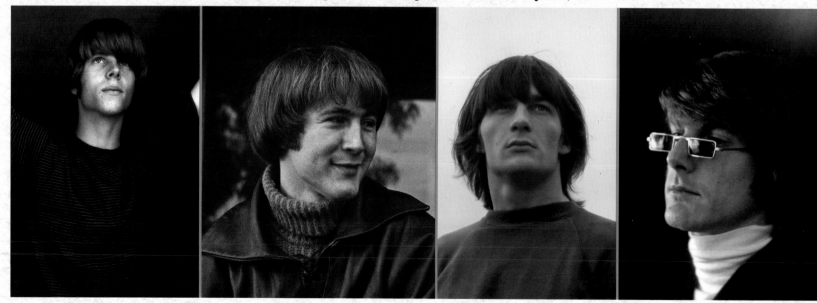

him, but he okay-ed it and we were able to release it.

The Byrds first heard it all together on KFWB, when they were in a station wagon they bought from the folk singer Odetta. They had to pull over. And David, who had been anti-Dylan all along—the next time we went to Ciro's, I see him outside on the sidewalk, explaining to some young girl the deep meaning of Dylan and all that stuff. Like he was the expert . . .

Dylan got up onstage and played the harmonica. He gave me permission to use a photo I took of him and the Byrds on the back of their first LP. I wasn't really surprised with what he came up with after that.

Bob Dylan at a press conference at Columbia Records, Hollywood, 1965.

"The Bells of Rhymney" is my all-time favorite Byrds song. What song best describes the Byrds? I would say that one, because of the vocals on it, the harmony. Because of the way we approached the song. We had turned into a band with our own style. We went from doing Bob Dylan material, and then we take "The Bells of Rhymney," with our own signature rendition of it. It's not like Pete Seeger at all. It's our own thing. Michael Clarke was a lazy drummer, but when he was on, he was great. And he's playing these cymbals. A great experience. I just love that cut.

The breakthrough record was "Mr. Tambourine Man,"

CHRIS HILLMAN: I do have to say, all five of us were learning how to play—once again, coming out of the folk thing and plugging in. McGuinn was the most seasoned musician, and we all sort of worked off of him. Jim had impeccable time. Great sense of time. McGuinn's style, and that minimalist thing of playing that was so good. He played the melody.

I remember that the Columbia studio was a union room. The engineers had shirts and ties on. Mandatory breaks every three hours. Terry [Melcher] was a good guy. I didn't really get to know him. I was shy. Columbia was comfortable to record in. Terry was good. I liked him. I will say this—on the Byrds albums as the bass player, I was not placed back in the mix. Sometimes it worked.

The Byrds play Dylan—it was a natural fit after "Mr. Tambourine Man." I'm not a big fan of the Wrecking Crew's track of "Mr. Tambourine Man." It's way too slick for me. Yes, we probably could have cut it. I don't know if we would have had the success. And I understand completely, from a business sense, why Columbia and Terry brought in good session guys to cut a good track. "Let's hedge our bets here, and let's get this thing and get it as best we can." That's fine, but not my favorite Byrds record.

Advertisement for the KFWB Beach Boys Summer Spectacular in the *KFWB/98 Hitline* newspaper, 1965.

but the breakthrough album was *Turn! Turn! Turn!* The single record is the most recognizable Byrds song, way over "Mr. Tambourine Man," with all due respect. That's the Byrds song people always remember. It was the LP cover I autographed the most.

JIM McGUINN: I remember one time, Dylan took me aside. I went over to the hotel he was staying at, and he said, "You know, I used to think of you as just an imitator, but I heard 'Lay Down Your Weary Tune,' and listened closely—you're doing something that wasn't there before. That's really good."

BILL MUMY: Yeah, the Byrds were "my band" back in the mid-sixties. I used to draw their logo—you know, the one from *5D*—on my notebooks and stuff. Marta Kristen, who played my sister, Judy, on *Lost in Space*, turned me on to the Byrds in 1965. She turned me on to Dylan, too. I would have found 'em on my own, but I'll always thank her for that. See, it was folk music that made music the most important thing in my life. Specifically, the Kingston Trio's catalog. Of course, I came into that a bit late, but when it hit me, it hit me turbo hard.

I was a folk music fanatic by 1965. Kingston Trio, Pete Seeger, that kind of stuff. One of the things about the Kingston Trio, besides the fact that they had fourteen Top 10 albums—four at the *same time* in 1959—was they had amazing harmony. Especially the original trio, with Dave Guard, before John Stewart replaced him in 1962. Dave

Bill Mumy performing "Tijuana Jail" at the Hollywood Bowl to promote *Lost in Space*, 1965.

The Kingston Trio (Bob Shane, John Stewart, and Nick Reynolds), 1967.

Guard was the genius in that band. His harmony parts were all over the place. Like Crosby's in the Byrds. So when I heard the Byrds doing folk songs, with these really interesting harmony parts that Crosby created, I was hooked. Also, they had electric energy, and it just got you more excited. Hey, the sixties were truly special! The very first electric guitar I ever bought was a Rickenbacker. I still have 'em both. The Byrds were a big influence on me.

I played the Hollywood Bowl in 1965. It was my very first gig ever. It's been downhill ever since! It was Scout Day. The bowl was packed with Boy Scouts, Girl Scouts, Cub Scouts, and Brownies. Packed. *Lost in Space* had just started airing, and there I was, promoting the series onstage at the Hollywood Bowl, in that crazy silver spacesuit with an acoustic guitar. Art Linkletter was the emcee of the show. He introduced me and I walked out and played the Kingston Trio's "Tijuana Jail"! A song about going to Mexico and gambling and drinking and being thrown in jail! Isn't that great? What blows my mind is the fact that no one—not my parents, not the promoters, no one—suggested I play a different song. I could've played "This Land Is Your Land" or something a bit more "appropriate," so to speak. But nope! I played "Tijuana Jail." That cracks me up. We did eighty-four episodes of *Lost in Space* from 1965 through 1968. The first season was in black and white, and the rest were color. Big-time color.

A TOWN WITH PITY

IAN WHITCOMB: In July of 1965, I played the KFWB Beach Boys Summer Spectacular at the Hollywood Bowl. The Byrds, Dino, Desi and Billy, Donna Loren, Sonny and Cher, the Kinks, Sam the Sham and the Pharaohs, the Sir Douglas Quintet, the Righteous Brothers. By that time, I was with a booking agency, GAC—General Artists Corporation, who must have got me on. A terrific bill. My brother, Robin, played drums on the live shows for Sonny and Cher. A few months after this extravaganza, I played at the legendary It's Boss, the short-lived rock club on the site of the old Ciro's.

Ian Whitcomb on the set of *Shivaree*, 1965.

During 1965 and '66, I appeared on all the daily television music programs in the Los Angeles market. *Shebang!*, hosted by Casey Kasem, *The Lloyd Thaxton Show*, *Shivaree* with Gene Weed, and Dick Clark's *American Bandstand*. My faithful publicist and friend, George Sherlock from Tower Records, took me around to promote "You Turn Me On." The single went Top 10 in the United States. In fact, it was an American girl who said to me, "You turn me on," and that's where I got the idea for the song. The Standells were also on Tower, and we did dates together. Gypsy Boots was on the label. I also visited all the local radio stations, like KRLA, KHJ, and KFWB, where, in 1966, I participated in a *Talk-In* with DJ B. Mitchell Reed, along with Chad Stuart, Jeremy Clyde, Derek Taylor, and Doug Sahm—a group interview on the AM dial, where we discussed topics like the Vietnam War.

I had been a guest several times on producer Jack Good's TV series, *Shindig!*, that was filmed in Hollywood at ABC-TV. Jack had a background in drama at Oxford. When he did the earlier *Oh Boy!* television music series in England, he had everything organized and synchronized. So Jack saw the dramatic potential of rock 'n' roll. To that point, it hadn't been exploited or explored in this country. You simply had teenage kids dancing with each other on the Dick Clark shows. Jack had this dramatic view. The *Shindig!* shows were done live, and the backing tracks of the music were done on Melrose Avenue at Nashville West, next to Nickodell Restaurant near Paramount Studios. It took a week to make a *Shindig!*

In 1966, I was living in publicist Derek Taylor's old house in Nichols Canyon. Doug Weston, the owner of the Troubadour club, showed up and asked me to perform. Doug and I went to David Abell and rented a lovely upright piano. I was the first person to bring a piano into his room. I started off with the old songs, backed by Somebody's Children, and [for the] second half, I would do my ragtime stuff on the piano. I went down quite well. Among the people who came to see me were author Christopher Isherwood and artists David Hockney and Don Bachardy.

I'm a music historian who plays rock 'n' roll, ragtime, and Tin Pan Alley. Leiber and Stoller produced a few sessions on me. I've played behind Del Shannon, Frankie Ford, and Roy Orbison's band, the Candymen. I've played piano with Big Joe Turner at the Ice House in Pasadena and Big Mama Thornton at the Hollywood Bowl. Eubie Blake came to see me headline at the Ash Grove. I've played with Big Jay McNeely all over the world.

CHAPTER 12

GÖTTERDÄMMERUNG

Ike Turner was born in Clarksdale, Mississippi, not far from where the devil shook hands with Robert Johnson. In 1951, he produced "Rocket 88," with singer Jackie Brenston fronting Turner's ferocious R & B band, the Kings of Rhythm. The band was a model for the stripped-down, midsize groups that would dominate the fifties, with Turner playing piano behind Brenston's vocals, accompanied by tenor saxophone and drums. At the song's center was a potent new sound: the distorted guitar. It was a "race record" smash; many consider "Rocket 88" to be the very first rock 'n' roll record.

Turner was also a talent scout, discovering B.B. King and Howlin' Wolf. In 1956, he met Anna Mae Bullock, a teenager from Brownsville, Tennessee, who was singing in talent shows and a gospel choir in Knoxville. She joined the Kings of Rhythm. At the urging of Juggy Murray of Sue Records, Turner teamed with Bullock, soon to be rechristened Tina Turner, on "A Fool in Love," which hit big. Ike had written it for a singer who never showed up for the recording session. But Tina knew it and nailed it, and soon, the train was leaving the station.

In October 1960, Ike and Tina appeared on American Bandstand. The following year, the duo ruled the regional airwaves with "I Idolize You" and "It's Gonna Work Out Fine." Ike then assembled a girl group, the

Ikettes, who charted with "Gone, Gone, Gone." It was now time for the Ike and Tina Turner Revue.

TINA TURNER: Ike and I haven't got the time to develop as songwriters, 'cause we spend so much time in the studio and on the road. There's a lot of good music to be covered. Ike selects the songs, and there's a tremendous amount of preparation for our tours. I never felt we've used sex as a gimmick in our program. It's important today, because people who pay to see a show want a little of everything. The sexual portion of our show isn't planned; it just happens. It works out well visually, and it always seems to get the most audience response. Everybody needs an image. There's a million groups out today—flipping, smoke bombs, dancing—fortunately, everybody can't be sexy. We've discussed it a thousand times . . . the miniskirts, and see-through dresses. People's minds do wander.

For years, we've gotten reviews that seem to dwell on the sexual aspect of the show. I've never felt people gaining sexuality after seeing our show, but I like them to remember what they have just seen. I've never really thought of our show as being aggressive. Even as wild as I am, I know that I maintain my femininity. People have always told me that.

Above: Ike and Tina Turner at the Moulin Rouge for a taping of *The Big T.N.T. Show*, Hollywood, 1965.
Opposite: Ike and Tina Turner onstage with DJ Jimmy Byrd, circa 1961.

KIRK SILSBEE: They toured relentlessly. In L.A., they played the black clubs, the rock clubs, and the teen clubs. They even performed in bowling alleys!

I think that Ike is a very underrated guitarist. I know Jimi Hendrix heard him. Ike was really stretching boundaries on instrumentals like "The New Breed."

First of all, Ike was a real bandleader. And you didn't always get real bandleaders in R & B. You might have gotten artists who cut with good studio outfits, but if they were lucky enough to get hit records—and I'm talking about the R & B world—they were thrown out on the road and at the mercy of hastily assembled traveling bands or house bands that might not know their material. That wasn't the way Ike operated. He kept a highly disciplined, cutting-edge playing and recording unit that could go on the road at a moment's notice and play the shit out of the music the way it was supposed to be heard.

Ike had this band, and he was generating material like mad. He could write and produce it. He had this

great singer in Tina, and he had a very good backup unit. So he was like Phil Spector, if Phil was performing. They met with Spector on the "River Deep—Mountain High" session, after he saw them in action at *The Big T.N.T. Show* filmed concert in 1965.

By Spector's own reckoning, "River Deep—Mountain High" was his magnum opus. It wasn't a Wall of Sound, it was an avalanche, with twenty-one musicians and twenty-one background singers. Handel's Messiah was a nursery rhyme compared to the sonic assault Spector unleashed on this track. Co-written with Jeff Barry and Ellie Greenwich, it begins with a rumble and then erupts in a roar, pushing Tina Turner to apoplectic heights. Spector demanded literally dozens of vocal takes, leaving Turner a frazzled, depleted mess. Among the session players on the date were Leon Russell, Carol Kaye, Earl Palmer, Glen Campbell, and Jim Gordon.

DONOVAN: THE INFINITE MIND

DONOVAN: It was 1966, and I played that May—a week at the Trip club on Sunset. All Hollywood turned up. New pals . . . I met the Mamas and the Papas and Cyrus Faryar of the MFQ, who played the wonderful electric violin on "Celeste" when I recorded it in CBS Studios for the *Sunshine Superman* album.

Peer Music was and still is my music publishing family. Ralph Peer supported me all the way, and I am so grateful, as I learned early music publishing is the beginning of this music business, and is the center of it all today.

Mickie Most, my Brit producer, and I went into Columbia Records recording "Season of the Witch." The sound engineers in white coats! Like doctors. As we recorded "Season of the Witch," Mickie said to one engineer, "Turn the bass level up." The two in white coats said they needed a conference on this. They left the studio control room. They returned and said they couldn't turn up the bass, as it was going into the red on the dial. Mickie said, "Look guys, your boss, Clive Davis, just gave me a million dollars to record three

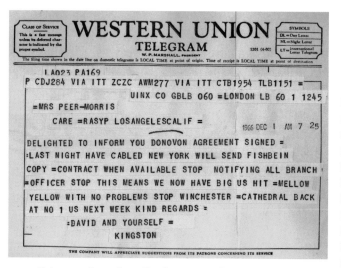

Telegram from Peer Music announcing Donovan's "Mellow Yellow" record, 1966.

artists. Do you think if I asked him for a little more bass, he would give it to me?" The bass was turned up. A real *Spinal Tap* moment, long before the film of the same name.

Decades later, "River Deep—Mountain High" looms large in the pop pantheon. Rolling Stone listed it as the thirty-third greatest song in the history of rock 'n' roll. Although it barely cracked the Top 100 in 1966 (it was #88 on the Billboard chart), it would go Top 5 in England. The public's indifference was a devastating blow to Spector, speeding him toward that dark night of the soul. For a man of such peerless self-confidence, the song's failure provoked an equally epic retreat into what became his "wilderness years." Spector appearances were as rare as yeti sightings; the teenage tycoon of pop fell into full retreat, a looming blackness patiently waiting to claim the legacy.

JACK NITZSCHE: I knew ["River Deep—Mountain High"] was a great song. We did the rhythm track in two different three-hour sessions. Even during the cutting of the track, when she was putting on a scratch vocal, Tina was singing along as we cut it, and was so into it on the high notes. Oh man, she was great, doing a rough scratch vocal as the musicians really kicked the rhythm section in the ass. Once in a while, a vocalist would run through a song, but this time Tina made everybody play better.

Phil [had] said, "I've got a song for Tina." I went to Phil's house and went over the arrangement, note by note. When I first heard the intro, I didn't like it very much, but once it was being recorded, it all made sense. It was real good.

DAN KESSEL: The sessions for "You've Lost That Lovin' Feelin'" were monumental, but the sessions for "River Deep—Mountain High" were even beyond that. The lobby at Gold Star was jammed full of celebrities and other Hollywood types. I didn't do handclaps or play percussion on that one, preferring instead to hover in the rarified atmosphere of being near Phil in the control booth. While my stepmom, B. J. Baker, soared like a flaming Valkyrie in the heart of the vocal section, and my dad, Barney Kessel, blasted away on his 1959 Danelectro within the massive depths of the three-piece bass section of this incredible Spector Philharmonic, with Tina exploding like a cosmic supernova, Phil nudged me and asked, "Can Mitch Miller do this?"

Recording session at Hollywood's Gold Star Studios for "Paradise," produced by Phil Spector, 1965. Seated musicians: (*from left*) Lyle Ritz, Jim Yester, Henry Diltz, Barney Kessel, and Tommy Tedesco. Standing: (*far left*) Don Randi.

Ike and Tina Turner with Phil Spector at Gold Star Sudios, Hollywood, 1966.

DON PEAKE: Tina was not vibing with us. She was in the booth with Ike. We were playing, and we thought this was the greatest song ever recorded and into it. We were so proud of it. We were stunned when it flopped. You understand that when you work with someone like Phil, you are actually part of their family, their history, and you are also part of their dreams. It wasn't just playing on a date [and saying], "Give me my money."

George Harrison provided a jacket blurb for the 1969 re-release of the "River Deep—Mountain High" album: "It is a perfect record from start to finish. You couldn't improve on it." John Lennon called it a "masterpiece." In 1969, Spector himself said that he only made "River Deep—Mountain High" to "do something experimental."

BONES HOWE: I had worked with Ike and Tina at Studio B at Radio Recorders, and Ike used to pay in cash. Ike had the girls—and he paraded the girls. I liked Ike. He was a good guy, and I had a good time working for him.

I didn't get to know Phillip until later, 'cause he was working at Gold Star and I was at Radio Recorders, and then I went to United. I knew who he was. I met him a couple of times. Then, in 1966, he called me up

and was doing a Tina Turner album and wanted to do the whole orchestra live, and Larry Levine at Gold Star couldn't do it. So Larry called me and asked, "Do we think we can do this at Studio A at United?" "Absolutely." I did four or six tracks on that Ike and Tina Turner album, including "A Love Like Yours (Don't Come Knockin' Every Day)." Larry came over and clued me in on how to set up the Wall of Sound tape reverb echo, and all that stuff.

I had some idea of what Stan Ross and Larry Levine had to go through at Gold Star to make Phil's records. It was tape reverb and the chamber. I knew what it was. But doing it and finding a way to make it work on a record is a different thing. I knew what it was, technically. For one thing, Phil had this vision of what the sound should be like—and it was his sound. You'd hear a baritone saxophone suddenly pop out. It just had all of these wonderful things happening in his tracks that worked with his recordings and his artists. Phil knew the song meant something. People were buying songs, not sound.

TINA TURNER: We toured for years with all the English groups, and I always liked what they were singing about. The biggest change started happening when we were working around L.A. in 1966 and ran into Phil Spector.

He wanted to record me, and when we cut "River Deep—Mountain High," Mick Jagger was in Gold Star Studios. After hearing the song, he wanted us to do their fall tour of England with the Stones and Yardbirds.

ANDREW LOOG OLDHAM: The '66 tour with Ike and Tina Turner and the Yardbirds was a give-something-back-to-the-fans type of thing. Ike and Tina were a seventeen-piece review; you were not making money putting them on the bill. On top of that, Tina had had the Phil Spector record in July, "River Deep—Mountain High," that we had championed. And if we, the Stones and I, were not going to bring them over, nobody else was, and the UK deserved to see what we had been fortunate enough to witness in the U.S. Long John Baldry was the host of that tour. We had so much music on the bill, we could only offer him the compère spot.

TINA TURNER: The English weren't used to seeing girls with high heels performing, and I think they were shocked a bit. In June of 1967, the Ike and Tina Turner Revue opened for the Monkees at the Hollywood Bowl.

ANDREW LOOG OLDHAM: Phil Spector had so many firsts. His "To Know Him Is to Love Him" was a fifties garage equal of Les Paul and Mary Ford. His early sixties run with the Crystals and the Ronettes set the audio standard for so many . . . and we are all still humming that standard. When I first heard "You've Lost That Lovin' Feelin" in Phil's New York office, I thought I might be listening to three records being played at once. "River Deep—Mountain High" was his traumatized pop finale, apart from a great curtain call with John [Lennon] and George [Harrison]. It's not an accident that Dennis Hopper took the pictures of Ike and Tina and Phil. All of them, save Tina, were dancing to the same headstone.

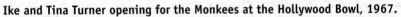

Ike and Tina Turner opening for the Monkees at the Hollywood Bowl, 1967.

CHAPTER 13

AND THE HITS JUST KEEP ON COMIN'!

RUSS REGAN: In 1965, KHJ changed their format to Boss Radio with Bill Drake and Gene Chenault. I loved the RKO radio programmer, Bill Drake. He understood programming as well as anyone I ever met. He understood one thing: Play the hits, and keep the talk down to a minimum. Bill understood the repetition of Top 30. He called me and explained to me, before KHJ went Boss Radio, that he was going to go up against KRLA and KFWB. "We're gonna do it." I told him, after he mentioned Boss Radio, "Bill, I'm not a radio programmer. I'm a record promotion man. And kids ain't using the term "Boss" anymore. Boss is old hat." Bill says to me, "I'm bringing it back." And he did.

Bill Drake envisioned a new radio concept wherein personalities vied with the songs themselves for the listener's interest. Dave Diamond was one of the nine original "Boss Jocks" hired by Drake to build 93 KHJ AM in Los Angeles into a ratings power. Diamond had laid plenty of pipe: WKGN in Knoxville, Tennessee; WIL in St. Louis, Missouri; KOIL in Omaha, Nebraska; and KBTR in Denver, Colorado. He arrived at KHJ in 1965, where he pioneered the inclusion of album selections within the Boss Radio playlist.

DAVE DIAMOND: I knew exactly where all the music was coming from in the late fifties and early sixties. I loved Ricky Nelson, Jan and Dean, Timi Yuro, the Beach Boys, and Jack Nitzsche's "The Lonely Surfer." I knew that stuff was happening out of L.A. and Hollywood. My goal was to get to the West Coast, even when I was in Omaha.

Somebody brought me a tape of an L.A. radio station, maybe KFWB, and I stood there listening to it and said, "This is where I've got to go. I've got to be in Los Angeles."

I loved Phil Spector's stuff. That Wall of Sound—that new sound. It held me, because I had spent so much time in production rooms, making radio promo spots . . . I knew what he was doing. I thought about taking all those layers of echo, and you could make a record sound any way you wanted. I had echo on my radio station in Knoxville in 1961—the whole station in echo. It sounded so different [from] any other station, and no one knew how I did it.

At KHJ, I did the 6:00 to 9:00 PM shift. We went to number one in six weeks. Then Phil started coming to my weekly talent shows at the Tiger's Tail, the former home of the Crescendo and Interlude, around the time the room became the Trip. One night, I had Phil onstage with the Righteous Brothers, Jan and Dean, Sonny and Cher, Dewey Martin from Buffalo Springfield on drums, Brian Wilson, and Ian Whitcomb, backed by my house band, Harvey and the Beau Jives. Everybody wailing on "You've Lost That Lovin' Feelin'."

In 1966, Dave Diamond introduced Nancy Sinatra's high-steppin' sensation, "These Boots Are Made for Walkin'," to the world.

DAVE DIAMOND: I always liked Nancy. She'd write me letters when I was on the air in St. Louis, and I'd play her records. Nothing would happen. When "These Boots Are Made for Walkin'" came through, I knew it was a

Opposite: **Gene Norman's Crescendo nightclub in West Hollywood, early 1960s.**

hit. Lee Hazlewood wrote it, and Billy Strange arranged it. I called the promotion man at Warner Brothers Reprise, a real good-lookin' surfer guy, and said, "Hey, you got a hit with Nancy Sinatra! Can you give me a box of records?" Because, in those days, two or three plays on a record, man, it started to scratch.

Nothing happened. One week, then two weeks, and I didn't hear anything. Frank [Sinatra] was playing at the Sands in Las Vegas, so I sent him a telegram. I had never met him. "Nancy has a hit with 'These Boots Are Made for Walkin'" (stop) Can't get records (stop) No cooperation from Warner Brothers Reprise."

Man, the next day, some guy from the label comes by with two boxes of records, trying to kiss my ass all over the place. I guess Frank called there and just raised holy hell. "Who is this guy, Dave Diamond? Nancy tells me he has a big radio show and you're not cooperating with him!" The records show up and I play it and keep playing it for six weeks, and finally the sales start to show and finally KHJ goes on it. And then KRLA, and then it goes number one.

Then they had a big thank-you party at Martoni's in Hollywood. I was invited, of course. There were so many phony freaks around Nancy when I got there, I couldn't even get to her to say hello. So I go to the upstairs level, and there's just a few people up there and Frank is standing there. I order a drink, and he's looking the other way. So I finally just walk over and say, "I'm the impudent bastard that sent you the telegram about Nancy." And he looked at me and responded, "Holy balls, man! Wow. You're Dave Diamond?" "Yeah." "That was really a great move on your part." Then, a while later, my pal, Russ Regan, found "That's Life" for Frank to record.

RUSS REGAN: At Loma Records, I was general manager, and I gave "That's Life" to Frank Sinatra to cut. Kelly Gordon, a songwriter, first gave it to me. He played a little piano. Kelly brought me the demo of "That's Life," which had already been recorded. It was just a hit in Houston, Texas. Kelly wanted to record it, but I told him it was a Frank Sinatra hit. [He said,] "Be my guest." So I went around my office—it was next door to Mo Ostin. "Mo, let me play you this song. I think it's a hit for Frank Sinatra." Mo, God bless him, puts it on, and says, "Russ, this is a smash for Frank Sinatra." He says to his secretary and

Dave Diamond on Sunset Strip Tue.

The Crescendo on the Sunset Strip will have a Diamond-studded Tiger Room every Tuesday night. KHJ dj Dave Diamond has been signed to act as official host and master of ceremonies. The 6-9 pm-er introduces acts and 'name' guest stars whom he obtains from KHJ.

Newspaper advertisement for KHJ DJ Dave Diamond's new music series, held at the Crescendo nightclub in West Hollywood, 1965.

assistant, "Donna. Get me ABC Messenger Service."

He sent the dub over to Frank Sinatra. It went to his home after he called Frank. He had the direct line. Two days later, Mo Ostin calls me on the intercom. "You sitting down? Frank loves the song. He's gonna do it." Initially, Jimmy Bowen was going to produce it, but he got Ernie Freeman because he felt there was an R & B kind of feel. So we all went to United Western. Frank did it in two takes. Never met him, [but] I watch it go down. Jimmy Bowen acknowledged me. I walked [out] onto Sunset Boulevard. "Thank you, God. This is a smash!"

Frank was my idol. The record got released thirty days later. It took off like a rocket ship. By October '66, it was a Top 4 record on the pop charts and number one on the R & B charts. That could only happen because it was done in L.A.

Then Frank flew me and Mo to Las Vegas, where he was playing the Sands Hotel. Mo and I took his wife, Mia Farrow, to dinner at the Flamingo to see Trini Lopez. He was also on Reprise, and she was a Trini Lopez fan. Then we came to the midnight show of Frank at the Sands, and we're sitting ringside. Right? And he belted out "That's Life," and I thought I'd died and gone to heaven. Incredible show. It was his anthem before "My Way" replaced it.

After the show, we were all invited to have a 2:00 AM supper at the Chinese restaurant at the Sands Hotel. Sinatra is sitting next to me. I'm calling him "Mr.

Sinatra." He asks, "Can I call you Russ?" "Sure!" Everyone at the table knew I found the song.

Mo and I flew back home at 10:00 AM the next day. Two weeks go by after this incredible night, and I walk into Martoni's restaurant to hang out with the record company guys. And there is Frank Sinatra, sitting there with Jilly Rizzo and his guys at a booth. I walk up to him [and say,] "Hi, Mr. Sinatra." [He says,] "Get lost, kid!" So I start walking way—my heart was broken. [Then I hear,] "Get back here, Russ! I know who you are." Frank Sinatra got me good.

BONES HOWE: I would go to KHJ and sit in the booth and watch the Real Don Steele and Robert W. Morgan. They were my friends.

Don Steele and guys like him loved radio. Being in the booth with Steele. He never came down. He was on high all the way, and screamed all these wonderful gimmicks that nobody else did, 'cause he was a madman when he was on the air. Of course, he'd go to Martoni's and drink, and he was always sober when he was in that booth. He drank gallons of coffee and was like one of those hyper DJ guys.

THE REAL DON STEELE

DON STEELE: My father was a truck driver, and my mother booked big bands out of the local Musicians Union 47 in Hollywood. I'd go with her to gigs and sit in the pit. I graduated from Hollywood High School. As a matter of fact, when I got out of the U.S. Air Force, there were two things open: I could either rob banks, or I thought I'd kind of like to be a radio announcer. I studied at the Don Martin Broadcasting School.

I began in the Corona, California, market. Later I was working in Omaha, Nebraska, as the *Don Steele Affair.* One day, after a year, the program director said, "Why don't you call yourself 'the Real Don Steele'?" People started calling me that on the street. That's a phonetic thing. The act of certain words and formations of sound.

I started in April 1965 at KHJ. Took me seven years to get here. Every half an hour we'd have an ID: "This is KHJ Los Angeles." The Boss Radio format requires more detail, and you must give the time. And at that point, I can give a title while I intro a record. I came up with some catchphrases, like: "It's 3:00 in Boss Angeles!" "It ain't that bad if you're fired at 3:30!" "You gotta flaunt it at 4:00!" "Spread your love at 5:30!" "We're gonna kick it out here on a fractious Friday!" "Tina Delgado is alive,

The Real Don Steele at the KHJ studio, Hollywood, 1968.

alive!" That's the catchphrase of all time. I used that in Portland, Oregon. All of a sudden, it was all over town. I don't have any idea why, but I know when it's a hit. I can feel it. Then I feel what can I say that hasn't already been said. Then I'd try to get it said on my show or somewhere.

I didn't know how hard it was and how much you had to really dedicate yourself to do it. But as it came out, now I'm glad I did. The honing and the polishing—that was necessary for me. And I had to be stone-cold dedicated. What a wonderful thing it must be to enjoy your job. To have fun working. I mean, not many people get that break.

The Real Don Steele taking his radio shift at KHJ following DJ Sam Riddle, Hollywood, 1968.

The radio world in L.A. was the Wild West. Everybody was after everybody else's ratings. Believe me. It was like a baseball game, and KHJ wanted to crush KRLA. One of the ideas behind KHJ was that the music keeps coming. So, except for the little short commercial breaks, they butted those records one up against the other, and talked over the intros and did promos over intros. Which is why you got to hear an extra song or two per hour, and a lot of good stuff. Steele's talk and intros were like pieces unto themselves. I'd tune in just to hear them!

I met Bill Drake, who programmed the RKO chain and consulted on the playlist. He had been a disc jockey and loved being a DJ, but his thing was that he analyzed format. He was the guy who understood that format had a big effect upon the listening audience. He engineered that Boss Radio format, where the music was going all the time and the commercials were snuck in.

You can't make good rock 'n' roll records if you don't listen to the radio, and I listened to the radio all the time when I wasn't in the studio. The one wonderful experience is when you've heard your own record on the radio, and you know what you've done and hear what it sounds like. But, of course, by the time I was doing that, I had done records for Lou Adler and others and heard them on the radio. I knew what to do to make a record sound good on the radio. So that was a key.

Let me tell you what my audience is. It's four girls in a Volkswagen Bug, listening to the music in a six-by-nine oval speaker in their car, going sixty miles an hour on the freeways. That's what it's about. Not about great speakers and hi-fi. Your audience was fourteen- to eighteen-year-old girls, mostly. They were the ones who bought the records.

None of us really knew how much influence the transistor radio was gonna have. The transistor radio was for the ball games. Studio guys had the thing in their pocket and an earphone; while they were recording, [they] were really listening to the Dodger game. What you had to do was listen to the radio and know what your records were gonna sound like when they got played. That's how people went and bought them.

This is how loose AM radio was back then. Herb Alpert and I had known each other. He was sort of on the fringe of the jazz world. I got a call from him in 1966, and he wanted to do a session at Western Studio 3. "I've signed this Brazilian band, and I've got to do a single record with them. I'm going through the Brazil '66 songs now, and I've got to get through this in three hours."

So we go into the studio, and we do this song called "The Joker" from a Broadway show. Now, we've got half an hour and have to do a B-side. Sergio Mendes says, "I've got this song that we do that everybody likes. Let's put it on the B-side." [It was] "Mais Que Nada."

I loved that session. The percussion elements—those were real players, not studio players. The difference between them playing "The Joker" and then, when they got cut loose, "Mais Que Nada" . . . it was completely different, and just wonderful. It had so much energy. It carried the other side.

Jerry [Moss] was a terrific promotion man. He took the "The Joker" record out and played it to a DJ, who said to him, "What's on the other side?" He spun it. "We'll put that on the radio." Can you imagine?

The wonderful thing, later, about FM was that it was much truer to the studio mix than it was on KHJ, coming out of little car radios and all the rest of that. Because it was very squelched, very limited on AM.

DAVE HULL: The music of KRLA was really programmed by Reb Foster and Dick Moreland. The new sounds. This is just before psychedelic music hit AM—1965, early '66.

When KHJ came on the scene in 1965, it took them really into 1967 to kick us, and basically, they just hammered the music. No talk, no fun, just music, and it worked. It simply worked.

And then in '67, FM radio, and B. Mitchell Reed. The actress Loretta Young told her daughter and two sons, "You are not to listen to those FM people. You kids are allowed to listen to that funny guy Dave Hull, but not to go to B. Mitchell Reed and all those people on FM." That was a direct quote from her son Chris to me, several years ago.

MICHAEL JACKSON: I started in Springfield, Massachusetts, at $125 a week for my work in television and radio. To supplement my income, I did sock hops and record hops at high schools and town halls. And you know something, I envied a man named Joe Smith, a DJ on the air in the Boston market who made $200 at a record hop while I only made $50. Joe was on WBZ, and later did a brief stint on KFWB in L.A. before eventually becoming president of Capitol Records.

I packed up and went to San Francisco. First, I was on a Top 40 station, KYA, the Boss of the Bay. I loved San Francisco, and was given the name "Michael Scotland in Scotland's Yard" by KYA program director Les Crane. He signed me to do the morning show, but he didn't tell me until I got there that "morning" began at one minute after midnight. That lasted for a handful of months. I then revolted, and he said to use my own name. Crane was fired soon, to be followed by me being fired. It was a fun and adventurous time.

Then I went to KEWB, where I got a job doing the overnight shift. Chuck Blore ran the station, along with KFWB in Hollywood. I only played one song in my entire year and a half on KEWB. That one recording was Presley's "Blue Suede Shoes," which brought me threats. Hence, controversial talk radio was born. Gary Owens and Casey Kasem were on the station, real pros. I totally phased out spinning records and began talking with the callers.

TIME magazine discovered me, and wrote a page and a half—a wonderful, glowing article that called me "The All Night Psychiatrist." I received an offer from KHJ in L.A. I had a six-month stint as a TV host on a late-night show and early evening *Hootenanny* program. I loved the great American folk music of the past and present, with artists like Pete Seeger, Peter, Paul and Mary, and the Kingston Trio, among others. Talk was always the goal.

In those days, we didn't have computers or much in the way of assistants. I felt very privileged to be there. I was the new boy in town, and was very young and very foreign. I knew that I was going to become an American, which didn't mean sounding like an American. Every American does that. I realized that my voice would be easily recognized, and that was the key.

In Hollywood, my first date was with Anna Kashfi, who was separated from Marlon Brando. Thereafter, I tried to date every would-be starlet, but that's another story. By spring 1965, I left KHJ because they became Boss Radio. I then went over to KNX, a CBS affiliate, to do talk radio.

I was invited by film mogul Jack Warner for lunch at the studio. He was most hospitable. His basic advice to me was that I talked too much. "Well that's my job, sir."

MICHAEL JACKSON: BORN TO TALK AND LISTEN TO THE SONGWRITERS

Long before his innovative and pioneering thirty-two-year talk radio stint at KABC, the intelligent and charming England-born radio personality, Michael Jackson, did a weekly show on Radio Luxemburg called *It's Record Time*, sponsored by EMI. His first stop in the States was in Springfield, Massachusetts, at WHYN radio and television. Michael then travelled to the West Coast, landing at KYA and KEWB in San Francisco. He then made it

Michael Jackson in Los Angeles, circa 1972.

to Southern California in 1962, becoming a fixture in the Los Angeles radio market.

Jackson was on KHJ in 1965 for six months, on the 7:00–midnight shift. At the station were Steve Allen and his wife, Jayne Meadows, with Chick Hearn announcing the L.A. Lakers basketball games. Ratings were low, the station changed formats, and Boss Radio started in their Melrose Avenue studio. A stop at KNX in 1966 followed, and then his three-decade-plus slot at KABC ended. Upon his departure from the station, Jackson landed at KRLA, another former rock music channel now in the talk radio business.

In the early eighties, Michael received a star on the Hollywood Walk of Fame. The recipient of seven Emmy Awards, he was also inducted into the Radio Hall of Fame in Chicago.

He replied, "I mean, you won't survive if you keep trying to do things of substance all the while." I was on the air four hours a day, every day. He meant well, I think. Little did I know I was going to marry the daughter of one of his biggest talents, Alan Ladd, who never made a film that wasn't profitable.

When I met my wife-to-be, I was doing a show on KNX and got a call from movie producer A. C. Lyles at Paramount, who invited me to a screening of a film. Afterwards, I was invited to a party for some coffee and dessert. At the Ladd house, my wife-to-be, Alana, opened the front door. The next night, the Ladd family threw a birthday dinner for Mr. Lyles, which, surprisingly, I was invited to. A month later I called Alana for a date, and on that first date, I proposed. And it has worked.

One of our first dates after we got married was at Gus Kahn's widow's house, Grace Kahn. Sitting at the table between Alana and myself was a delightful man who said, "Do you have a favorite piece of music?" Both Alana and I responded at the same time, "Long Ago and Far Away." And he said, "Thank you. I wrote that with Jerome Kern." It was Ira Gershwin.

Hollywood was a movie and TV town before it became a music town as well. Alana Ladd and I were engaged during the 1965 Watts Riots. On our first date, we were booked to see Harry Belafonte at the Greek Theater, but it was canceled. This was a period just before the new rock bands started writing all their own material. I would have music and songwriting people on my program. Yip Harburg, who wrote "Somewhere Over the Rainbow," said to me, and began to cry over the air, "Nobody wants pretty words anymore."

In 1966, I went to KNX on Sunset Boulevard, the studio where Groucho Marx and *You Bet Your Life* was done. And there was a recording studio on the premises, and all the new bands, like the Byrds, were there recording for the Columbia label. Terry Melcher was their producer, and his mother, Doris Day, was a fan of mine. KNX had Robert Q. Lewis and Bob Crane on the staff. We were a team of real pros, and enjoyed each other.

I used anybody I could find who had talent on the air. So I was welcome most places. I got to meet many, many people. My closest friend from L.A., based on being here in the entertainment world, was Danny Kaye. He had a hit record ["D-O-D-G-E-R-S Song (Oh, Really? No O'Malley)"] on the Reprise label in 1962. I got

to meet everybody. I'm friends with the songwriter Leslie Bricusse. He wrote Sammy Davis Jr.'s "What Kind of Fool Am I?" and Shirley Bassey's "Goldfinger."

Over the decades, I booked my own guests on my show. I had interviews with countless songwriters, musicians, and vocalists alongside economist Milton Friedman, Israeli military leader Moshe Dayan, politician Henry Kissinger, and comedian and actress Lily Tomlin. Ray Charles, Louis Armstrong, Neil Diamond, Ella Fitzgerald, Linda Ronstadt, the Kingston Trio. Julie Andrews, Diana Ross, Sammy Cahn, Michael Feinstein, Harry Belafonte, Gene Autry, and, in the eighties, a lengthy discussion with Jello Biafra on the censorship of rock music and lyrics.

I met a lot of record company presidents in the sixties and seventies. Joe Smith, Allen Livingston from Capitol, and later, in 1979, a guest on my KABC radio show was David Braun, then president of Polygram Records.

You see, in the sixties we weren't in a celebrity-obsessed world. Not at all. In those days, you didn't put people on a pedestal overnight and then chop them down. They love the chopping down. We live in a world now where you listen to news, and it's followed by entertainment shows that try and cover the same stories.

When the other Michael Jackson died in 2009, many fans covered what they thought was his star with flowers. However, it was my star, not his. If it could have brought him back, he could have had my star—he earned it.

Over and over, Los Angeles has proven itself to be the place where the stone hits the water, causing a ripple effect around the world with music, television, radio, films, and communication of all sorts. I feel blessed to be here.

In 1963, Johnny Rivers was playing Gazzarri's nightclub on La Cienega Boulevard. By 1964, he had a one-year contract at the Whisky a Go Go from owner Elmer Valentine.

LOU ADLER: I [was] going to see Don Rickles at the Slate Brothers. I'd come a little late for the first show and a little early for the second show, and [was] looking for a place to hang around until the second show. A half a block away was a club called Gazzarri's. I went in for a drink, and Rivers is onstage with just a drummer, Eddie

Rubin. He's in a suit and tie, and everyone else in the place are in suits and ties, and he's playing rock 'n' roll and everyone is dancing. I hadn't seen people of that age or of that cut dancing to rock 'n' roll since the twist.

During the break, he came up and [said he] was thinking of cutting a live album at Gazzarri's. Was I interested in producing it? "Yes!" Don Kirshner at Aldon Music, who I was working for at the time, heard it and didn't like it. I never got around to mixing it. Then Rivers got a job from Elmer Valentine to open the Whisky a Go Go.

Johnny Rivers performing at the Whisky a Go Go in Hollywood, 1965.

Adler then cut a "live" album with Rivers at the Whisky over the course of two nights, adding some studio overdubs with an audience of three hundred invited people, including the Blossoms, for Imperial Records. Cover versions of Chuck Berry's "Memphis" and Mose Allison's "Seventh Son" put Rivers on the charts. "Secret Agent Man" and "Poor Side of Town" followed, the latter becoming a number-one hit in November 1966.

BONES HOWE: P. F. Sloan and Steve Barri, the writers of "Secret Agent Man," were my friends. I got them together with Rivers and Louie. [They said,] "Wow! We got Rivers to cut one of our songs." Rivers had a real good voice.

P. F. SLOAN: The original title was "Danger Man." What happened was that I made a demo of "Secret Agent Man," just an instrumental version of it for a TV show. The Ventures heard the demo of just the guitar version, and they put it out. And, thank God, it was a big hit for them. At this time, I had only just written thirty seconds of the song lyric, because it was only for the TV show *The Prisoner.* It was a huge television show in England. They had a different theme song in England. Someone stuck their head into the music publishing office where I was working. "Hey. Can you write thirty seconds of a song

for a TV show?" So I wrote that in-between breakfast.

BONES HOWE: Rivers was a performer first. He learned from the road. He knew how to play in front of an audience. He was a good performer before he was a recording artist. He came into the recording studio and was really raw when we did "Memphis" and "Maybelline." We all caught a great period in time.

The rhythm section had a lot to do with the Rivers records. Mickey Jones was the drummer on the first Rivers sessions, and Joe Osborn on bass. But that was part of Rivers's thing. He liked that country R & B.

Boy, he hit the record and radio market at just the right time. Lou had the idea of bringing in go-go girls and background vocalists. That was part of something that was going on. So we did those things with the hand-claps over them, but the rhythm section was really strong, and Johnny could deliver those tunes.

LOU ADLER: Rivers had started writing, and we were getting ready to record his next album, *Changes.* Up until that time, he hadn't written. He started the song "Poor Side of Town," and called me. "I'm sort of stuck on the bridge and the third verse. Do you have any ideas?" I worked on it separately and gave him what I had. That was a number-one record for him, and the first song he had ever written as a recording artist.

Johnny Rivers is—and it might be cliché, it's used in a lot of ways—but he's an underrated artist. I mean, we must have had fourteen, fifteen Top 10 records. He's one of those artists who always knew what was right for him. That's him. Choosing old material that had already been recorded, like "Memphis" and "Maybelline" . . . Berry Gordy told me that the Rivers covers of the Motown records, like "Tracks of My Tears" and "Baby I Need Your Lovin'," they outsold the originals.

CHAPTER 14

SAFE AND WARM IN L.A.

BRIAN WILSON: Just before we began collaborating on *Pet Sounds*, I asked Tony Asher what it was like writing commercials for an advertising company. It seemed like interesting work. I said, "You should be good with words if you can do that." He said, "I'm pretty good with words." Out of nowhere, I said, "Would you like to work with me on some songs and write some lyrics?" "I'll give it a try." Tony Asher is a cool kind of guy, a little soft-spoken. His attitude is just right for creativity, and just right to work with.

I don't remember the recording session of "God Only Knows." Too far in the past to remember. I mean, [it was,] "Here is your part . . . okay, here is your part . . . okay." Somehow, we got "God Only Knows" done. The record spoke for itself. It was a religious experience. Carl and I were into prayer; we held prayer sessions in our house on Laurel Way. "Dear God. Please let us bring music to people." It happened. A cool trip. A lot of people say to me that *Pet Sounds* got them through high school or college.

Barney Kessel did the introduction to the song "Wouldn't It Be Nice." Glen Campbell was also there. I said to myself, "I'm going to have these guys play directly into the board instead of going out into the studio." That's how we got that sound. I also did that on "California Girls." My brother, Carl, played a twelve-string on that, and we plugged him into the console and he did his thing. Every now and then, I'll do that. It is something I can't quite describe, but it is much more mellow than an amp.

BONES HOWE: The best record made during the whole era was *Pet Sounds*. In the case of Brian Wilson, it was a whole room full of people playing together. Brian was a different kind of music maker. He was so far ahead, he wasn't in the race. Poor Chuck Britz, the engineer, had to figure out how to get all that sound on the tracks. I remember going in when they were recording *Pet Sounds* and having to wade through all of those musicians: two drummers, seven guitar players, pianos, and Bill Pittman and others filling the spaces in-between—and poor Chuck, in that little room. Everyone had to be close together, and there wasn't a time lag from one place to another. So getting that on the tracks and mixing them with Brian was really part of putting the paint on the canvas.

Brian, like Spector, liked to mix in mono. They were made to play on the radio, which was mono. They were made to sound good on the radio.

Drummer and Wrecking Crew principal Hal Blaine has probably enjoyed more hit parade success than anyone who ever counted out, "One, two, three, four." He rolled behind Spector, Brian Wilson, Frank Sinatra, Elvis Presley, and countless others on "MacArthur Park," "Mr. Tambourine Man," and "Strangers in the Night."

HAL BLAINE: Many times, Brian would just have a chord sheet. And somebody would run off a bunch of copies, enough for each guy, and then we would more or less make our own notes as to what sounded like a break. We would go from there. Try different things. A little louder here, a little softer there. In a relatively short time, the

Opposite: Brian Wilson and Van Dyke Parks at a recording session for *SMiLE* at Western Recorders, Hollywood, circa 1966/1967.

The Beach Boys at Brian Wilson's home in Bel Air,
circa 1966/1967: *(clockwise from top left)* Dennis Wilson,
Al Jardine, Bruce Johnston, Brian Wilson,
Carl Wilson, and Mike Love.

String orchestra recording session for Brian Wilson's *SMiLE*
album at Western Recorders, Hollywood, circa 1966/1967.

arrangement would come together. We could sit down and write out our own parts; we were kind of individual arrangers. Yet it took Brian to give us the general picture and the material, of course. The song is the story. Brian started using voices in rock 'n' roll. That's what made most of us [studio musicians] really perk up. It was really beautiful blending. It set a trend.

In those days, all musicians in the big orchestras wore blazers and neckties. There was no talking or whispering. You kept your eye on the conductor. We came along as the crew who were going to wreck music; they thought we were nuts. We wore Levis and T-shirts. We smoked cigarettes. There was no booze. Although musicians were famous for drugs, there were no drugs. We were straight, responsible, reliable people, and we did know what music was all about.

After leaving their respective folk groups, the Mugwumps and the New Journeymen, in New York, singer Denny Doherty and singer-songwriter John Phillips formed a new group with John's wife, Michelle, and Cass Elliot. The four were briefly known as the Magic Circle before they settled on the Mamas and the Papas. Signed to Dunhill Records by producer Lou Adler, the band issued its first single, "Go Where You Wanna Go," in 1965. "California Dreamin'" hit the charts soon after, and their debut LP, If You Can Believe Your Eyes and Ears, *landed at number one on the* Billboard *Top 200. "Monday, Monday" was the third single from this momentous debut, and garnered the foursome a U.S. number-one hit.*

Looking back, the meteoric triumph of the Mamas and Papas appears as mythical as the proverbial genie granting three wishes. Their trajectory from clean-cut folkies to acid-addled pop aristocrats is both a cautionary tale— be careful what you wish for—and a validation of pure talent and ceaseless ambition. Their reckless indulgences have long since passed into tabloid infamy. What is worth celebrating, of course, is their singular weave of melody and harmony that soothed the ear like velvet. How it came to be is the quintessential L.A. story.

KIM FOWLEY: In 1965, I tried to sign the Mamas and the Papas to GNP Records. I got a phone call from Cass Elliot, who I had met through James Hendricks, a songwriter. I hung out with her. She smoked pot. I didn't. She wanted to know how the town worked.

Gene Norman at GNP was my boss. I really respected Gene. I was A&R there at the time. [I told him,] "I just discovered a new band." "What do they want?" "Two hundred and fifty dollars a month. Plus they will do clerical." "No new artist is worth $250 a month." So I called Nik Venet, who was at Mira Records, and I was going to be involved in the publishing. Nik helped produce "Hey Joe" by the Leaves on the label. They sang over the telephone. Nik had previously met John when he was in the Journeymen, a Capitol act. John Phillips has a great gift for harmony in his songwriting. Nik was going to take

them over to Mira the following Monday for a 3:00 PM meeting to see Randy Wood, who dated my stepmother. He was formerly with Vee-Jay Records. Nik gave John a check for $150 to hold them over until the meeting. They called up, looking for some grass to calm themselves down, and Barry McGuire didn't have any. This is just before Barry hit with "Eve of Destruction."

Then Lou Adler met the group through Barry, and he signed them on the spot for three grand. They never showed up for that Mira meeting and Nik said, "Somebody must have grabbed them."

I saw John Phillips a year later at a listening party for "Daydream" by the Lovin' Spoonful. I said to John, "Why don't you pay back Nik Venet the $150 that he gave you that was going to carry the group over until that Mira meeting?" John then sent the check to Nik, who framed it and never cashed it. I loved the records Adler and Bones Howe subsequently did with them.

BONES HOWE: I was in the room with Lou when he first heard the Mamas and the Papas. It was in the back room at Studio 2 at Western Recorders. John had a guitar and sang four songs for us. The mix of those four voices was so amazing. You didn't need to do much in terms of enhancement. We doubled their voices up, but it really was a great sound.

When I was an engineer, I was there to serve the producer and the music. I never lost sight of that. I did what I was told, except I found ways I thought benefited the performance of the musicians in the studio. I made suggestions, like putting Cass and Michelle on one side and Denny and John on the other side. "Let's do it this way and see how it works." Those became concrete formats, because what I found out is that if you put the guys close enough together, they'll play better. Not only that, the sound will be better, because the sound doesn't have to travel as far to the other microphone. It's all about an ensemble sound.

Sometimes Lou would ask me about guys. Like on "California Dreamin'." He did not want to put a saxophone on it. He didn't want a guitar solo. John [Phillips] said something about a flute. I said,

Photo used on the original cover for the Mamas and the Papas' *If You Can Believe Your Eyes and Ears*, 1966.

**Bones Howe at the board at
Western Recorders, Hollywood, 1968.**

"Bud Shank is in the back room doing a session. Bud Shank will play." Lou said alto flute, and Bud had [one]. I asked Bud to come into Studio 3 for our session, and he made it in one or two takes.

When you put a rhythm section together, it has to be a rhythm section. It's got to be a section and be able to communicate in such a way that they play together. That's what those guys did. For me, they were the best, and I heard rhythm sections from the East and they always sounded disconnected. I always give Lou credit for being my production mentor. During the "I Saw Her Again" session, I didn't erase the previous vocal, and the playback went: "I saw her again . . . " Lou said, "That's great!" At that moment, I understood trusting your gut.

LOU ADLER: That's all John's amazing arranging. You could hear it in the old Journeymen albums, the group that he was in before, which included Scott McKenzie and one other fellow [Richard Weissman]. Even then, his arranging was too far-out for folk music. I mean, you couldn't listen to it and say, "This is a folk group." He was doing such far-out things. Grittier.

JOHN PHILLIPS: I didn't recognize that until Scott McKenzie came out to L.A. and bought a bunch of the Journeymen records . . . I suddenly realized the Mamas and the Papas were a culmination of about seven or eight years' work in an arranging style that came together with these particular voices who were able to execute this style in a proper way.

LOU ADLER: I think the key element is the vocal arranging of John and his songwriting, without a doubt. And three very trained voices, musically, and the determination on Michelle's part, who is not as musical as the other three. The individual styling of Cass is something out of the twenties or forties, like Tin Pan Alley. The style of the Mamas and the Papas was once described as "the girls chasing the boys"—vocally, that is.

JOHN PHILLIPS: For a long time, I was very influenced by four-part harmony. Well-arranged two-part harmony, moving in opposite directions, and with contrapuntal lines following, gave you a four-part harmony effect. But at the same time, it kept the strength of the two-part harmony. Two-part harmony lines working against each other would give you the four parts, but all at the same time. So, you maintain strength continually. Other than the Four Freshmen, the Hi-Lo's had the sound of four-part all the way.

Lou Adler, 1965.

Songwriting is a very physical process. I just stay up for a few days. I usually lose a lot of weight, you know. By then, all the impurities have been taken out, and your mind is free from the last couple of months of whatever you've written last, and real things start happening. Real lyrics start coming out. You are very tired and emotional, and you get to feel real emotion. That's when the writing really starts. As far as the words and music itself, I don't have a plan. Sometimes I can sit down and write a song in twenty minutes, and sometimes it takes me a month to finish a song. Usually, the twenty-minute songs are much more provocative than the month-long songs, because I've overworked it by that time. "Monday, Monday" was a twenty-minute song. So was "San Francisco" [for Scott McKenzie].

JOE OSBORN: John was in charge. He worked out the vocal parts and everything. That's where he spent most of his time. The band just used to play what they felt, but John would zero in with vocal parts. There really wasn't a singer in the bunch, but together, they made a sound. John knew what he wanted to hear, but Lou, I think he probably spent a lot of time with John before the session. Because he would know the song, and he would know what John had in mind. But he left it up to John to relay that to us. Lou would come in once in

John Phillips at a sound check for KHJ's Appreciation Concert for the Braille Institute at the Hollywood Bowl, 1966.

a while and wanted to know if everyone had their parts. He would start to make suggestions as we got into it—for Hal Blaine to play a fill, to go into here—but nothing really specific to play. Lou left it alone. That's what made him one of the good producers, because he knew what musicians to put together, and then left them alone.

LOU ADLER: When you heard the result come over the speakers, it didn't matter what you went through to get it. The job of a producer is part psychologist, part catalyst—certainly [on] the music end. It's a lot of things. You're locked away in a studio for quite a while, and in the case of the Mamas and the Papas, these four people exposed every so often, you have to be a psychologist at that point.

The Mamas and the Papas taping a television appearance on ABC's *Where The Action Is* in San Diego, 1966.

In 1965, Howard Kaylan was a student at UCLA. That was his day job. At night, he co-led the Turtles, who were about to take off.

"I had a radio show as a college DJ," Kaylan said. "My program was called Afternoons With Howie the K. The songs I played were basically records I brought from home. The things they had at the station were basically just Top 40 crap. I would play something around the Beatles' Rubber Soul. I would spin the B-side of the Swinging Blue Jeans record. Then the Turtles started to happen."

With harmonies from founding partner Mark Volman, Kaylan lent his warm tenor to a series of memorable pop music gems, earning nine Top 10 singles over the 1965–1970 period. Their cover of Bob Dylan's "It Ain't Me Babe," out on White Whale Records in September 1965, was engineered and produced by Bones Howe, who then crafted their own rendition of "Eve of Destruction," a P. F. Sloan song made popular by Barry McGuire and produced by Lou Adler for the Dunhill label in the summer of '65.

P. F. SLOAN: I played guitar and harmonica on "Eve of Destruction." I was on a tour in London of my own, "Eve of Destruction" was number one, and the Grass Roots' "Where Were You When I Needed You," [which] I wrote, was in the Top 10.

I went to one of the clubs. McCartney was there, and [he] asked me, "What's this load of rubbish about the 'Eve of Destruction'? I talked to John Lennon, and Lennon thinks this is a load of rubbish. Won't have none of it."

MARK VOLMAN: After we were on the radio, we took up residency in Hollywood at the Whisky, which was the top of the heap among the local clubs. A KHJ DJ, Sam

NOTES FROM MAMA MICHELLE

MICHELLE PHILLIPS: I was born when we were living in Boyle Heights. East L.A. Aliso Village. Lou Adler is from Boyle Heights, too. I first started listening to radio station KFWB at Thomas Starr King Junior High School, and then while attending John Marshall High School.

John and I had never heard ourselves sing with anything more than one guitar when we went to audition for Lou. So, when he put together Hal Blaine, Joe Osborn, Larry Knechtel, and engineer Bones Howe, when we heard ourselves with a band, it was amazing! It just inspired us more and more. And you know, I think we were very lucky that we picked a lot of good material.

I think that we put a lot of energy into making the material great. John was such a perfectionist, and so was Lou. That was a big romance. John and Lou were perfectly suited for each other. They bounced off each other. They really appreciated each other's gifts.

When we were starting our first album, I suggested we do a Jerry Leiber and Mike Stoller song, "I'm a Hog For You Baby," that I knew from the Coasters. When

Michelle Phillips, Cass Elliot, and Hal Blaine (*on drums*) at a sound check for a KHJ Appreciation Concert at the Hollywood Bowl, 1966.

Left: Denny Doherty onstage at the Melodyland Theater in Anaheim, 1966. *Right:* John Phillips at a recording session at Western Recorders, Hollywood, early 1966.

I sang it for them, they all laughed at me. "Oh God, you've got to be kidding." But they'd never heard it. And you know what, then I sang the Shirelles' "Will You Love Me Tomorrow" for them. And John went, "I don't know . . ." [So I said,] "Okay. I got another one. 'Dedicated to the One I Love.'" I sang that for John, and it was like his eyes lit up and his head exploded. And he responded. "I like that. Let's get the lyrics and the key for it." Then he took that record, and made it his own. You know, it doesn't sound like anything the Shirelles did. John took that song, and he knew what to do with it. He knew how to arrange it and make it a wonderful record for us.

The stuff that we decided to cover was great. I mean, if you listen to our version of "Dancing in the Street," or "My Girl," or the Beatles song, "I Call Your Name," those are great covers. Because John knew that, with our vocal blend, we could make those songs great. Listen to the backgrounds in "My Girl." I know the Temptations did a fantastic version of it, but you gotta listen to our version of it, too.

We decided to do "Dream a Little Dream of Me." That was really a song that had been co-written by a friend of my father's, Fabian Andre, when we were living there in Mexico City.

When Fabian died on New Year's Eve of '66, I found out about it in '67, and I told John. "Oh my God! He wrote one of my favorite songs, 'Dream a Little Dream of Me.'" We started to work it up. It just sort of happened, you know? What if I didn't know Fabian had died? That song had been a hit before. It had been a hit twice. But we brought it back and gave it a whole new life.

When John gave you a part, you had to learn these incredibly difficult parts. He would say things like, "You'll thank me for this someday." He would keep us in the studio, doing take after take until it was perfect. We would already be complaining an hour before we finished. "But that's the perfect take, John! It's not going to get any better than that." "Yes it is." And there was just so much material.

I came home one day in 1966 or '67 and turned on the television, and a special from Vietnam was being broadcast. The camera panned across this audience of soldiers and marines who were fighting in Vietnam. There is such a look on their faces. This is just right in the middle of this horrendous war, and you can see it just etched on their faces. Then the camera pans across them, and there is this huge banner that says "California Dreamin'." That just shook me to my core. It became a destination anthem. I'm the co-writer of that song.

Riddle, put on shows at It's Boss, and we had done Sam Riddle dance party shows like *9th Street West*. It continued with the DJ Reb Foster connection from KRLA. The Tiger's Tail was a good place for us to find our connection to Hollywood with Bito Lido's and Gazzarri's. The Byrds were at the Trip, and we sort of took up residency at the Tiger's Tail, which for over a decade before us was Gene Norman's Crescendo and Interlude [clubs]. KBLA DJ Dave Diamond had shows there that we played.

The Turtles would go on to enjoy global success; their signature hit, "Happy Together" moved the Beatles' "Penny Lane" out of the number-one slot in America in February 1967. The group sold 41 million records and had nine Top 10 hits of their own.

CHIP DOUGLAS: "Happy Together" came in as a demo in 1966. It was written by Garry Bonner and Alan Gordon. The song had been all over town, and everyone had passed on it, including Gary Puckett and the Union Gap. Nobody wanted it.

White Whale Records was down at the end of Sunset Boulevard. It came to them last. Howard [Kaylan] and Mark [Volman] looked at each other when Lee Lasseff and Ted Feigin played it for the guys. "Listen to this." Howard and Mark's eyes got big as saucers. They

P. F. Sloan at the KFRC Fantasy Faire and Magic Mountain Music Festival at Mt. Tamalpais, 1967.

FROM WESTCHESTER TO MANCHESTER

HOWARD KAYLAN: On the Turtles' first trip to England in 1967, we met the Beatles. Graham Nash took us to the Speakeasy Club. Lennon and McCartney sang "Happy Together" at the table. Paul and I also traded verses on Don and Dewey's "Justine."

I met Jimi Hendrix. He got me so high on grass in a club that I puked on his suit. But he did come to see our show that the Turtles did at the Speakeasy. I left the club and wanted to go back home. "I gotta get out of this country. I gotta go back home where somebody is waiting for me and they know who I am."

Brian Jones then asked me for an autograph, and I signed it. I didn't really look up when I did it. I almost did one of those double takes where you look behind you to see who he was really talking to, 'cause I didn't think it was me. He was so sincere. I was very shocked. I didn't realize he was a fan of West Coast pop music, or that he cared at all about harmony stuff, let alone that he was a collector of it. And really big into the Mamas and the Papas and the Association. Anybody on the West Coast singing harmonies—he knew their stuff backward and forward.

He loved Jewel Akens. His "The Birds and the Bees" was done at Gold Star. Brian was the only guy in the Stones, besides Andrew Loog Oldham, who was into West Coast music. Andrew, I love. I love Andrew Loog Oldham. His liner notes on the Stones albums, I loved from the get-go, even more than I loved the records. And I knew there was something deeper in the man that heard a different Stones than I was hearing. Truly. I was hearing the pop stuff. He was hearing the deep cuts, and loving them. I guess you have to be in his position. We were on his [Immediate] label briefly in the sixties, with "You Baby."

went, "Okay!" They knew it was for them.

Howard and Mark were the ones initially attracted to the demo of "Happy Together." I happened to be in the group at the time, playing bass, lucky thing. We worked it out and went on the road, polished it up a bit. Somewhere along the line, I got the idea to put in this big instrumental part where we go up and down vocally in the middle. "That will be cool. What do you think?" "Yeah!" So everybody kind of made up their own vocal parts there. When we went in the studio, I thought, "I'll arrange a pad of four-part harmony when the chorus hits." It's in the background to give the big depth. Today, they do the same thing with a vocalizer or some synthesizer machine to give you the big depth. We didn't have those back then. "Okay. I'll write out the chords in four-part harmony."

Everybody had a little something to do with it. We did it at Sunset Sound. Produced by Joe Wissert and engineered by Bruce Botnick. Johnny Barbata came up with some drum fills. Howard has this special little crying thing in his voice, almost like Tammy Wynette would do—and just that beautiful teenage tone and right on pitch and right on the money.

HOWARD KAYLAN: Gold Star felt and sounded different from any other L.A. studio. You could literally smell the tubes inside the mixing board as they heated up. There was a richness to the sound that Western and United, our usual studios, never had. Those two rooms sounded clean, while Gold Star felt fat and funky. Perhaps we were all reading too much of the Spector legacy into the room, but I don't think so. Our recordings from Gold Star always just sounded better to me. I miss that room.

HENRY DILTZ: Phil Spector came to see the MFQ play at the Trip. Our manager, Herb Cohen, had spoken with

Bob Lind in McCabe's Guitar Shop at the Troubadour, West Hollywood, 1966.

Phil and told him to check us out. I know that Phil wanted to work with the Lovin' Spoonful. It was right at the time he was working with the Ronettes, the Righteous Brothers, and, a bit later, Ike and Tina Turner. He wanted to produce some of the new folk rock music that was happening.

Phil would come down to the Trip and bring his twelve-string guitar and jam and play with us on "Spanish Harlem," a tune he co-wrote with Jerry Leiber. It was fantastic. He was great. We would back him.

Phil signed us to a record deal, and then suggested "This Could Be the Night." When he sat around the piano, he would play these big fat chords and we would harmonize, you know. He would give us notes to sing, and make a chord. He was trying to find the right song for us, and trying to get a feel on what we would do. Then he found "This Could Be the Night" by Harry Nilsson. It was all written, but then he put his own spin on it.

We went to Gold Star with him and recorded with the Wall of Sound people. Just myself on banjo and Jerry Yester on guitar were on the instrumental track. The MFQ's Chip Douglas and Cyrus Faryar both sang with us on it, and I had the lead. Jack Nitzsche was the arranger.

Phil presided over a well-oiled music-making machine. There's a lot of musicians, but they are playing simple lines in unison, producing a fat sound. Eventually, it became the theme to *The Big T.N.T. Show*, which had Donovan, the Byrds, Joan Baez, the Ronettes, Ray Charles, and others. We later recorded "Night Time Girl" with Phil at Gold Star, with Jack Nitzsche's arrangement. The song had these great banjo chords. Al Kooper wrote it.

I also played banjo on Bob Lind's "Elusive Butterfly" that Nitzsche arranged—listen to those strings—and a couple of other sessions with Phil, the Ronettes' "Paradise" and the Righteous Brothers' "Ebb Tide." I sat between Jerry Yester, Barney Kessel, and Tommy Tedesco. It was a thrill being part of that whole thing.

CHAPTER 15

A LOON AND A BEAR

Local radio was feeling groovy in the summer of '66. The Top 30 was percolating with the sounds of "electrical bananas" and "excitations." So imagine their nervous breakdown when the Mothers of Invention's Freak Out!, a double LP on Verve Records, landed on their desks. The brainchild of guitarist/composer/sonic anarchist Frank Zappa and producer Tom Wilson (Dylan's corner man), Freak Out! made "Z" the hippest letter in the alphabet. Adults now had something to be genuinely concerned about.

Toward the end of 1965 and early 1966, the Frank Zappa-led band was in flux, with new members joining (Elliot Ingber), other new members joining and leaving (Alice Stuart, Henry Vestine, Jim Guercio), and still other members leaving and then re-joining (Ray Collins). Denny Bruce was enlisted as the original drummer in Zappa's outfit, doing shows and re-hearsing with Zappa and bandmates in East Hollywood for six months.

DENNY BRUCE: When I did come on board, Jimmy Carl Black and Roy Estrada were there from the beginning. Frank could not get hired because his music was not danceable enough for clubs at that time. Like Johnny Rivers and Trini Lopez. He had seen, and so had I, the Gauchos from Fresno, who had two drummers in the band. Jim Doval, the leader, knew the business, and knew how to get people on the floor and shake their booty.

The group did a live album for ABC-Paramount and played the Trip and Pandora's Box. The Gauchos got on the *Shindig!* TV show. They were damn good—all Chicanos, but one of the drummers was white, named Kelly, who I got to know a little bit. When I did hook up with Frank, he mentioned how much the two drummer idea made sense to him. As he said, "The Gauchos make me want to dance, and I do not dance."

KIM FOWLEY: The first time I had heard about Frank Zappa was when he co-wrote "Memories of El Monte" by the reformed Penguins. Zappa visited Art Laboe's Original Sound and knew the engineer, Paul Buff. He was a mentor to Frank, and they were good friends from Cucamonga. That's the real teacher of Frank Zappa. Paul did "Bustin' Surfboards" by the Tornadoes, and the surf music classic "Wipe Out."

My impression of Zappa was "John Cage-obsessed doo-wop guy with emotional leanings toward East L.A. Latin and black culture, making fun of white people who were superficial and shallow." Which, of course, was cool.

It was at Canter's restaurant one night in early 1966 that I marched in, doing my rounds, and there was

Above: Denny Bruce in Hollywood, 1966.
Opposite: Frank Zappa in Herb Cohen's rehearsal room on Sunset Boulevard, Hollywood, 1971.

The Mothers of Invention with Kim Fowley (*center*) at the Whisky a Go Go in West Hollywood, 1967.

Elliot Ingber, sitting with Frank Zappa. I saw the hustle, because, obviously, when I walked in, Elliot said to Zappa, "This guy here has the juke vibe." I knew all the code moves. "Elliot here says you're God onstage." "He's right! I can tear up a crowd. I'm not the greatest singer in the world, but I know how to control an audience and hypnotize them."

Elliot Ingber was in the Gamblers with bassist Larry Taylor. Nik Venet produced after they were with Phil Harvey, and cut "Moon Dawg" and "LSD-25" in 1959 for World Pacific. Ingber on bass. Guitarist Don Peake toured with Sandy "Teen Beat" Nelson.

Zappa was another guy in the mid-sixties standing around in Laurel Canyon clothes. Nothing more, nothing less. Somewhere between a beatnik and a farmer. So we went that night, someplace where they had their equipment, and he said, "Play something!" I made up a song on the spot, and he said, "You're in the band if you wanna be."

The first gig we did was in a venue, a building on Santa Monica Boulevard near the intersection of Crescent Heights. They used to have music there, where people and independent promoters would rent it and four-wall it. Two hundred, three hundred people. The Mothers of Invention went in. I came on for two or three songs. It was raga music, jazz changes, Roland Kirk, R & B, atonal, mantra, rock.

I was able to not only follow what Frank and Elliot were doing, along with Roy Estrada and Jimmy Carl Black, I was [also] able to move the audience. I looked like the scarecrow of Oz meets Frankenstein. So how could I, as a two-bit hustler/one-hit wonder, get up and control an audience of skeptical hippie morons from Laurel Canyon and the street? Frank never could understand how I did it. Why I did it. But he did understand that he saw it happening, and felt it happen.

In October, Herb Cohen became the group's manager. He encouraged them to join the Musicians' Union—an expensive move, but one that improved their ability to get work. They were then booked at clubs like the Whisky a Go Go and the Trip. It was at one of these shows at the Whisky that MGM/Verve Records producer Tom Wilson stumbled upon them in late 1965, an event that eventually got them signed to a record contract the following March. The deal was signed on March 1st, and nine days later, the band was in the TTG Recorders studio to record Freak Out! *Recording took three days, and the album was completed on March 12th.*

KIM FOWLEY: Frank said, "We're going in the studio to do what we did tonight. We're gonna turn the street loose in there, and you can come down and make noise if you want."

I walked into the studio with jazz pianist Les McCann and Danny Hutton. I had lived earlier in the attic of a house owned by his mother. Danny had already had his own hit with "Roses and Rainbows." In comes Mac Rebennack—later Dr. John—who I knew from Gold Star. I did the vocal arrangements that night when he played piano. I sang "Help, I'm a Rock" and "Who Are the Brain Police?" with Frank. So we did that album. I received a "hypophone" credit. That's where you grab your throat and sing.

Ray Collins, great singer. Tremendous. He was the Roger Daltrey, and Frank was the Peter Townshend. I liked Roy Estrada. Zappa was like James Brown. He knew how to pick a band of sidemen. He knew how to get ensemble-playing done. Like Sly Stone, too.

Frank wasn't a producer that night. Tom Wilson was. You have to understand the dynamic. He was Harvard-educated, and acted like a professor of literature from Harvard or Yale. He had produced Dylan's "Like a Rolling Stone," and jazz artists.

It's funny, he was officiating in the control room, but he never came out on the floor where we were. Then Frank would run back and forth between the floor and control room with Tom Wilson. But there were over a hundred people there.

The Mothers of Invention outside the Whisky a Go Go in West Hollywood, 1968.

TTG Studios was a giant cheeseburger box with high ceilings, owned by a sound engineer, an Israeli named Ami Hadani, who built studios and worked with Wilson and Zappa on *Freak Out!* and *Absolutely Free*. Bill Parr built and designed the TTG board in the big film-scoring room upstairs.

For *Freak Out!*, we were there all night. We didn't get paid. We did it because Frank convinced us it was historical, and that we were on the cusp of something important. We all bought into it. We all wanted to go have breakfast. That was more important.

The *Freak Out!* album, to me, was John Cage meets 1920s France. A Josephine Baker version of art is anything that you can get away with.

I also sang and performed with Zappa and the Mothers of Invention a year later at the Whisky a Go Go, for a live album that was recorded but never released. Mick Jagger was in the audience that night.

HOWARD KAYLAN: I went to the Whisky a Go Go one night, and someone actually went around and passed out flyers, telling people [about] the Freak Out. Nobody knew what a Freak Out was.

I go to the Freak Out that night. There are two or three rooms that are being used simultaneously, and Frank had tape recorders going in all of them. There are different tracks being played in all of them, and people are doing different things in every room. Frank would put some guys in one room, and some in another. The environment was more Soupy Sales than, say, Spike Jones.

He's creating his own scenarios. He's making people go up to the mike and either rant in their own language, or getting them to say things. I think I was doing a little bit of both. Then I went into another room, where it seemed to be like a orgy, and that's where [Tom] Wilson was. I knew who he was. I was aware that he was the guy who produced Dylan and many other gems. They were just recording random couples and noises, and people who had not met each other before. Frank would actually direct them physically. A touch here. A grope here. "Say something about it." Almost like he was directing a movie. It was surreal and great. I really wanted to be a part of it. It was so outside of my normal, structured thing.

I had no idea, and still don't know, how much stuff was ever going to be used. Brilliant editing job. Still a masterpiece, in my mind. But as far as the commerciality of the venture, I didn't really think for a minute that it had any potential whatsoever. I'm sure he didn't think my idiot pop songs had any potential whatsoever.

As the album was being prepared for release, the band had a name change forced on them by MGM, which was uncomfortable with "the Mothers." At the time, however, the change appeared to be only for the record company. At the June Fillmore shows, Bill Graham continued to introduce them simply as the Mothers.

RICK ROSAS: When I heard the first Mothers of Invention album, *Freak Out!*, I then freaked out. "Help, I'm a Rock." Just great. I had no idea until later that Zappa loved doo-wop and worshiped East L.A. It didn't dawn on me, his link to East L.A.

Canned Heat was formed in 1966, after evolving from its South Bay jug band origins. The band—Bob "the Bear" Hite on vocals and harmonica, Henry Vestine on guitar, Alan "Blind Owl" Wilson on guitar and harmonica, Larry Taylor on bass, and Frank Cook on drums—recorded its debut Liberty album, Canned Heat, *in 1967. Fito de la Parra replaced Cooke for their second LP,* Boogie with Canned Heat, *which spawned two hot singles, "On the Road Again" and "Going Up the Country."*

Canned Heat promotional supplement, 1968.

For many middle-class white boys, Canned Heat was their introduction to four-to-the-floor and no messin' around. They were inexhaustible road dogs—grimy, greasy apostles of the blues who mixed some fatback funk into their tasty blend of Southside deep delta and roadhouse grooves. When "the Bear," all three hundred pounds of pork butt, began prowling the stage, it was time to feast—and bring plenty of napkins.

FITO DE LA PARRA: In 1965, I came up from Mexico with my band. We played at the Sea Witch, at the Daisy for the movie stars, and at the Troubadour. I saw Hollywood for the first time. That's when I first met Skip Taylor, who later produced and managed us. He was an agent at William Morris. We always admired the Chicano bands from East L.A., like Cannibal and the Headhunters, Thee Midniters, Chan Romero. The producer, Eddie Davis. That's one of the reasons why we decided to try our luck in Hollywood. Music from East L.A. and Montebello could go Top 40. They were Chicanos, and brothers of ours.

In the early and mid-sixties, I heard American music, R & B, Johnny Otis on the radio, and Wolfman Jack on XERB when he broadcasted out of Mexico. Wolfman later became a friend of Canned Heat. We would hear the heavy shit, not the Top 40 that everybody else was listening to. He educated us right from Rio Grande. He played a lot of R & B, and that was part of the education we were getting, besides Jan and Dean and Herman's Hermits. We first met Wolfman when we performed at the Hollywood Bowl at a ninety-nine-cent radio station event.

LARRY TAYLOR: Bob brought in Alan, who had a strong influence on the country blues part of it. In my case, I'm a jazzer. I'm a jazz listener, and jazz lover, and a hardcore blues-style rock 'n' roller. That's where I'm comin' out of. I played a lot of slide guitar and a lot of Alan-type stuff. I was deeply influenced by him. With Canned Heat, we were stretching out, experimenting. In the studio, we stretched out more than most bands at that time. Live, it stretched out even more, expounding on a different level than you did in the studio. That was new.

"What's Happening!" column by DJ Larry McCormick in the *KFWB/98 Hitline* newspaper, 1966.

JUNE 28, 1966

WHAT'S HAPPENING!
By LARRY McCORMICK — KFWB Good Guy

About six months ago, KFWB was host to several groups of advertising people (Bows and Genuflections) at one of the Sunset Strips' most famous niteries. Management, figuring wisely that we Deejays would not be quite enough entertainment, (Heavens, what an understatement!) decided to shell out for some people with talent. First, they got Go-Go Dancers, and they were. . .uh. . .well. . .talented, and then they got a musical group.

McCORMICK

The title, "musical group" is not nearly enough to describe them, although they DO sing and play. And they do sing and play songs most of the modern generation has heard before; at least they SOUND like the same songs, until you stop and listen. That is when you discover that R & R Standards are suddenly parodies and the original material molds to form very hard hitting social statements.

No, they are not beatniks, vietniks, bums, protest marchers or dirty speech advocates, but they do seem to feel that many of today's accepted conventions, values and demands on the individual are like invisible shackles which only serve to hamper the enjoyment of life. They call themselves "The Mothers Of Invention", which itself is unconventional (but very inventional) since there is not a mother in the group.

Their biggest put-down is for people who are "lame" (trans.: unaware. . .un-hip) Those who are unaware of the problems and people, developements, trends and, yes enjoyments that exist all around them. People whom, they seem to say, stay so locked in a prison of convention and conformity, that they never really know WHAT'S HAPPENING"

They also have a place in their hearts (?) for those who go through the same hum-drum existence day in and day out, referring to them as "plastic people". Included in this "bag" are those whom the need to conform has robbed of emotion to point of being so inhibited that they don't live at ALL. (Hence, "plastic" people)

If there is anything "The Mothers Of Invention" are NOT, either in song or appearance, it's inhibited. Their garb is, well, you'll just have to see them. Their performances are equally shaking. These performances are probably best summed up in an excerpt from the liner notes of their new album (about which I'll say more later): "Frank Zappa is the leader . . . sometimes he sings . . . sometimes he plays the guitar. . .sometimes he talks to the audience. . . sometimes there is trouble . . . . ."

The group includes Frank Zappa, Ray Collins, Jim Black, Roy Estrada and Elliot Ingber, and their new album is called "Freak Out". Now before YOU put THEM down as degenerates (or something) perhaps I had better give you their definition of "freaking out." Again, from the album liner notes: "Freaking out, on a personal level, is a process whereby an individual casts off outmoded and restricted standards of thinking, dress, and social etiquette in order to express, creatively, his relationship to his immediate environment and the social structure as a whole. Less perceptive individuals have referred to us who have chosen this way of thinking and feeling as "freaks". When any number of these "freaks gather and express themselves through music or dance, it is generally referred to as a "freak out."

I hope you will have a chance to hear the new album by the "Mothers of Invention" or that better still, you will get a chance to see them in person, because that way they can play upon your reaction and the experience is thereby heightened. You may find the "Mothers" appealing, or you may find them revolting. Of one thing I am sure: You will find them to have some of the same qualities attributed to a popular potato chip; "Eenteresting; provocateef", and like potato chips, rather salty.

CHAPTER 16

COLORED BALLS FALLING

PAUL BODY: In a time of the rise of the guitar player—the sixties— Johnny Echols was right up there with the heavyweights. He wasn't flashy, but he was good. On the Sunset Strip at that time, he was the best. He could do that Byrds thing, and then he could rock it, and then he could jump into a total jazz bag. He could do whatever it took to get the song over. On top of that, he sung a mean vocal at the beginning of the song that became "Revelation." In other words, he could play the guitar like ringing the bell, and if Arthur [Lee] was the soul of Love and Bryan [MacLean] was the heart, Johnny Echols was the heart and soul.

Paul Body at home in Monrovia, 1967.

JOHNNY ECHOLS: The Coasters made an impression, because I took guitar lessons from a neighbor down the street from us, and it was Adolph Jacobs, the guitarist. I was listening to KB-CA-FM, the local jazz station, and KGFJ-AM, the soul and R & B station, and the new rock on KFWB. What I did was kind of meld these two music forms together.

Arthur started coming to my shows. I would take him around to gigs I played with Henry Vestine and Larry Taylor, before they had Canned Heat. We had a group that played frat parties when we were, like, age fifteen.

Johnny Echols was born in Memphis, Tennessee, in the same hospital as his future bandmate and fellow Pisces, Arthur Lee. They lived across the street from each other. Their parents were all schoolteachers, and both families moved to the Adams District of South Central Los Angeles. Music figured prominently in their households. Jazz players, like saxophonists Charles Lloyd and Frank Strozier, and guitarist Gabor Szabo, were family friends. Echols even hung with Ornette Coleman. Like so many of his peers, he seized upon the guitar to give voice to his musical ideas.

Soon, these young, unknown strivers were moving in some fast company, first jamming with Little Richard and Jimi Hendrix, then with Jimmy James, who was backing the O'Jays at L.A.'s California Club on Santa Barbara Avenue.

The band was joined by Allan Talbert on saxophone and drummer Roland Davis, another school chum, on keyboards. Billy Preston also joined the group, and Lee, who was garnering a reputation as an organ and conga player, became the lead singer. They changed their name to the LAGs—short for "L.A. Group"—as a nod to the popular

Opposite: **Johnny Echols (left) and Arthur Lee performing with Love at the Hullabaloo, Hollywood, 1968.**

instrumental outfit Booker T. and the MG's, and recorded a single, "Soul Food."

JOHNNY ECHOLS: We were into surf music. The Beach Boys. I really liked Dick Dale. We actually played some of our songs, including one called "The Ninth Wave" and "Rumble-Still-Skin."

In 1964 and '65, the LAGs took up residency at Cappy's in North Hollywood. They eventually landed a singles deal with the instrumental "Rumble-Still-Skin" for Capitol Records, after Lee was directed to the offices by Kim Fowley, then employed by Ardmore-Beechwood Music. The LAGs subsequently evolved into the American Four and recorded "Luci Baines" for Del-Fi Records, owned by Bob Keane.

JOHNNY ECHOLS: In 1964, '65, we were playing out in Montebello at this place called the Beverly Bowl, and we started to develop a large following. There was a friend across the street, Alan Collins. He had a club up in Hollywood, the Brave New World. By then, we were called the Grass Roots.

I also then started realizing even more how important guitars and amps were to sound. I met Don Peake at Wallichs Music City in Hollywood, and he takes us down the street to his house on Rossmore. Don had this 1959 Fender Bassman amp. He played this thing for us, and I noticed the sound. Don introduced us to that sound, because the over-driven harmonics and the tubes . . . that amplifier was probably one of the first ones that really had that blues sound. So Don hooked me up with that, and I went and got one like that. Then I got a Stratosphere guitar. There was this guy out in Hawthorne who was a country music player. I had the Stratosphere, but at that time, it only had a mandolin neck on it.

Then I went off to Carvin Guitars—I had their catalog—and got a neck made out there. So I was able to put a twelve-string neck on the six-string, and that started me using it. Guitarists like Joe Maphis had used them, but they didn't use twelve strings. He was using a mandolin and a six-string. That was the country sound. So I think I was probably one of the first people who did marry a twelve-string neck to the six-string neck.

I had more options, and could play and go between the necks. I could play twelve-string parts, and then go on to six-string parts and not have to continue to pick up one instrument and put down another, because I could always keep it in tune. 'Cause I'm playing them both together. There was another reason—they just looked so damn cool! Nobody else was playing that, and it just gave us that extra little something.

Before we met guitarist Bryan MacLean—he was a roadie then for the Byrds—we had guitarist Bobby Beausoleil. We stopped covering other people and doing our own songs.

BRYAN MACLEAN: I had planned to be a gallery artist. See, I only came into music at age seventeen or eighteen, which is kind of late. David Crosby and I became close friends. He took me under his wing, more or less, and I became the original Byrds roadie before they got a road manager.

The Byrds opened for the Rolling Stones in Long Beach, in 1965. "Mr. Tambourine Man" hadn't quite broken yet. David Crosby was my mentor, my dear friend. I don't really understand what it is; I was an obnoxious, bratty little kid, but for some reason, he took me under his wing and was a tremendous influence. I made him into such an idol because of his voice and melodic sense that, initially, I began to really, you know, copy him.

Multiple exposures of the Love band members by photographer Guy Webster in his Beverly Hills studio, 1966.

Frank Zappa was a very dear friend and a very strong influence on me. Frank played this big, fat Barney Kessel Gibson guitar hollow body. He was the first one that started to show me how to actually play guitar. In other words, he gave me the basic principle, 'cause I had never had any kind of formal theory or music. He started to show me. "You know, the basic thing that you want to do is, don't think that you are playing licks, but think of it as a melody." He played melodic lead. Both of us were into Stravinsky. At one point of time, he invited me to be in the band. We were not Love yet. Still the Grass Roots.

The actual first song I ever wrote was "Orange Skies," but that was from Jim McGuinn's guitar solo in "The Bells of Rhymney." I did the exact guitar solo, verbatim, and I just wrote a song over that. I didn't know I could write a song. And the song came out.

There was a dispute over the ownership of the band name "Grass Roots." It was already in use by the Grass Roots, who were recording for the Dunhill label with their version of Bob Dylan's "Ballad of a Thin Man." An alternative was required. Among the discarded: Summer's Children, the Domino Effect, and the Coalition.

They arrived at their new name while driving along Beverly Boulevard. A billboard advertising Luv Brassieres caught their attention. Arthur had previously worked on the premises. Bryan felt that "Luv" would be appropriate for a band name, and Lee suggested "Love," with no "the" in front. At their next gig, they tossed the name at their loyal fans, who loudly approved.

Jerry Hopkins, a writer for the Los Angeles Free Press, *and his associate, Doug Lyon, became the Love's "managers." In late 1965, the duo steered the band to Art Laboe's Original Sound recording studios on Sunset Boulevard to record demos of "My Little Red Book" and "Hey Joe."*

JOHNNY ECHOLS: We did the first unreleased Love album at Gold Star, and for some reason, it hasn't resurfaced. It was to serve as our demo. We had contract offers from MCA [Decca]. We were thinking of signing with them, and Columbia, and we chose not to because of the simple reason that Elektra Records was the only company that would let us own our publishing and masters. We learned that from Little Richard. "Do not let them take your music." So I insisted.

Ronnie Haran, who booked talent at the Whisky a Go Go from 1965 to 1968, asked Elektra Records label owner Jac Holzman to come see Love. Record company talent scouts, such as MGM's David Anderle, had already witnessed them in action at Bito Lido's. Immediately after their Whisky set, Holzman offered the band's manager, Herbie Cohen, a deal for $5,000.

In January 1966, Love, now with Ken Forssi on bass and drummer Alban "Snoopy" Pfisterer replacing Don Conka (immortalized later in Lee's "Signed D.C."), recorded their debut album at Sunset Sound, produced by Holzman with Mark Abramson and engineered by Bruce Botnick.

JOHNNY ECHOLS: For what we needed to get on tape, we had to do it live, because we needed the sound to bleed into the other mikes. We needed the overtones; we needed the sound bouncing off the walls. We needed a distorted sound, not a clean sound.

"Can't Explain" started as a bluesy, Stones-y kind of riff. I had not known that the Stones had the song "What a Shame." Then I hear it, and I think, "Damn. This song sounds very similar, so we're gonna have to do a whole lot of work on it." So we changed all the lyrics that were similar to what they did and came up with a kind of chimey, jangly guitar. I noticed on the radio, especially on KRLA and KFWB, that Byrdsy guitar sound seemed to cut through everything, the traffic. I was trying for a guitar that had a really high treble, so that it would cut through everything else.

Bryan's "Come Softly to Me" blew my mind. We started putting a jazzy beat to it, because Bryan's songs were very much show tunes. We had to do a lot of tinkering with the songs to get them to fit in the mold that we were trying to create for Love.

In January of 1967, Love's long-awaited follow-up album, Da Capo, *arrived.*

JOHNNY ECHOLS: I knew we were not doing disposable pop music. We wanted to play rock music and do it as serious music, like the Beatles were doing.

My role with Arthur and Bryan was basically an ombudsman to kind of keep these two personalities happening. So I knew that from the very start. They would

MIDNIGHT SUN

Los Angeles native Bruce Botnick is a sound engineer and a record producer, which is sort of like saying Keith Richards plays rhythm guitar. At age eighteen, Botnick talked his way into a job at Liberty Records in Hollywood, where he subsequently recorded Bud Shank, Bobby Vee, Johnny Burnette, Jackie DeShannon, Leon Russell, David Gates, and Jack Nitzsche. He then moved to Sunset Sound, hired as a mixer initially to do children's albums for Disney.

Botnick engineered the entire Doors catalog, as well as Love's first two albums. He produced their seminal *Forever Changes* LP in 1967, and co-produced the Doors' *L.A. Woman* in 1971. Botnick was at the mixing desk with Buffalo Springfield, the Turtles, the Beach Boys, and Marvin Gaye.

HARVEY KUBERNIK: So many monumental albums were recorded at Sunset Sound. The Rolling Stones mixed *Beggars Banquet* and *Exile on Main St.* there.

BRUCE BOTNICK: It was built by a man named Alan Emig, who came from Columbia Records. He was a well-known mixer there, and designed a custom-built, fourteen-input console for Sunset Sound.

Tooti Camarata, a trumpet player and an arranger [who] did big band stuff in the forties and fifties, had a friendship with Disney, and he decided to build a studio to handle the Disney records and all the movies, like *20,000 Leagues Under the Sea.*

HK: What did the room bring to the recordings you engineered or produced?

---

have been at loggerheads all the time. Because they liked the same chicks, if you listen to some of the songs. There was always that strong tension between the two of them, and I was always stuck there in the middle, kind of keeping the peace but also drawing the best out of them that I could. Otherwise, you know, Bryan was very much a show tune kind of guy. I knew we could not release show tunes, so we had to do a lot of work on his songs to meld them into something that was acceptable to an audience that we were developing.

[The song] "7 and 7 Is" took forever to do. I had all the treble turned up on my guitar, plus I have this vibrato the drummer has to play in time to. That was the problem with poor Snoopy; he could not keep up with it, because it was like playing with a click track. Of course, nobody played with a click track back then, but he had to keep up with this vibrato, and if he lagged behind even a little bit, then the song was off. So that was preconceived. We knew what we were doing.

I took a lead vocal on "Revelation." I would do that on a lot of songs. A lot of songs that you think are doubled, like "My Little Red Book," you are hearing both Arthur and I sing. So, several songs were like that.

In 1966, the Beach Boys launched Brother Records, Inc., becoming one of the first bands to found its own record label. The group's members were its shareholders, and Capitol Records was its distribution partner.

BRIAN WILSON: I worked with Van Dyke Parks on *SMiLE,* an album after *Pet Sounds.* Working with him is not easy at all, because he is a perfectionist. He wants it his way, and the right way. So, I go, "Yes, Van Dyke." He'd say, "Okay, but that's not what I had in mind." He's a gentleman and a scholar. A very bright person. When I heard "Heroes and Villains" on the radio, I thought to myself, "Hey! I did that with Van Dyke!"

On "Good Vibrations," Mike [Love] came over to my Laurel Way house. On the piano and that [writing] session, I could not envision the whole recording. The title came from my mother. She said, "Dogs bark at humans because they think of good vibrations. They pick up on bad vibrations, but don't mind picking up good vibrations." My mother got the title for it.

We started at Gold Star with the verses. Then we went to Western Studio and did the chorus background. Then we went to Sunset Sound to get the bridges, and

BB: Well, the room was very unique. Tooti Camarata did something that nobody had done in this country—he built an isolation booth for the vocals. Later on, I convinced him to take the mono disc mastering system and move it into the back, behind what became Studio 2. We turned that into a very large isolation booth, which we used to put strings in. That's one of the things that worked so well for Jack Nitzsche, because we were able to put six strings in there and get full isolation live. It was great.

With the strings being in the large isolation booth, the drums didn't suffer, so we were able to make tighter and punchier rhythm tracks than any of the other studios in town. 'Cause everybody did everything live in those days. You did your vocals live. You did your strings and your brass live, and the rhythm section. This was a big deal. Then add to it the amazing echo chamber that Alan Emig designed. It's still phenomenal, having survived a fire. That chamber was like the chamber at Capitol Studios and Gold Star Studios.

HK: The recording consoles?

BB: It was all tube. At one point, Alan had worked with Bill Putnam, who had helped design the two preamps in all the Universal Audio consoles. So when he came to Sunset Sound, he took it a step further and built this custom board with some of that circuitry and the two preamps. So it really sounded great.

United Recording Studios, Western Recorders, Gold Star, Sunset Sound, RCA . . . they were terrific rooms. There was a commonality between them. They all had the same loud speakers, which were Altec Lansing 604s. So you could walk from studio to studio and know what the hell you were hearing. Some rooms had more bottoms than others, but still, the general, overall sound was the same. So you could take your tape, and go to another room.

then we went back to Western to get the second half of the bridge, and over to Columbia on Sunset, where they had an eight-track machine for the vocals. I was completely blown away at the prospect that we could put the theremin on the far right and the cello on the far left. Carl [Wilson] said, "Why don't we use a cello?" I replied, "Well, good idea." So we called a cello player to come to the studio. We had him play the part. Came right in and did it. Van Dyke and I also talked about the role of the cello on "Good Vibrations."

At the playback, all the guys said, "Hey, Brian. This is a number-one record." I said, "You know what? I agree. I think this is gonna be a number-one record." Mike's bass part was the one. Mike's voice on it was the thing that sold me on it. Mike's singing got us famous. Because his voice has a quality to it that goes hand in hand with the song. He was the appropriate singer for the song.

ANDREW LOOG OLDHAM: "Good Vibrations" was brilliant, but cold. Genius has to function with a beat in the third ear, and his third ear was on Ritalin. A lot of folks went along for the ride because it was pretentious, or at least lofty. And, in a way, that belonged to the times. We had had the sex, drugs, and rock 'n' roll, and now we desperately wanted to make a difference, be it at Kent State or Grosvenor Square. So, in a very warped way, Brian was on the money. I liked the Beach Boys again with *Wild Honey* and *20/20*.

PHIL SPECTOR: I've always been flattered that Brian continues to say nice things about me and keeps recording my songs. Brian is a very sweet guy and a nice human being. I'm glad he's coming out of his shell. I think he got caught in a trap with "Good Vibrations." I think he got condemned more than condoned. He became a prisoner instead of a poet. He had the plaudits, the accolades, and touched the masses. I know music is a very important thing to him, besides a vocation. It became cluttered the last few years. Your attitude is in the grooves, and it's a very personal thing. But Brian thrived on competition.

I remember when "Fun, Fun, Fun" came out. He wasn't interested in the money, but a Top 10 record. He wanted to know how the song would do against the Beatles, and if KFWB would play it. But I never saw Brian as a competitor.

CHAPTER 17

THE LEFT HAND OF DARKNESS

Ray Manzarek spent his childhood in Chicago. He studied classical piano, but his ear was drawn to the city's rich jazz and blues heritage. By the time his family relocated to Redondo Beach in Southern California, Manzarek was testing the musical waters—a little Horace Silver-inflected jazz trio here, some steamin' Otis Spann-styled blues there. He fronted Rick and the Ravens, a juke-jointy outfit with just enough cohesion to provide an entry into the record business. There was also a magpie intelligence at work; behind those studious, wire-rimmed glasses, Manzarek pursued a degree in cinematography at UCLA's prestigious school of film.

Manzarek's chance encounter with his former film school classmate—a certain James Morrison—is shrouded in the mists of Avalon. In hindsight, it more often played like something out of the Brother's Grimm. Ably assisted by guitarist Robby Krieger's liquid lead lines and drummer John Densmore's Trane-chasin' rhythm, these intrepid seekers coalesced around the shamanistic influences of William Blake and Bertholt Brecht, Muddy Waters and Bill Evans.

Morrison fancied himself a poet, not a pop singer, but his narcissism knew no limits. He proved to be an intoxicating stage figure. Taking their name from Aldous Huxley's mescaline memoir, The Doors of Perception, *the band labored to find currency within the teeming Sunset Strip community. But Morrison threw caution (and Oedipus) to the wind one fateful night at the Whisky a Go Go. Their reputation as the devil's disciples was sealed, and with it came unimaginable highs and unfathomable lows. After five coruscating years, their sun exploded; the background radiation persists to this day.*

RAY MANZAREK: "Moonlight Drive" is really a seminal, or a signpost song. It's the first song Jim Morrison sang to me on the beach. It had been after we graduated UCLA. "What have you been doing?" "I've been writing songs." "Sing me a song." "I'm shy." "You're not shy. Stop it. There's nobody here. Just you and me. I'm not judging your voice. I just want to hear the song. Besides, you used to sing with Rick and the Ravens at the Turkey Joint West and did 'Louie Louie' until you could not talk."

I had been in a fabulous recording studio before, at World Pacific on Third Street in L.A. That's where we cut the Doors' demo, along with some Rick and the Ravens songs.

JOHN DENSMORE: I had to work harder on the tempo, because Ray's left hand was the bass. When he took a solo, he'd get excited and speed up. [I'd say,] "Hold it back. Hold it back." But without a separate guy doing bass line runs and grooves, there are holes. "Okay. I'm going in." Sometimes I didn't do anything. That was my territory, between the beats.

Ray had a previous relationship with World Pacific Records and Dick Bock, who owned the label and released Ravi Shankar albums in the U.S. We got a couple hours of free studio time at their recording studios, and that's when we got to make a demo in 1965. On the way into the studio, Ravi Shankar was leaving with Alla Rakha, my idol, with these little tabla drums. Robby and I went to Ravi Shankar's Kinnara School of Indian Music.

You hear the Indian thing in techno stuff now. That came in, and it was deep, and it's still around. "The End"

Opposite: **Jim Morrison at the Hollywood Bowl, 1968.**

The Doors at the Whisky a Go Go, West Hollywood, 1966.

was a raga tune. So [in] maybe 1966, 1967, I was noticing in the traditional Indian ragas [that] you gotta wait for your climax. It's not a quickie, you know. So that was the influence.

RAY MANZAREK: Sunset Sound was a very hip recording studio. It was an excellent recording studio—four tracks. Paul Rothchild and Bruce Botnick. Never had met Bruce before. Paul was the producer.

Rothchild and Botnick are Door #5 and Door #6. There's four Doors in the band, and two Doors in the control room. They were always there, always twisting the knobs and really being on top of it. A couple of high IQ guys. We couldn't have done it without them. So, it was a great combination of six guys. That first album was basically the four Doors and the two other Doors in the control room making the sound. We made the music. They made the sound, and they did an absolutely brilliant job. It was a real joy, and a great learning experience.

Rothchild and Botnick were two alchemists with sound. We were the alchemical music makers, but they were alchemists with sound—adding a bit of this, a bit of that. Some reverb. Some high end. They were making this evil witches brew concoction as we went along. The sound just got better and better.

I was the bass player of the Doors. When it came to recording, I played a Fender Rhodes keyboard bass. The instrument was great in person because it had a deep, rich sound and moved a lot of air. But in the recording studio, it lacked a pluck. It did not have the attack that a bass guitar would have, especially if you played a bass guitar with a pick. So, on some of the songs, we brought in an actual bass player, Larry Knechtel, who played the same bass line that I played on "Light My Fire," doubling my bass line. They could then get rid of my bass part and use the nice sound that Larry Knechtel got—the click and the bottom. Well, the whole thing took ten days. "Light My Fire" was two takes. "The End" was two takes.

First of all, the left hand created that hypnotic Doors

Ray Manzarek performing at the Cal State Los Angeles gymnasium, 1967.

secret to the Doors' hypnotic sound comes out of the left-hand keyboard bass. Meanwhile, the right hand thinks it's Johann Sebastian Bach.

A fifth person, another physical element onstage, would have taken away the diamond with Morrison at the point. As we faced the audience, Morrison was at the point, Densmore was at the point behind Robby and I, who were point left and point right—a four-sided diamond, the purity of the diamond shape, rather than some kind of pentagram star thing. A fifth element would have confused it.

DJ, song sniffer, and writer Dave Diamond joined the Burbank-based radio station KBLA in early 1966, after program director Bruce Wendell hired him over Christmas of 1965. Starting that year, Diamond hosted a three-hour Stones City *program on Sunday nights. In 1967, he introduced* The Diamond Mine, *a show that mixed British and American psychedelic rock, social commentary, and especially the new music from Los Angeles bands including Love, the Rising Sons, the Seeds, and the Doors. Diamond was instrumental in steering Elektra Records' Jac Holzman to see the Doors at the Whisky a Go Go, and was the first disc jockey in the U.S. to spin*

sound. For instance, during the "Light My Fire" solo section, it's an A-minor triad to a B-minor triad that just repeats like the same sorta modal chord structure Coltrane used in "My Favorite Things." My left hand is playing the same thing over and over, while the right hand is playing filigrees, comping behind Robby, punctuating with single notes. When I'm soloing, I'm playing anything I want to play, and that bass line just keeps on going. It never varies, and it never stops. Over and over, like tribal drumming, or Howlin' Wolf playing one of his songs without any chord changes. On and on and on. The same pattern.

Now, if I were to have added a live bass player to play that, the guy would have lost interest after two minutes. So I think the

John Densmore after performing at the Cal State Los Angeles gymnasium, 1967.

Jim Morrison and Robby Krieger performing at the Cal State Los Angeles gymnasium, 1967.

"Light My Fire." Diamond soon suggested an edited version single from the lengthy LP track.

DAVE DIAMOND: It was serendipity, how I met the Doors. I was on a date with a girl in early 1966 on a Sunday night, and she wanted to see a new group called the Doors. We went to the London Fog, right near the Whisky a Go Go. This place was no bigger than a fuckin' kitchen. This was music I didn't quite understand. Then they played "Light My Fire," and it kind of hit me. So I went back the next night by myself and sat way back and listened to them again. I thought, "Oh my God! I get it." So I went back the next night and waited until they got done, and tried to sign them to an independent record contract. They said they would meet me and talk about it.

So we met at the International House of Pancakes in Glendale. I was living on Los Feliz Boulevard. We had breakfast, and I told them what the deal was: I would make a record, and we would shop it around, and we would play it on KBLA. Because I could play what I wanted, too. I would buy the time so it would be legal. They thought it over, and finally Morrison says, "You know, well, we think that we're going to be really big. So we want to get on a big label." I said, "If that's what you want to do, I'll make a phone call."

I get up and go to the counter where you cash out, and telephone Jac Holzman at Elektra. I didn't really know him, but I had been playing his Love LP on my show. "Jac, this is Dave Diamond. Listen, I've got a group, and I want to sign 'em but they won't sign with me because I'm an independent. This is gonna be a million-selling thing, and it's a different kind of group." Jac was doing different kinds of folk music—the Paul Butterfield Blues Band and Love. I'm sure Jac knew I was playing Love on KBLA, and that's one of the reasons I called him.

So Jac came to listen to the Doors at the Whisky, and signed them. I had played their demo acetate months earlier. They played a couple of high school gigs for me, and I think a show at the Red Velvet Club. I was on their debut album. I spun "Twentieth Century Fox."

"Break On Through," their first single, really didn't make it. Robby [Krieger] and John [Densmore] come over to my place, checking my fan mail and reading all the letters [that said,] "Play the Doors!" I'd get fifty or sixty letters a day, 'cause I was spinning this new stuff. People were just going nuts. They never had heard this kind of music.

One day, they come over, and they are both all sullen and gloom. "'Break On Through' stiffed. We don't know what to do, and the record company won't do this and that." I said, "Have them put out 'Light My Fire.'" They said, "They won't do it because it's too long. No one will play that long a record." So I took them over to KBLA and showed them how to edit it down, removing the long instrumental passage. "Take that to Jac Holzman, and you'll have a number-one hit." And that's what they did.

JOHN DENSMORE: Robby and I went to a local DJ's apartment—Dave Diamond from KBLA—and he said it was a hit, but [added,] "You have to edit this down." So we pressed Paul Rothchild, and he just whacked at it, and all of us felt [that] the cut was kind of brutal. But then, we became the darlings of the FM radio stations, who played the long version. That jump-started the whole FM underground, "we're cooler" scene. Which was very cool.

HOME IS THE HUNTED

DON PEAKE: I met the Doors in Laurel Canyon. [They] were across the street from me on Wonderland Avenue. It was so loud, I started complaining. They had a Vox organ in there, and the whole house was rocking. I took Ray Manzarek to court, and the city attorney made him turn it down. I said, "I play recording sessions and get up in the morning, and they played all night."

I knew Frank Zappa from the neighborhood. Incredible bandleader. He was writing modern classical music. All that stuff he did with the time signatures and everything . . . he was really a classical composer to me. Avant garde.

DAVE DIAMOND: When "Light My Fire" reached number one, I called the office. "Hey, I want to hire the Doors for the Valley Music Theater." "Okay." "I pay scale, you know." Their manager said, "Oh no. We gotta have ten grand." "Ten grand, man? I can't pay that much on the deal." So we argued, and I was really getting pissed off. "I did a lot for this band, and now I can't even talk to them." Their manager said, "Let me talk to Morrison." Then he comes back and says, "Jim likes the idea. He thinks it's great. We'll do a Dave Diamond thank-you concert." I paid them $750, and I made $12,000 on the deal.

Jim Morrison and Robby Krieger performing at the Cal State Los Angeles gymnasium, 1967.

CHAPTER 18

EXPECTING TO CHART

Buffalo Springfield cut their self-titled debut LP at Gold Star, with managers Charlie Greene and Brian Stone handling the production. Upon its December 1966 release, the album featured "Baby Don't Scold Me" by Stephen Stills. But in its second pressing, out in spring 1967, the track had been replaced with "For What It's Worth," a sticker on the front cover announcing the addition of the hit single.

Premiered at a benefit concert for KBLA at the Santa Monica Civic Auditorium the previous November, Stephen Stills's protest dirge gave voice to the rising current of disaffected youths. The song was a kind of "audio vérité"; an angry gathering of kids had "occupied" the entrance to Laurel Canyon, at the intersection of Crescent Heights and Sunset Boulevard. They resented and resisted—by force, ultimately—the LAPD's imposition of an evening curfew. If it didn't rise to the level of an Arab Spring, it did alert the Man to an inchoate movement rallying around such contentious issues as Vietnam, women's rights, civil rights, and the paramount right of the young to be taken seriously.

This was, to a very real extent, ignited by the plaintive resonance of a single guitar note, tolling like a bell at midnight. Its success as a radio favorite, generational anthem, and pop culture cliché was, like many defining moments of the transgressive sixties, a product of old-school professionals guiding their intemperate young charges through the painstaking hard work

of sounding spontaneous. Amazing what the theater of the imagination can do with the help of a well-placed microphone.

STAN ROSS: I was in Gold Star with engineer Tom May, working with Sonny Bono on "Sunset Symphony." Charlie Greene and Brian Stone called and said Buffalo Springfield had wanted to cut that night, too, but the studio wasn't available. I then received a call at 11:30 that night: "We're in trouble. We're sitting here, and nothing is happening." Tom May and I went over to the Columbia

Above: **Buffalo Springfield at the Third Eye club, Redondo Beach, 1966.** ♪ *Opposite:* **Neil Young at a KHJ promotion, Malibu, 1966.**

studio. The kids were on the floor, having a good time. I had two hours, and I had to get some sleep for a session tomorrow morning.

I had a great idea for the drum rhythm. I thought the drummer shouldn't use his foot, and wanted someone to use a hand mallet. I wanted to take the guitar and wrap some paper around the frets, and I wanted a backbeat. Not using the drum, but using the backbeat of the frets of the guitar. That's a sound and technique I worked on at Gold Star many years ago—a very crispy, wonderful sound. After we got the track together, it's 2:00 AM. I said, "Look, guys, all you got to do is get the vocals around here, and put some fills in-between the vocals."

The next morning, I got a phone call from [Atlantic Records'] Ahmet Ertegun. "I got the record. I want you and Phil Spector to listen to two mixes and tell me which mix you like." So Phil came down to Gold Star. CBS sent over mix one and mix two. Phil and I listened, looked at each other, and agreed. That's the record that came out.

Spector is subsequently thanked on the back cover credits of Buffalo Springfield Again, *hand-drawn by musician and photographer Henry Diltz.*

"Despite impressive songwriting and musical performances, the album suffered from lackluster production resulting in an overall vapid sound," contends John Einarson, author of the book For What It's Worth: The Story of Buffalo Springfield. *"Balances were off from track to track, the fidelity flat, the bass sound lost, and harmonies buried. Overall, the album lacked presence or definition owing to the inexperience of producers Greene and Stone. The bass and drums are totally dull, and the guitars have no sparkle or strength."*

RICHIE FURAY: Who knows what may have happened, had we had someone like George Martin producing? We learned some hard lessons from that experience, vowing to exert greater control over our recordings in future.

We had the vocal parts and harmonies worked out on these things. There was some real innovation going on.

Richie Furay at Gold Star Studios, Hollywood, 1966.

Walking into Gold Star Studios, with all the history, and hearing our music coming through those speakers, even though it's a four-track, was bigger than life.

We were always comfortable singing someone else's song early on. The first album and some of the second, you can hear that the cohesiveness was a group effort. There was not the possessiveness of, "This is my song, this is my baby. I'm singing it because I wrote it." Early on, there was this, "What does this sound like with you singing?" I know we tried "Mr. Soul" with everybody singing, and it sounded best with Neil. The individual members brought their own take on what was being presented to the song. We liked the Beatles, with John and Paul singing harmony. Stephen and I did a lot of that unison singing that we picked up from the Beatles. But then, there was a lot of experimentation.

The band was that first album, and it was never captured again. That album represented the five of us together, in the studio. After that, it started to fall apart. It got worse with the next two albums. There were a lot of people being used other than the five of us.

Buffalo Springfield's world became dislodged in January 1967. Bassist Bruce Palmer got into some immigration problems, and was deported back to Canada. During this period, the group employed various fill-in bass players—Ken Kolbun, Jim Fielder, and Bobby West—on session dates from January to May, when they were ostensibly recording their second album. The working title was Stampede. *They remained at Gold Star until late May, when Bruce returned. Then Neil quit in early June, before returning in August to record demos for "One More Sign," "The Rent Is Always Due," "Round and Round," and "Old Laughing Lady" by himself at Gold Star.*

Buffalo Springfield then started taking their action to Sunset Sound, where they discovered engineers Bruce Botnick and Jim Messina. The venue would become their studio of choice for Buffalo Springfield Again, *as well as tracks for their next album,* Last Time Around. *The Young demo "Down, Down, Down" was later re-recorded for his Jim*

Messina-engineered Buffalo Springfield sound collage, "Broken Arrow," on Buffalo Springfield Again. *Young's "Old Laughing Lady" copyright would surface on his solo album, courtesy of arranger/producer Jack Nitzsche.*

RICHIE FURAY: I was amazed at some of the demos that Stephen [Stills] and I did. We had the vocal parts and harmonies worked out on these things. There was some real innovation going on. The quality of the demos underscores the writing. You can hear a song evolve. Even shows what Ahmet Ertegun saw in the band.

He also encouraged us to learn the board. So we'd go in, and we would record 'em like some of the vocals were going to be done. Ahmet had heart and soul for the band. "Make these demos. Do whatever you need to do to make the product." Because of him, the band got launched a lot quicker than maybe it could have. He definitely saw something in this band right away.

BRUCE BOTNICK: On their second album, *Buffalo Springfield Again*, the songs were so strong, and so were the performances. We had two lead guitar players, Stills and Young, two prolific writers, and there was constant tension between the two—creative tension that would manifest itself in either one of them, you know, losing it for a few minutes. Then they would get back together and hug like crazy, and do the songs. Again, it was about performance.

During the period of the sixties and into the seventies, the focus was on the joy of getting the songs out. We'd be recording a song, and Stephen would say to Neil, "Hey, man, I just got a new idea for a song," or, "It isn't finished, but what do you think?" Neil would say, "Hey, that's great. Did you think about doing that there?" So this went on constantly.

You have to realize that when Buffalo Springfield came into the studio, they were rehearsed. They had played their music live. Double sets at nightclubs. Same thing as the Doors. That's one of the reasons we were able to get good performances.

Neil Young was never a prima donna. In fact, none of the guys were prima donnas, when it came to recording them. Everyone was serious about recording the music. Jack Nitzsche was a part of this. He's the one who brought Buffalo Springfield to me. I was there for "Expecting to

Stephen Stills and Neil Young, San Francisco, 1967.

Fly," and then wound up doing "Bluebird" and three or four others. Maybe "Rock and Roll Woman." "Expecting to Fly" was a real Jack extravaganza. If you listen to it today . . . I wonder how Neil would have done it without that arrangement.

RUSS TITELMAN: This was after Jack made the Bob Lind record "Elusive Butterfly." So the string parts had similar qualities, because it's a Nitzsche arrangement and production. Don Randi on electric piano. "Expecting to Fly" [features the] Wrecking Crew band.

I did a lot of sessions with Jack and Buffalo Springfield. Jack and I used to go and see them at the Whisky, and up in San Francisco. They cut at Sunset Sound a lot, where "Expecting to Fly" was done. I got hired to do the gig. Jack and I became really close friends, just spent an awful lot of time together. I was at Jack's house in Nichols Canyon when they wrote the arrangement. Jack had the snare drum, you know, playing two and four through all the odd time signatures. Neil was there. He was great.

DAVE DIAMOND: I met Buffalo Springfield through their drummer, Dewey Martin. He was a good friend, and we ran together in a Hollywood circle. Dewey gave me an acetate of their album, *Buffalo Springfield Again*, when I was briefly on radio station KFWB—before they went all talk and news. Dewey came by the back door to the station on Hollywood Boulevard with the other group members for an interview.

Left: Richie Furay and Dewey Martin at a KHJ promotion, Malibu, 1966. ♪ *Right:* Acetate copy of *Buffalo Springfield Again*, autographed by KFWB DJ Dave Diamond, 1968.

MARK GUERRERO: Next to the Beatles, Buffalo Springfield is my all-time favorite band. Richard Rosas and I saw them at the Cal State Los Angeles gymnasium in 1967, for probably two dollars. We were about seventeen. They kicked ass on this show. We loved "Uno Mundo."

THE DREAM CAME TRUE

RICK ROSAS: We saw Buffalo Springfield live at Cal State L.A., and we went to the goodbye concert in Long Beach. It was pretty heavy. I was so young. It was really good, but I was hoping it could be a little bit better. They were a recording band to me. Back in those days, I don't think they had guitar tuners or really good sound systems. The PA equipment was pretty bad back at the time. We were still knocked out by them. I went backstage and saw a white Econoline van with the name "Buffalo Springfield" printed on the door. Wow!

Many years go by, and I end up playing with Neil [Young] in his Bluenotes group. "This Bud's For You." I did play with Neil at a little Mexican restaurant nightclub near East L.A., in Montebello on Garfield. We went down there one night because the sax player, Steve Lawrence, used to play there. "Let's play a little club!" "Hey, let's do it!" We were at SIR, rehearsing. Next thing I know, we grabbed a few amps and went down there, set up, and played. It was hilarious. Neil later did a version of "Farmer John" on a Crazy Horse album.

I later played with Neil on his solo albums and tours, and then, Crosby, Stills, Nash and Young. I played the Hollywood Bowl. On those concerts, there was a little mellow section in the show where Ben Keith played steel guitar and I played Stephen Stills's bass, which he named Grandma. David Crosby gave it to him. I think it's a '58 Precision bass. That was the bass Stephen played on "Suite: Judy Blue Eyes."

All during my tours and recording with Neil, he and I would talk about Buffalo Springfield. I never hid my excitement about Buffalo Springfield and loved to talk to him about that band, sometimes over a couple of glasses of wine. He embraced the band. He loved it. Neil would talk about it as much as he could remember. He drove around in one of his first tour buses with the Buffalo Springfield logo on the back. He probably knew I went to the last Buffalo Springfield concert. Earlier this decade, Neil put together the *Buffalo Springfield* box set. That was his baby.

Then I got the phone call to be in the reformed Buffalo Springfield. A couple of years ago I was sort of depressed, 'cause I wasn't working and nothing much

Latin rhythms. Being Chicanos from East L.A., hearing Stephen Stills singing in Spanish! We loved him for that.

Our band, Mark and the Escorts, recorded at Gold Star. [We said,] "We need to record something there." So I called them and booked a four-hour session that cost eighty dollars. I still have a piece of paper that has "Gold Star" on it. At this time, we were called "Nineteen Eighty-Four," after the George Orwell book. We cut two songs, including one of mine called "Amber Waves," a really psychedelic, weird, acid kind of rock thing. B minor to G minor, and all this Eric Clapton-style fuzz sustain lead guitar. This band evolved into Men From S.O.U.N.D. from 1966 to '68. We covered "Hung Upside Down," "Mr. Soul," "Bluebird," and "Rock and Roll Woman."

"Amber Waves" LP by Nineteen Eighty-Four.

Rick Rosas and I saw the last Buffalo Springfield show, in May 1968 in Long Beach. The one memory I have of the show is that, when they were in the middle of a Stills song, a security guard came onstage and stopped the music, telling people that they were getting too close to the stage and to move back. Stills got pissed off and threw his guitar. This guy had the audacity to stop the band. "Stop the music! Stop the music!" It was very sad, and they broke up.

Buffalo Springfield re-formed in 2011, and took to the road featuring Neil Young, Stephen Stills, Richie Furay, drummer Joe Vitale, and Rick Rosas on bass. The tickets cost more than two dollars.

was going on. Neil was doing his own thing. Then I get a call from Bonnie at Lookout Management. "I've got [manager] Elliot [Roberts] on the line for you, and we have a two-way call with Neil." So they both got on the phone. "How you doing?" "Fine." "Well, we've got some news for you. Welcome to the Buffalo Springfield." I just said, "Oh my God! You're pulling my leg." They started laughing, and Neil said, "Rick, I can see your smile on your face right now." It was the biggest grin I had had in years. Probably one of the most exciting moments in my life. That's where it started.

Neil's tours had Buffalo Springfield tunes, but this was Buffalo Springfield and the front line of Neil, Stephen, and Richie. I was a huge fan of Poco. They knocked me out. They were tight, and the harmonies were impeccable. Always loved Richie's songs and voice.

I was already a graduate of Neil Young University. That gave me a tremendous amount of confidence to take on this job. Dewey Martin and Bruce Palmer were definitely part of the original sound. I did my best to try and emulate Bruce to the best of my ability. I tried to play some of the parts, because they worked so well.

The shows were magic. Neil used some vintage Buffalo Springfield gear—a couple of his guitars.

I had never met Richie prior to our four rehearsals for Buffalo Springfield at the Bridge Concert. We rehearsed in Menlo Park, just outside of San Francisco. We came in on a Monday. The gear was all set up. Richie was just the sweetest man in the world. Still is. He was so nice. A wonderful man. He was beaming, and so excited about Buffalo Springfield. I thought *I* was excited. He was smiling every day. Then Neil started counting off songs that are in my DNA. It is a dream to me—more than that, an incredible experience playing stuff that I've always wanted to play with him and Buffalo Springfield. Even in rehearsal, and on our short tour, I further realized the sound they get from the three of them.

They have this sound that is hard to describe. The blend of the voices. So much magic. I don't think at rehearsals we had a set list, per se. We just tried out songs that they all wanted to do and knew. Maybe a couple didn't work, but we finally got a set together that really jelled and seemed to make sense. And some deep catalog things, like "Broken Arrow."

Left: Chris Hillman and producer Terry Melcher at Columbia Records, Hollywood, 1965. ♪ *Right:* KRLA promotional item for Buffalo Springfield's proposed second album, *Stampede.* ♪
Bottom: Buffalo Springfield performing at KHJ's Appreciation Concert for the United Negro College Fund at the Hollywood Bowl, 1967.

HERE THEY COME! FROM BOISE TO SUNSET

by GARY PIG GOLD

Paul Revere and his Raiders, straight out of the northwest wildwoods, swung forth the most colorful, classiest, *hardest* pop L.A. had ever seen, let alone heard. While "Madman Markus" Lindsay's pipes could more than hold their own against Messrs. Jagger and even Burdon, behind him, the Raiders themselves always boasted a Yardbird-challenging string of expert, uniform guitarsmen.

The AM dial-busting, seven-inch wonders that Mark Lindsay and Terry Melcher wrote and/or produced for the band offered the kind of glimmering, slicing sounds the latter could only sometimes pull off with fellow Columbians the Byrds. The Raiders' definitive, pre-Monkee "(I'm Not Your) Steppin' Stone," the uber-bubblegummed "Mr. Sun, Mr. Moon," the hard 'n' heavy "Just Seventeen" (which, when sent to press and radio with a blank label, tricked even *Rolling Stone* into thinking a new Zeppelin track was being leaked), and the band's monumental, career-defining "Him or Me (What's It Gonna Be)" are the kinds of three-minute masterworks Los Angeles inexplicably

Paul Revere and the Raiders, 1966.
"I wanted to take them out of their uniforms for this shooting," said photographer Guy Webster.

Paul Revere (*center*) on the set of *Happening '68*, Hollywood, 1968.

never ever learned to embrace with at least Doors and Springfield levels of respect.

Yes, most unfortunately, like their all-stomping British brethren the Dave Clark Five, perhaps an occasionally questionable choice of onstage wardrobe forever doomed the Raiders in the Cool Quotient sweepstakes. That, and/or their *anti*-drug (highly unusual for the time) monster "Kicks." But if you can dare, just one peek behind Paul and pals' tricornered hats reveals a nifty, tough, *and* bitchin' band that had few, if any, equals in the creative revolution that was Top 40-driven L.A.

CHAPTER 19

CIRCUS BOYZ

Davy Jones was already in the Monkees before producers Bob Rafelson and Bert Schneider held auditions in Hollywood. Jones was a contract player with Screen Gems-Columbia, and had been seen onstage at the Music Center in Los Angeles when writers Paul Mazursky and Larry Tucker said to him, "We're going to write a show for you." After Micky Dolenz, Peter Tork, and Michael Nesmith were cast in the television series, it was up to the golden ears of music supervisor Don Kirshner and Lester Sill at Screen Gems to select the songs for the group to record around their television and touring activities.

The NBC series The Monkees debuted on September 12, 1966. What could have—should have—been a national embarrassment became an instant sensation. With so many ways for it to have gone wrong, there was only one way for it to have gone right—with great songs!

Micky Dolenz, Don Kirshner, and Davy Jones at RCA Studios, Hollywood, 1966.

DAVY JONES: Screen Gems was looking for a project for me, and *The Monkees* came along. They looked at all kinds of people. There was talk about Stephen Stills auditioning and being turned down because he had bad teeth. Screen Gems had a TV series with Paul Petersen, *The Donna Reed Show*, and he used to sing and make records. It was a great way of selling records. So they held auditions, everyone did screen tests, and they ended up with Mike Nesmith, Peter Tork, Micky Dolenz, and me—the Monkees. Initially, Peter and Mike were more the musicians, and Micky and I were the actors. We became four actors and four musicians.

Don Kirshner was a hell of a guy. He had his whole company—Carole King, Neil Diamond, Harry Nilsson, Neil Sedaka, Carole Bayer, Leiber and Stoller, Barry Mann, Cynthia Weil, Tommy Boyce, Bobby Hart, and many, many others writing tunes for the Monkees. He was a very honorable man who had an idea. He always followed the same format. He executed it well within the Monkees' project, but I think that the show's producers, Bert Schneider and Bob Rafelson, didn't want anyone to take any success from them. That's why Don ended up being ousted and being paid off. It was the same thing that happened to Paul Mazursky and Larry Tucker, who wrote the pilot. They also were phased out. They never really got the credit they should have gotten.

"Last Train to Clarksville" was our first single, and a

Opposite: Davy Jones at a sound check at the Hollywood Bowl, 1967.

Left: Micky Dolenz on location in Marina Del Rey, 1968. ♪ *Middle left:* Davy Jones, Hollywood, 1967.
Middle right: Michael Nesmith on the set of *The Monkees*, Hollywood, 1967. ♪ *Right:* Peter Tork on location in Marina Del Rey, 1968.

lot of trouble was started over it because Donnie Kirshner, our music supervisor, and Bert Schneider and Bob Rafelson, started arguing immediately over who was responsible for the success of the Monkees. They never even considered that Mike, Micky, Peter, and I could have had something to do with it. But the record was out, and it was a hit before the TV show started. There was a great promotional campaign. They changed the name of Del Mar to Clarksville for the day. KHJ, the radio station, rented a train for the day, and they took five hundred contest winners. They put us in a helicopter, and they flew us onto a beach down there, where all the contest winners were waiting. We did four different concerts for them in one of the baggage carriages on the train, on the way back to Los Angeles. They ushered them in, a hundred at a time.

Well, there were session players, and there were musicians. I have seen many different musicians playing in the Beatles recording sessions, and on the Beach Boys, and the Mamas and the Papas, and the Lovin' Spoonful, [and] the Association. A lot of these bands used side men.

Chip Douglas was always a very big fan of the Monkees. He was responsible for "Daydream Believer," a song John Stewart wrote, and an album we were all very proud of called *Headquarters*. But the Monkees were always looked down upon, because we used other musicians on our albums, and we were not so good with our own instruments. It was a thing the press got onto at the time.

Whenever Carole King wrote a tune, she then put the track down, and Micky sometimes sounded like Carole King, the way she wanted it to sound. I was sort of a reflection of Tommy Boyce, what he wanted me to

Chip Douglas playing new material for Davy Jones in his dressing room at Screen Gems-Columbia Studios, Hollywood, 1967.

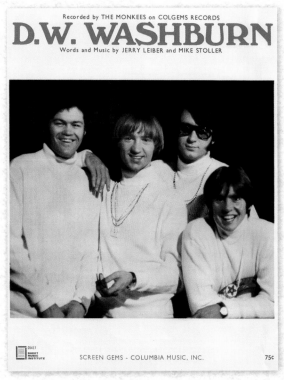

"D.W. Washburn" sheet music, 1968.

Kaye, Glen Campbell, and drummer Hal Blaine. James Burton, fresh from blazing behind Ricky Nelson, flavored Mike Nesmith's pioneering country-pop most especially. It is James who is the object of Nesmith's "Play, magic fingers!" demand during "Papa Gene's Blues." Similarly, Everly stick man Jim Gordon powered Monkee tracks clear through '68's "D.W. Washburn."

The Monkees even let the songwriters themselves craft their wares long past the usual demo-only stage. Practically from the pilot episode onwards, Tommy Boyce and Bobby Hart, along with their backing musicians, the Candy Store Prophets, provided tracks for most first-year Monkee productions, and backed the Prefabs during their earliest stage appearances. Harry Nilsson and even Carole King were on hand, and on instruments, when many of their compositions were cut. Even several Buffalo Springfields can be heard on Monkees recordings.

sound like. Basically, we were at the mercy of the track, and at the mercy of the producers.

In 1962, Lester Sill had teamed with Phil Spector to create their label, Philles Records, formed from the first parts of their respective names, Phil and Les. By 1964, Sill had been hired as a consultant for Screen Gems-Columbia Music. He then ascended to the position of president at their newly created Colgems Records.

GARY PIG GOLD: In carefully conceiving, crafting, and then launching the Monkees, Bob Rafelson and Bert Schneider were wise enough to surround them with the best musical support team possible. In L.A., in '65, '66, that meant Spector's crew whenever possible—Carol

LESTER SILL: The whole Monkees thing was laid out and planned. Before we went to Victor—even though Victor was a natural because the records were on RCA, and NBC

Left: Michael Nesmith with recording engineer Hank Cicalo at RCA Studios, Hollywood, 1967.
Right: Bobby Hart (*left*) and Tommy Boyce in Laurel Canyon, 1969.

owns RCA—we had auditions with all the record companies. Capitol presented an audition to us, as did all the major labels, but we had a good feeling about the Victor situation by being able to tie it in with the network and the record company. The radio was a normal thing, but it was much easier to promote because of the television exposure.

Unused concert ticket to a Monkees concert at the Hollywood Bowl, 1967.

We sat with NBC and told them we were going to start a new label and put the Monkees on that label. So we divested ourselves of the Colpix label. We just took everything back from all the distributors and started Colgems, which was distributed through RCA Victor. It was a joint venture between Screen Gems, the television division of Columbia Pictures, and RCA Victor between 1966 and 1971.

The first producer that we selected was Snuff Garrett, and that didn't quite work out. There was a personality conflict. Snuff and the boys just didn't get along, even though Snuff, to me, was one of the finest producers around. We put Tommy [Boyce] and Bobby [Hart] on the project, and they came through. In the meantime, Don Kirshner, who ran this whole operation, was in New York and sort of lying back a little bit. I have a feeling that Don wanted to wait to see whether or not it was going to be successful before he stepped in. We called one of

Micky Dolenz at a sound check at the Hollywood Bowl, 1967.

the record executives from RCA into the studio and played it for him. He said, "Fine, we'll make the deal. Go ahead with it." The single "Last Train to Clarksville" became a hit right away in a few weeks, about six weeks before the show came on. *The Monkees* came on, and the record exploded.

The show premiers in September, the album's out in October, and by the end of November, I'm sitting in the RCA Victor offices with Steve Sholes and Donnie, and Steve told us that their album sales had reached 2,800,000. It was phenomenal.

MICKY DOLENZ: My primary career had been an actor up to that time. But by the time I had the interview with the Monkees, I'd already been in three groups. I played rhythm guitar in one, and sang lead and backup in the others. I'd recorded; I'd already had three sessions at the time, one with Glen Campbell playing guitar for me as my session musician. That was that "Don't Do It" record.

I don't recall being too concerned about being cast as a drummer, because I had approached the show as an actor. The auditions for the show were screen tests, improvisation, acting, music, and singing. I did "Johnny B. Goode," playing guitar, for my audition piece. But, knowing the business, I knew that the way the characters fell in together would be up to the producers. I really hadn't thought about it much or cared. They knew I could play guitar. Davy didn't play any instrument, really. Also, they wanted him up there in the front as a front-piece, a showpiece.

Mike had had a lot of experience in bands, playing guitar. I suspect that he had probably lobbied quite heavily, obviously, to play guitar. Peter also was a very accomplished musician on a number of instruments. I think it kind of just happened by default. There wasn't anybody left. I looked a bit like a drummer, and I acted a bit crazy. So there I was, cast as the drummer. I said, "Fine. When do my lessons start?" [*Laughs.*] In all respect, it was not brain surgery.

"Pleasant Valley Sunday" was one of the best tracks we did. Outside of Chip Douglas playing bass and Eddie Hoh on drums, it's all us. By that time, we were doing an

Above left: The Monkees on the "Southwest" set of their TV series at Fred Niles Studios, Chicago, 1967.
Above right: The Monkees on the "rainbow" set of *The Monkees*, Chicago, 1967.
Bottom: Michael Nesmith and Jack Nicholson backstage at a 1968 Monkees concert in Salt Lake City.
Nicholson co-wrote the band's feature-length movie, *Head*.

awful lot of it. Mike and Peter were always playing guitar and bass, and Peter on keyboards, right from day one. I had to learn to play the drums, quick. You have a unique style. My drums were set up left-handed. I'm left-footed and right-handed.

CHIP DOUGLAS: I found "Pleasant Valley Sunday" on a demo when I was at Screen Gems. It's a wild record, but it wasn't quite as wild on Carole King's demo. It was a little mellower and smoother. Not quite as fast. I don't know why I got the idea to speed it up, but somewhere I was sitting around with my guitar and came up with that guitar lick to start it off with. I would memorize these demos, and listen to them enough and get the words into my head, and then start to play it and kind of come up with my own thing, and [get] ideas for who would sing what. I would think, "Micky can hit these high notes on this thing and this key," and Carole did it in a different key, I believe. I was struck by all of her vocals. She's a great singer, and the demos she did were all very well put together and simple, yet they had a whole band in 'em— piano, bass, guitar, and drums, usually.

This was a great song, and we were lookin' for some

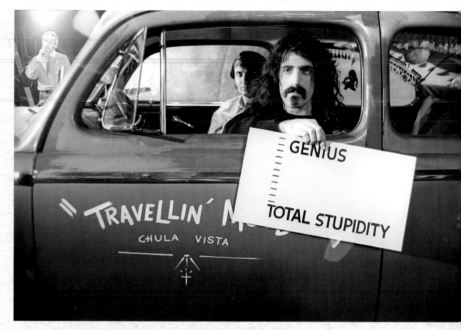

Michael Nesmith and Frank Zappa on the set of *The Monkees*, Hollywood, 1967.

sort of protest thing. I think George Harrison's "I Want to Tell You" was a subconscious influence. As it is played on the guitar, the note intervals are similar. The Beatles' riff uses the low E and A strings, and mine, which is faster and a different pattern, used the low A and D strings

INSIDE THE SONIC CAGE

HANK CICALO: I had worked with [arranger] Shorty Rogers a number of times. I had done some projects with Shorty for Lester Sill. They were looking for an engineer to work with the Monkees, and my name came up. That's how I fell into the project.

I had a meeting with Lester, Bobby Hart, and Tommy Boyce. We went out and had lunch or dinner, and they discussed what the project was about, and they were just about doing the pilot. Nobody knew what was going on. It was going to be a TV show with a lot of music, and that's all I knew about it. I got along with Tommy and Bobby; they were nice guys, and a lot of fun. The one song I didn't engineer was "Last Train to Clarksville," which was done by Dave Hassinger. I'd be booked for a month at a time, doing just the Monkees' things.

It was a lot of work. There was always this endless

pressure of trying to do three or four musical numbers for each show while they were still shooting. We were working long hours at night, and whoever wasn't shooting the next day could stay longer and do a vocal or this kind of thing or that kind of thing, working Saturdays and Sundays. For that period, because of the hours we were working at night, and also mixing, and also going through a very interesting change at that time, we would do a track on three-track or four-track, and then go from one machine to another machine, adding a vocal. We also went from four-track, to eight-track, to sixteen-track in that two-year period. It was the very beginning of multi-track, and we all progressed in a new medium as well. We were able to stack voices and double up voices without losing quality. It was a very interesting period.

The Monkees **director Bob Rafelson (***left***) and producer Bert Schneider at RCA Studios, Chicago, 1967.**

must be told, now that she has released her demo of it in 2012.

DANIEL WEIZMANN: Gerry Goffin and Carole King wrote it in New Jersey about a street called Pleasant Valley Way, a gentle homage to Lennon and McCartney imitators. But Goffin and King had already done time with Screen Gems and co-wrote "Just Once in My Life" with Spector—the California dream was in their blood—and "Pleasant Valley Sunday" is just loaded with all the paradoxes of the West Coast.

For starters, the song itself is *meta*. Well, it's the Monkees themselves who bridge the gap between that garage band and that television. They're a TV band finally playing their own instruments. For the Monkees' generation, the line between reality and screen fantasy has been erased once and for all. Moreover, the song has a *knowing* quality, teasing out the problem of post-war prosperity with supreme ambivalence. Pretty amazing, when you think that these lyrics are directed at the readers of *Tiger Beat*. Yet all but the very youngest kids got it intuitively, and the soul revolution was televised after all. "Pleasant Valley Sunday" is the natural flipside of the Beatles' "Penny Lane"—a swift drive to the groomed cul de sac at the end of American capitalism. We're a long way from the promise of Brian's beach.

to kick off the tune.

I will say, I got the bridge all backwards on the Monkees version from her demo. I memorized it wrong on the bridge, and kind of got the lines turned around. I'm not sure if Carole was really happy about that. But the story

Finally, it's the song's fade—realized in the studio by producer Chip Douglas and engineer Hank Cicalo—that makes it a pop art masterpiece. These are Spector's minions at the knobs; the vocals drown in a rising and crashing tidal wave of echo and reverberation and alienation, which refuses to let you know whether you are slipping into dream or waking from a nightmare.

KHJ'S "BOSS 30" RECORDS IN SOUTHERN CALIFORNIA!

ISSUE NO. 81 — PREVIEWED JANUARY 18, 1967

Last Week	This Week	TITLE	ARTIST	LABEL	Weeks On Boss 30
(1)	1.	I'M A BELIEVER/STEPPIN' STONE	The Monkees	Colgems	8
(2)	2.	TELL IT LIKE IT IS	Aaron Neville	Parlo	6
(3)	3.	GEORGY GIRL	The Seekers	Capitol	5
(9)	4.	PRETTY BALLERINA	The Left Banke	Smash	3
(7)	5.	FOR WHAT IT'S WORTH	The Buffalo Springfield	Atco	4
(21)	6.	KIND OF A DRAG	The Buckinghams	USA	3
(15)	7.	98.6	Keith	Mercury	3
(22)	8.	RUBY TUESDAY	The Rolling Stones	London	2
(4)	9.	SNOOPY Vs. THE RED BARON	The Royal Guardsmen	Laurie	8
(10)	10.	THE BEAT GOES ON	Sonny & Cher	Atco	4
(6)	11.	WEDDING BELL BLUES	Laura Nyro	Verve	8
(12)	12.	SUGAR TOWN	Nancy Sinatra	Reprise	7
(24)	13.	MR. FARMER	The Seeds	GNP Crescendo	2
(11)	14.	FULL MEASURE	The Lovin' Spoonful	Kama Sutra	7
(13)	15.	KNIGHT IN RUSTY ARMOUR	Peter & Gordon	Capitol	5
(5)	16.	STANDING IN THE SHADOWS OF LOVE	The Four Tops	Motown	7
(8)	17.	HELLO HELLO	The Sopwith "Camel"	Kama Sutra	6
(23)	18.	IT MAY BE WINTER OUTSIDE	Felice Taylor	Mustang	5
(18)	19.	WORDS OF LOVE	The Mamas & The Papas	Dunhill	6
(20)	20.	SINGLE GIRL	Sandy Posey	MGM	7
(17)	21.	THERE'S GOT TO BE A WORD!	The Innocence	Kama Sutra	8
(28)	22.	I HAD TOO MUCH TO DREAM (Last Night)	The Electric Prunes	Reprise	2
(26)	23.	GIMME SOME LOVIN'	The Spencer Davis Group	United Artists	2
(25)	24.	GREEN, GREEN GRASS OF HOME	Tom Jones	Parrot	2
(27)	25.	I'VE PASSED THIS WAY BEFORE	Jimmy Ruffin	Soul	3
(30)	26.	(WE AIN'T GOT) NOTHIN' YET	The Blues Magoos	Mercury	2
(29)	27.	NIKI HOEKY	P. J. Proby	Liberty	3
(HB)	28.	MUSIC TO WATCH GIRLS BY	The Bob Crewe Generation	dynoVoice	1
(HB)	29.	LOVE IS HERE AND NOW YOU'RE GONE	The Supremes	Motown	1
(HB)	30.	SO YOU WANT TO BE A ROCK 'N' ROLL STAR	The Byrds	Columbia	1

THE POPULARITY OF RECORDS LISTED HEREIN IS THE OPINION OF KHJ BASED ON ITS SURVEY OF RECORD SALES IN SOUTHERN CALIFORNIA CORRELATED WITH LISTENER REQUESTS.

KHJ radio survey, 1967.

"THIS IS THE LOVE CROWD, RIGHT?"

In 1967, record producer and Ode Records label owner Lou Adler, along with John Phillips of the Mamas and the Papas, undertook an unprecedented and wildly ambitious endeavor, co-producing the Monterey International Pop Festival, held on June 16, 17, and 18 in Monterey, California. It was the first—and, for many, the greatest—music festival ever, featuring the best in pop, rock, blues, psychedelia, and sitars. The thirty-two acts from the U.S. and England, a veritable survey of the KHJ Boss Thirty, included the Association, Johnny Rivers, Laura Nyro, Lou Rawls, Buffalo Springfield, the Byrds, Canned Heat, and the Who, performing day and night over that weekend. When the audience awakened on Monday morning, everyone agreed that it had been a dream come true.

Russ Giguere of the Association with his wife, Bertie, in the seating area of the Monterey International Pop Festival, just hours before the landmark 1967 event began.

TOMMY BOYCE: David Gates was a songwriter for Screen Gems. "Saturday's Child" was the first song he ever had recorded. We were working on the first album, 'cause everyone else in the world would not work on the Monkees. They all turned it down. We were fired twice, and quit three times. It's true. So we're in there recording, and our boss, Lester Sill, hands Bobby and me the lead sheet and says, "Learn to like this."

Firesign Theatre button promoting their own 1972 presidential candidate, "Papoon."

BOBBY HART: Bob Rafelson and Bert Schneider knew what they were doing. They were the brainchildren behind the Monkees. There was other input around them, and they took ideas from people. But they were the people who got it done. Rafelson really wanted to be director, and he was a brilliant director, which he proved later on with many hit films. Schneider was the new bright boy on the lot, as far as the production . . . Mr. Producer-type. It was a brilliant combination.

PHIL PROCTOR: In June of 1967, David Ossman, Phil Austin, and I were doing *Radio Free Oz* on KRLA radio, while Peter Bergman was on a two-week trip to Turkey and I was at Monterey. I did phone-ins to KRLA from the festival. I was with the *East Village Other*, covering Hollywood and L.A. I had seen harassment of longhairs, the incident on the Sunset Strip at Pandora's Box.

The Monterey International Pop Festival was a new world in front of me. The one pervasive memory that I have from that weekend was being surrounded by like-minded people. That was lacking from New York at the time. Working as I did for this East Village newspaper, which was quite an artistic paper—they had an understanding that a new society was on the brink of expressing itself. That was a youth society, a new generation that was more artistically and emotionally focused than the previous generation. That was the main vibration up there at the festival—a terrific feeling of unity. It was not political at all. It was really a relief to be in a musical setting outdoors.

I remember the weather was wonderful and, yes, people were smoking pot and stuff like that. But it was not a druggie festival. It was a celebration of pop music.

At Monterey, there were hippie entrepreneurs. That was all part of taking power and control of the culture in a positive way. There wasn't the kind of corruption and super management manipulation that took over later, that led to all kinds of disputes about recording contracts and all that stuff. It was much more heartfelt. It was like, "Why can't we benefit all of us?" For quite a while, the industry gave us honest royalty reports. The companies were run by music men. A&R people, not lawyers.

That was one of the reasons we had a feeling of community and family that grew around the burgeoning recording industry. Because, at a certain point, that industry was a beacon of the expression of good will and freedom of thought that could be expressed through the medium of take-home recordings.

I had known David Crosby from my contact with actors Peter Fonda and Brandon De Wilde, so it was easy to connect with those guys again. Our group, Firesign Theatre, would share a record producer, Gary Usher, with the Byrds. We recorded at the Columbia Records studio on Sunset Boulevard, where they, and Chad and Jeremy, Simon and Garfunkel, Janis Joplin and Big Brother and the Holding Company, and Donovan also recorded. Donovan was supposed to play at Monterey, but had a visa problem in England.

The youth revolution—and believe me, that's what it was—when you were in the middle of it, was unstoppable. It was definitely a pervasive spirit, where a new generation realized that it had a cultural power. That was expressed, oddly enough, in the growing success of the phonograph record. We were right in the middle, where the 45 went to LP, and AM radio to FM radio. Both of

Brian Jones at the Monterey International Pop Festival, 1967.

Jim McGuinn performing at the CAFF (California Action for Fact and Freedom) benefit concert at Valley Music Theater in Woodland Hills, California, 1967.

those things allowed more liberty and freedom. Because commercial AM radio had gone about as far as it could go. Right? People were crying for a more personal expression of artistry in the privacy of one's own home, and the phonograph record afforded that. Because, basically, you couldn't censor it to the degree that AM radio was censored. FM radio was the same way. Suddenly, there was free speech, if you will. The growing Pacifica radio chains and the small campus stations . . . suddenly radio became a tool of cultural propagation, of new thought, and New Age thinking, and new music. It did not need the support of monolithic, capitalistic, or corporate powers in order to reach an audience. FM radio and the Monterey International Pop Festival did not come out of management. All of that came later.

PETE TOWNSHEND: We were pretty scared. We'd done a package in New York with Cream, and it seemed as though we'd missed a beat. We were still displaying Union Jacks and smashing guitars, while Cream played proper music and had Afro haircuts and flowery outfits. Jimi had already hit in the UK.

JOHNNY RIVERS: The vibe of the festival was very mellow, and kind of the theme of the whole thing. It was a gathering of tribes, and hadn't really gotten to the wild hippie stage yet. The "Summer of Love" was the summer that came after that. It wasn't going to be frantic [or] out of control, but everyone digging on the music, because there was such a variety of it.

Six weeks before Monterey, I had done the Hollywood Bowl with Buffalo Springfield and the Supremes. Jimmy Webb was in my band for Monterey on keyboard. John Phillips and Lou Adler worked well together, and you have to give them credit. Not only did they pull it off, but they did it in good style. It came off without a hitch, man.

MICHELLE PHILLIPS: Monterey Pop was so beautiful. It was convenient for the artists, as well as the audience. Practically everyone had a seat, and if not, people were lined up beside a fence, and they could hear and see. The weather had a lot to do with it, too, and it was this beautiful, almost spring weather. Also, the fact that there weren't *too* many people . . . I don't know how many people came through Monterey that weekend, but it was very manageable. You also didn't have a lot of drug freak-outs. It was lovely.

John Phillips, Lou Adler, and Dick Moreland backstage at the Anaheim Convention Center for a Bee Gees, Spanky and Our Gang, and Vanilla Fudge concert, 1968.

RAVI SHANKAR: I was recording for Dick Bock's World Pacific Records. Some of my recordings with jazz musicians are on that label. About my performing, I can only tell you what I've heard, not once, but a thousand times. It comes from a man who is a porter at the airport, or the immigration officer, and they say one thing, which I always get tears in my eyes about: "Thank you for what you gave us through your music." This has always been the case. That's what I want to do through my music, to give them, as much as is possible, love and peace and the feeling of all the different sentiments that we have, starting from romantic to playful, to happiness, to speed, to virtuosity and fun . . . and, finally, something which is most important to me, the spiritual.

The Mamas and the Papas performing at the Hollywood Bowl, 1967.

ANDREW LOOG OLDHAM: These white kids in the audience were in school. We all grew from the diversity presented in those three days. I put [the Rolling Stones'] *Flowers* together when I was working at the Monterey International Pop Festival. I just asked Lou Adler if he minded me co-opting the Monterey team of [photographer] Guy Webster and [artist] Tom Wilkes. He did not, and they did *Flowers*. In 2010, I just saw that *Flowers* logo in a children's store next door to Dragon Herbs on Wilshire and Fourth in Santa Monica, California. Exact same thing on a kiddie's T-shirt. The good work lasts in amazing ways.

ROBERT MARCHESE: The biggest-selling album of that whole event was Jimi Hendrix and Otis Redding [*Historic Performances Recorded at the Monterey International Pop Festival*]. The liner notes by Ralph J. Gleason said it took both of them from rumor to legend. Before Monterey, Hendrix had done his first real studio recording session at Gold Star, and Otis had come to Hollywood a few years previously to record before he officially joined Stax Records.

At Monterey, people started seeing the dollars. Prime example: [manager] Albert Grossman smiling at Janis Joplin, knowing he's got a million dollars there. After Monterey, when Hendrix played the Hollywood Bowl, Mo Ostin and Joe Smith from Reprise were sitting right in front of me. Beside them were two little white chicks, like Valley beach bunny blondes. Hendrix started playing. Believe me, they started wetting their pants. I leaned into Mo's ear and Joe's ear, and said, "This is why you got millions of dollars staring you in your face. This is the first time these two chicks ever got turned on by a black cat [*laughs*]. He doesn't carry a razor blade; he's awfully good lookin'.

Tim Buckley on the set of *The Monkees*, Hollywood, 1967.

AL KOOPER: I was the assistant stage manager at the festival. Two things came out of Monterey. [Bassist] Jim Fielder. I knew him because of Tim Buckley and Mothers of Invention. These are things that first took place in New York. When I went out to L.A., I was looking for musicians for my new band. I bumped into him and ran it by him. He procured a drummer, Sandy Konikoff, and we played together.

Directly after Monterey, I went to the Big Sur Folk Festival on the grounds of the Esalen Institute and played with Sandy and Jim. We performed some of my new songs—"I Can't Quit Her" and "My Days Are Numbered." Then, the Blood, Sweat and Tears album, *Child Is the Father to the Man*.

I wrote "I Can't Quit Her" at the 9000 building on Sunset Boulevard, in a songwriting office. I remember I stopped in the middle when I was writing the bridge, because I came up with "proselytized," and I didn't know what it meant. So I had to go find a dictionary in the building and look it up, and it meant exactly what I wanted it to mean. It was serendipitous.

I also included songs by Randy Newman, Harry Nilsson, and Tim Buckley. I picked all the songs. Well, first of all, Randy Newman and I wrote for the same publisher, January Music, and I played on a version of "Just One Smile" [Gene Pitney], so I knew the song very well. I knew all of Randy's songs by the demos I'd get up at the publisher. I knew Randy Newman way before you did, or anybody did. I never met him, but the demos were so wacky, it was just compelling—his voice was so strange, and the whole conception was so strange. I just was really floored by it. So I always wanted to do that song. That was my chance.

By the time we did that album, "Without Her" from Harry Nilsson was my obsessive song. His version. I played it all the time. I could not get sick of it. It was incredible. I wanted to record it, so I had to write another arrangement because, you know . . . 'cause his was fantastic. So I made it into a bossa nova. "Morning Glory" from Tim Buckley. There was just a question of finding a song for Steve [Katz] to sing, so I suggested that to Steve, and he bought it.

ANDREW LOOG OLDHAM: Al Kooper always knew when to hit the road. He knew that 1650 and the Brill Building were still pulling a four-hanky movie over the British Invasion, so he headed west and shacked up on Sunset and wrote himself into the continuing movement of American song. Then, courtesy of Chip Monck, he stopped off and grabbed a piece of the Monterey Pop Festival. Thus re-engaged, he headed back east and formed and scored with Blood, Sweat and Tears, whilst holding down an A&R and staff producer gig his mum must have been proud of with Clive at the Black Rock. Let us not forget his A&R championing of the Zombies in 1968, and the "Time of the Season."

CHRIS HILLMAN: The '67 Monterey International Pop Festival was fabulous. The greatest rock festival ever. I'm sorry—not Woodstock. Not the Isle of Wight. It was Monterey.

In August 1969, I was living in the San Fernando Valley, in a house with Gram Parsons. The news came on about Woodstock. I said to Gram, "That's no Monterey!" And it wasn't. We were almost chuckling. I'm not denigrating it or putting it down. Monterey was the best.

Also, on the other side of the coin, I've always felt that 1969 was the turning point—when it got edgy. Meaning, it got a little dark. Here's the point. In '67, I was playing Monterey. In 1968, McGuinn and I [the Byrds] did a fundraiser for Robert F. Kennedy in downtown at the L.A. Sports Arena, when he was running in the California primary, just a couple of months before he died. This is when things really changed. Then, in 1969, I played Altamont. My God. Within a couple-year period.

JERRY WEXLER: I went to Monterey, and in 1969, I got the rights to the Woodstock soundtrack that came out on our Cotillion label, a subsidiary of Atlantic. There was a lawyer named Paul Marshall who used to be our in-house council, but we parted ways. Nevertheless, he called me up. "Listen. Are you interested in Woodstock?" It was going to take place in two weeks. Who the hell knew what Woodstock was going to be? He said I could have the rights for $7,000. I thought about it, and bought it for seven grand. I figured, seven grand? Let me take a shot. And that was it. I should have grabbed the film rights, too, but Warner got them. Thank God I bought Woodstock.

David Crosby and Jim McGuinn of the Byrds performing at the CAFF (California Action for Fact and Freedom) benefit concert at Valley Music Theater in Woodland Hills, California, 1967.

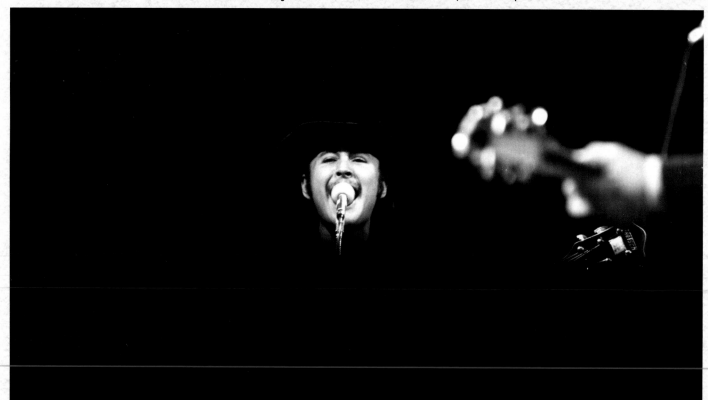

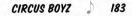
ROSEMARIE AND CRITTER WENT TO THE SHOW

DONOVAN: The Hollywood Bowl, in 1967, was divine for my music. I filled the place up twice. Open to the stars, I was creating the Ritual Donovan. That was when I was titled "the Prince of Flower Power." The teachings of the masters of the ages. I channeled into the new youth millions, as my service this incarnation was poet and rock shaman. The Hollywood Bowl was the launch of the mission that George Harrison and I would take on, more than any of our brothers and sisters of the music fraternity.

The album *Donovan in Concert* in

1968 was recorded at the Anaheim Convention Center. I had my little wonder band, so Mickie [Most] and I recorded it. Probably one of the first few live concert albums of the late sixties. I did "Saturday Night," a rare song, and with Harold McNair on flute, we performed some of the gentle nature ballads and children's fantasy songs. I remember that I was pioneering so many things taken for granted now, like good sound systems and lighting, and real security.

Donovan at a KHJ Appreciation Concert at the Hollywood Bowl, 1966.

In 1967, Jim McGuinn changed his name to Roger McGuinn at the suggestion of a guru in Indonesia who mentioned that a new name would vibrate better with the universe. McGuinn, a sci-fi fan who was also into gadgets, chose Roger because it was used to signal "okay" in radio messages.

That year, the Byrds landed on the charts again with "Eight Miles High." No song seemed more emblematic of the "Summer of Love," with its mosaic of enigmatic words and trippy dissonance. Next to the Beatles' "Tomorrow Never Knows," it was the perfect record to relax with and float downstream.

CHRIS HILLMAN: Engineer Dave Hassinger did a version of "Eight Miles High" and got a little more of an edgy feel. The fact that this was the first time the Byrds had stepped away from the Columbia embryonic building . . . it's very hard to tell the difference [between] the "Eight Miles High" versions, but the one we did at RCA had a little bit more edge because we felt a little freer, and we hit a homer with it.

Then Columbia said, "We will not accept this because it was not recorded at our studio." In those days, that was the law. Recording in Hollywood then, and at

our age at the time, and not being aware personally . . . I didn't think about the environment being an influence. A studio was good anywhere. I didn't care about the technical part if it was a comfortable place to work, and the engineer was quick and got sounds that were good. But it was in Hollywood at RCA, where the Stones did their albums from 1964 to '66. So when you came to record in those days, you didn't go to Santa Monica or the San Fernando Valley. You went to Hollywood. That's where the studios were.

ROGER McGUINN: We were on the road, and I had bought a Phillips cassette recorder in London. It was such a new invention at the time that there were no prerecorded cassettes on the market, but I had a couple of blanks that I picked up. We stopped somewhere in the Midwest—Crosby knew somebody there. So we went over to this guy's house, and he had the latest Ravi Shankar and [Coltrane's] *Africa/Brass*. I dubbed that on one side of the cassette, and Ravi Shankar on the other. We strapped the cassette player to a Fender amp on the bus, and we just kept turning the cassette over and over and listened to that thing for a month on the road. We loved that music, which influenced "Eight Miles High" later.

The break on "Eight Miles High" was a deliberate attempt to emulate John Coltrane, like sort of a tribute to him, if you will. We had heard Ravi Shankar earlier. I had a physical response to that Coltrane album the first time I heard it. It felt like a white-hot poker was searing through my chest. It cut deep into me, and it was a little painful. But I loved it. It just opened up some areas in my heart and head that I hadn't known about.

CHRIS HILLMAN: Roger and I wrote "So You Want to Be a Rock 'n' Roll Star" at my house in Laurel Canyon in late 1966. He lived over the canyon, and I called him up. I said, "I got a song," and asked him to come over. Part of the bridge to that song was influenced from his working with Miriam Makeba. Hugh Masekela would later play trumpet on that recording session.

I really started writing songs after Crosby and I were on a Hugh Masekela session that he was doing with this South African gal, Letta Mbulu. A wonder singer. All the musicians were South African, with the exception of [percussionist] Big Black. I played bass on a demo session. Such warm, loving people. There was a great piano player named Cecil Bernard. Very inspirational.

Doing the Masekela sessions for, I believe, two days, got me going. "Time Between" was the first song I wrote after coming home from the session the first night. "Have You Seen Her Face" was inspired by a blind date Crosby set me up with, and probably other young ladies I had met.

Then we had Clarence White come in and play on *Younger Than Yesterday.* David was a good rhythm guitarist. Roger was a great collaborator. He could write songs with myself, Gene [Clark], and David.

KIRK SILSBEE: Most AM radio jocks of the 1960s used airtime to cultivate their own images between records; very few put the music first. Foremost among the latter was B.

Mitchell Reed. He was what Jerry Wexler would have called "a herald and an enunciator of the new music."

As part of Chuck Blore's original "Seven Swingin' Gentlemen" of the wildly successful Color Radio format on KFWB, Reed spun jazz and Sinatra along with the pop of the day, from 1958 to early 1963. Returning to his native New York during the first shots of the British Invasion, Mitch—Burton Mitchell Goldberg, to his mother—became a WMCA Good Guy. But he returned to KFWB in 1965, catching the exploding Hollywood Renaissance of Love, Byrds, Springfield, Doors, Spirit, Sweetwater, et al.

On his show, *The Wide Wide Weird World of BMR,* Reed dipped into album cuts, premiered *Strange Days* by the Doors in its entirety, programmed special Dylan and Stones shows, interviewed the Strawberry Alarm Clock, routinely played all of the Who records before any other L.A. programmer, gave us tasty curveballs like Yaphet Kotto's "Have You Ever Seen the Blues," and announced the David Crosby/Stephen Stills alliance called the Frozen Noses. Between cuts, Reed got Crosby to explain his dissatisfaction with the mix on "Lady Friend," peeled back the layers of Paul Simon's lyrics to "Fakin' It," gave a sly nod to Cass Elliot's bare-ass centerfold in *Cheetah,* invoked Sir Thomas Beecham after the sublime string

The Byrds and Hugh Masekela performing at the KFRC Fantasy Faire and Magic Mountain Music Festival at Mt. Tamalpais, 1967.

ending to "How Can I Be Sure" by the Rascals, and applauded a student walk-out at Marshall High over a cancelled Sunshine Company appearance. In the context of his show, Reed could make ad copy sound hip.

He was the one AM DJ who made the transition to the underground FM format with his legendary stints at KPPC and KMET. There, he continued to point the way as he programmed and commented. It was guerilla musicology, with Mitch dropping gems like, "Show me a blues man, and I'll show you a train song in his past."

One of his loyal listeners, Rich Tuskewicz of Inglewood, recalls the day that Reed died, in 1983: "I felt like I lost a friend that day. Listening to him always made me feel like I was just so aware of what was happening." To his listeners, BMR meant "Better Music Radio."

In October of 1967, the Doors released their second album, Strange Days. *Expectations were high, and the competition stiff—particularly from one of their own stablemates.*

RAY MANZAREK: Jim got his chops together. By then, he could sing, man. That throat had opened up, and that man was singing.

Doug Lubahn is the studio bassist on the album. Doug and I worked very closely together. I showed him what I wanted on the bass parts, and he would play it and improvise on what I had shown him and expand upon it. He was adding his own little touch to it that made it extra exciting for all of us to be there. He was just a great stoner/hippie/good guy.

I knew Jim was a great poet. There's no doubt about that. See, that's why we put the band together in the first place. It was going to be poetry, together with rock 'n' roll. Not like poetry and jazz. Or, like, it was poetry and jazz from the fifties, except we were doing poetry and rock 'n' roll. Our version of rock 'n' roll was whatever you could bring to the table. Robby, bring your flamenco guitar. Robby, bring that bottleneck guitar; bring that sitar tuning. John, bring your marching drums, and your snares, and your four-on-the-floor. Ray, bring your classical training, and your blues training, and your jazz training. Jim, bring your Southern Gothic poetry, your Arthur Rimbaud poetry. It all works in rock 'n' roll.

JOHN DENSMORE: I noticed that, with Elvin Jones and John Coltrane, there was communication. So I thought, "I'm gonna keep the beat. That's our job as drummers. But I'm gonna try and talk to Jim during the music." Like "When the Music's Over." That's Elvin. I knew I wasn't playing jazz.

At Valley State College, one of the ethnological music instructors was Fred Katz, who was the cello player for the Chico Hamilton jazz quintet. I saw Chico at the Lighthouse and stole one of his cymbal things, [which] I used in "The End."

I wasn't thinking cinematic, but certainly Ray and Jim, coming out of the UCLA Film School, were cinematic dudes. That's for sure. I mean, I hear the world; filmmakers see it.

Then came Love's Forever Changes, *released in November 1967. Dark, brooding, and pensive, it sent a shiver through pop music's consciousness. Hailed for its creative daring, it was thus doomed to cult classic status.*

JOHNNY ECHOLS: We started with kind of an idea, after hearing the Beatles' *Sgt. Pepper's.* We decided that we wanted to do something that had horns and strings. We knew, from the very start, how this album was going to be the thing that defined us. It was either that we were gonna take off and just go all the way, or something was gonna have to happen. We were getting bored of the three-minute rock tune, and wanted to push it.

We knew with *Sgt. Pepper's* that there was a whole new sonic thing going on. Absolutely. The material and concepts of an outline for it were written before we went into the studio. Arthur was not very much of a guitar player. He could play a few chords and basically would sing the songs to me, play the outline of them. Then I would get together with Kenny, and we would work out some structure for the song. Bryan had a way, kind of a counterpoint that he would do with his finger picking, that would work against what we were playing. We would always have the rehearsals with Kenny and me first, and then Michael Stuart. We would rehearse with acoustic instruments, sometimes at a friend of ours, Joe Clark's house in the Valley. Or sometimes we would rehearse in the daytime at the Whisky.

BRYAN MACLEAN: When I was growing up, my mother was an exquisitely beautiful, talented artist who also studied flamenco. I would be doing my homework, and she would be doing her castanets. In the midst of that, I had that influence. I think "Alone Again Or" was like the third or second song I wrote.

Forever Changes, to me, is astonishing. I mean, nobody planned anything. We were kind of caught, and I don't want to oversimplify and say it was just because we were at the right place at the right time. But it was, in a sense, so perfect, you know, for any kind of clean slate. In other words, if you wanted to initiate something, that was the perfect time to innovate. In that point of time, it was very open, and what we did was straight off the press. I was into Rogers and Hammerstein and Lerner and Loewe.

Love was a pure, unmitigated expression of exactly what was going on. We weren't posturing. We weren't trying to prove anything. What you saw was exactly what you got.

JOHNNY ECHOLS: Arthur was writing some absolutely phenomenal lyrics. I was knocked on my ass, because I'm expecting the pedestrian, the same old stuff that I'd heard before. Then I start reading these lyrics, and this isn't the Arthur I know—a dude that I'd fought and wrestled to the ground. This was a poet. I am listening to this poetry, and it was absolutely shocking, because it just came out of fuckin' nowhere. It was only for this brief

Poster for a fundraiser for Robert F. Kennedy at the L.A. Sports Arena, 1968.

period of time.

Forever Changes could only happen in L.A., and could only happen at that particular point in time, because you had that cosmopolitan freedom; you didn't have people put into little categories and boxes. You could hear blues one night, and go hear rock and go hear experimental or avant garde jazz, or whatever. If you listened to the radio then, the DJs were playing Herb Alpert and the Tijuana Brass, Dick Dale, and Frank Sinatra, all on the same radio station. So you were exposed to whole different genres.

During the recording, there was a mutiny going on. Bryan wanted more of his songs on the album. Initially, *Forever Changes* was meant to be a two-album set. Then, towards the time to get to the studio, Jac Holzman said, "No, we can't afford it." They were gonna do another album right behind it. Everybody was upset that we had worked on all of this music, and now we're not using it. Elektra booked the studio and said, "We'll bring in the Wrecking Crew, and they'll play the music." So that's what they did. They played for maybe less than ten minutes, and we knew that it just could not work. So those dudes were asked to go, and the only ones that stayed were Carol Kaye, Don Randi, Jim Gordon, and Hal Blaine, who played the drums on one song. Carole played on one song, and Don Randi played with us on a couple of songs—"Bummer in the Summer," and I think "Old Man." That was it.

See, this was the weird thing. We didn't know for certain that Elektra was gonna come through, because they didn't come through with the double album thing. We're basically playing in the dark, and kept leaving room for imaginary strings and imaginary horns. So we're doing this all in our head, and no charts or anything. "How will this sound if there isn't a horn?" I don't think anybody has recorded a record like that.

John Fleck and Michael Stewart were different players. Michael is one of the finest drummers on this planet. He just knew exactly what to play. He's a percussionist, but a deft percussionist. He's not one playing all over the solo. [Don] Conka was one of the finest drummers I've ever known, but he could not have played *Forever Changes* because he did not have the light touch Michael Stewart had.

The magic of *Forever Changes* is that it is unexpected. It just came all of a sudden, like the atom bomb. You are dealing with regular TNT explosions, and all of a sudden you've got an atomic bomb. It just pushed the envelope so far outside of the mainstream that it took a while. Now, if it had been released in the last few years, it would have done a whole, whole lot better commercially, 'cause people are ready for that. But back then, people were just kind of stunned. Everything was just different—the way the horns were done, the way the jazz was blended in with folk music, blended in with kind of show tunes and rock 'n' roll—but also because of the times we were living in. We had the civil rights movement. We had the Vietnam War. There were assassinations. Martin Luther King Jr. in Memphis. Robert F. Kennedy in Los Angeles. So there, we got a rose coming out of all this shit, and it is blooming. It is kind of permeating the air with sweetness.

SANDY ROBERTSON: When I first heard Love's "Alone Again Or," I thought I'd put on a Herb Alpert record by mistake. Love were so different—an acquired taste worth persevering with. When you "got" them, you wondered why it took your ears so long, why nobody else could blend elements alchemically like they could. Decades later, only the Stalk-Forrest Group album comes close.

When I heard the solo on "Your Mind and We Belong Together," it was a revelation. On that one song, he did what the heavy metal dudes aspired to, not only several years ahead in time but light years ahead in raw passion; the sort of mad intensity Ron Asheton would bring

to the Stooges comes to mind. That he could make it fit into the unlikely setting of Arthur's graceful music shows he was an essential component of the Love template of stylistic fragmentation within single tunes. That's only one song, only one of the styles he could play! Johnny Echols—wow!

BRUCE BOTNICK: I'll say I had to fight for Bryan to be heard, because I recognized the songwriting ability.

Arthur was Arthur, and that's the way it was. But he did recognize the songs, and as you know, he sang quite a few of Bryan's songs. Because his ego would not allow there to be two singers in the band. He allowed Bryan one or two, like "Old Man," that Bryan sang. But I loved Bryan. I thought he was very sensitive, and he was a perfect foil for Arthur and the ying and the yang of the songwriting. I really think that's what really made the band. It's sort of like Jagger and Richards. They had two different approaches, but when put together, it was beautiful.

I produced *Forever Changes* and then had a fight with Arthur. I called Jac [Holzman]. There was a point where Arthur had basically imposed his will so physically upon the band that they couldn't move without his telling them what to do, and they didn't have any confidence. When we went into the studio, they couldn't play. I made a decision. I called Jac up and said, "This is what I want to do," and he said, "I support you. Let's see what happens." He had worked with the Wrecking Crew.

On the two songs the Wrecking Crew did, Arthur told everybody what to play. All the parts. They didn't make it up. The band wasn't that creative. The guys in Love, when this was going down, they were terrifically upset about it. They came to me and said, "Can we have another chance? We'll get our act together." And they did. That's when we recorded the rest of the album.

It's the songs. They are wonderful. Listen to the melodies and the words. Even today, when I listen to it, I am amazed by it. It's sort of like I almost don't remember being there. I do remember all the recording, the overdubbing, and where we did it. Doing some vocals at Leon Russell's house—things like that. I think I did the whole album for, like, $12,000.

CHAPTER 20

UP, UP, AND ALL THE WAY

BONES HOWE: On January 1, 1967, I made up my mind to be a record producer and stop being a drummer and engineer for hire. Lou got angry with me—until I had a number-one hit record with "Windy."

Jimmy Yester of the Association gave me a reel of tape by songwriter Ruthann Friedman . . . must have been twenty songs on it. I was a studio guy, and the production was a lot of it for me. Any live performance was just a recreation. The record, to me, was how you heard it on the car radio. "Windy" was cut on four-track. I tried to find the things I loved about a song, and enhanced them. It was percussive in nature. The bass part on "Windy" is partially percussion; a marimba is in there. I'm sure the complex harmonies that ended up in the records I made were because of my jazz upbringing. I always loved the sound of those kind of chords, whether they were horns playing or people singing.

I was also a musician. I was playing at the time and doing all these different things. I played on the Grass Roots' "Where Were You When I Needed You." They ended up using the demo version. I offered the Association "MacArthur Park" from Jimmy Webb, and they passed.

Johnny Rivers had fallen hard for the 5th Dimension, a vocal ensemble of Marilyn McCoo, Billy Davis Jr., Florence LaRue, Lamonte McLemore, and Ron Townson, once named the Hi-Fi's, and then the Versatiles. Rivers signed them to his Soul City label, distributed by Imperial Records. Rivers also contracted songwriter Jimmy Webb to

his music publishing house. With Rivers producing, Bones Howe behind the board, and those seamless voices giving lift to Webb's artful melody and words, it was a sweet deal for all of them.

JIMMY WEBB: I was a kid out of Oklahoma who headed to Hollywood to become a songwriter. My heroes were Burt Bacharach, Vaughan Williams—ah, *The Lark Ascending*—and Johnny Mercer. My dad, a hard-down military man who spoke one syllable at a time, gave me forty bucks and wished me luck. Even though the Beatles had turned the music world upside down by writing their own songs, I knew there was still a place for me. They used strings. Buddy Holly used strings. Leiber and Stoller used strings. I wrote those kind of songs.

I walked in off the street to Motown's Jobete publishers in Hollywood with a bunch of songs I knew were good. The receptionist laughed—"Honey, you know you're at Motown, don't you?" "Yes, ma'am." She gave my tape to a fella who actually listened to it while I sat in reception. He called me in, and I was suddenly, incomprehensibly, a professional songwriter! They paid me forty-five dollars a song—big money. It was a great education. Even the Supremes covered one of my tunes. Johnny Rivers bought my contract out for $15,000, which he subsequently deducted from my publishing monies. All part of an education. Johnny recognized hits, had great ears, and insisted my release from Motown included "By the Time I Get to Phoenix," "Up, Up and Away," and "Didn't We."

"Up, Up and Away" was written to be the theme to

Opposite: **The 5th Dimension with Bones Howe (*center*) and Jimmy Webb (*right*) at Western Recorders, Hollywood, 1967.**

a throwaway teen movie, like one of those beach blanket flicks. A movie producer wanted to do something similar, but make it all about balloons . . . only in Hollywood. He asked me to write a little theme tune, and I just went with it. Sometimes a balloon is simply a balloon. I stole the opening from the Association's "Along Comes Mary," almost note for note.

BONES HOWE: Johnny Rivers asked me if I would be interested in producing the next 5th Dimension album. "Yeah!" But, first thing, I'm to do an album with Jimmy Webb called *The Magic Garden*. "He wants to do a big orchestra." "If you're willing to pay for it, I know what to do. We will go into the big studio at United and record together."

When work began on the 5th Dimension album, Rivers suggested they cover "Go Where You Wanna Go." Howe selected "Paper Cup" and "Carpet Man" by Webb, as well as scripture from the Laura Nyro songbook, including "Wedding Bell Blues," "Stoned Soul Picnic," "Sweet Blindness," and "Save the Country."

Jimmy Webb, Hollywood, 1968.

The 5th Dimension at KHJ's Appreciation Concert for the United Negro College Fund at the Hollywood Bowl, 1967.

The Association at a recording session
at Western Recorders, Hollywood, 1968.

BONES HOWE: I was actively working with music publishers. I found Neil Sedaka's "Puppet Man" and "Wor-
kin' On a Groovy Thing," and "California Soul" by Val-
erie Simpson and Nickolas Ashford.

From one record to the next, I began to find things
that could get played on the radio. Jimmy would sit down
at the piano and play his songs live, with these beautiful
harmonies. There were no demos. He was the hippest
songwriter in town. All of his songs have major sev-
enths and major ninths and elevenths—all those altered
chords, like you find in jazz. So that was what I thought
was very attractive. He also wrote beautiful melodies.
Suddenly, here is a guy doing all these hip chord changes
in a pop song. Somebody once introduced themselves to
me and said, "You're Bones Howe. You work with Jimmy
Webb." "Yes." "How does he sleep with all that music in
his head?"

I heard Laura Nyro's "Wedding Bell Blues" on KHJ
radio, because Bill Drake, the RKO programmer, liked
the record. Then I saw Laura at the Monterey Pop Festival in 1967. I mixed the Association and Mamas and the
Papas live sets. I thought Laura was amazing, and it was
almost jazz, what she was doing. Laura was different. She
had some L.A. studio musicians with her at Monterey,

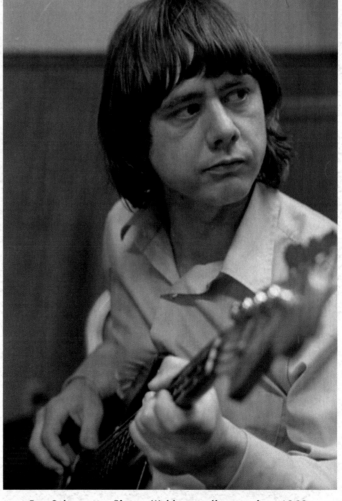

Joe Osborn at a Jimmy Webb recording session, 1968.

IT CAME FROM BURBANK

DAVE DIAMOND: L.A. AM radio, from 1965 to 1968, was very competitive. DJs hardly spoke to each other, even on the same station. Casey Kasem was really nice. Don Steele was hard to get to know, but I liked him.

I went to Martoni's, a restaurant, bar, and watering hole for the music and record business where people went to be seen. It was actually the place where Sonny Bono and Cher, in 1965, were asked to leave one night by one of the owners because of his wardrobe. Sonny then wrote about the incident in "Laugh at Me." That became a big hit.

Martoni's was the place where Sal the bartender told me that DJ Tom Donahue in San Francisco was listening to my free-form shift on the radio in early 1966, when KBLA first started, as he was readying FM. Somebody had told him in town that "Dave Diamond has taken a completely different direction than all the other radio stations in L.A., and he's creating a sensation." I heard it from several people that "Donahue has been down here, listening to you." Then I hear about him going to San Francisco and taking credit for starting it. That really pissed me off.

KRLA DJs like Reb Foster told me, "I love listening to it, but I'd

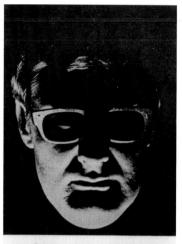

DAVE DIAMOND

Above: **Dave Diamond sticker.**
Below: **The Seeds' *A Web of Sound* LP cover, 1966.**

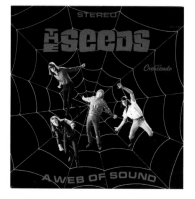

The Real Don Steele riding a camel for a KHJ promotion, Hollywood, 1969.

never let you do that on my station." Everybody else said, "I'd never let him do that." Shit, I started showing up in the ratings and beat them.

When I did radio, I thought it had to be exciting. Very exciting, and very well-produced. The music had to be hard-driving. I liked ballads, too. It just had to turn me on. FM radio, out here in late 1966, '67, and '68 . . . I had already done it on KBLA, introducing free-form radio and programming album cuts. Man, I played the Seeds' *A Web of Sound* LP, and the long track, "Up in Her Room." Then everybody later started doing it, and I thought they were really phony.

Then KBLA decided to go country in June of 1967. I had a two-and-a-half-year contract, and the company that was buying the station didn't want to pay me off. So Bruce Wendell called me in one day and said, "Hey, this station has been sold. They're going to go country. I don't know what is going to happen." He took me back to the record library, opened it up, gave me the key, and said, "It's all yours, buddy."

I had to pay my rent. Bill Drake brought me up to KFRC in San Francisco, from 1968 to 1971. Drake came to me just as my brand new shift at KFWB folded. My phone rang. "Are you interested in San Francisco?" So I grabbed it. I didn't have any offers. L.A. is a nasty town when you are out of work. Just awful. Bill offered me a nice deal there, and a contract, and I took it. I was number one there, and the station was number one. I brought some of L.A. to San Francisco. Drake had a different playlist in San Francisco than he did anywhere else. I just wasn't tempted to go on FM and do what I'd already done. I was back in town on KRLA in 1971.

like Hal Blaine, who also worked with Johnny Rivers. R & B radio stations played her song "Stoned Soul Picnic," that I also did with the 5th Dimension at Wally Heider's studio. It was a number-one R & B hit. I kept exploring the Nyro and Webb mines. I kept finding stuff I loved, and it got easier when we got rolling on it.

On "Stoned Soul Picnic," we had complex five-part harmonies. I'm a big believer in using as few microphones as possible for singers. I wanted Marilyn as the lead on the later singles, and Bill was the lead on most of the 5th's albums. He had some Wilson Pickett in his voice that made him unique.

"One Less Bell to Answer" was a number-one record. It's a Burt Bacharach and Hal David composition that was initially done by Keely Smith.

Hal Blaine was on everything, and Joe Osborn . . . I discovered Joe doing those Johnny Rivers records with Lou Adler. Mickey Jones was the drummer on the first Rivers sessions, and Joe Osborn. He played the bass the way I thought, as a jazz player, rock 'n' roll players should play the bass. Joe and Hal, together, really had the lock

and the feel. Then Dennis Budimir and Tommy Tedesco—jazz guys on guitar.

That's kind of how I built a rhythm section. A lot of it was conversation. I always started my session in the room. The lead sheets would go out, but I always started with the guys and stood out there with them as they ran the first tune. I hated the disembodied voice that came from the control room to the floor, telling everybody what to do.

The 5th Dimension were in New York, and somebody had given them tickets to see the show *Hair*. They told me about an amazing song called "Aquarius." "We can do that song, and it will be a big hit." I listened to the song, and felt it wasn't a whole song. I went to New York with my wife, Melodie, and we went to see *Hair*. I'm watching this thing unfold, and I realize "Aquarius" is simply an introduction to the show. It doesn't go anywhere. Then "The Flesh Failures (Let the Sunshine In)" begins—a downer of a song, talking about civilization going to hell. But then there's the chorus, with three bars being repeated. "Oh, shit! That's how we do it."

FROM BRITAIN, WITH LOVE

LORD TIM HUDSON: Oh, Dave Diamond was brilliant! *The Diamond Mine* made him the hottest DJ in the country. Humble Harve was great, too. All of these people were characters! It was a moment in time when you had all of these great radio personalities. Then they squashed the great characters and gave all of the power to management. That allowed the FM stations to flourish, and the DJs on those stations didn't have any personality.

How did I get into radio? I was in London, working with the Moody Blues. I went to a party, and on one couch was B. Mitchell Reed, James Coburn, and Pete Kameron [former Weavers road manager and future Who road manager, responsible for sending advance Who acetates to BMR]. I asked BMR to send me some R & B records for the Stones, because they weren't writing much of anything yet. He sent me "Go Now" by Bessie Banks, and it took about twenty-four hours to turn that into a Moody Blues record. I still

love that record.

Anyway, James Coburn said, "We need an English DJ in America!" I was in Montreal, and Lee Bartel called me to go on the air at KCBQ in San Diego. Then the Beatles invited me to go on their '65 tour with them. When I was in Hollywood, an agent named Seymour took me to all of the radio stations: KHJ, KRLA, KFWB, and KBLA, too! At KFWB, they said, "You'll be the first million dollar DJ!"

BMR was the Steve McQueen of radio. He mentored me. My boss at KFWB was Bill Wheatley, and the worst thing he did was take Mitch off the nighttime roster and move him to the morning slot. He wasn't a morning person at all. I was the hot young kid on the block. With the two of us on at night, back-to-back, it would have been incredible! The DJs on those stations didn't have any personality, but AM radio was a great training ground.

JAMES BROWN! Sports Arena: Jan. 1

"MR. DYNAMITE" IN ACTION! — The explosive James Brown, enjoying the biggest year of his career, will ignite 1966 with a New Year's Day concert at L.A. Sports Arena. Above, he sets off sparks of laughter with Magnificent Montague and Hunter Hancock, popular disk jockeys at KGFJ, the radio station sponsoring event.

Rhythm 'n' News article about an upcoming James Brown concert at the Los Angeles Sports Arena, 1966.

But I couldn't do this until I got permission from the music publisher. I went to United Artists, who had the copyright. I played the two things for the 5th Dimension and told them we'll do the chorus at the end.

I also had Bob Alcivar, a vocal arranger, on the team. We worked closely together. Bob would sit at the piano with each member and teach them their part—a huge asset. I couldn't go forward with any song until he figured out what key would be best for each singer.

On "Aquarius," Alcivar exclaimed, "They're in different keys! How are we going to get these things together?" "We're gonna hook them together like two trains. We will record them separately, and I will find a way to put them together, with Hal Blaine on drums." I mixed it and put it together. We put strings and horns and stuff on it, and put it together. It was more like building and architecture.

One time, I'm sitting at Martoni's, and RKO radio programmer Bill Drake walks up to the booth. "You know, the Soul City label sent me a copy of your new record with the 5th Dimension's 'Aquarius.'" "What do you think of it, Bill?" "You know something? It's a hit, but it's too long." Think of a DJ sitting there and waiting for the hour straight up. He's got two and a half minutes to put something in before he goes straight to the Coppertone commercial. He's got to pick something out of the rack to stick in. They sequence their own shows. Bill said, "If there is any way you can get me a short version of it, I'd put it right on the air."

I finished my dinner, went back to the studio, and cut a 2:39 version of

Charles Wright and the Watts 103rd Street Rhythm Band, Los Angeles, 1969.

it. It was under three minutes. The next day, I went to the promo guy at Soul City. I had acetates of it. "This is the next 5th Dimension hit." It was on the radio the next day.

I did what Bill asked me to do, and he did what he said he would do. That was how close the music people were to the radio station. You didn't have to go through the whole screening at KRLA. Basically, KRLA was just listening to KHJ to see what to put on.

KIM FOWLEY: "Magnificent Montague" ruled KGFJ from 1965 to 1970. He spun it all: Percy Mayfield, Lou Rawls, Sam Cooke, Patti Drew, the Rivingtons, Gloria Jones, Dusty Springfield, the Flirtations, Sandie Shaw, the Rascals, Barbara Lewis, Roy Hamilton, the Valentinos, Bobby Womack, Brenton Wood, James Brown, Earl Dean Smith, the Impressions, Rotary Connection, Pat and Lolly Vegas, the Packers, Eric Burdon and War, the Googie Rene Combo, Bill Withers, and Charles Wright and the Watts 103rd Street Rhythm Band. His playlist had Dobie Gray's "On the Dance Floor," "Dr. Love" by Bobby Sheen, "Oo Wee Baby" from Fred Hughes, "The Bells" by the Young Hearts, and Bob and Earl's "Harlem Shuffle." Plus the Vee-Jay, Duke/Peacock, Sue, Chess, Kent, Philles, Soul, Imperial, Motown, and Stax labels.

Tom Reed was also on KGFJ. You could still hear, in the nearby Inland Empire area, all the L.A. R & B and pop music radio stations out in Pomona and Riverside—including KMEN, the AM radio station John Peel was on in 1964. [That was] right before he brought the new sounds of Southern California to England, a period just after he came out west from Dallas, Texas. I later produced a Gene Vincent album for his Dandelion label.

I was a DJ on KPPC, the Pasadena-based hip radio station, in late 1967 for one seventy-two-hour period over a weekend, but got axed because I played an Otis Redding campaign song for 1968 Democratic presidential candidate Hubert Humphrey. It was "The Huckle-Buck" with Hubert Humphrey lyrics. I also programmed Country Joe and the Fish's "I-Feel-Like-I'm-Fixin'-to-Die Rag" right afterwards. Back to back. The program director fired me on the spot. "Leave the building, now!" I then gave the address of the radio station over the airwaves, and a thousand kids showed up in the parking lot to party and support me.

Radio formats, until the beginning of FM radio, would play anything good. Then FM radio came along and messed it up, the same way *Downbeat* magazine messed up jazz. The critics showed up. A bit later, in 1968, *Rolling Stone* magazine showed up, and all of a sudden had to put an intellectual meaning and enforce a culture on something that was supposed to be wild, crazy, fun, and illuminating.

The standard of music was amazing, and everyone was under thirty years of age. FM radio became more prominent, with playlists broadcasting albums instead of singles that AM stations programmed. There was a window, through 1967, where Peanut Butter Conspiracy was on playlists with the Beatles. But there were so many bands, and the brain cannot comprehend and absorb it all, and if you were sixteen years old then, you didn't have money to buy thousands of records every week. So, a lot of people just got lost in the shuffle that were wonderful.

KIRK SILSBEE: One day in December 1966, the visionary composer and producer David Axelrod was driving to the Capitol Tower on Vine Street for a recording date. His radio was tuned to KGFJ, and Axelrod heard the Magnificent Montague cue one of his latest productions: "Mercy, Mercy, Mercy" by the Cannonball Adderley Quintet. He was initially tickled that a jazz cut was getting AM radio attention. Pianist Joe Zawinul's compelling, funky blues changes on an electric piano in front of an appreciative audience made for a natural turntable hit. But Axelrod's gratification turned to annoyance, then horror, as Montague programmed the record no less than seven times in a row.

"The major labels were terrified of payola," Axelrod would later explain. Stopping at a pay phone, he called the station, desperate to get Montague on the line. "Man—lighten up!" Axelrod loved the airplay, but seven times in a row? "People are gonna think some weird shit is goin' down, and Capitol can't sit still for that," he told Montague. The DJ was always open to quid pro quo arrangements concerning records, but this one was a freebie; he genuinely loved "Mercy, Mercy, Mercy."

A year later, Axelrod would write and produce one of the first conceptual rock albums: the Electric Prunes' *Mass in F Minor*, followed by his own *Songs of Innocence*. The rock audience didn't quite know what to do with the former, but the latter birthed the fusion genre, mixing jazz, rock, soul, and classical forms. Van Dyke Parks responded with his ambitious *Song Cycle* before John Tartaglia and Michel Colombier followed suit. *Songs of Innocence* and its successor, *Songs of Experience*, not only opened a horizon of sonic possibilities, but later provided pastures of plenty for electronic plunder by hip-hop auteurs.

RUSS REGAN: In December of 1966, I went to Uni Records. MCA executive Ned Tanen called me. There was an agent at MCA, John Hyde, who worked on *The Lloyd Thaxton Show*. MCA had the show, and I used to take records to Lloyd, and John Hyde ends up working for Ned Tanen. One day, Lew Wasserman says to Ned, "I want to start a new record label, Universal City Records, to go up against Decca, because Decca is old hat and we got to start something new. Ned, I want you to run it." He's not happy about who is going to be the national promotion man for Uni. John Hyde says, "I know this guy, Russ Regan, who would be a great guy for this." So I met with Ned and John at the old Cock 'n Bull on Sunset Boulevard. Ned Tanen, an hour and a half later, says, "You're hired. You want the job, you got it."

I was a promotion man for six months, with no hits that were being picked by a group of A&R. Ned then said, "Russ, I think I made a mistake when I brought you here. Lew says I got $100,000 left to get this label off the ground. We've gone through $900,000. Can you do it?"

"Yes. But I have to pick the hits." "You're the new general manager of Uni."

The first record I picked was by the Rainy Daze—"That Acapulco Gold," which Dave Diamond sent to me. It took off, we sold 150,000 copies, and Bill Gavin, in his trade magazine, said it was a high grade of marijuana we were advertising. The record then died a slow death. Dave Diamond then calls me and says, "I have a record they will never figure out." "Send it over." Frank Slay produced it, and brought it to me. I purchased "Incense and Peppermints" for $2,500 by a basically unknown group called Strawberry Alarm Clock. We put it out, and after three weeks, I get a call from Henry Stone, the distributor in Miami. "I just wanted to call you and tell you it's number one in Sarasota, Florida, and if it can be number one here, it can be number one anywhere."

I went to see Bill Drake at his office and said, "Bill, this is make it or break it time for me. This record is number one in Sarasota, Florida. You got to trust me and just put it on KHJ for me. If it doesn't hit in three weeks, take it off." It took off like a rocket ship and became number one near the end of the year—my first million-selling record.

Then came FM radio. In 1966, '67, it was like being a CD manufacturer watching digital downloads come into the picture. "What the hell is going on here? What is this new technology? What is this new distribution system? They are now distributing more music on FM instead of AM radio?"

Bill Drake at Uni Records in West Hollywood, 1969.

HE'S NOT JUST A SESSION MAN ANYMORE

Glen Campbell was born in Billstown, Arkansas, on April 22, 1936, and moved to Los Angeles in 1960 from Albuquerque, New Mexico. His first recording date was a Jerry Fuller song that Sam Cooke recorded. Campbell then inked to a publishing company, American Music, that DJ and music publisher Cliffie Stone oversaw for Gene Autry. He eventually issued his own 45, "Turn Around, Look At Me," which appeared on Dick Clark's *American Bandstand*. Campbell then became a Capitol Records recording artist with a Brian Wilson and Russ Titelman song, "Guess I'm Dumb," produced by Nik Venet. Campbell was Brian Wilson's road replacement on the Beach Boys tours, playing bass in the band after Brian suffered a nervous breakdown in '64. He charted with a cover of Buffy Sainte-Marie's "Universal Soldier," which landed him a booking on *Shindig!* Campbell's stock rose dramatically with the 1967 release of "Gentle on My Mind," a John Hartford song. Wrecking Crew veteran and Capitol Records staff producer/arranger Al De Lory collaborated with Campbell on four Jimmy Webb-penned pop anthems: "By the Time I Get to Phoenix," "Wichita Lineman," "Galveston," and "Where's the Playground Susie."

John Stewart and Glen Campbell on the set of *The Glen Campbell Goodtime Hour*, Los Angeles, 1969.

JIMMY WEBB: Glen Campbell became my voice. I first heard him on a transistor radio while I was riding a tractor in Oklahoma. I was fourteen years old. Ten years later, I'm in a Hollywood recording studio, and he's singing "Wichita Lineman." Go figure. I was one lucky bastard.

GLEN CAMPBELL: Being a studio cat proved a financially rewarding job. Music is the most labeled, segregated, and filed form in the U.S. I was cutting records six and seven years before "Gentle On My Mind" and "By the Time I Get to Phoenix" happened. I was not labeled then.

AL DE LORY: Brian Wilson seemed to have a certain confidence, and he was going for it. I did that on my records, too; I must have got stuff from him and Phil Spector along the way. Brian and Phil did it the way they thought it should be, and I learned to do the same thing. Get good material together, and cut it. Brian was turned on by what he was doing—making the best possible sounds. I got ideas from him and Phil, boldness, in a sense . . . creating that wonderful thing, chart and arrangement, without any pressure or influences.

CHAPTER 21

IT WAS A MELLOW YELLOW YEAR

How quickly the flower children wilted. If 1967 was imbued with the promise of peace and love, 1968 quickly put paid to that utopian fantasy. It was a year riddled with deep hurt, dashed hopes, and social and political upheaval. Musicians were equally flummoxed—"Are we pop stars, or are we artists?" Only their dope dealers knew for sure. That year, as if to acknowledge the search for clarity of purpose, the Doors released Waiting for the Sun.

RAY MANZAREK: "Hello, I Love You" had been around for a while. Jim wrote on the beach when we used to live down in Venice. My wife, Dorothy, would go off to work, and Jim and I would wander over to Muscle Beach. He was gorgeous. Man, he was perfect. He was a guy who had opened the doors of perception and made a blend of the American Indian and the American cowboy.

Somebody, invariably Robby or Jim, would come up with the original idea for a song. But boy, the four of us would get together and change, modify, and polish the songs.

That was a time when we started questioning the government. That was all based on the war in Vietnam. "Why are we in Vietnam? Why are we fighting these people?" "The Unknown Soldier" and "Five to One." "Not to Touch the Earth"—ecology was very, very big. We were all trying to save the planet. The sun was the energy, the supreme energy. The Establishment, as we called it—the squares, as they were called in the fifties—were trying to stop drug use, the smoking of marijuana. They were trying to stop any kind of organic fertilizer. The word "organic," to them, meant hippies, radical potheads, and people who wanted to leave behind the organized religions and start some new tribal religion based on American Indian folklore. That's indeed what we were. We called ourselves "the new tribe." We were working in the future space. By our third album, we were in the future. Many things have come to pass that Jim Morrison wrote about.

In May 1968, Columbia Records released the album Super Session, *featuring Al Kooper, Michael Bloomfield, and Stephen Stills. All three were in a period of transition: Kooper had just been unceremoniously dumped by Blood, Sweat and Tears (a group he started); Bloomfield was hanging around after his stint with the Electric Flag; and Stills had just put the kibosh on Buffalo*

Above: Jim Morrison's handwritten track list for the *Waiting for the Sun* **album, 1968.**
Opposite: Ray Manzarek at the Hollywood Bowl, 1968.

Springfield. Aided and abetted by pianist Barry Goldberg, bassist Harvey Brooks, and drummer "Fast" Eddie Hoh, the trio's Super Session *marked the first time in rock 'n' roll that a jam session earned its wings as a fully realized, let alone best-selling, album project. The album moved 450,000 copies, reaching number eleven in* Billboard. *FM radio jumped on it.*

AL KOOPER: I had no expectations for that record. I mean, just none whatsoever. I just did it because I had a job as a producer, and I had no one to produce. I went in because I thought Michael and I should make a record together, considering how our careers ran parallel, and also because we were friends and it would be fun to work together. Michael brought Eddie Hoh in, and I brought in Harvey Brooks. I said, "You pick the drummer. I'll pick the bass player." Again, sort of like a Blue Note concept.

The most important thing is the playing of the two principals, Bloomfield and Stills. It's timeless. Bloomfield's stuff is some of the greatest blues-playing ever. It was a great period of time, and there were great minds geographically located in the same place. There was a lot of freedom out on the West Coast, but frankly, *Super Session* could have been recorded anywhere.

Also, know that the Columbia studio was a union

shop, so there were breaks every three hours. One time, I was sitting in my car in the parking lot, smoking a joint, and guitarist Jesse Ed Davis knocked on my window. He invited me to a session he was doing with Taj Mahal. I ended up playing organ and piano on a couple of tracks on the Taj Mahal album *The Natch'l Blues*.

After *Super Session*, I then found Shuggie Otis on an album called *Cold Shot* by his father, Johnny, on the Kent label. "God, he plays great!" So I got in touch with Johnny Otis, and I went to his house. Then Don Harris came in during our chat—Shuggie was there—and the three of us played. Johnny played vibes, I played piano, Don played violin, and Shuggie [played] guitar in his living room.

Kooper Session: Al Kooper Introduces Shuggie Otis was subsequently released by Epic Records in 1970. Johnny Otis, who published his first book, Listen to the Lambs, *in 1968, had his own album on Epic,* The Johnny Otis Show Live at Monterey!, *in 1970. Johnny Otis would then produce* Here Comes Shuggie Otis *in 1970, and Shuggie's* Freedom Flight *in 1971.*

The Byrds' fifth album, The Notorious Byrd Brothers, *was released in January of 1968. Producer Gary Usher made extensive use of studio effects, including phasing and flanging techniques, and the album incorporated both pedal steel guitar and Moog synthesizer. Original band member and cofounder Gene Clark, who had split from the outfit in 1966, came back for a month of recording before bailing again. David Crosby was fired in October 1967, and drummer Michael Clarke flew the coop midway through recording and then returned upon completion. The first single from the album was their attempt at the Gerry Goffin and Carole King tune, "Goin' Back."*

ROGER McGUINN: Gary Usher got the tune, brought it to us in the studio, and played it for us as a demo. I didn't know of Carole King, even though I had worked in the Brill Building earlier on. I had never heard of the Goffin/ King songwriting team, but I loved the tune and thought it was really good. Gary explained that these were Tin Pan Alley writers who had just kind of taken a sabbatical and had come back and revamped their style to be more

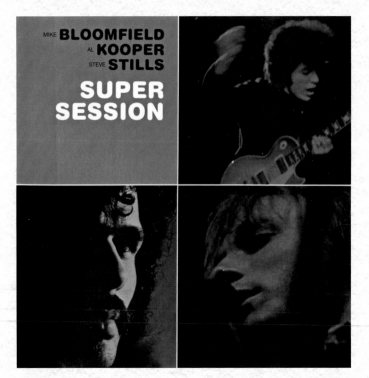

Booklet for the CD reissue of *Super Session*.

Los Angeles Free Press advertisement for Shuggie Otis, 1969.

I HOPE NORTY'S OR ARON'S WILL STOCK IT

On August 30, 1968, the Byrds' *Sweetheart of the Rodeo* long-player hit the record stores. Though it received praise from many critics, who found its warm, down-home feel a soothing respite from the increasing "heaviness" of the rock scene, many fans blanched at the band's embrace of country music, personified by shit-kickin' good old boys in Levis and cowboy shirts—a far cry from the hipster uniform of love beads, granny glasses, and suede boots. At a time of great social and political tumult, the Byrds had become perversely retrograde—or so it would have appeared.

contemporary, like we were doing. So it really fit well, I thought. We learned it and put a kind of dreamy quality into it.

Gary Usher was wonderful, a very creative guy. I really enjoyed our [previous] producer, Terry Melcher, but Gary had some tricks up his sleeve that Terry didn't have, more technological stuff. Terry was more, like, nuts and bolts—get the sound, the big AM radio sound. Gary was more alternative and into experimenting with, like, getting the phase shifter for "Old John Robertson." Chris [Hillman] and I knocked that off "So You Want to Be a Rock 'n' Roll Star" in very late 1966, at his house.

CHRIS HILLMAN: Gary Usher was an incredibly gifted producer to work with, especially at the very end of *The Notorious Byrd Brothers*, when it was just McGuinn and I trying to finish it. Gary worked with us as another band member. Good ideas. I don't have a problem with "Goin' Back." Gary brought in a song that fit us like a glove. It was perfect. It's Roger and I singing lead. It's a little too pretty, but it's okay.

ROGER McGUINN: My idea was very ambitious. It was going to be the origins and the history of music, if you will, from the beginning—the dawn of man up to the present day, incorporating Elizabethan music and how that came over to the Appalachians and got distilled into folk music, country music, rock 'n' roll, and the African blend. It was to cover everything, including jazz, and finally go off into space music and synthesizers and go off the top into the future. But I couldn't get anybody to go along with me, and got outvoted. I thought it would be a nice thing to put in one package and have it all there.

The Byrds had already begun to explore the marriage of country and the rock world. Clarence White added a bluegrass touch, coupled with a rock 'n' roll beat, on "Time Between Us" from their 1966 Younger than Yesterday *LP. He's also on their* The Notorious Byrd Brothers *long-player. Going back to 1965, the Byrds waxed folksy country on "Oh! Susannah" and "Satisfied Mind," a Porter Wagoner song, and brought a bluegrass feel to "Mr. Spaceman." So McGuinn and company weren't introduced,*

let alone steered, to country music by their new recruit, Gram Parsons.

Chris Hillman met Parsons in a bank and invited him to the Byrds' rehearsal room in West Hollywood, a little office space that McGuinn rented.

ROGER McGUINN: We were rehearsing, and Gram came in. There was a keyboard of some kind, and I asked Gram if he could play any McCoy Tyner, because I wanted to continue in the vein of "Eight Miles High" jazz fusion with a Coltrane kind of thing. He sat down and played a little Floyd Cramer-style piano, and I thought, "This guy's got talent. We can work with him." That was my original thought—not knowing that he had another agenda, and that Chris and he were, like, kinda in cahoots and going to sway the whole thing into country music. But I really liked country music. Having come up in folk, I always considered country music, especially Hank Williams and the traditional country music that Gram was into, a part of folk music. So it wasn't alien to me.

I started harmonizing with Gram, and he and I had a good blend. I was getting into it. It was fun. He and I had a lot of fun for a long time, up until he left.

When Sweetheart *was first released, it sounded like something that DJ Tennessee Ernie Ford would have spun in the late fifties on country radio station KMPC. Many Byrds loyalists missed the jangle of McGuinn's Rickenbacker guitar, not appreciating the wholesome beauty of a Martin D-45.*

ROGER McGUINN: Some people were heartbroken, because they didn't hear the Rickenbacker. But those people didn't show up to the gigs. The people we got were into it, and they liked it. There was a fan base that was gonna go along with us, no matter what

Michael Clarke and Chris Hillman at Columbia Records, Hollywood, 1965.

we did. There was nothing like it before.

We all got along great with the musicians in Nashville. I mean, we had cowboy hats and boots. I loved it. We were just role-playing. Even Gram. He wasn't that kind of kid. He was a folkie. He was a preppie. Basically, Gram got turned on to Elvis when he was ten years old, and that changed his life. He wanted to be a rock star,

Roger McGuinn at Columbia Studios in Hollywood, 1965.

which he eventually became. Then he got into country—he got into Buck Owens, and he got into Waylon and Willie. I think what he really wanted to do was get rid of me and get a steel guitar player.

The Byrds doing Dylan continued with *Sweetheart of the Rodeo.* "Nothing Was Delivered" and "You Ain't Goin' Nowhere" were cut. Chris got the demos of those songs in the mail. Dylan, as a songwriter, was so much better than everyone. We had been out of touch for a few years, and it was interesting that at this same period, he was going in the same musical direction we were. Gary Usher, the producer, was amazing when he was doing this. He was a tech head for the time, and very innovative.

CHRIS HILLMAN: *Sweetheart of the Rodeo* is an okay record. Gram brought two great sings to the mix: "One Hundred Years from Now" and "Hickory Wind." Really, two of his greatest songs.

I still think "Time Between" on *Younger Than Yesterday* was our country rock song of the time. That's when we started doing that stuff. We had Clarence White come in and play on *Younger Than Yesterday.* I'm not taking credit for any of that. Rick Nelson deserves credit in the country rock thing, too—big credit, way beyond anybody else. But you know how this business works.

ROGER McGUINN: We didn't have any resistance from the record company when we did *Sweetheart of the Rodeo.* The radio station visits were in the old business model. I don't think we were very welcome to bring *Sweetheart* to radio stations. DJs like B. Mitchell Reed on KMET, who we knew, couldn't play *Sweetheart* on their shows. They had radio restrictions. Even if it was their own personal taste, they weren't going to play it.

CHAPTER 22

MEET ME AT SUNSET AND FAIRFAX

Between 1967 and 1969, a handful of ticketless love-ins were held in Southern California. These peaceful meet-and-greets combined live music, often from unsigned bands, with meditation, frolicking, food, and good vibes in public parks, where smoking was not illegal. The first love-in (a term coined by L.A. radio legend Peter Bergman) took place at Elysian Park during spring 1967; others were held in Griffith Park, where Jefferson Airplane and the Moody Blues performed.

KIM FOWLEY: I was an emcee, and also got to sing and jam with bands when the scheduled musicians got caught in traffic jams, weren't there, or canceled. They would start at 6:00 AM, when Dennis Wilson would show up. Billy Hinsche, from Dino, Desi and Billy, was always there. They were stage hands. There was a group meditation. Some people may have been on LSD. Teenage Allen Ginsberg clones would go, "Ommmm . . ."

There were bands like the Peanut Butter Conspiracy, Clear Light, and Kaleidoscope. Lesser groups, like the Ashes, would all play to mostly disinterested people. The later it got, the better the bands got. It went on to 2:00 AM. Everybody got laid. I got action. There were mattresses under the stairs for the musicians, the crew, and the emcees to have sex with chicks who were naked, running around on acid. There were a lot of great girls, with good teeth that weren't yellow yet from taking penicillin and tetracycline to clear up their acne. I was also booking and calling bands, 'cause I knew park pussy was gonna be there. White chicks in West L.A. drove east of La Brea then, because they were curious.

Cleo Knight was there with Green Power, a sort of hippie food collective that fed everyone. He was genuine. Gypsy Boots was always around. John Carpenter was very important. Great guy. Genius. He was the music editor of the *Los Angeles Free Press*. He had a better brain than Bill Graham, but he just did it for the love of the music and the gathering. Carpenter was the secret weapon, and organized everybody. John supposedly made a deal with the cops. "As long as you guys keep it orderly and you get the kids to pick up the trash at the end of the night, we won't bother you. If you're not doing fornification in public, and there's no drugs, drinking, or fights. Have a good day."

Sometimes there would be a lost dog or a lost kid, or somebody was parked illegally and about to be towed away. That was as severe as it got. I learned crowd control at the love-ins.

ALEX DEL ZOPPO: Our very first public gig as Sweetwater was a huge love-in near the merry-go-round in Griffith Park. We had changed our goal of playing the Whisky after we went to the Monterey International Pop Festival, and decided to strive for those big outdoor events instead.

Our first opportunity for such a thing was a love-in that was going to be big—it was sponsored by the *L.A. Free Press* and a radio station I can't remember. They had full-page ads in the Freep for it, which had Iron Butterfly and Phil Ochs on the bill. They'd already had hits by that time. It was emceed by DJ Elliot Mintz.

Our guru, Harvey Gerst, who hung with all the major peeps at the Troubadour and had written with the Byrds,

Opposite: **Barry McGuire at a Griffith Park love-in, Los Angeles, 1967.**

Left: Sweetwater at a Griffith Park love-in, Los Angeles, 1967.
Right: KPFK DJ and host Elliot Mintz at a Griffith Park love-in, Los Angeles, 1967.

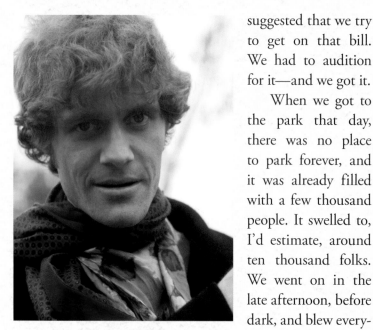

**Kim Fowley at a Griffith Park
love-in, Los Angeles, 1967.**

suggested that we try to get on that bill. We had to audition for it—and we got it.

When we got to the park that day, there was no place to park forever, and it was already filled with a few thousand people. It swelled to, I'd estimate, around ten thousand folks. We went on in the late afternoon, before dark, and blew everyone's mind, mainly because of us being so different in every way from all the other acts. After we played, we got an encore—at our first gig.

Elliot asked if we had management or representation. When we said no, he recommended someone, which eventually led to us signing with our long-time manager, Bruce Glatman.

We played another love-in fairly soon after that, in Elysian Park, which was cool, but didn't seem to be as well-organized. We told [Glatman] that we loved those open-air, free-flowing events, and he steered us to nearly every one that happened circa '67.

We did play the Whisky off and on for a few months, actually—two sets a night, sharpening our chops and gaining a fan base, and eventually getting signed there by Mo Ostin to Reprise when we opened for Janis and Big Brother.

**Concert poster for the Grateful Dead, Jefferson Airplane, and
Canned Heat at the Kaleidoscope in Hollywood, 1967.**

Left: **Cyrus Faryar, Barry McGuire, Renais Faryar, Lynn Taylor, and Fred Williams at a Griffith Park love-in, Los Angeles, 1967.**
Right: **Van Dyke Parks and Phil Ochs at the Renaissance Pleasure Faire, Thousand Oaks, 1967.**

Collage in the window of Lucy's El Adobe Café
in Hollywood, 1968.

HARRY E. NORTHUP: First of all, it was free. They were joyful and wild, and they fed us. There seemed to be one every few weeks. Cleo Knight always had cold turkey sandwiches and mashed potatoes. Some of my friends were dropping downers, drinking red wine, and dancing. There were always characters, like General Hershey Bar and General Wastemoreland, and they would add to the general anti-war feeling that permeated the love-ins. It was a nice, lazy day in the park. The way people were dressed was different from 1965 and '66. Short-hairs, long-hairs, bikers, jocks around the picnic tables. Lots of bell-bottoms and patchouli oil.

I lived in Santa Monica, and there were some stoner surfers from the Midwest who knew every event in town. They would say, "Love-in at Elysian Park," go there, and just drop mescaline. There was a feeling of togetherness. You had the children of conformist parents there who added a sense of rebellion. There was a time when people thought love could actually conquer the world. People really didn't realize you had to go out and get a job and make a buck.

The local media could never really get a handle on how to cover a love-in. The dream that existed around town in 1967 and 1968 was partially shattered in June of '68, when Robert F. Kennedy was murdered in Los Angeles.

Left: Henry Diltz playing a flute at the Renaissance Pleasure Faire, Agoura Hills, 1968.
Right: Peter Bergman of the Firesign Theatre at the Farm, Burbank, 1969.

JIM KELTNER: In the spring and summer of 1968, I was playing with the Charlie Smalls Trio. Charlie sang and played piano, and he wrote "The Wiz" a few years later. Wilton Felder was the bass player, and we had two great girl singers. We worked the Daisy Club in Beverly Hills several times. We were scheduled to play the night Robert F. Kennedy was shot. Kennedy was coming to the Daisy that night for his victory party.

At some point, I noticed our band break was taking

Charlie Smalls with Davy Jones on the set of
***The Monkees*, Hollywood, 1967.**

too long. I asked Wilton, who was sitting in the back reading his bible, what he thought was going on. He said, "I don't know. Everyone is up in the coat room." They were gathered, watching a little television. Someone came out and said, "It's over for tonight. Bobby Kennedy has been shot." I don't remember anything else after that.

The very next day, they talked about Sirhan B. Sirhan, and his address in the Altadena-Pasadena area was in the newspaper. He lived nearby, two streets down. I called out to my wife, Cynthia, "Hey, the guy who killed Kennedy lived on Howard Street." Then, in an article, they mentioned that he worked as a box boy at Weidner's health food store on Lake Street. And I'm going, "What? I used to stumble over him on weekends as he was bent down stocking the shelves in the little aisles." It bowled me over. What kind of weird and horrible coincidence is that? I'm supposed to play for Bobby Kennedy that night, and the guy who is the box boy at my health food store takes him out!

ANDREW LOOG OLDHAM: In 1967, along came an audience, now pretty high on a regular basis, that was going to be around for a while and could be targeted and marketed to. And voilà! The twelve-inch LP, as opposed to the 45 RPM single, became the opus moderandi. Quite frankly, I was more than a little lost with this change of events, though fortunately most of the acts I worked

Left: Promotional item for the Cheetah, 1967. ♪ *Middle:* Promotional poster for the Newport '69 Pop Festival, 1969.
Right: Flier for the Newport '69 Pop Festival.

Above left: Advertisement for the Fantasy Faire and Magic
Mountain Music Festival in the *Los Angeles Free Press*, 1967.
Above right: Handbill for the 1969 Palm Springs Pop Festival.
Left: Promotional item in the *Los Angeles Free Press* for
Kaleidoscope appearing at the Magic Mushroom club, 1967.

with, in particular the Small Faces, were not. They held my hand through the storm. During '67, this music was merging with the new love and peace movement that was starting to stand up to the Vietnam War—something, it should be said, that it did not do for long enough, retreating into the picket-fence comfortability of Cat Stevens, Carole King, Joni Mitchell, James Taylor, and Crosby, Stills, Nash & Anybody, whilst the war still had another few years to run.

New York and San Francisco had the Fillmores, Philadelphia had the Electric Circus, and in Los Angeles, the venue that best showcased the roiling rock music setting was the Shrine Exposition Hall, a warehouse space that provided a pivotal setting for the most ambitious new bands. Within this world were the Pinnacle concerts.

A magical and spiritual-infused live music period began in November 1967, when the Pinnacle dance concerts took place in downtown Los Angeles. Three former USC students—Marc Chase, Sepp Donahower, and John Van Hamersveld—and a consortium of students from UCLA, Otis, and Chouinard conceived and promoted visiting acts and local talent. It was the new, hip community in the City of the Angels, where art, film, and music collided—and provided. Pinnacle advertising was primarily word-of-mouth, via announcements in the Los Angeles Free Press *and point-of-purchase fliers given out at record stores, head shops, and other concerts.*

The Pinnacle and Shrine collaboration was an environment of chance, trust, and sound—a respite from a confusing era. Just about all the admission ducats were purchased on the night of the show. The only real concern at a Pinnacle happening was whether the girl at the box office window had enough small bill and coin change in her cigar box to break your ten-dollar or twenty-dollar bill after your ticket buy.

KIRK SILSBEE: It was brief, but it was incandescent—only fourteen concerts in all. The Shrine Exposition Hall was a trade show space, and its use for dance concerts was ground that had already been broken by the *Freak Out!* concerts of July and September 1966, by Frank Zappa. It seemed to be a place where would-be concert promoters grazed; the Doors had already played there in January of 1967, with Iron Butterfly and Sweetwater.

Frank Zappa at the Santa Monica Civic Auditorium, 1970.

The first of the Pinnacle concerts came in November of 1967, and that wonderful poster by John Van Hamersveld promised "Amazing Electric Wonders" with Buffalo Springfield, the Grateful Dead, and Blue Cheer. Throughout the Pinnacle history—which was short but very intense—Van Hamersveld's posters rivaled anything seen by the San Francisco artists working for the Fillmore and Avalon Ballroom for graphic ingenuity. A few of the later Pinnacle posters were farmed out to Rick Griffin, Victor Moscoso, Bob Fried, Bob Schnepf, and Neon Park.

Little Richard at the Whisky a Go Go, West Hollywood, 1970.

It's important to remember that the Pinnacle shows were dance concerts. There was an ordinance that barred dancing in Sunset Strip clubs like the Whisky. But people could dance at the Cheetah in Venice and at the Pinnacle shows, and that's one of the reasons they were so successful.

Pinnacle was not the Fillmore South. There were only fourteen concerts, and sometimes it was months between shows. Pinnacle didn't feel the need to present every weekend, so the bills didn't have a lot of no-name bands. They presented Hendrix, Cream, the Who, Traffic, the L.A. debut of the Jeff Beck Group, the Chambers Brothers, Pink Floyd, Peter Green's Fleetwood Mac, and the Yardbirds' last L.A. appearance. One bill had the Butterfield Blues Band, the Velvet Underground, and Sly and the Family Stone. That show covered a lot of stylistic ground! It was music that was too big for a club, yet it preceded the era of arena and stadium rock.

Pinnacle had an exceptional light show, Single Wing Turquoise Bird Lights. Sepp Donahower and Marc Chase were not happy with what they were seeing around town, so Sepp got his USC roommate, Caleb Deschanel, involved in the formation of a house light show operation. Sepp even paid Caleb to go around town and shoot 16 mm film for the Single Wing shows, which employed many simultaneous projectors.

There were a bunch of people who moved in and out of Single Wing; two of them were George Lucas and Charlie Lippincott. Charlie would later handle the merchandising and promotion for *Star Wars*. Sometimes they would run old movies, like the *Flash Gordon* serials, backwards, with several overlays. The light show was an explosion of color and images—always moving, and fairly mind-boggling.

The Pinnacle producers were visionaries who developed the dance concerts as events. They weren't owned by or aided much by the L.A. radio stations. The USC campus next door had KUSC and a hippie music show, *Underground Airbag*. On the AM dial, KRLA had DJ Johnny Hayes. He hosted a late-night program, *Collage*, which programmed the non-Top 40 rock music that was being presented in the Pinnacle shows. Then KRLA advertised its own Scenic Sounds-produced concerts at the Santa Monica Civic Auditorium that the station co-sponsored. So the bands that played the Pinnacle gatherings got radio airplay after midnight.

By the summer of 1968, the historic run of Pinnacle shows came to an end. Their last production was in July of that year: the Paul Butterfield Blues Band, the Velvet Underground, Sly and the Family Stone, and the Rockets.

Donahower continued in concert promotions in 1970 with Pacific Presentations, then Avalon Productions. He even promoted the Rolling Stones' June 1972 appearance at the Hollywood Palladium.

The Newport Pop Festival was held on August 3rd and 4th, 1968, at the Orange County Fairgrounds in Costa Mesa, California, and drew approximately one hundred and forty thousand people. Tiny Tim, Sonny and Cher, Electric Flag, Canned Heat, Iron Butterfly, Blue Cheer, Jefferson Airplane, Grateful Dead, the Byrds, and Quicksilver Messenger Service were among the acts presented. KHJ DJ Harvey "Humble Harve" Miller hosted the festival, along with Wavy Gravy.

Other Southland live music rooms, like the Cheetah and the Kaleidoscope, were also defunct by November 1968. The Los Angeles Forum, the Anaheim Convention Center, the Los Angeles Sports Arena, and the Long Beach Auditorium/Arena were now the regular halls for touring attractions. In 1969, from January to September, the Pasadena Rose Palace began to serve as a rock concert facility around its annual float construction. It was a sweaty ballroom that hosted Lee Michaels, Iron Butterfly, John Mayall and the Bluesbreakers, Deep Purple, Led Zeppelin, the Byrds, the Grateful Dead, and Joe Cocker.

A further tipping point in the local musical climate

Lee Michaels in Simi Valley, circa 1968.

and concert-going festival experience occurred in the San Fernando Valley during the weekend of June 20–22, 1969. There, Newport '69 took place at Devonshire Downs, a former racetrack that was part of the north campus at San Fernando Valley State College (now Cal State Northridge). Spirit, Taj Mahal, the Edwin Hawkins Singers, Ike and Tina Turner, Lee Michaels, Sweetwater, Southwind, Three Dog Night, the Chambers Brothers, Albert King, Steppenwolf, Brenton Wood, the Byrds, Poco, Grass Roots, the Jimi Hendrix Experience, Joe Cocker, Jethro Tull, Eric Burdon, Creedence Clearwater, and many other acts played to nearly one hundred and fifty thousand visitors. Janis Joplin even came onstage, and took a bow.

ED CASSIDY: The band [Spirit] had to be seen to be believed. Our LPs were pale by comparison. It was unique in a way, soft on record, and our stage thing was so concrete that more people got into us for that reason.

The band was definitely ahead of the times in many areas. I even played differently than most of the rock drummers—a bastardized version of rock, incorporating my own trip. We were exploring new ways of improvisation; Randy [California] and I were keen on that.

The thing that was successful about Spirit was that we didn't try to contrive any of the elements that appeared in the music. We weren't rock 'n' rollers, and we weren't jazz. It just happened.

In 1970, the Olympic Auditorium became a concert setting again for shows by Little Richard and Frank Zappa. The landmark downtown Los Angeles venue, which opened in 1925, had been home to prestigious boxing and wrestling events, as well as a showcase for the Los Angeles roller derby team, the T-Birds. While the Olympic was an occasional venue for sporadic rock concerts, the Ash Grove, on Melrose Avenue in West Hollywood, was a continual roots music hotbed of intergenerational artists from its 1958 founding to its demise in the early 1970s.

The Chambers Brothers at the Hollywood Bowl, 1968.

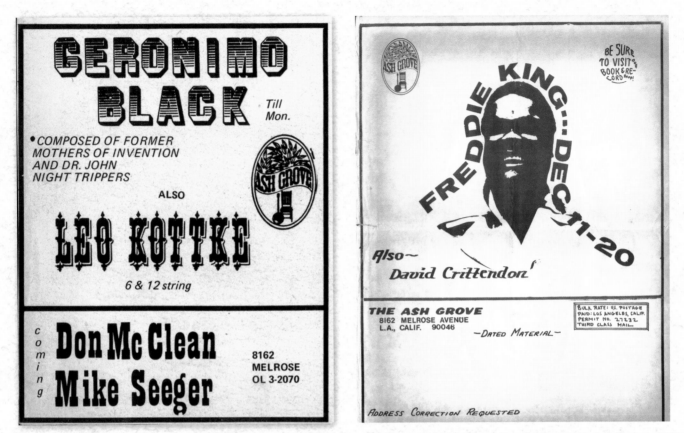

Top left: Advertisement in the *Los Angeles Free Press* for performances by Geronimo Black and Leo Kottke at the Ash Grove, 1969.
Top right: Ash Grove flier featuring Freddie King and David Crittendon, 1969.
Bottom left: Ash Grove flier, 1967. ♪ *Bottom right:* Advertisement in the *Los Angeles Free Press* for performances by the Firesign Theatre and Taj Mahal at the Ash Grove, 1970.

THE ASH GROVE

by KIRK SILSBEE

In 1958, 22-year-old Ed Pearl borrowed $10,000 and opened a hundred-seat room on Melrose Avenue in West Hollywood. It was the era of Beat coffee houses, but the Ash Grove, as Pearl called it, far outlived all the other espresso garrets because of his booking policy. It became the most important West Coast outpost for folk, blues, and ethnic and roots music of all kinds.

Outside of the biggest names, like Pete Seeger, Joan Baez, and Ravi Shankar (whom Pearl presented in local concert venues), virtually every active folk and blues performer passed through the Ash Grove until closing in 1974. In New York, Pearl met Bob Dylan in 1961.

"He knew all about the Ash Grove," Pearl recalled in 2008, "and he said he dreamed of coming out here more than anything. So, I had him all booked. Then he called me up and said, 'Ed, I've got a chance to make a record for John Hammond at Columbia Records. What should I do?'"

Odetta, Guy Carawan, Phil Ochs, the Limelighters, Bud and Travis, the Stoneman Family, Tom Paxton, the Jim Kweskin Jug Band, the Byrds, and John Fahey all played the Ash Grove. Future jazz composer Carla Bley first found the nerve to lead a piano trio there. It was also the most consistent local showcase for authentic blues. The durable duo Brownie McGhee and Sonny Terry first met there, as did Lightnin' Hopkins and Big Joe Williams. It's where Magic Sam played his last gig, and where Albert King, Mississippi John Hurt, Son House, Reverend Gary Davis, Mance Lipscomb, Jesse Fuller, Clifton Chenier, Muddy Waters, and Howlin' Wolf all played. Flat-pick master Doc Watson first encountered bluegrass progenitor Bill Monroe at the Ash Grove. The Chambers Brothers, Taj Mahal, the Rising Sons, the Kentucky Colonels, Ry Cooder, Canned Heat, Rod Piazza,

Rising Sons at Guy Webster's studio in Beverly Hills, 1965.

Linda Ronstadt, and Dave Alvin all gestated at the club.

It was also hospitable to Lawrence Lipton's poetry and jazz shows. It was where comic monologist Hugh Romney worked before he became known as Wavy Gravy; where blacklisted screenwriter Dalton Trumbo read aloud; where Holly Near first sang her songs. It was the stage laboratory for the Firesign Theatre, and the place where Michael McKean and David L. Lander performed with the Credibility Gap. It was where a cappella giants the Persuasions first sung in Los Angeles, and where the San Francisco Mime Troupe and El Teatro Campesino appeared regularly.

When New Orleans drummer Earl Palmer came to L.A. to produce records for

Ash Grove flier, 1967.

the Aladdin label, he played the Ash Grove with Buddy Collette's jazz band in 1959. It preceded Palmer's fabled career in the Hollywood studios, and he considered that interlude his "jazz peak."

Ed Michel was the house bassist at the club long before he became a celebrated jazz and blues record producer. Michel cut his first albums at the club, one of which was a live recording by transplanted Mississippians the Chambers Brothers. When it was discovered that a technical glitch had marred the tape, they cheerfully re-took the stage and sang another set.

After the Dillards drove to L.A. in a '49 Hudson in 1962, their first Ash Grove appearance resulted in a record deal with Elektra. A recurring role on *The Andy Griffith Show* soon followed.

UCLA ethnomusicology student Barry Hansen, later known as radio's Dr. Demento, worked the sound and lights at the club in the mid-1960s. Future blues scholar/journalist/broadcaster Mary Katherine Aldin kept the books. Blues harmonica titan George "Harmonica" Smith taught Taj Mahal, Rod Piazza, James Harman, and Louie Lista the finer points of blues harmonica. The club provided a vital testing ground and showcase for emerging rock bands like the Rising Sons, the Red Roosters, the Nitty Gritty Dirt Band, Kaleidoscope, Canned Heat, and Spirit.

The Ash Grove was a mandatory stop for young British Invaders with a thirst for authentic blues. When Eric Burdon heard Lightnin' Hopkins at the club, he considered it a spiritual pilgrimage. John Mayall was similarly gratified to find a stronghold for blues culture. Mick Jagger personally thanked Pearl after hearing Taj Mahal, and subsequently added the blues omnivore to their television special, *The Rolling Stones Rock and Roll Circus.*

Ash Grove flier for the Rising Sons, 1965.

The Ash Grove was also a hotbed of leftist political activism of every stripe. It was an embarkation point for Southern-bound Freedom Ride buses. Civil rights, voting rights for eighteen-year-olds, feminism, black nationalism, anti-Vietnam activism, and migrant workers' concerns were as much a part of the club as the music.

Problems with the LAPD were ongoing, and the Ash Grove was under continual pressure. Pearl noted that there were five fistfights in the club's history, proudly adding that he participated in three of them.

The Watts Riots of 1965 added a layer of irony to the club's fortunes. Police recruits were suddenly scarce, so the department advertised in the Southern states. Those young patrolmen appreciated that the club booked Doc Watson, the Carter Family, and the bluegrass players, and stopped in to listen. The nearby precinct house sent runaways to the club, because they could get help there.

Passions ignited by the extreme political currents that swirled around the Ash Grove drew the hostility from reactionary groups. No less than three break-ins and arsons—in 1969, 1972, and 1974—forced Pearl to close.

Two subsequent attempts to relocate the Ash Grove, first to Santa Monica Boulevard in 1988, and then to the Santa Monica Pier in 1996, proved short-lived. But the club's legacy can scarcely be measured. Countless great moments occurred, like the time in 1966 when young bluesnik John Hammond shared the bill with Howlin' Wolf. After singing Robert Johnson's "Terraplane Blues" in his opening set, Wolf summoned Hammond upstairs to the dressing room and demanded, "Where the fuck you learn to play that?" After a command reprise of the song, Wolf hissed, "Man, that's evil."

CHAPTER 23

THE KING HAS ENTERED THE BUILDING

Steve Binder had directed NBC television specials on Leslie Uggums, Harry Belafonte, and Petula Clark. He directed the television shows Jazz Scene USA, The Steve Allen Show, and the memorable T.A.M.I. Show, a rock 'n' roll theatrical extravaganza film hosted by Jan and Dean and starring James Brown, the Rolling Stones, Lesley Gore, the Miracles, the Supremes, and Chuck Berry. Binder also directed the NBC weekly pop music series Hullabaloo. He was young, wore turtlenecks, and won the confidence of nervous network executives desperate for that coveted demographic: the all-too-fickle teenager.

The Singer Sewing Machine Company had sponsored a 1967 Herb Alpert television special, and Elvis Presley hadn't toured in years. NBC floated the idea of another small-screen product, which seemed like an ideal way to keep the brand fresh. Presley's manager, the omnivorous Colonel Tom Parker, lobbied for a traditional Christmas show. Presley was steered toward Binder and his partner, recording engineer/record producer Bones Howe, whom Elvis had worked with years earlier at Radio Recorders in Hollywood.

The management and creative team all agreed that this Presley special would shine the spotlight solely on Elvis, with no special guest stars and no holiday theme. Parker also agreed not to demand repertoire focused exclusively on Presley-controlled copyrights, although Parker did subsequently publish "If I Can Dream," the hit record that emerged from the broadcast.

Acetate label copy of Elvis Presley's "If I Can Dream," 1968.

STEVE BINDER: Elvis would come to our offices every day on Sunset and Larrabee. We were rehearsing one evening, and the television was on in Bones's office, and Bobby Kennedy was assassinated. We stopped rehearsal and watched the TV set. We spent the entire night sitting around, until five o'clock in the morning. Elvis played the guitar and picked, not strummed, and talked about the assassinations of John F. Kennedy in Dallas and Martin Luther King Jr. the previous April in Memphis. Those are the kind of things that bond people.

We had a great team, with Bones Howe and Bill Cole, NBC's head of audio. In those days, unless you had a union card, you weren't supposed to participate. But Bill had no problem working with Bones. In fact, they worked great together and learned together the difference between making records and television audio. All of a sudden, they were learning about the contemporary music business. In those days, everyone said television was a visual media, and the sound sucks on those tiny little two-and-a-half-inch speakers. What they didn't realize was that the whole world was listening to car radios and transistor radios and not complaining because their speakers were probably an inch and a half [laughs]. It was all about how you approached the music—that was really the difference between good sound and bad sound—and the fact that we married the music industry with the television industry into one cohesive [form of] entertainment.

Opposite: **Steve Binder and Elvis Presley at a rehearsal for the '68 Comeback Special, Burbank, 1968.**

The musical director was Billy Goldenberg, who had replaced Billy Strange. I first met him when I was directing *Hullabaloo*. He was given free rein to assemble an all-star orchestra. He enlisted musicians from both the NBC stable and the Wrecking Crew.

DON RANDI: I got the call from Billy Goldenberg. Half the people on the sessions were Wrecking Crew. He was playing with some musicians he never met face to face, but the fact was that we could do the music instantly, and it made it easier for everybody else. A band that plays together and listens to each other doesn't have to do twenty takes. On the NBC special, they didn't have the time to spend sixteen hours on getting a drum track, or something like that. You had to move along. I've always had the facility to play music on my feet. That comes from many late night shifts at Sherry's Jazz Club.

In a way, the sessions we did, it was Elvis Presley meets the Wrecking Crew—Tommy Tedesco, Larry Knechtel, Hal Blaine, Mike Deasy. We played together a lot. So it's like any band that plays together a long time. Tommy Morgan is on harmonica. He composed music for a *Twilight Zone* episode in the very early sixties, and was on *Pet Sounds* in 1966. Chuck Berghofer on bass. The percussionists were John Cyr and Elliot Franks. Frank DeVito was the bongo player on the NBC stuff and studio. I did hundreds of dates with Hal Blaine.

I guess we were all taking Elvis into a different world. It was a completely different thing for him from the Memphis band. Just having the Blossoms on the sessions . . . Elvis loved the Blossoms. He knew Darlene Love from her work with Ray Charles.

There were a lot of Leiber and Stoller songs: "Hound Dog," "Jailhouse Rock," "Trouble," "Little Egypt," "Love Me," "Saved," and "Santa Claus Is Back in Town."

BONES HOWE: On the sit-down section, Bill Cole was the NBC-TV audio guy, and I said, "Here's what we got to do. Here's what we want." So he set it up, and all we did was make sure all the mikes were hot. It was television done live. It's like making a

mono record. It's how I began my career. You mix it all together. Bill Cole had done it a dozen times with other people.

When Elvis came offstage with the black leather suit, he was soaking wet. The suit was stuck to him, and Bill Belew, the costume designer, had to get a seam ripper to get it off him. It was so tight and wet. The seams were cut, and it had to be peeled off him.

You know, that live section is probably the closest to seeing what Elvis was like all the time. He was a great singer. I'm a believer that you set everything up, and then it either happens or it doesn't. You set up the best situation you possibly can, and then you let it happen. If everything comes together, it's amazing. A lot of times, it doesn't come together.

BILLY GOLDENBERG: We did "Guitar Man," and there was this strange sound he had never heard. Elvis walked out into the studio and around to the musicians. He always called me "Billy, my boy." He said, "What's this?" I said, "That's a French horn." He said, "Do you think I can sing with that?" I said, "Of course. You wanna try?" "Yeah, I really want to try." We didn't do anything but "Guitar Man" for three or four hours, because he was getting so excited by all of it. I knew, by the end of the evening, that we had it.

We were on our way to something. "Guitar Man" was the force behind all of it. It was extremely exciting writing for the NBC staff orchestra and the studio musicians. The orchestra was wonderful. I had worked with them on films and dramatic things. I hand-picked people I had done previous work with.

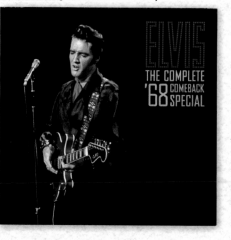

Booklet for the CD reissue of Elvis Presley's *'68 Comeback Special.*

BONES HOWE: I produced and engineered the Presley special at United and did the pre-records. When it was time to do the Presley pre-records, this was the place, because he was gonna sing live.

Elvis nailed "If I Can Dream." He was a great performer, with his hand taped to the microphone and complete with knee drops in front of the string section! He got all these violinists with their mouths hanging open.

With some artists, you can kind of plug in what the record is gonna sound like. But with Elvis, you sort of were relying on him to perform this piece. And he did.

I gave him a hand microphone placed on a long cable, 'cause I knew he was gonna walk around in the studio and not stand in one place. He loved being in the middle of a bunch of guys around him. They were like his audience. Not many takes—not more than four or five. He heard it for the first time with the orchestra, right then and there. He didn't wear headphones, standing in the middle of the orchestra. It's like being on a stage in Las Vegas. But, of course, he hadn't done Vegas then.

DAN KESSEL: Bones used a nice amount of limiting to help with controlling the inconsistent volume peaks on Elvis's vocal, but still had to keep his eyes glued to the VU meter so he could ride the lead vocal signal to keep Elvis from dropping and peaking. Bones, being the skilled

pro that he is, started working on a mix right after the recording session, while the musicians were still packing up. When he had completed a thoroughly great-sounding mix, which he declared was the "final mix," Colonel Parker leaned across the board and nudged up the fader next to the strip of masking tape which had a star drawn on it [Elvis's vocal] and said, "There's your final mix."

BONES HOWE: He sang "Memories" live, but then I did a track and he sang it afterwards. He wanted to sing it really, really softly. We turned the lights out in the studio after the orchestra went home. With TV, you have to have a track on everything. I turned the lights off in the studio, and he just stood out in the studio and sang it all by himself in the dark, and we made two takes. The second one is the one that is in the show.

As for the durability of the *'68 Comeback Special . . .* you start with an icon, and there is no doubt that Elvis

Recording session at Western Recorders in 1968 for Elvis Presley's "A Little Less Conversation,"
including: (*left to right*) John Bahler, B. J. Baker, Presley, Sally Stevens, and Bob Tebow.

Presley is an icon. Then you surround him with a really good idea. A *really* good idea. It's like bringing a great song to an artist. You surround him with a crew and professional people who know how to deliver the baby. Steve Binder, the director, was Mr. Television. We know what he went through with live TV. Now you know what I went through with live recording. Just put those two guys together in a room with a great artist.

The thing about it is that you wait for the opportunities to put all this stuff together, and every now and then you get a chance. We got somebody who was burning to happen. He was liked a caged-up animal. He had done all those stupid movies. He was ready to be led out, and he came out screaming. If you just go back to the first meeting . . . think, if we'd had to do a Christmas special. So they throw us out of the office. So we don't do an Elvis Presley Christmas. Okay. You gotta take your chances. That's the other thing. If you believe in yourself and you believe you can do these things, then take your chances.

STEVE BINDER: "Memories" becomes a prophetic statement. The same writers, Billy Strange and Mac Davis, also penned "A Little Less Conversation."

I always felt, during the *'68 Comeback Special*, [that] Elvis rediscovered himself. You could see it on his face, and you could see it in his body language all the way through it.

I played Elvis the sixty-minute show in a screening room, before the December 3rd broadcast, when the NBC network got their biggest total viewing audience and the season's number-one rated show. Elvis told me, "Steve, it's the greatest thing I've ever done in my life. I give you my word—I will never sing a song I don't believe in."

By January of 1969, "If I Can Dream" was a number-twelve hit record, and the '68 Comeback Special soundtrack was in the Top 10. When Elvis headlined at the International Hotel in Las Vegas, "Memories" was included in his opening night performance. Mac Davis then wrote "In the Ghetto," a big hit record for Elvis in 1969.

RICHARD CARPENTER: I started listening to music at age three. My dad had a great record collection—78s—that I pored through. They were made of shellac, and I broke a couple of them, thinking that it was the end of me.

I devoured everything I heard on the radio. I particularly liked Mary Ford and Les Paul, and Patti Page. I loved melody above all else. My classical piano training informed my love of arrangement and orchestration. You can take any song that was a hit, change the arrangement, and you end up with nothing.

Well, to make a long story short, Karen and I made

DOWNEY SOFT

The new soft rock sound finds its apotheosis in Downey, a suburb in Southern California. Vocalist-drummer Karen Carpenter and her brother, pianist Richard, triumphed at a 1966 Battle of the Bands contest at the Hollywood Bowl. They played a pastiche of jazz and classical stylings, but in their hearts they longed to be pop stars. They caught the ear of the Wrecking Crew's Joe Osborn and signed to his Magic Lamp label.

Karen and Richard were mentored by Professor Frank Pooler, the choral director at Cal State Long Beach who helped shape their signature vocal blend. After refining their sound for a couple of years, they met A&M Records' Herb Alpert, who, in April of 1968, had a number-one vocal record with "This Guy's In Love with You," a song written by Burt Bacharach and Hal David. Richard insisted the group be billed and recorded as "Carpenters," a nod to Jefferson Airplane and Buffalo Springfield. With their hipster redentials in order, the label released their first album, *Offering*, in 1969. Professor Pooler would co-write with Richard Carpenter a new seasonal standard, "Merry Christmas Darling."

As of 2008, their combined sales of singles and albums hit a total of one hundred million units, which is a lot cooler than simply being hip.

Left: Karen Carpenter during an interview at KHJ, Los Angeles, 1973. ♪ *Right:* Richard Carpenter at KHJ, Los Angeles, 1973.

a demo. We met a chap named Joe Osborn, a premier session electric bass man on the West Coast. He had a garage studio, and we got to know him. Karen and I did the tracks, and every now and again he'd play bass. We did a lot of ping-ponging, if you know what I'm talking about, because you're only dealing with four tracks, and here are all these voices—like twelve.

It was a pretty good demo. It was turned down by just about every label in town, but Herb Alpert heard it, and he thought there was something there, so we signed to A&M in April of 1969. The first single, at least, got on the charts. That's more than most debut singles do, but it was not a hit. The second one, which came out in May of 1970, was a monster. That was it. It was hard to describe. We believed we had what it took, and just

didn't give up. Then, of course, you start to worry about what you're going to follow it up with, like every recording artist.

I was—and still am—fanatical about listening for details in songs. The first time I heard the Beatles was on KRLA in 1963—"From Me to You." The first chorus has a group harmony, and the second time, it's a two-part harmony. It was subtle, but it made the song interesting. The lyric was nothing, really, real "Moon in June" stuff, but the arrangement was really clever. I always strove to find the right detail for Carpenters music. Bacharach's demo for "Close to You" was straight eighths—yeesh! I changed the beat entirely around to accommodate Karen's knack for rhythmic punctuation. You can hear it in her drum fills and in her vocal delivery.

By 1969, rock music had infiltrated that last bastion of musical convention: the soundtrack. The Beatles' A Hard Day's Night *had nabbed an Oscar in 1964, but the suave sounds of Henry Mancini and Elmer Bernstein still held sway. With the release of the* Easy Rider *soundtrack, however, the movie studios and record labels came to a startling realization— their products were increasingly addressing the same audience. Why not double down with an "underground" soundtrack to a film equally outré?*

No movie depicted this union of lurid sight and sound quite like Mick Jagger's feature film debut, Performance. *Shot in the fall of 1968 and released by Warner Bros. (over their categorical objections) in 1970, the film had a soundtrack that reeked of trippin' gone wild; it was sensual and malevolent in equal measures. For many, the Jagger-Richards contribution, "Memo from Turner," might as well be the best Stones song they never recorded. Fortunately, their longtime musical confederate, Jack Nitzsche, was brought on to supervise the score.*

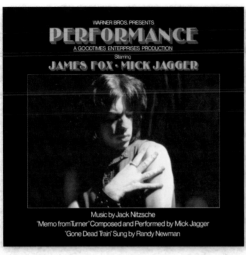

Artwork submission considered for the UK
Performance **soundtrack album cover.**
Artist unknown.

RUSS TITELMAN: I worked with Jack on the *Performance* soundtrack. It's, like, a defining moment, I think, in movie score history. What he did is just so unusual and groundbreaking in a lot of ways. There hadn't been a soundtrack like that before.

I wrote "Gone Dead Train" with Jack, and Randy Newman sang it. Jack called me up and said, "Come on over. We have to write a song for this picture." I wrote the melody, and he wrote the lyrics. I wrote that song on guitar. We finished it in a couple of hours, I think. Sort of like a white boy's version of a Chuck Berry song, in a way.

They had the track of "Memo from Turner" with Mick's vocal done in England. Donald Cammell, the director, didn't like it. So he said, "Why don't you guys play it?" So we had Jagger's voice on click, and we played live to that as if he were there singing. We ran it once or twice. I played the Keith Richards rhythm guitar, Ry Cooder played the slide, and Randy Newman played the organ. Bobby West was the bass player. He was great. It's

a unique kind of bass part for anything having to do with the Rolling Stones, because it's like an R & B James Jamerson bass part. I believe it's Gene Parsons on drums. We cut it at United Studios, in Room B. That was it.

"Memo from Turner" is a great thing. Actually, Jack had to be away, and he said, "Go mix it." I was just terrified. "What?" So I went in, and it wasn't so difficult, because it was sort of pre-mixed on the tape. "Gone Dead Train," we cut live with Randy singing.

I was there for the whole thing. We saw the screenings. It was so fantastic, what Jack brought to the overall sound. He had, like, a woodwind quintet, tamboura and veena. The Last Poets were used; it was their recording. Buffy Sainte-Marie, with mouthbow solos. The choral stuff he added, and the use of the Moog synthesizer . . . these scary, foreboding sounds, and surrounded by rock 'n' roll instruments. The Harry Flowers cue is a great cue. It's like Muzak, but it's the coolest Muzak you ever heard. In every case, he did something magical. If you listen closely, Lowell George appears, uncredited, as well.

JACK NITZSCHE: This is the only movie I have ever done where nobody interfered. Nobody. [Director] Donald Cammell would drop by the studio once in a while. He let me do whatever I wanted. I put all kinds of weird shit in that score. It was amazing. To this day, I'll be in a restaurant, or walking down a street, or leaving a screening on a lot somewhere, like at Paramount, and someone will yell out "*Performance*!" Billy Friedkin saw me walking and, [from] across the street, yelled, "*Performance*! The greatest use of music in a motion picture ever!"

MERRY CLAYTON: Jack called me at home from the studio in the Los Angeles area one night where I lived with my husband, Curtis Amy. Curtis told him I was just about ready to go to sleep. See, I was pregnant, but Jack insisted that he had to talk to me about this Stones session immediately. Curtis then woke me up. Jack was on the line. "Merry, I really need you to do this part. There is no other singer who can do this. Please." I worked with Jack on the *Performance* soundtrack, and with Neil Young in 1968 or '69.

Okay . . . I was really tired that night, but I got up, put on my coat, and got in the car with Curtis. Later that evening we drove up from L.A. to Hollywood where the studio was located, on La Cienega.

When she arrived, Clayton was greeted warmly by Jagger. Seeing him in the flesh, Clayton said to Jagger, "Man, I thought you was a man, but you nothing but a skinny little boy!"

MERRY CLAYTON: They played me the song and asked if I could put a little somethin' on it. I said, "Stop the song and tell me what all this stuff means" before I went any further. I said, "I'm gonna put my vocal on it, and I'm gonna leave, 'cause this is a real high part and I will be wettin' myself if I sing any higher!" 'Cause my stomach was a little bit heavy.

So, we went in and did it. Matter of fact, I did it three times. I didn't do an overdub. Mick's vocal was already on it at a playback, and I recall he did a bit of touching up after I left. But they got what they wanted. I said, "It was so nice meeting you guys." "Oh, Merry, you sound incredible. We just love you." I was walkin' out the door as they were talkin'. "Okay. Love you guys, too! See you some other time." I got in the car with my husband, who took me right home, and I went right upstairs to bed. That was the "Gimme Shelter" session.

Just before she split the scene of the rhyme, Clayton politely inquired about payment procedure and credit for her work. Very swiftly, the Stones' legal team generated an agreement.

FUTURE SHOCK

Before singer Merry Clayton's torrid vocals were paired with Mick Jagger's on "Gimme Shelter," Clayton had already shared a microphone with Bobby Darin and Pearl Bailey, and had been a member of Ray Charles's Raelettes from 1966 to 1968. Clayton's official introduction to the Rolling Stones began half a decade earlier, in 1964, when the band, along with Andrew Loog Oldham, went to a Jack Nitzsche-produced session at the RCA studio where Clayton was recording.

Before the Stones embarked on their November 1969 U.S. tour, Jagger, Keith Richards, producer Jimmy Miller, and engineer Glyn Johns prepared the basic track for "Gimme Shelter" at Olympic Studios in England. They then booked time at L.A.'s Elektra Studios with assistant engineer Bruce Botnick.

Jack Nitzsche suggested Clayton for "Gimme Shelter" to augment Richards, who sang on the recording as well. Miller played percussion on the session, and lead vocalist Jagger overdubbed harmonica to drummer Charlie Watts, pianist Nicky Hopkins, and bassist Bill Wyman.

Merry Clayton, 1970.

Mick Jagger on *The Ed Sullivan Show*, Los Angeles, 1969.

MERRY CLAYTON: Next thing I knew, lawyers had talked, and everything was cool. It was a go on the record. Then, immediately, I heard "Gimme Shelter" on the radio in Los Angeles. It's a powerful track.

My dad, who was a bishop—I call him "Reverend Doctor Daddy"—heard it and said, "Merry, what is this line in the song about rape and the murder?" "Well, dad, that's part of the song." He laughed. "Boy, they're really singing them different these days . . . "

"Gimme Shelter" was previewed on that Rolling Stones '69 trek. I heard the song for the first time at the November 8th concert at the Inglewood Forum, a week or so before it was commercially available. I sat in the lodge section with my brother, Kenny, and our friend, Bob Sherman. I was stunned by this scary, prophetic warning Jagger sang to us at 3:30 AM.

America soon heard the same warning—with a difference. On November 18, 1969, the Rolling Stones taped a telerecorded spot for The Ed Sullivan Show *at Television City in Hollywood, broadcast on November 23rd. The band had invited Little Richard to the studio. He came in a green suit.*

The Sullivan *broadcast utilized the prerecorded "Gimme Shelter" track from* Let It Bleed, *including Merry Clayton's voice. However, the tape jammed during a backstage playback as Jagger was singing live, so Mick and the Stones basically lip-synced to Merry Clayton for the "Gimme Shelter" debut to a national audience.*

In 1970, Clayton recorded her own version of "Gimme Shelter," produced by Lou Adler for his Ode Records label.

RUSS TITELMAN: Lowell George was a flute player, and a Japanese shakuhachi flute player. In fact, Lowell could play anything that he picked up. I met him at the Kinnara School of Music—Ravi Shankar's school. I studied sitar for a year. George Harrison came by, and we were briefly introduced. I would produce him years later.

In 1969, Lowell was playing with the Mothers of Invention and rehearsing Little Feat. Lowell and I became best friends, so we spent all our time together. He was rehearsing the new band and played with Fraternity of Man, with Elliot Ingber and Richie Hayward. He put together Little Feat. He had Roy Estrada and himself and [was] rehearsing in this little room on Sunset Boulevard. Lowell played me the songs he was writing, and I thought they were great. "Willin'" and "Truck Stop Girl."

Lowell was going to sign with Gabriel Mekler's Lizard Records label. I said to him, "I don't think that's a good idea. Let's go to Lenny [Waronker] at Warner Bros. Records. Let's go to Lenny first." So I took Billy [Payne] and Lowell after I called Lenny, and told him I wanted him to hear this stuff. We went to his office, a little cubical, practically like the size of the cubical we used to write in, only a little bigger. He had a miserable little spinet piano in there, not completely in tune. So Lowell, Billy, and I went to the office. Lowell brought a guitar; Billy played piano. They played "Truck Stop Girl," "Willin'," "Brides of Jesus." They got done doing those songs, and Lenny said, "Go upstairs and make a deal with Mo."

That's how it happened. That's how innocent those days were, too. They didn't have to do a showcase. Lenny said, "Go make a deal with Mo." Lenny was, like, the best song man of anybody. He got it immediately. That was it.

When I finished the first record, I played it for Jack [Nitzsche], and he loved that record. Jack thought I did a great job on it.

Titelman first started working for Warner Bros. as a producer in 1970, then joined the label as a staff producer in July 1971.

KIM FOWLEY: I saw B.B. King play in downtown Los Angeles in the late sixties, when you could only hear his records, like "Lucille" and "How Blue Can You Get," on KBCA-FM or KGFJ on AM. I first met B.B. in 1959, when he was on Kent Records and I was a food runner for Dee Clark at the Watkins Hotel in L.A. I was

working for DJ Alan Freed on KDAY in 1960. I ran into B.B. in the lobby of the hotel. I had a concept about a black Lowell Thomas travelogue of American history locations through the decades. B.B. then invited me to his house near South Central L.A. on a Sunday, and his wife cooked barbecue for us. We sat and talked about it.

There he was, in L.A., listening to a nineteen-year-old guy lay out a convoluted concept about decade of time travel through America. Nothing ever happened. That he actually spent hours on one long day talking about it to me, and I got a free meal out of it . . . B.B. and his wife were very kind to a nineteen-year-old, non-focused hustler.

B.B. is a great performer and an excellent songwriter. I worked and wrote tunes with Leon Russell in the

HE WENT TO HOLLYWOOD HIGH SCHOOL

In 1969, Little Feat was formed by Lowell George and keyboardist Bill Payne when George was a member of Frank Zappa's Mothers of Invention, after Payne had auditioned for Zappa. They were joined by drummer Richie Hayward and bassist Roy Estrada. Russ Titelman then brought Little Feat to the attention of Warner Bros. Records.

Lowell George at former Monkee Peter Tork's recording session in Hollywood, 1970.

Johnny Otis at the Ash Grove, West Hollywood, 1970.

late seventies. B.B. did his song, "Hummingbird." Leon told me, "I make solo albums so I can get covers by significant artists."

MARSHALL CHESS: Blues always had an audience in Los Angeles. Etta James—"the Queen of Soul." They were calling her that before Aretha [Franklin]. She's just great . . . singing in church. She's a real L.A. girl, a street girl. Johnny Otis initially broke her out on Modern Records. In 1960, Etta came to Chess and our Argo label, and had another hit in '61 with "At Last." During 1967 came "Tell Mama." Both great records. Chess, in 1965, had Fontella Bass's "Rescue Me," followed by Billy Stewart, with "Summertime" in 1966, both of them hits. They were in rotation on all of the pop and R & B radio stations in Southern California. The drummer on "Summertime" is Maurice White. I saw early genius in him, long before Earth, Wind and Fire.

Muddy Waters played the Troubadour and the Ash Grove. When Muddy Waters' *Electric Mud* came out in 1968, I had a very good group of radio people, and sent it around. My alternative guys. They all got on it heavy. So the album took off and blew up. I think we shipped over 100,000 units in the first month. It was the biggest album Muddy had ever had. A blues album, at that time . . . and everyone loved it, including Muddy. We were in the record business and we liked that it was selling, ya know?

At that time, I was very aware and very on top of

alternative FM radio. I drove across the United States visiting FM DJs like Tom Donahue and Bobby Mitchell in San Francisco. I'd meet all the DJs on radio stations in Los Angeles, like KMET and KPPC. These guys would be smoking joints on their shift, and they'd take an album right from your arm and play it immediately, five times on the air!

KMET would also spin Buddy Guy and an album I did with Rotary Connection. I knew Minnie Riperton when she was in a black R & B group on Chess, the Gems. Charles Stepney and Curtis Mayfield are the two major geniuses of Chicago. Not just arrangers. Brilliant geniuses. I loved them!

I loved Ewart Abner of Vee-Jay Records. Oh man, when my dad got the award at the Rock and Roll Hall of Fame, I asked that Ewart be the presenter.

FM radio was a godsend for the blues. The big commercial AM stations would not play the records at all, except some black stations. I decided to repackage Chess to that market that was getting stoned and going deep. It was a big boost when the English groups covered the music earlier, on records and at their shows. We loved it,

Ike and Tina Turner at the Inglewood Forum, 1969.

CROSSING THE SLAUSON LINE

B.B. King's "Paying the Cost to Be the Boss," on the Bluesway/ABC record label, was a Top 10 R & B hit in 1968, and it was popular on the KGFJ radio station. King's opening slot at the Rolling Stones' November 8, 1969, show at the Inglewood Forum was a career-altering opportunity. On that cosmic night in 1969, King played in front of music reviewers, rack jobbers, DJs, guitarists, booking agents, and paying folks who had never heard, let alone seen, him in action. King was worshiped onstage in Inglewood that evening. It was a moment in which he knew that, by the following Christmas, his next half a century of dates and live bookings were going to be taken care of.

In late 1969, King hit the pop charts with the mournful "The Thrill Is Gone" and, in 1970, "Hummingbird." He then headlined the Whisky a Go Go in 1971.

B.B. King at the Inglewood Forum, 1969.

and something we thought could never happen. Muddy Waters and B.B. King really dug white people doin' their stuff. Bill Graham at the Fillmore was the greatest for the blues artists of that era, having B.B. King and Muddy Waters on his bills. The Stones were having B.B. King and Ike and Tina Turner on their entire 1969 U.S. tour.

In 1970, I became president of Rolling Stones Records. In 1972, I had a house in L.A during the Stones' Sunset Sound recording sessions for *Exile on Main St.* I remember taking "Tumbling Dice" to local radio when it was called "Good Time Women."

The Rolling Stones at the Inglewood Forum, 1969.

CHAPTER 24

IT'S THE SINGER AND THE SONG

In pop music, as in Newtonian physics, for every action there is an equal and opposite reaction. The late sixties had seen the rise of the power trio—blues-based, volume-addled outfits like Cream, the Jimi Hendrix Experience, Led Zeppelin, and the Who (the latter two were indeed power trios, with a lead vocalist). This surge in amplitude drove adolescent boys into headbanging paroxysms, but left their girlfriends to stew in long lines at the restroom, moaning about endless drum solos and "too many notes!" All that yearning neediness was being squandered in the mindless worship of the Marshall stack—but not for long.

By November 1970, Hendrix had exited in a ghastly gurgle, Clapton was rendered prostrate by his own opiated demons, and even Plant and Page began tempering their own rock god pomposity with gentle musings about "Going to California" with a mandolin in hand. Like marmosets amongst the megasaurs, the dulcet strum of an acoustic guitar and the minor chord voicings of a lowly pianist began to emerge. Sensitivity had seized the pop consciousness.

The soundscape was now receptive to the peaceful, easy feelings of "Sweet Baby James"—the aching earnestness of Jackson Browne, the emotional transparency of Elton John, and the oblique intimacies of Joni Mitchell. Whether nurtured in the canopies of Laurel Canyon or a bedsit in London, pop's newest idols were on a journey to the center of themselves. Sometimes the trip provided no direction home, as in the heartbreaking instance of England's Nick Drake. Others, like the uber-disciplined Carole King, were too buoyed by life to let their sentiments overwhelm them. The songs were often plain-spoken to a fault—bland on brown. However, at its best, this latest development in the mercurial world of pop and rock grafted an invaluable thoughtfulness and crafty restraint to music which was sagging under the weight of its own excessiveness.

The voluble hub of the singer-songwriter movement was Doug Weston's iconic West Hollywood nightclub, the Troubadour. It was an arcadia for anyone with gumption, a

Above left: Troubadour marquee, West Hollywood, 1970.
Above right: Doug Weston touting a Joni Mitchell show outside the Troubadour, West Hollywood, 1972.
Opposite: Joni Mitchell at her home on Lookout Mountain Avenue in Laurel Canyon, 1970.

Left: James Taylor at the Farm in Burbank, 1969. ♪ *Right:* Jackson Browne playing piano in his home, Hollywood, 1971.

Guild guitar, and a capacity to turn tenderness into a call to arms. It was here, in a modest showroom affronted by a garrulous bar scene, that Elton John rocketed to stardom, where King, Browne, James Taylor, Randy Newman, Glenn Frey, and Don Henley brought their unaffected (though keenly strategized) blend of country, folk, and pop together before a listenership craving a sound as revealing as a diary entry.

Before these transplants secured a booking at the Troubadour, Emitt Rhodes delivered on that stage. His self-titled debut LP on ABC-Dunhill Records was the talk of the town in 1970. The singer and songwriter played all the instruments and produced the album inside his Hawthorne home with Harvey Bruce, his A&R man. He also engineered it, assisted by mix-down engineers Keith Olsen, a former Music Machine bassist, and Curt Boettcher, who arranged the Association's "Along Comes Mary" and then produced the group's "Cherish."

DON RANDI: There was a pop music world before the singer-songwriter that featured the arranger. Then the musicians started to write their own songs. That goes

back to Bob Dylan. The transition was the beginning of the end of all the live recordings, too, because everything was changing. When the multiple track started, that was good in the beginning because we did need more tracks. I noticed the new generation that was coming up was much more tuned in to what was going on, whether it be political or musical. They were better musically. They had played in clubs, and the songs got better.

You got to realize, though, [that] the Motown Records era, with Smokey Robinson and those guys, was so brilliant that it was hard to top that. Lee Hazlewood was great. There were great country writers around that were starting to move into the rock 'n' roll thing with the "story songs." The kids were more educated, and the subject matter got better to write about, 'cause it was freer and they didn't have to be afraid to stay within 2:50. "You can't go past three minutes." They had agents and managers, and the budgets started to get larger, too. We would go in and do an album for $10,000. It was unheard of.

KIM FOWLEY: The emergence of the songwriter who sang . . . the soft rock world from 1969 to 1973 comes out of

Left: Laura Nyro playing piano at a Crosby, Stills, Nash and Young rehearsal on a Warner Brothers soundstage, Burbank, 1970. *Right:* Linda Ronstadt performing at the Troubadour in West Hollywood, 1970.

David Bowie's androgyny and Ozzy Osborne's evil. People needed relief. So the guy on a stool appeared, holding a guitar and singing to girls who were afraid of a penis. Sensitivity is how those guys got laid, and that's how they got paid.

DANIEL WEIZMANN: The effect of marijuana on male testosterone levels seems to have made a big cultural impact on songwriting in those years. From folk rock to soft rock, these dudes are coming toward a new companionship with women, where the whole heavy boy-girl power struggle has been cooled. The Doors were erotic, Buffalo Springfield wistful, but by the time you get to Poco and James Taylor, it's like the slings and arrows of competition, possession, obsession, and the cruel side of heartbreak was gone. Nobody was writing "Night and Day" and "I've Got You Under My Skin" in those years.

Before Carole King recorded her landmark Tapestry *album with producer Lou Adler, she had already left a*

queenly imprint on the sound of the early sixties. With her writing partner and soon-to-be husband Gerry Goffin, King ruled the roost of AM radio with such genre-defining hits as "Will You Love Me Tomorrow" (the Shirelles), "Up on the Roof" (the Drifters), and "Hey, Girl" (Freddie Scott). King also collaborated with Howie Greenfield on "Crying in the Rain," which Lou Adler produced for the Everly Brothers. King's own record on the Aldon Music-spawned Dimension label, "It Might As Well Rain Until September," reached number three on the UK charts in 1962 and Top 30 in the U.S.

In the mid-sixties, King, Goffin, and New York Post music columnist Al Aronowitz founded their own short-lived, New Jersey-based record label, Tomorrow Records. Charles Larkey, who recorded for the label as a bassist for the Myddle Class, eventually became King's second husband after her marriage to Goffin dissolved. King and Larkey relocated to Southern California, finding inspiration in Hollywood's rustic Laurel Canyon area. In 1968, they founded the City, a trio rounded out by New York musician Danny "Kootch" Kortchmar. Jim Gordon served as guest drummer on the City's sessions that yielded one LP, the

Adler-produced Now That Everything's Been Said. *King chose not to tour at the time, partially due to stage fright, which hampered the album's commercial success. However, it did include songs later popularized by the Byrds ("Wasn't Born to Follow") and Blood, Sweat and Tears ("Hi-De-Ho").*

The seeds had been planted, however; King was finally emboldened to pursue a solo career, unencumbered by any expectations other than honoring her own ear. In 1970, King released her debut solo LP, Writer, *produced by John Fischbach. Her follow-up, 1971's* Tapestry, *wasn't just the biggest album of the year—it made the earth move and continues to rumble to this very day.*

Lou Adler and Berklee College of Music student/guitarist S. Ti Muntarbhorn at a Carole King concert in the Boston Music Hall, 1973.

LOU ADLER: Going back to my early days with Sam Cooke and Bumps Blackwell, the first thing that Bumps, Sam's producer, did was take Herb [Alpert] and me to school. Bumps made us go through stacks of demos, made us break them down. "What was good about the first verse? The second verse? The bridge? How do you make the transition from bridge to third verse? Lyrics? Melody?"

From the beginning, I was a song man. The song was very important to me. That's why working with Carole King on the potential songs for *Tapestry* was so amazing, to hear her sing and play on piano fourteen or fifteen songs of that quality. Twelve of those songs would end up on *Tapestry*.

THE HONORABLE VOLTAIRE PERKINS NEVER RAN IT DOWN LIKE THIS

JAMES CUSHING: People say that the singer-songwriter genre happened because people were recovering from the sixties, but I think there's another reason—California adopted the "no fault divorce" law in July 1970, and then the rest of the country followed suit. Before that time, it was really hard to get a divorce. You had to prove so many things, hire lawyers to get photographs, like Jake Gittes in *Chinatown*. Prior to 1970, the California Supreme Court ruled that, from now on, there will be exactly two reasons for divorce: incurable insanity or irreconcilable differences.

This new law had enormous impact on everyone—the people who made the music, who listened to the music, who sold the music, their secretaries, their lawyers, and the listeners with their radios. All of a sudden, none of them had to worry about hiring a divorce detective. Now, if you got sick and tired of your spouse, you could get divorced right away. So it seemed that everybody got divorced.

From an observer's viewpoint, divorce can be very liberating for both parties, but, according to psychologists, it's the equivalent of a death in the family, in terms of personal trauma. So everybody's newly liberated, but traumatized. In light of this situation, James Taylor singing "You've Got a Friend" sounds really good. But Jim Morrison singing "Break On Through" does not sound as good, because you've just broken on through to the other side of the conventional life, and now that you've broken on through, you're stuck with the fact that it's broken, and you broke it. I hope you like it broken. That's what you wanted. Oh, but you feel a strange nostalgia for the unbroken? You've got a friend.

HANK CICALO: The A&M studio had a Howard Holzer special-made console. You could really punch his board. The only thing I had to worry about was tape. There was no noise reduction in those days. Everything was supporting that voice and that piano. That's where the nucleus of the whole album was. No matter what happened in that room, it had to support it.

I met Carole when she wrote songs for the Monkees, with whom I did four or five albums. The writer becoming the recording artist or star seemed to be a natural path. To see them grow was special, but we were all growing—the producers, the record companies.

Lou had an incredible feeling for songs. He could listen to a tune and go, "That's not it. Let's go on to the next one." Carole's demos sounded like records. They were wonderful. I thought her piano-playing was great; she knew when to lay out, and when to hit it. So when her vocals came in, the spaces were always in the right places.

Right: Carole King in Beverly Hills, just before the release of her debut solo album, *Writer*, 1969. *Bottom:* Carole King performing at the Troubadour in West Hollywood, 1970.

CHAPTER 25

ON HIS CAROUSEL

By 1968, singer Graham Nash had become disenchanted with the direction his band, the Hollies, was headed in. Their most recent album, Butterfly, featured his most ambitious songwriting and vocal arranging. Their record producer chafed at its edginess, as did the other band members, who embraced the hit-making mantra above all else. The group had survived the first British Invasion; their lambent harmonies and pitch-perfect tunefulness provided an arresting counterpoint to the warp-speed gyrations of mid-sixties pop. But there was ferment in the air. The first wave of teen sensations had crested, and in their aftermath, a stronger, more authentic cohort of talent had reassembled, unabashed and uncompromising. Nash was ripe for the plucking.

That year, at the end of an American tour, the Hollies performed at the Whisky a Go Go. In the audience were Davy Jones, John Sebastian, Michael Nesmith, Henry Diltz, David Crosby, members of the Mamas and the Papas, and Stephen Stills. Immediately after the show, Nash was chauffeured down Sunset Boulevard in Stephen Stills's Bentley. In the car, Stills turned to Crosby and nodded toward Graham. "Which one of us is going to steal him?" he asked.

GRAHAM NASH: Ashley Kozak was Donovan's manager, and Donovan was the one who taught me to fingerpick. It was Donovan who gave me my first inkling that I could be an independent artist. I was still in the Hollies, of course, and both Ashley and Donovan encouraged me to keep writing and make a record myself.

Nash officially left the Hollies and threw in his lot with David Crosby and Stephen Stills. Woodshedding in Laurel Canyon, they discovered a potent symmetry in their words and music. It was the sound of comfort and joy.

Working with producer Paul Rothchild, the trio recorded "You Don't Have to Cry" and "Helplessly Hoping." Dissatisfied with the results, they decided to produce themselves.

GRAHAM NASH: We got in Crosby's Volkswagen van, drove up to Wally

Above: The Hollies, New York City, 1966. ♪ *Opposite:* Graham Nash outside Gary Burden's house, Los Angeles, 1969.

Heider Studios, and brought our guitars and amps out and started to make the record. It was small, and it was funky. I'd never met the engineer, Bill Halverson.

BILL HALVERSON: I was a big band guy and a vocal group guy who was in love with the Four Freshmen and the Hi-Lo's, which really served me helping the Beach Boys and set me up for Crosby, Stills and Nash. In 1968, I engineered the Cream "Badge" session at Heider 3 with [George] Harrison and [Eric] Clapton and everybody. So I had some real good history with Atlantic Records. I had done, to [that] point, a lot of sessions, but not a full album. So I asked the person at the booking office if I could put my name on the Crosby, Stills and Nash album. They said they'd get back to me, and they said okay.

GRAHAM NASH: We knew that we had fabulous songs. When I first heard "Suite: Judy Blue Eyes," I couldn't believe it. As a songwriter and as a performer, I could not believe this song. It was stunning in its composition. It went this way, and then it went that way, then it sped up, then it slowed down, and then it peaked. I couldn't wait to record it. As a matter of fact, when we got to the end of the album—I think we had mixed three-quarters of it—Stephen comes into the studio and he goes, "I wanna re-cut it." I said, "What?" "Yeah. I'm not sure that we got it." "I got it. It gets me. If you want to re-cut it, fantastic. Let's go to it." We spent twenty-two hours re-recording "Suite," and never used it.

Mama Cass sings on "Pre-Road Downs." We found a spot for her to join us on a vocal.

Crosby, Stills and Nash shipped in May 1969 and became the record of the summer of '69. It got constant airplay on FM radio formats, spawning two Top 30 singles with Graham Nash's "Marrakesh Express" and Stephen Stills's "Suite: Judy Blue Eyes." Other highlights included Crosby's bluesy "Long Time Gone," Stills's folk-rocking "49 Bye-Byes," and "Wooden Ships," a sci-fi fantasy penned by Crosby, Stills, and Jefferson Airplane's Paul Kantner.

Crosby, Stills and Nash at a recording session at Wally Heider Studios, Hollywood, 1969.

ROGER STEFFENS: The *Crosby, Stills and Nash* debut is one of the greatest albums in the history of rock. Those exquisite harmonies and lilting lyrics . . . that was what we played in Saigon, when attacks were taking place around us. It just cooled everyone out. "Lady of the Island" and "Guinevere"—so hauntingly soothing, yet edgy.

MARK GUERRERO: Richard [Rosas] and I saw Neil Young and Crazy Horse a bunch of times at the Troubadour. We saw Crosby, Stills, Nash and Young's first week at the Greek Theater in 1969—caught them several times, and even snuck in a couple of times. The debut *CSN* . . . to this day, one of my

Crazy Horse outside the Santa Monica Civic Auditorium, 1970.

favorite albums. The harmonies were beautiful. It was so great, and there was so much talent. Stills was at the height of his talent. Neil was even higher than he was in Buffalo Springfield. Stills played a lot of instruments on that album, and the drums were laid on later. It is a different vibe when the drums are overdubbed.

I love the *CSN* album and *Déjà Vu*, but when I heard them at the Greek, I was slightly disappointed. The harmonies could never sound as good as on the record, because the harmonies were doubled on the record. They were perfect, what Neil added for the *Déjà Vu* second album. Again, great songs.

I bought the Crosby, Stills, Nash and Young *4 Way Street*

Crosby, Stills, Nash and Young at Balboa Stadium, San Diego, 1969.

Neil Young at Broken Arrow Ranch in Northern California, 1971.

album, heard it once, and didn't hear it much again. I don't know why.

BILL MUMY: I also was there at the Greek Theater where Crosby, Stills and Nash debuted in 1969 with Joni Mitchell as opening act. Wow. Truly brilliant. I can still hear them singing "Blackbird" in my head. Yep. I was there at the Troubadour for many Neil Young solo acoustic sets, and I was there the night he and Crazy Horse took that stage for the first time. Man, were they loud! They were rough, and they were primal and magnificent.

MARK GUERRERO: I played Neil Young's first solo album every day. I love "I've Been Waiting for You." I also liked his second album, *Everybody Knows This Is Nowhere*, which was totally different. "Cinnamon Girl," "Down by the River"—again, great songs and great passion. Crazy Horse was a funky-ass little group. Basically, it was a garage band, but it works. Simple works for him better. He wouldn't want the Wrecking Crew.

Neil's guitar-playing is interesting. He can be sloppy. Right? He's not that technical. But his passion, you know, and the grit, and the tone, and his style, is what makes him great.

I loved *After the Gold Rush*. My favorite Neil Young solo album. Heard the shit out of it. I loved stuff like "Tell Me Why" and "I Believe in You."

I loved *Harvest*. I liked the songs, the style of the musicians that made up the Stray Gators, and the sound of the album. *Harvest* was the culmination of Neil's first four albums, which are still my favorite Neil Young albums. They were all great, yet very different from each other.

Crazy Horse offered a 1971 debut LP with producer-keyboardist Jack Nitzsche, who joined on electric piano in early 1970. They were first introduced in 1969 as Neil Young's backing band on his second solo album, Everybody Knows This Is Nowhere. *Young had jammed with the Rockets earlier during a Whisky a Go Go show, and*

then enlisted band members Danny Whitten, Billy Talbot, and Ralph Molina to record with him on Everybody Knows This Is Nowhere. *From the opening notes of "Cinnamon Girl" to the closing strains of "Cowgirl in the Sand," Young's alliance with Crazy Horse was forged—one tune on the LP is aptly titled "Running Dry (Requiem for the Rockets)."*

The origins of Crazy Horse go back to 1962, when bassist Billy Talbot and lead singer and guitarist Danny Whitten first met in Los Angeles. They recorded a single for the Valiant label, "Can't Help Loving That Girl." Eventually, after adding some members, they became the Rockets and recorded an album for the White Whale label.

"The chemistry was really great," said Talbot, who met Whitten at the Peppermint West club in '62. "However, those things happen. The Rockets were a jam band—someone would play two chords and we'd soar on that for hours. As we became Crazy Horse, Ralph, Danny, and I were still always a group, not studio musicians. That's what we were able to bring to Neil. And then, on tour, that's where we really developed a following. There seemed to be more to it than just playing rock 'n' roll—there was a spiritual presence and connection with the audience."

After their first Warner Reprise album, Crazy Horse, *they followed with* Loose.

BILL MUMY: The Troubadour was only a few miles away from my house in Cheviot Hills. Each week, a new act would be there, from Tuesday through Sunday, and I was drawn to the Troub like a moth to a flame. I even walked there when I couldn't get a ride and didn't have my driver's license yet.

I was at the Troubadour the week Richie Furay and Jimmy Messina debuted their new band, Pogo. I'd been heavily into country rock since the Byrds first hinted at it on their great *Younger than Yesterday* album, and I'd dug what Michael Nesmith had brought to the Monkees in that style. The Lovin' Spoonful, Rick Nelson, Dillard and Clark—all seasoned their rock with some country.

But no one kicked country rock ass like Pogo did. What a fucking powerful, great live band!

Richie Furay, center stage, singing so strong and high with a huge smile on his face . . . there was no way not to love that guy! Bassist Randy Meisner, soon to become a founding Eagle, singing even higher than Richie and laying down a very solid groove with drummer George Grantham, singing *even* higher—it was almost like the dude was on helium. Jim Messina lookin' cool and pickin' turbo twangy hot licks on a vintage Fender Telecaster, bettered only by Clarence White in the Byrds at that time. Last, but certainly not least, absolutely stealing the show, set after set, was Rusty Young on pedal steel guitar, making that instrument rock like it never had before. He made it sound like a Hammond B-3 at times. His lead riffs were astonishing, and his supporting mellower bits sat perfectly in the songs. Amazing players and singers.

Like the original Lovin' Spoonful from that other coast, Poco [formerly Pogo] reeked of having a great time onstage. Their sense of joy was contagious. I saw them every time they played the Troubadour back in the day. The lineup changed with Meisner leaving and Messina quickly taking over the bass chores, then that seat [went] to another future Eagle, Timmy B. Schmit.

Poco in the Orange County countryside, 1970.

Then Messina departed, which was a major loss, to be replaced by the capable Paul Cotton. Regardless of who was in the band, as long as it was Richie and Rusty, it was Poco. They proved they were the real deal every time I saw them live. But for some sorry reason, Poco didn't translate as well on vinyl. The great, well-deserved commercial success that went to Buffalo Springfield alumnus Stephen Stills with Crosby, Stills and Nash—and Neil Young as a solo artist, with Crazy Horse and with Crosby, Stills, Nash and Young—eluded the effervescent Mr. Furay. It's a hard business, as Wild Man Fischer told me ten million times.

I caught Loggins and Messina at an early gig, too. A bit too sweet for me, but cool nonetheless. Joni, Cat Stevens, Carly Simon, James Taylor, Livingston Taylor, Arlo Guthrie, John Stewart, John Sebastian, Dan Hicks and the Hot Licks, Rick Nelson, Jim Croce, Hoyt Axton . . . the list goes on and on. They all played Doug Weston's Troubadour, and I was lucky enough to be there. It was a good thing. A real good thing.

HOWARD KAYLAN: Because I was so much a part of the L.A. scene, I would go to places like the Troubadour to see Tim Buckley with Herb [Cohen]. He knew that I loved Tim Buckley. Oh my God . . . as early as you can go back to his "Pleasant Street." I loved him so much. And I loved him as a human. I just thought he was a special person, and such a gentle soul. Tim had this sadness and this mystery in his eyes that were canyons deep, man. You could look there and see the oldest and most disturbed soul I have ever known. Ever, ever.

JOHN WARE: Linda [Ronstadt] had, and has, an incredible voice—an instrument like almost no other singer, yes, but she also was, to me, a living band instrument without ever "showing off" her chops. In 1968, Chris Darrow came to my house in Claremont, where he also lived, and suggested I call "this girl singer" he'd heard at the Troubadour. He was in the Nitty Gritty Dirt Band at the time and knew me as a guitar player, but he guessed I was still a drummer, and a drummer from Oklahoma at that. Armed with an invitation to come to her house in Santa Monica, I knocked on her door with an audition ahead. She opened and said, "Hey, I know you!" Indeed, we had met a couple of years earlier when I was in a

Linda Ronstadt in Topanga Canyon, 1968.

short-lived group with Levon Helm, Jesse Ed Davis, and Junior Markham that rehearsed in the house in which she lived. Somehow, I never auditioned that day.

For the next few years, on and off, I was a permanent student in the Roundie Grad School of Country Rock. She thought I was the answer to the question, "Where do the best country rock drummers come from?" True or not, her belief in my playing put me on a serious pathway that led to Michael Nesmith, who wrote her first radio hit, and to Emmylou Harris, who I met with Linda, and both of those doors opened to big personal career steps.

Linda is the dean of the school. Her absolutely spot-on taste made the L.A. music scene of the early seventies what it was. One more aside—I've always had the same mixes in my monitor onstage: kick, snare, bass guitar . . . except with Linda. I *always* had her voice beside me. I so looked forward to every show we played, to hear that voice . . . truly inspirational. *The* sound of L.A. country rock.

CHRIS DARROW: Nik Venet made a lot of things happen in this town. I first met him when Linda [Ronstadt] and the Stone Poneys were on *American Bandstand*. I was with the Nitty Gritty Dirt Band that afternoon.

As a teenager, he had an office in the Brill Building with his good friend Bobby Darin. Nik and Bobby were the executive producers on Wayne Newton's "Danke Schoen." As a staff producer and talent scout, Nik signed the Beach Boys to Capitol Records, and Lou Rawls and Glen Campbell as solo recording artists, to the label. Nik was an early supporter of Johnny Rivers, and set up his debut LP. Nik [produced] "Love Her" for the Walker Brothers, a Barry Mann tune with a great arrangement by Jack Nitzsche, which helped relocate the group to England in 1965. Venet signed the Stone Poneys to Capitol.

Nik was responsible for delivering Fred Neil's song, "Everybody's Talking," to the movie *Midnight Cowboy*, that Harry Nilsson sung on screen. Nik was involved with Frank Zappa during *Lumpy Gravy* for MGM. Venet was in the studio with Orson Welles, Jim Croce, the Four Preps, Clara Ward, Rick Nelson, and Dory Previn. Nik produced John Stewart's *California Bloodlines*. He was the executive producer of Don McLean's *American Pie* at United Artists. I worked with him there. Nik Venet is one of the most overlooked label executives and producers in the history of modern popular music.

ANDREW LOOG OLDHAM: Tony Curtis once said to me, "Somebody has to open the door." Brian Wilson should sing harmonies with stacked vocals to Nik Venet every day.

DON PEAKE: In late '68, things were different. Atco put out the album *Gris-Gris* from Dr. John, the Night Tripper. Mac Rebennack was now Dr. John. I had played with Mac on Sonny and Cher record dates, and a Moulin Rouge show. That's when Mac said his famous quote. President John F. Kennedy had been assassinated in November 1963. Sonny came backstage, and we're all standing there. Leon Russell, Dr. John, maybe Mike Post. Sonny says, "We've been asked to play for Mrs. Kennedy, and we're going to New York." Mac turns to me, and he goes, "Them politicians. The scurviest dudes on the set."

JAMES CUSHING: The near-simultaneous arrivals of Dr. John and Captain Beefheart [Don Van Vliet], and their underground artist status on the FM dial, established them both as visionaries. Beefheart was born in the area, but Dr. John relocated here to become himself. The theatricality of Hollywood helped make their personae possible—and I mean real personae, not merely recording contract stage names.

In L.A., both artists were free to be themselves and push the boundaries. In the case of Dr. John, who brought New Orleans mojo to town via the Wrecking Crew and with arranger Harold Battiste, the result was a brilliant debut LP, *Gris-Gris,* and its equally wild follow-up, *Babylon.* Humble Pie would cover "I Walk on Gilded Splinters." That song title was a signal for all of us to investigate other sides of our once-confined or restricted journey. They both drew on New Orleans and the cosmos, but the recordings were brewed and done in Hollywood, California.

Beefheart's music and vision reflect Ornette Coleman, Son House, and his own experience as a painter and sculptor. Beefheart was never a retail seller; his early work landed on the regional FM radio dial, and got filed under "underground artist." Both Beefheart and Dr. John sing with gargly-gravelly voices that still scare away the casual listener, but both men became enormously influential on songwriters and vocalists as diverse as Tom Waits and Johnny Rotten.

Beefheart's sensibility has always struck me as the perfect embodiment of the kind of surrealism unique to Southern California, especially the San Fernando Valley,

Nik Venet (*second from left*) with the Stone Poneys at Capitol Studios, Hollywood, 1968.

OUR GUY FROM CLAREMONT, ALWAYS DEEP IN THE ORBIT

CHRIS DARROW: During November of 1967, Mike Nesmith was still in the Monkees, and recorded his first solo album, *The Wichita Train Whistle Sings*, for Dot Records. It was an all-instrumental album of Nesmith's material that featured a fifty-one-piece orchestra, including many of the famed Wrecking Crew. Shorty Rogers was the arranger of the project. Rogers arranged a couple of tracks on our album, *Rare Junk*, when I was in the Nitty Gritty Dirt Band.

The Corvettes in the Hollywood Hills, 1968.

In 1969, Jeff Hanna, my partner from the Nitty Gritty Dirt Band, and I decided to form our own band doing original material. We recruited John Ware on drums and John London on bass to fill out the lineup. We called ourselves the Corvettes. Mike Nesmith, who was a dear friend of London's and had a production deal with Dot Records, liked our stuff and signed us up to the label. I was thrilled to be associated with one of the great record labels of my childhood. The second single, "Beware of Time," was the second cut on a recently released CD devoted to the history of country rock, *Country and West Coast: The Birth of Country Rock*, on ACE Records. We have the second cut on the CD following the Everly Brothers. Unfortunately, our two singles for Dot Records failed to chart.

Linda Ronstadt, who had just had a hit with Nesmith's "Different Drum," was looking for a band to go on tour with her. Since we had no work, Michael suggested that Linda come to one of our rehearsals and check us out. We were on the road with her in a week's time and, for a while, were billed as Linda Ronstadt and the Corvettes, and would perform one of our songs every set. Jeff eventually reformed

Chris Darrow playing his guitar in Claremont, California, 1966.

the Dirt Band, and future Eagle Bernie Leadon took Hanna's place. I believe the Corvettes were Linda's finest touring band, and set the sound for her emerging country rock career.

In 1969, while based in New York for a summer and staying at the Chelsea Hotel, we recorded two songs on a super session album called *Music from Free Creek*. We flew in famed L.A. pedal steel player Red Rhodes to play on our two tracks. One night, while waiting for bandmate Bernie Leadon in the foyer of the Chelsea, I met Peter Asher while he was checking into the hotel. He was on his way to Los Angeles to become head of A&R at MGM Records. Asher had just left the Beatles' record label, Apple Records. I went up, introduced myself, and invited him down to the Bitter End to see us play. He admitted to being a big Ronstadt fan and showed up that evening for the gig. That night was the beginning of a relationship with Peter for both Linda and myself. He loved the Corvettes, and was interested in signing us.

However, at the end of our stay, Bernie got a call from Gram Parsons asking him to join the Flying Burrito Brothers, which he took. Soon after, Mike Nesmith called Ware and London to form a band called the First National Band with him and Red Rhodes. This is when I first decided to become a solo artist. Asher agreed to sign me to a solo deal at MGM, but he was soon let go after his arrival. In 1972, I released my first solo album on Fantasy Records called *Artist Proof*, produced by Denny Bruce, Michael O'Connor, and myself.

Also during our stay that summer at the Chelsea, Linda asked me if I would be interested in being musical director for her next album. The main aspect of this job was finding material that would be suitable for her to record. We chose to drive up to Woodstock, hang out, and see if we could round up some material from the East Coast songwriting contingent. While staying at the Mill Stream Inn, we proceeded to make a list of our favorite old songs and look for new, original ones. One night, Maria Muldaur came by to visit and sang us a song that just took our breath away. It was called "Heart Like a Wheel," by Anna McGarrigle of the McGarrigle Sisters.

Over the course of our stay, I suggested a number songs for Linda that came from my record collection, which included "You're No Good" by Betty Everett and "The Tracks of My Tears" by Smokey Robinson and the Miracles, both of which I had performed with my pre-Kaleidoscope band, the Floggs, circa 1965. Also, one of my all-time favorite songs, "The Dark End of the Street" became another one I was pushing for.

Alas, there was ultimately no interest in the songs we presented to her producer, and the album ended up taking a different turn. However, I played with Linda for about three years after that, until I began pursuing my own solo career.

After moving to L.A., Peter Asher didn't know anyone in the studio scene there, so he asked me for

Red Rhodes playing pedal steel guitar at former Monkee Peter Tork's recording session in Hollywood, 1970.

suggestions as to where to record, and musicians he could use with an artist that he had brought with him from Apple, James Taylor. I suggested Sunset Sound with my favorite engineer, Bill Lazrus, and Russ Kunkel on drums, and also future Eagle Randy Meisner on bass.

In December of 1969, I would play fiddle on the Asher-produced *Sweet Baby James*, by the aforementioned James Taylor. In addition to working with Ronstadt at the time, I also performed and recorded three albums with former Kingston Trio member and writer of the Monkees' "Daydream Believer," John Stewart. John asked me to introduce him to Asher, which resulted in Peter producing Stewart's 1970 release, *Willard*. I played fiddle on the title track.

In 1974, Linda released "You're No Good" and "The Dark End of the Street" on her album, *Heart Like a Wheel*, named after the title song. This would be the first of many Asher/Ronstadt collaborations, and probably the best. It went to number one on the charts and sold over two million copies at the time. It took almost five years to prove we were right about the material.

Linda Ronstadt has one of the most effortless and alluring voices ever to record in popular American music. It's too bad that she doesn't get more credit for her contribution and development of country rock in the late sixties and early seventies in California.

Left: **Chris Darrow with the Floggs in Claremont, California, 1966.**
Right: **Jennifer Warnes and Claudia Lennear at a recording session for Chris Darrow's *Artist Proof* at Crystal Sound, Hollywood, 1972.**

where his masterpiece *Trout Mask Replica* was written and partly recorded in 1969. It's a surrealism that finds primitive magic within the most banal settings.

BILL INGLOT: In late 1969, the stage was being set for solo artists. James Taylor, Leon Russell, Elton John—his first 1970 Troubadour shows in L.A.—and then something like the Paul McCartney and Emitt Rhodes first solo albums. So it sort of creates that strange world in the very early seventies, where even Marc Benno gets to make solo records, because he plays rhythm guitar on the Doors' *L.A. Woman*. The table is really set by the success of *McCartney*. Then Carole King from the City group, to *Writer*, and then *Tapestry*. Soft rock happened because hard rock happened. Karen Carpenter was an underrated singer, and an underrated drummer.

You also have the case of the group Bread. Session guys and a Screen Gems staff writer. The thing with Bread is they were signed as a band, and obviously David Gates wrote the hits and then became the hit writer, even though I think the other guys could write songs. The fact that they had to write under pseudonyms just to get stuff placed with people . . . that must have made an interesting band dynamic.

IAN WHITCOMB: In the very late sixties, the music changed around the city. Delaney Bramlett, with Delaney and Bonnie. David Gates and Larry Knechtel had Bread. Leon Russell as a solo—a case where he was a short-haired session man piano player on *Shindig!*, then you suddenly find him with this long hair and this quasi-persona, this mysterious creature behind that hair and hat.

JIM KELTNER: In October of 1968, I got a call from Delaney and Bonnie, who asked me to sub for Jimmy Karstein at Snoopy's Opera House, a little club in the valley. At the time, I was recording with Gabor Szabo, and playing gigs with him at places like Shelly's Manne-Hole in Hollywood and the Lighthouse in Hermosa Beach. Then in February '69, they asked me to do Delaney and Bonnie's *Accept No Substitute* album at Elektra.

Leon played piano on everything but "When the Battle Is Over," which was Dr. John, Mac Rebennack. It was a song Mac wrote with Jesse Hill.

There was a fusion of the Southern people beginning to play with the Hollywood cats. Everyone at the time was being influenced by that scene. George Harrison loved that Delaney and Bonnie LP when he heard an advance acetate of it, and tried to get it on Apple Records. Delaney and Bonnie had tremendous magic and chemistry. I was playing with Delaney and Bonnie at the Thee Experience club on Sunset, and Jimi Hendrix came in two different nights to jam with us.

Then, in 1970, a bunch of us did Joe Cocker's *Mad Dogs and Englishmen*. Jimmy Gordon and I played drums together. It was a very strong band, and the record that came out was very successful.

By that time, I had played with Leon quite a lot, and knew his style. It was real easy to play with Leon in those days. He played very percussive, and with an amazing gospel feel. In 1972, we did Leon's big hit, "Tight Rope," from his *Carny* album.

Around that same period, I played on Dave Mason's *Alone Together* LP on Blue Thumb Records. The producer was Tommy Li Puma. I always loved Dave's playing and singing. I also really liked the way Jim Capaldi played with Dave in *Traffic*. Jimmy Gordon played on "Only You Know and I Know," and interestingly, I had played on Delaney and Bonnie's version earlier. On "World in Changes," I got to play my ride cymbal that I had just bought from Pro Drum Shop on Vine. It was a cracked K. Zildjian that Tony Williams had traded in for a new one while he was in town with Miles Davis earlier.

Carl Radle, Jesse Ed Davis, and I had recorded some Dylan tunes with Leon as the Tulsa Tops, which we did at Leon's home studio in North Hollywood. "A Hard Rain's A-Gonna Fall" is my favorite. Later, while I was living in London, Leon called me and asked if I could come to New York to record with Dylan. We did "Watching the River Flow" and "When I Paint My Masterpiece" on March 17, 1971.

A couple of years later, I played with Bob on his recording of "Knockin' On Heaven's Door" that we did on the big soundstage at Warner Bros. in Burbank. Roger McGuinn played pump organ on that session, and to this day, I cry when I hear Bob's version. It's been covered so many times, but Bob's is the only one that gets to me.

During 1971, I did the "Bangladesh" studio single with George Harrison and Phil Spector at Wally Heider's Studio 4 in Hollywood, and that August, we all did the

CHRIS HILLMAN'S WORDS-EYE VIEW OF LIFE IN THE FLYING BURRITO BROTHERS

CHRIS HILLMAN: The original concept was as plain as day. Here we are, in 1969. We wanted to do country stuff. The first two years with Gram [Parsons] was very good, very productive, and on the same page. He was confident. I was a musician. He wasn't a musician. Gram was a charismatic figure. He was an interesting man at the time. I'm not saying he was a great singer. He wasn't. He was a good singer on a couple of tracks, probably on the first album.

I knew Gram and I would always cherish a couple of years when we really worked together. But it turned into Caine and Abel at that point. And about the trust fund—that was the downfall of Gram. He was handicapped big time with the annual stipend of $55,000. Because—this is what I have said, and you've read it before—it was a Tennessee Williams play. A tragedy in front of my eyes. I was young, but I was smart enough and well-read enough to go, "This is like some Southern Gothic, Faulkneresque, Tennessee Williams thing unfolding here." As I started to lose him.

We were sloppy, the Burritos with Gram. I had just come out of a band that recorded "Eight Miles High," that went from doing Bob Dylan songs to being able to do a song like that—to doing something that musical. To be on par with the Who or the Beatles. The point is, we became a really tight, good band. I'm in the Burritos, and I'm looking at it, [and] it should be perfectly tight, but it wasn't. We didn't put any time into it. I must say—and I'm not patting myself on the back—when Gram left, Bernie [Leadon] and I took that band and we tightened it up and we made it a good band.

Flying Burrito Brothers concert poster drawn by Chris Darrow, 1970.

When Bernie left, we lasted another six or eight months. It became a musical band then.

Did it have the magic that Gram offered? Not really. I still was learning how to sing. Gram was an interesting guy. He had that thing. I don't know what the attraction is, other than that he died in such a mysterious way. Yes, he did some good songs. He had a bunch of good songs. Two songs, "Hot Burrito #1" and "Hot Burrito #2," those are Chris Ethridge songs. Chris Ethridge brought those in, and Gram helped finish 'em. "She"—another great song. Ethridge and Parsons, as well. With all due respect to Gram, he was a good collaborator. We collaborated well, and Gram collaborated well with Chris Ethridge and Bob Buchanan on "Hickory Wind." But they don't get the credit.

So, I always say the Burritos were an interesting band. It was like I was in a Mexican circus. It was funny. I mean, with Gram, it was really extremely entertaining most of the time—until he got so drugged out we had to get rid of him. He was a great guy, and had a great sense of humor.

Chris Hillman and Gram Parsons playing cards at Peter Tork's house in Laurel Canyon, 1968.

two Bangladesh shows in New York. It spawned a great live album set that George and Phil put together.

In November of '71, I recorded with Ry Cooder for the first time on his album, *Into the Purple Valley*. It was done at the Western complex Studio 3 and Amigo (Warner) studio in North Hollywood. That was the beginning of a great musical relationship with Ry.

JAMES CUSHING: Leon Russell, like so many of the deepest L.A. musicians, came from somewhere else—Lawton, Oklahoma—and he brought all the blues and country western and gospel soul the Midwest holds with him. I think of him as a son of Ray Charles. On piano and as a singer, Russell understands Charles's ecumenical spirit profoundly, but it is rare for Charles's influence to result in work of such distinctive originality. Russell's four LPs, made between 1969 and 1972—*Asylum Choir II, Leon Russell, Leon Russell and the Shelter People*, and *Carny*—hold up as least as well as Charles's own records of the period, and in his work with Delaney and Bonnie Bramlett, Joe Cocker, Bob Dylan, George Harrison, the Rolling Stones, and the Concert for Bangladesh, he never loses his own lonely, honky-tonk identity.

IAN HUNTER: My thing was Leon. The piano playing. "Ghetto" was the first time I heard him. It was on a Delaney and Bonnie record. I just couldn't believe it. It was gospel rock. It was unbelievable. I know where he got it from, like Dr. John and a couple of other people, but for me, the style of playing . . . the feel. I went home and tried to do that for months. I tried to learn that song for months. I got near it, but never got it right.

In 1965, native Angeleno Danny Hutton was on the pop charts with his self-penned "Roses and Rainbows." Drummer Earl Palmer was featured with other session stalwarts at Sunset Sound for his "Funny How Love Can Be" follow-up. He also worked for Hanna-Barbera Music as an A&R man. Hutton was a studio maven, eager to learn from the best on both sides of the recording console. His window of opportunity opened when he joined two other vocalists who were equally savvy and ambitious.

Three Dog Night emerged in 1968, led by three vocalists: Danny Hutton, Chuck Negron, and Cory Wells, known around town for his soul-style singing with the Enemies. The group and backing outfit secured their first record deal with the Dunhill Records label after an audition at the Troubadour. Their repertoire introduced several L.A.-based songwriters whose own careers were about to explode: Randy Newman with "Mama Told Me Not to Come," Harry Nilsson with "One," Neil Young with "The Loner," Danny Whitten with "Let It Go," Hoyt Axton with "Joy to the World" and "Never Been to Spain," and Paul Williams with "An Old Fashioned Love Song" and "Out in the Country."

Reviewing demo material during a visit to England in 1969, Hutton met Elton John after a telephone call to the Dick James Music publishing office in London. John and his songwriting partner, Bernie Taupin, were staff writers for James at the time. John

Leon Russell at the Concert for Bangladesh at Madison Square Garden, New York City, 1971.

came up to Hutton's hotel room with several acetate song demos, and Hutton hastily arranged for John to attend Three Dog Night's Marquee Club show (he posed as a roadie after a mix-up on the guest list). Three Dog Night would eventually cover two Elton John/Bernie Taupin tunes, "Lady Samantha" and "Your Song," after Hutton brought them to their producer, Gabriel Mekler.

GARY STEWART: Three Dog Night's legacy was having both the AM and the FM radio world. Look at their first four albums—you can see tracks by Moby Grape, Spooky Tooth, Traffic, the Band, and Argent. The songwriters that they introduced, as well—Elton John and Bernie Taupin, Laura Nyro, Hoyt Axton, Neil Young, and Randy Newman—they were selling out 17,000-seat arenas, like the Forum, at a time when AM artists weren't able to sell out big gigs.

Danny Hutton outside the *Shivaree* set, Hollywood, 1965.

KIM FOWLEY: Danny Hutton used to tout Elton in 1969, and earlier [he] was my driver. I recorded him for Challenge and Invictor Records. His mother was my landlady. Danny was, and is, cool.

In the late summer of 1970, I was living in Sweden. I was at an outdoor music festival and onstage with P.J. Proby. We followed the Move. Elton was there and playing piano with Blue Mink at the time. They followed us. Elton said to me, "I remember you when you were on *Tops of the Pops*, singing 'They're Coming to Take Me Away, Ha-Haaa!'" I was on that 1966 TV show in England, with Los Bravos and the Small Faces. I told Elton, at that 1970 festival in Sweden, "Pay attention to Danny Hutton when you come to town. He will steer you through L.A., and you will survive because of him." I wished him luck. That was a Saturday night, and on the following Monday he left for Hollywood.

Before his Troubadour shows, Elton did come up to Danny's house on Lookout Mountain and played piano. Danny also took Elton for his first Hollywood meal, at Billy James's Black Rabbit Inn.

Elton John first came to America in August 1970 to perform at the Troubadour in L.A., headlining a six-night, sold-out engagement over David Ackles. He had just been signed to Uni Records by visionary talent scout and label head Russ Regan.

Three Dog Night performing at the Miami Pop Festival at the Gulfstream Park Racetrack in Hallendale, Florida, 1968.

RUSS REGAN: Uni was on 8255 Sunset Boulevard. I would eat breakfast at the Continental Hyatt House Hotel every morning.

Lenny Hodes was a song-plugger for Dick James Music. I knew of Dick James—he was the Beatles' publisher—but had never met him. Lenny bought me this record and said, "DJM has a licensing deal with Larry Uttal of Bell Records, and they passed. I've shopped this everywhere, and it's been turned down by five record companies. They think he sounds like Jose Feliciano." Lenny was with Roger Greenaway, who also touted him.

I took it, and around six o'clock that night, I put it on. It was the *Empty Sky* album.

Elton John debuting at the Troubadour, West Hollywood, 1970.

when I shut the record label down for a couple of hours and brought in the employees, sales and marketing, A&R, everybody—thirty people sitting on the floor of my office. I looked up to the sky and said, "Thank you, God." I had never heard an album that good in my life. I played the album, and everybody went out of their minds. It hadn't even been out in England yet. I equated that *Elton John* album to *Pet Sounds*. It was so good. The arrangements by Paul Buckmaster were important, and Gus Dudgeon was a great producer.

I went back with publicist Norman Winter, who did the PR and was head of publicity at Uni/MCA.

"Oh my God," I thought, "This guy is good. What the hell is the problem?" I loved his voice and the songs. "Skyline Pigeon" and stuff like that. "Lady Samantha" was in there. I called Lenny and said, "I like this artist. What's the deal?" He said, "If you like him, Russ, you got him for nothing." So I said, "I want him, and I want to sign him."

He calls me the next day and says, "I just talked to Dick James, and we have a deal. But Dick wants you to buy another act along with this kid. We're giving you Elton John for nothing, and Dick wants $10,000 for a band called Argosy." I replied, "Because you guys are so nice to give me Elton John for nothin', I'll buy this other master for $10,000."

Then, before I could put out *Empty Sky*, the advance of the *Elton John* album came to me in the mail. That's

He had handled Buffalo Springfield. From 1966 to 1968, I signed a lot of acts. The group Pleasure Fair, with Rob Royer. David Gates was hired as arranger and producer. They later formed the group Bread. And Hugh Masekela. We had an instrumental hit with "Grazing in the Grass" that was done at Gold Star. I signed a reggae artist, Desmond Dekker, who went Top 10 with "Israelites." Then Neil Diamond, Elton John, and Olivia Newton-John. Norman was there every step of the way as we planned Elton's invasion of America.

Elton then came to Hollywood in August with drummer Nigel Olsson and his bass player, Dee Murray. Bernie Taupin was there. Norman got a double-decker red English bus to pick the boys up at LAX, with a banner that read, "ELTON JOHN HAS ARRIVED." He then brought them back to the Continental Hyatt House

Hotel, where they were staying.

I had previously signed Neil Diamond to Uni Records, after his Bang Records contract was nullified. I knew Bert Burns at Bang, and he had a key man clause in his contract with Neil. When he died at the very end of December 1967, Neil was available. Ned Tanen at Uni then got a call from Neil's lawyer. Ned said to me, "Russ, what do you think of Neil Diamond?" "I love him!" "Russ, I'm warning you. He has been turned down by five record companies because he wants to have three albums a year, guaranteed." They considered him a singles artist. I said, "Let's give it to him. I want it." We put Neil on at the Troubadour in 1970 and did a live album, *Gold*, that Armin Steiner engineered. I thought Neil could be a great superstar, and I always focused on the songs. I was with him at the label through July 1972. Then Neil recorded *Hot August Night* the following month at the Greek Theater in '72, that Tom Catalano produced.

The day before Elton's Troubadour event, he went over to Neil Diamond's house in Coldwater Canyon. We got Neil to introduce Elton that first night at the Troubadour. I was so darn busy at the record label [that] I couldn't make the Troubadour sound check, so I sent Rick Frio, who was working for me at Uni. After the sound check, Rick calls me and says, "Russ, you're not gonna believe it. We got one here. We got one!"

At the Troubadour, on August 25, 1970, I was ringside for Elton. He played the house piano that Laura Nyro had used earlier, when she was at the club. I called everybody in town. There was Neil, Danny Hutton, Quincy Jones, Henry Mancini, Randy Newman, Graham Nash, David Crosby, Van Dyke Parks, Elton's booking agent Jerry Heller, Mike Love, music columnist Rodney Bingenheimer, photographer Kurt Ingham, and Robert Hilburn from the *L.A. Times*. He then wrote a huge review that helped break Elton. It happened at a time when a great review in a newspaper could help radio exposure. I didn't realize Elton John was a superstar until the Troubadour. Brian Wilson, Gordon Lightfoot, and Leon Russell came other nights. Leon and Denny Cordell had tried earlier to sign Elton to their Shelter Records label.

The first show was broadcast in conjunction with two local radio stations, including KPPC. It was a progressive underground station, and it spun albums and not just singles like most of the other radio stations.

I couldn't believe I was so lucky to have an artist like Elton John. It wasn't a feeling like when Brian [Wilson] would play me his records before they were released. It was beyond that. This was something euphoric. I was so high, I didn't come down for three days.

BRIAN WILSON: Danny Hutton brought Elton up to my house in Bel Air in 1970. Three Dog Night [had done] "Your Song," still my favorite Elton song. He had just played the Troubadour. I heard Elton was nervous to meet me when they rang the intercom system. I was nervous to see him! So I answered the buzzer and sang the first words of "Your Song" to Danny and Elton before they came up.

RUSS REGAN: I picked "Your Song" as the single. I knew FM radio would embrace Elton. I also helped arrange the *11-17-70* Elton John syndicated FM radio broadcast from New York. I gave it the green light. It was later released as an LP in America.

Russ Regan (*right*) presenting Neil Diamond with his gold record award in the Uni/MCA Records office, Universal City, 1969.

CHAPTER 26

THE SWAMP

Following their Vesuvian eruption into the pop music mainstream, the Doors charted a rocky course between the Scylla of Jim Morrison's poetic ramblings and the Charybdis of his impolitic behavior. The band continued to serve a volley of Top 10 hits, interspersed between long album track excursions that made their subsequent releases a rewarding but decidedly mixed affair. The quicksilver Mr. Morrison made for great PR copy, but played havoc with any creative or popular momentum for the group. In the end, the Doors remained an endless enigma, saints and charlatans dependent on Jimbo's tipple of choice.

ROBBY KRIEGER: Paul Rothchild brought in arranger Paul Harris to do the string and horn overdubs on *The Soft Parade*. I never liked the idea myself of strings and horns. It was an experiment. "Wild Child" is one of my favorites because it's live. That one didn't need strings or horns. "Touch Me" was originally called "Hit Me, Babe," and Jim thought people might take it literally on that [*laughs*].

Jim and I had a telepathic relationship. It was a perfect combo. That's how you make a great group. You have three, four, or five guys who come together and have that perfect intuitive relationship, and stuff comes out.

We played the Inglewood Forum in 1969, but didn't tour *The Soft Parade*. We only did it twice. It was another step for the Doors to try something different.

The reason I didn't like it was that I felt we were kind of doing the album for somebody else. But I definitely like how it came out. "The Soft Parade" song is an unusual piece of music. It's a suite of tunes all put together.

RAY MANZAREK: It was a blast to have saxophonist Curtis Amy in the studio. He played the solo on "Touch Me." That was the most fun part. You got to meet all these great musicians and hang out. They were our heroes. George Harrison came to one of our recording sessions.

Morrison Hotel was released in 1970. Critics hailed it as a return to form after the fever dream of *The Soft Parade*. The album's relentless grittiness is best captured in "Ship of Fools," wherein dystopia never rocked so hard.

Well, we had done our horns and strings experimentation. We had had a great time. I had a great time. Critically, it was our least-acclaimed album. However, it has stood the test of time, and there are many great songs on there. So, you know what? Let's go back to the blues. Let's get dark and funky. "Waiting for the Sun" was one of those songs with a great title, and the song took a while to jell.

Lonnie Mack was great, man. "Roadhouse Blues." He was either recording in the next studio, or working around us, or came down . . . I can't remember why he appeared. Paul Rothchild said, "Hey. This is Lonnie Mack."

Above: Handbill for a Doors concert at the Inglewood Forum, 1968.
Opposite: The Doors at the Morrison Hotel in downtown Los Angeles, 1969.

Ray Manzarek in the Doors' rehearsal room, West Hollywood, 1970.

He introduced him to Robby. "Hey, you wanna play some bass?" "I'd love to, guys." Simple as that. That was a great deal of fun. The album was definitely blues, Raymond Chandler. Downtown Los Angeles. Dalton Trumbo. John Fante. *City of Night* by John Rechy. The water and the beach down in Venice.

It was a barrelhouse album, and barrelhouse singing. He's smoking cigarettes. "Jesus Christ, Jim. Do you have to smoke cigarettes and drink booze?" He didn't say it, but it was like, "This is what a blues man does." Oh fuck. That's right. You're an old blues man.

We went downtown for the album cover, to the Hard Rock Café on skid row with Henry Diltz, and a flophouse called the Morrison Hotel. A sign read "$2.50 and up." It was definitely supposed to be a funky album, and you can see that on the inside photo and the front and back cover.

Robby Krieger in the Doors' rehearsal room, West Hollywood, 1970.

The Doors' L.A. Woman arrived in April 1971, co-produced by the group with Bruce Botnick. It was a collection of all original material, except for John Lee Hooker's "Crawling King Snake," which Hooker released on the Modern Records label in 1948.

BRUCE BOTNICK: I brought Jerry Scheff on bass in, because I had just done an album that he played on—Marc Benno's solo album. So I thought,

"Gee, guys. How 'bout if I bring in Jerry Scheff? Oh, by the way, he's Elvis Presley's bass player." Jim thought, "Wow. That's cool. I like that. I love Elvis." Then I suggested to Robby, "What would you think about bringing Marc Benno on rhythm guitar into some of the songs, so you'd be free and not have to do any overdubbing?" He said, "I like that a lot." He always had to do his rhythm part, and then play his solos separately.

It was done at the Doors' rehearsal space, not Sunset Sound or Elektra. We just wanted to get it on tape, going again for performance and not trying to be too perfect, for a little bit more raw approach.

Jim Morrison in the Doors' rehearsal room, West Hollywood, 1970.

JOHN DENSMORE: By the time we did *L.A. Woman*, we did no more than a couple of takes on everything. Jim was in the "bathroom," which was our vocal booth. Just pure passion and no perfection. Strip it down to the bare, raw roots. Elektra was a good studio.

John Densmore in the Doors' rehearsal room, West Hollywood, 1970.

I don't view drums as some do—as a venting rage. I go back to the Native American grandfather beat. If you don't have the good time feel and pulse, all the flash in the world is not going to mean anything, because there's no foundation. Playing drums, for

MY DOORS EXPERIENCE IN HOLLYWOOD

by Jan Alan Henderson

Growing up in the sixties above the Sunset Strip was an experience that defies description. In those days, everything was possible; the world of music had just turned the real world upside down. Fom 1965 to 1970, the Sunset Strip was my nocturnal home.

I remember seeing Ray Manzarek, Robby Krieger, John Densmore, and the late Jim Morrison at the Whisky a Go Go before their first record came out. At that time, music was basically tribal dance music, but that night, my fifteen-year-old world was turned inside out, and I was led to the Doors of Perception.

Before that, I tried to get into a sold-out gig at the London Fog. I ended up listening from the sidewalk, dodging the cops that were trolling for curfew violators. I was denied the visual impact of the band.

I remember walking into Gazzarri's midway through one of the Doors sets, and then, a year later, witnessed the phenomenon that the band had become one magical evening at the Hollywood Bowl. But none of this prepared me for my next encounter with the Doors—or, I should say, a Door.

The summer of 1969, I walked into Sunset Sound looking for a job. The first person I saw at the studio was a guy named Brad Pinkstaff. He was an apprentice engineer, the job I had hoped to get. We became fast friends, and I became his unpaid assistant, and worked on projects with him—*Lord Sutch and His Heavy Friends*, to name one.

One day, I walked into the Sunset Sound complex and someone said to me, "We need a vocal mike in Studio #2." So I went in and set up the mike, and walked out to the foyer. There, waiting for his call to put vocal tracks down, was Jim Morrison, with a gallon bottle of Red Mountain wine. A vocal overdub for *Morrison Hotel*. Now, I had heard of Jim's antics, but this afternoon, the Lizard King was nowhere to be found. Instead, I sat with Jim, had a glass of his wine, and talked about everyday things. He wanted to know about where I went to school and what my plans were. When I left the studio a short time later and walked down Sunset Boulevard, my feet weren't touching the ground, let alone the earth.

Later, Jim picked me up, hitchhiking up Laurel Canyon at Lookout Mountain, and drove me to Ventura Boulevard. As far as I'm concerned, Jim Morrison was a poet and unique performer, the likes of which we shall never see again.

me, is kind of meditative. It's centering. I'm trying to get back to the womb. The mother's heartbeat. The first drum we ever heard.

RAY MANZAREK: The recording of "L.A. Woman" is just a fast, L.A., kick-ass freeway driving song in the key of A, with barely any chord changes at all. It's like Neal Cassady, Jack Kerouac, and Allen Ginsberg heading from L.A. up to Bakersfield on the 5 Freeway.

There's "Riders on the Storm." It's the final classic, man. Let me see what I can do here. It was like "Light

Jim Morrison on the set of *The Smothers Brothers Comedy Hour*, Los Angeles, 1968.

My Fire." It just came to me, the bass line. It became this dark, moody, Sunset Strip, 1948 jazz joint.

The Turtles, who at one time preceded the Doors at the Whisky a Go Go in 1966, disbanded at the end of 1970.

Howard Kaylan and his partner, Mark Volman, turned down offers, including starring as Wolf and Claude in a local production of Hair *at the Aquarius Theatre. Instead, they opted to sign on as members of Frank Zappa's elite group of musical comedians, the Mothers of Invention.*

BRIAN WILSON AND HARVEY KUBERNIK: A CONVERSATION (SLIGHT RETURN)

HK: In 1969, the Beach Boys recorded "Break Away." The co-writer and lyricist is your father, Murry Wilson, who used the pseudonym "Reggie Dunbar" on the credits.

BW: My dad and I wrote it. He didn't want anyone to know that he wrote it with me. Believe it or not, we wrote some of it on my doorstep outside my house, and some sitting around at the piano. Sure, I was still friends with my dad after he didn't work with us anymore. He was a good buddy. It was after I heard a song by the Monkees. It was done at Sunset Sound Recorders.

HK: During 1969, 1970, and '71, you utilized drummer and percussionist Dennis Dragon on both the Beach Boys' *Sunflower* and *Surf's Up* albums.

BW: Yes. I gave him a couple of drum jobs.

HK: Actually, you gave him three gigs.

BW: Okay. Name them.

HK: "Disney Girls (1957)," the drum solo on "Susie Cincinnati," and "It's About Time." Dennis is the percussionist, and Earl Palmer is the drummer on the session.

BW: Right! Exactly!

HK: "Cool, Cool Water."

BW: Well, there is something special. The recording session was brilliant. Mike was absolutely brilliant. He was right on.

HK: "Don't Go Near the Water."

BW: Totally Alan's trip. I was not part of that. Same with "California Saga."

HK: "Forever."

BW: Oh, God. Well, I helped Dennis with the arrangement, and he wrote the song. A tearjerker. Dennis is an underrated music person.

HK: "Surf's Up."

BW: Van Dyke and I wrote that at my house. It was about eleven o'clock in the morning. We had a sandbox with a piano in it, and it took us thirty minutes to write. We just wrote it really spontaneously.

HK: "Feel Flows."

BW: That was Carl singing. Charles Lloyd is on it.

HK: I love your recording of "'Til I Die."

BW: Well, I put a B note in G major seventh chord and it was a third in the chord, and the note in the key of G resonates pretty well. Lyrically, I tried to put nature in there. Water, earth, rocks, and leaves.

HK: Did one of the principal guitar leads on "Marcella," a 1972 single from the Beach Boys' *Carl and the Passions—"So Tough,"* owe something to George Harrison's lead guitar part on "Let It Be"?

BW: Absolutely. Absolutely. Marcella was a Spanish chick that worked at a local massage parlor.

HK: One of my favorite tunes from *Sunflower* is "This Whole World." It has an ARP synthesizer and all sorts of bitchin' production going down with engineer Stephen Desper. But Brian, the recording is only like two minutes and twenty seconds!

BW: Harvey. A song is never finished.

Left: **The Turtles, 1969.** ♪ *Right:* **The Mothers of Invention outside Herb Cohen's rehearsal studio, Hollywood, 1971.**

Volman and Kaylan were now billed as "Phlorescent Leech and Eddie"; Kaylan was the former, and Volman, the latter. They were not allowed legal use of their own names until multiple Turtle lawsuits were settled. The duo went on to record and tour extensively with Zappa over a two-year period.

HOWARD KAYLAN: I followed Zappa's records. I worshiped *We're Only In It for the Money*—one of the greatest rock records of all time. The cover art, too. It was better to me than the Beatles were at the time. There was a lot more content. A lot more undertone. A lot more subplot. A lot more "wake up, America" kind of thing.

Whether it was real or imagined, I thought that Frank was the most brilliant writer since Dylan. I loved the Beatles stuff, and not to take away from it, but this was new. I wore out copies of it, even eight-track cartridges.

I certainly knew, with "Eddie, Are You Kidding?," that once that got recorded on *Just Another Band from L.A.*, it would be around, as "Happy Together" was around. I knew it. I know Frank connected with it, and if he laughed and we

got to record it, it would be around as any Zappa record would be around. I could never see that going out of favor.

We went into the rehearsal hall one afternoon, and Mark and I started to go through the routine. Frank listened to the routine, started laughing, and didn't know what it was. He tried to get us to explain to him about this little Eddie [Nalbandian], who was the owner of Zachary All Clothing on Wilshire Boulevard—a guy with a rack of suits who gives you a spiel on TV commercials late at night. Unbelievable. Frank just loved it and thought he could build a song from it right then and there.

To be a part of Frank's culture was even better than being a part of Frank's band, because you knew you were going to be immortalized.

Kaylan and Volman appeared on the Zappa albums Chunga's Revenge *and* Fillmore East – June 1971, *as well as the soundtrack to Zappa's surrealist film,* 200 Motels. *They were also featured on* Just Another Band from L.A., *recorded live at the Pauley Pavilion on the UCLA campus.*

Mark Volman and Howard Kaylan outside Gary Burden's studio in Venice, 1972.

GENE AGUILERA: To me, Zappa is tightly linked to the music of Los Angeles and the East L.A. music community. Always will be. When I first heard *Freak Out!*, I freaked out. Because there was a lot of doo-wop in there. There was a lot of Chicano in there. I felt he was sending me a direct message, right to my heart. He had Roy Estrada on bass. Chicano from the beginning. He has these songs like "Trouble Every Day," about the August 1965 Watts Riots. It was very L.A. He just didn't do these three-minute songs of love. He talked about a lot of politics. A darker shadow, the underbelly. Zappa sang of "going to El Monte Legion Stadium" and later, as a solo act, played the storied Olympic Auditorium. Even the title of the Mothers of Invention LP *Just Another Band from L.A.* appears resplendently in cholo lettering by Leo Limon. What a genius writer he was. I have Frank Zappa up on my wall.

Frank Zappa was injured during a concert in London in 1971, putting the Mothers on hold. Kaylan and Volman used the time to record their album, The Phlorescent Leech and Eddie, *for Reprise Records. They also sang on the first Steely Dan demo for a publishing company affiliated with ABC Records.*

HOWARD KAYLAN: In fact, the song was "Everyone's Gone to the Movies," that Roger Nichols engineered. That was the demo Donald [Fagen] and Walter [Becker] gave to ABC Records. Donald and Walter were the first guys who ever hired us to sing on their sessions. Donald didn't want to sing, because he thought he had a crappy voice.

Before any of that happened, we got the call asking if I wanted to be the lead singer of Steely Dan. "I would love it. I'm flattered, thrilled, and really love the songs you are writing. But Mark and I have done this as a team; we're writing songs as a team. I wouldn't feel right about leaving him." I still think I did the right thing. So I said no.

WALTER BECKER: I think when Donald and I started out, we were arrogant enough to think we would be successful, in spite of the fact that what we were doing was as far off the beaten path as it was. So we kind of had enough confidence in what we were doing to keep at it until we prevailed. We were probably successful in what we were trying to do in the seventies, at projecting a kind musical

persona that was not particularly, you know, tied to one or two or five individuals, and that was rather an outgrowth of our writing and recording style.

JELLO BIAFRA: Frank Zappa first played an important role with me with his band, the Mothers of Invention, which I didn't like in eighth grade, then totally loved in ninth grade. I was only beginning to realize that you could mix rock music with good lyrics—at least, lyrics that would upset the right people. Thus I got into Alice

---

LISTENING TO SAVOY BROWN AT THE SANTA MONICA CIVIC AUDITORIUM

by HARRY E. NORTHUP

If/if i if i/if i can can get/can get into in-/to the rhy/rhy/rhyth/rhythm of this/of this/of this/of this song/if i can get into the/rhythm of this song/if i can get/can get/can get/if i can get into the rhythm/ if i can get into the rhythm of/this of this/of this song/if i can get into the rhythm of this song/there is/there is/a possibility.

August 21, 1971 • Harry E. Northup
Copyright © 2012 Harry E. Northup

Kim Simmonds, founder and lead guitarist of Savoy Brown, 1989.

Cooper. Then Zappa hit all kinds of raw nerves, 'cause he was satirizing the same kind of people I had to go to school with and stuff.

I even tried to do a stage play of "Billy the Mountain" from *Just Another Band from L.A.* when I was in high school. But it was a class assignment, and some of the people were not into it at all. It didn't really come out very good.

Even then, Zappa wasn't just cynical about the people he called "plastic"; he went after the stupid side of the "Summer of Love," and the escapist side as well. And right there at the beginning, he was pointing to a possible government role in manipulating people through drug abuse. Frank was the first one who laid it out to me that it was possible to talk about these other things that concerned me but put it with interesting music at the same time. Of course, his sense of humor was amazing, and I saw a lot of people around me through the same lens that Zappa saw people.

Released in the spring of 1971, Graham Nash's emotionally charged solo work, Songs for Beginners, *followed in the wake of a temporary split with his bandmates, David Crosby and Stephen Stills.*

Nash's album is bookended by two protest songs: "Military Madness" and "Chicago," a piano-driven march on behalf of the Chicago Seven, then on trial for conspiracy and inciting to riot during the violent protests at the 1968 Democratic National Convention.

Nash realized that this album was an unexpected gift, after writing several songs about his breakup with Joni Mitchell ("Better Days," "Simple Man," and "I Used to Be King") and Stills's relationship with Judy Collins ("Wounded Bird"). Nash was inspired to keep writing. "I realized I could craft something special that you could listen to and could help you in your own life," he said. "At the time I wrote those songs, they were very hopeful. There was bleakness, but I tried to put an opening of light at the end."

David Crosby's solo LP, If I Could Only Remember My Name, *was in the record bins during 1971. Recorded in San Francisco, the album features musical contributions by some Bay Area music veterans, including members of the Grateful Dead and Jefferson Airplane: Jerry Garcia, Phil Lesh, Bill Kreutzmann, Mickey Hart, Jorma Kaukonen, Grace Slick, David Freiberg, and Paul Kantner.*

Joni Mitchell and Graham Nash, Big Bear, 1969.

It was nothing to rival the solo album sales figures of Nash and Stills, but Crosby's "Laughing," an aching lament for a generation's loss of faith, and "Cowboy Movie," an eight-minute surrealist dream, would be spun regularly on select FM radio stations.

In 1968, Ike and Tina Turner signed with the Beverly Hills-based Blue Thumb Records and had commercial success with their album Outta Season *and 1969's* The Hunter. *In 1970, they earned a Top 40 hit with their cover of Sly and the Family Stone's "I Want to Take You Higher." Later in the year, they moved to the Liberty label and charted with a frantic reworking of Creedence Clearwater's "Proud Mary."*

Tina Turner at the Whisky a Go Go, West Hollywood, 1970.

CHAPTER 27

GO WEST, YOUNG CLAN

*I*n 1968, Motown Records moved from Detroit to Los Angeles. Owner and founder Berry Gordy Jr. had a new vision, one that encompassed television and film production. Their new address was Hollywood. Not everyone in Motor City bought into it; the Funk Brothers were left to stew as a new roster of session aces converged around Hitsville West.

In August 1969, Diana Ross co-hosted a media event with Motown at the Daisy Club in Beverly Hills to introduce their newest discovery, the Jackson 5. The group—Tito, Jermaine, Marlon, Jackie, and Michael—and their parents lived in West Hollywood, with some members of the family attending Fairfax High School. Gordy assembled the Corporation, a consortium of songwriters, producers, and arrangers including Alphonzo Mizell, Freddie Perren, and Deke Richards, to craft infectious bubblegum soul like "I Want You Back," "ABC," and "The Love You Save." Puppy love never grooved so good.

In November, "I Want You Back" went to number one on the pop charts. The following month, the Jackson 5 appeared on The Ed Sullivan Show after the release of their debut LP; in January, they commanded the American Bandstand stage. From there, it was on to the L.A. Forum, performing before a sold-out frenzy. The next two years were a blur of television specials, concertizing, and chart-topping. It was an age of innocence, their precocious lead singer a paradigm of American exceptionalism—until it wasn't.

BERRY GORDY JR.: Michael Jackson—the greatest entertainer in the world and one of the smartest people and businessmen in the world. He conducted his own career, basically. He knew what he wanted. From nine years old, he was a thinker. I called him "Little Spongy," because he was like a sponge and he learned from everybody. He not only studied me, but he studied James Brown, Jackie Wilson, Marcel Marceau, Fred Astaire, Walt Disney.

DON PEAKE: I'm on a lot of the Jackson 5 records cut in Hollywood: "I Want You Back," "ABC," "The Love You Save." I was in a core session group that, in a sense, replaced the Funk Brothers, who did the Motown sessions in Detroit. We didn't want to replace them, but Berry Gordy moved out here.

Benjamin Barrett was a very powerful contractor. He worked with Gene Page a lot, and that's how he knew me, 'cause Gene always used me on Spector dates. Benjamin called me on the telephone. "Hey Don, Motown is moving to Los Angeles. I'm forming a staff band and want you to be one of the guitarists in the orchestra."

I went into the room, and there was David T. Walker playing guitar, Louie Shelton on guitar, and drummer Gene Pello. Some of the records have Paul Humphrey. He wasn't like Hal Blaine or Earl Palmer. He was very understated. He was chill. The pianist was Joe Sample, and the bass player was Wilton Felder, sax player for the Crusaders, but he played the bass for Motown.

Ben Barrett told me to go over to the mom-and-pop studio on Ventura and Colfax—Freddie Perren's studio. These were different sessions than with Spector and Brian Wilson. Freddie had us in a compact core group. It wasn't the five guitars, two pianos, two drummers, two

Opposite: **The Jackson 5 at home in Encino, 1971.**

bassists. This was more like Detroit combos, where the bass was featured. It was a whole different kind of music.

Playing with the Jackson 5 was just exciting. I had played with the Everly Brothers from 1961 to 1963, so I was into the harmony thing. I made all those Monkees records, like "Mary, Mary." I did the chart. I played on some, and arranged some. So, I was on the Monkees, Jackson 5, and then the Partridge Family.

Michael Jackson in the Motown Records office, Hollywood, 1971.

The kids were all there. I watched them do their vocals. Michael was magic. All of us looked at Michael and said, "Oh my God. This guy is amazing." We knew, like with "ABC," we were making a great record. Sometimes you can just tell. When I played on the Righteous Brothers' "You've Lost That Lovin' Feelin'," everybody in the room knew it was going to be monster. I played on so many songs by the Jackson 5, including a wonderful record, "Maybe Tomorrow," which has an electric sitar. That's me on the Danelectro.

We started recording down on Romaine Street, just south of Santa Monica Boulevard, near La Brea. The Motown studio, the Sunset Room. We also worked at the Crystal studio. It was a big room. The Motown studio was a little smaller. We did some Supremes records there with producer Frank Wilson.

KEITH RICHARDS: I have picked up as many hints on guitar playing as I can from Don Peake, who is the Everly Brothers guitarist. He really is a fantastic guitarist, and the great thing about him is that he is always ready to show me a few tricks.

As the sixties began, Los Angeles—the City of Quartz—began to shatter some very decisive socio-cultural lines that would come to define the decade. Hollywood had routinely played the apocalyptic card throughout the fifties with dozens of bug-eyed, sci-fi movie meltdowns; all manner of biblical and otherworldly plagues were brought upon the city.

In 1961, the devastation became unsettlingly real. Fire, fueled by the Santa Ana winds—"Devil Winds"—brought the wealthy enclave of Bel-Air to the brink of physical ruin. On December 14, 1963, the Baldwin Hills Reservoir cracked, and three hours later spilled 250 million gallons of water onto La Cienega (the Spanish word for swamp, ironically) Boulevard, destroying 277 homes and killing five people.

Concerned residents leaving the adjacent neighborhoods reached critical mass in the aftermath of the August 1965 Watts Riots, also known as the Watts rebellion. The six-day ordeal televised live (the first reality programming?) would end with thirty-four deaths, over 1,000 injuries, and nearly 600 buildings ruined or lost. Angelenos with money fled the inner city for the sprawling suburbs and their promise of good schools, good jobs, and a swimming pool in every backyard. The power nexus of the blue-rinsed old money—centered around the downtown region—soon faced competition from the burgeoning West Side, a nexus of Jewish wealth, entertainment industry muscle, and more liberal sensibilities brought on by the the maturing baby boomer generation.

Similarly, the San Fernando Valley was transformed from a parade of orange groves into a bastion of middle-class aspiration. Cheap land and plentiful water (think Chinatown) ensured that the vague outlines of waspy L.A. dissolved into the more pleasingly metaphoric "seven suburbs in search of a city."

The music scene was once again subjected to the heavy hand of the "thin blue line." Bands were subject to racial profiling by police and sheriff departments, particularly around their personal appearances on the local club and concert circuit. Newspapers and television outlets promoted suspicion on their broadcasts; you could always get ratings by plugging sex, drugs, and rock 'n' roll. The well-regarded newsman and commentator George Putnam asked nightly on TV, "It's ten o'clock. Where are your children?"

JOHNNY ECHOLS: When Arthur [Lee] and I went to Dorsey High School, there were no racial problems. Things were different there. We did not have that kind of chaos or animosity, or racial shit, pre-summer of the 1965 Watts Riots, or after it. It's so strange that it started later on. I think what happened was that there was an enclave there, and people were interested in bettering themselves and the community where Arthur and I lived. There were Japanese and white people living there, Hispanic, black, all in the same area. We're in the same Boy Scout troops, and we spent the night at each other's homes, ate at each other's houses. We never noticed any of that crap.

In the early and mid-sixties, the cops didn't mess with us, and we never got pulled over and hassled in our cars. We were cool, because L.A. was pretty cool and the cops were pretty cool, even then. They didn't do stuff or go out to just profile, unless you lived way over near Watts or South Central—they were probably hassling those people. But where we lived, it was such a cosmopolitan area that I rarely saw a cop car drive down Twenty-Seventh Street. They just didn't bother us.

Later, in Love, I was stopped after our show one night at the Whisky and frisked against the car on Sunset Boulevard. Love later did some dates, even gigged in Arizona—not the best sound systems, or having to use the house PA. There was another reason about why we didn't play out. It's a down reason, but the thing was, if we had been an all-black group, we would have been perfectly fine going through the South and Midwest. But since we were an integrated group and had a reputation for the girls coming up to our hotels, and stuff like that . . . when these girls would come into our rooms and stuff, the cops are always there watching to see who goes into the room, and checking IDs. We were told really quickly that if we were going to play in the South, we could find ourselves in some serious trouble.

JAMES CUSHING: In 1968, I heard about the death of Martin Luther King Jr. on KRLA. And later, in '68, Bobby Kennedy on KPPC. Then 1970 was Ruben Salazar and the police-led riot in East L.A. When the Esalen/encounter group/Synanon Game/therapeutic consciousness entered the period, a lot of buried racism came out, just as it has with the recent 2012 election of Barack Obama.

Plus, Vietnam contributed to an "Us vs. Them" mentality regarding police and non-police. The Black Panthers grabbed the spotlight later that year. They convinced enough white people that the apocalypse was nigh, and it was time to move to Simi Valley, Calabasas, or wherever.

Love's *Forever Changes* could be considered a political album, and so could the 1969 Crosby, Stills and Nash debut. There has always been the paradox of the leftist political consciousness being brought into the cosmopolitan world of Los Angeles by way of the entertainment business. The city has always been full of the tradition of massive contradiction, and that fact looms in the background of all its popular culture, particularly the R & B and jazz from Central Avenue. The rock and pop made in town were propelled to create singles and albums from this environment.

Perhaps Thee Midniters and Cannibal and the Headhunters were the earliest L.A. examples, but the new musicians getting record deals in the 1968–1972 era did not try and assimilate into the dominant white/mainstream culture. This was an example of the manifest desire to be true to yourself and your roots, not to assimilate.

The new political awareness could be overt and subtle at the same time. The Monkees were a subtly political band. Check out their feature movie, *Head*, but also the joy, silliness, and fun to be found in their 1966–1969 catalog. Joy has a political aspect; the freedom to be silly was one of the goals of the cultural revolution!

A handful of new groups in town coming from blues, jazz, and Latin perspectives got to make some statements: War, El Chicano, Charles Wright and the Watts 103rd Street Rhythm Band.

For a while, society, radio, and some record labels encouraged neighborhood celebration and ethnic pride with a political twist. The FM radio dial, especially KMET, would play long, extended LP tracks and items like "Compared to What" by Les McCann and Eddie Harris, which was openly political. One morning, I heard the fifteen-minute version of "Voodoo Child," by the Jimi Hendrix Experience, on KMET. The freedom to play the cosmic blues was another goal of the revolution!

When this music received airplay, it reached the multi-ethnic audience of Los Angeles by way of KHJ and KRLA. It was not just confined to KPFK-Pacifica or other hidden FM slots that we now know as National Public Radio. It had "commercial potential."

Alternative newspapers like the Los Angeles Free Press *were reporting regularly on the Chicano Moratorium, an anti-war movement of Mexican-American activists who opposed the Vietnam War. An August 29, 1970, march in East Los Angeles attracted over 30,000 demonstrators. Local police and citizens were alarmed. One hundred and fifty arrests were made and four people were killed, including journalist Ruben Salazar, a news director on Spanish television who penned columns for the* Los Angeles Times.

In 1967, East L.A.'s Thee Midniters recorded "The Ballad of Caesar Chavez," and in 1970, "Chicano Power." The Chicano rock and brown-eyed soul mixture of El Chicano and their monumental hit "Viva Tirado" on the Kapp label crossed the AM/FM radio divide, further ushering in Chicano consciousness to the Golden State culture in 1970. Their second platter, Revolucion, *contained the politically-charged tunes "Viva La Raza" and "Don't Put Me Down (If I'm Brown)."*

The good and groovy vibrations emanating from Boss Angeles radio were no longer just sunny, warm, safe, and white. Bands like War and Earth, Wind and Fire were now delivering a sound more representative of L.A.'s grittier streets.

War's origins go back to 1962, when Howard Scott (guitar and vocals) and Harold Brown's (drums, percussion, vocals) group, the Creators, operated out of Long Beach. Over the next few years, they added Charles Miller (sax, flute, percussion, vocals), Morris "B. B." Dickerson (bass and vocals), and Lonnie Jordan (organ, piano, vocals) from Compton. Joining the lineup next were harmonica player and vocalist Lee Oskar, and vocalist and conga and bongo player Papa Dee Allen, preparing a racially-mixed fusion of jazz, funk, rock, R & B, and Latin. They recorded a couple of 45s for the Dore label.

By 1968, the Creators had become Nightshift, performing backup duties at the Rag Doll club in North Hollywood for aspiring singer and Los Angeles Rams legendary defensive end David "Deacon" Jones.

Miller simultaneously was in the well-respected instrumental funk and psychedelic combo Señor Soul, residing at the Double Shot label. Their rendition of the Isley Brothers' "It's Your Thing" was a turntable favorite all over Southern California. (In 1970, Miller would do his last Señor Soul recording sessions with all his partners in War.) In 1969, they were spotted by record producer Jerry Goldstein of "Hang On Sloopy" fame, and the former lead singer of

Maurice White, Phillip Bailey, and Verdine White of Earth, Wind and Fire performing at the Forum in Inglewood, 1977.

the Animals, Eric Burdon. The sense of brotherhood and socio-political messages in the lyrics appealed to Burdon. Goldstein produced their debut MGM LP, Eric Burdon Declares "War," *in 1969. A single, "Spill the Wine" broke locally and nationally when they were first billed as Eric Burdon and War.*

In 1970, The Black Man's Burdon *was released. During a European tour, Burdon left, freeing the outfit to continue down their own path. Their first Goldstein-produced album on United Artists came shortly thereafter, simply titled* War. *In 1971, the band released* All Day Music, *and chart entries "All Day Music" and "Slippin' Into Darkness" followed. In 1972 came* The World Is a Ghetto, *which featured the smash hit, "The Cisco Kid."*

LONNIE JORDAN: People would always say we had a mixture of Latin, R & B, gospel, jazz, and reggae, and I told them, "Well, actually, you can just narrow it down to 'universal street music.'" It's like a mixed salad bowl of all genres. I know that some of our music back in the day, when the Vietnam War was happening, had an impact. I just didn't know that it would continue on today.

Former Chess Records studio drummer Maurice White came to Los Angeles from Chicago in 1970 to spearhead and guide Earth, Wind and Fire. Joe Wissert produced their Warner Bros. self-titled debut LP and The Need of Love *in 1971. They also provided the soundtrack for director*

Melvin Van Peebles's Sweet Sweetback's Baadasssss Song *on the Stax Records label.*

EW&F disbanded in 1972, only to reform again in 1973 under White's direction. A string of commercial and critically acclaimed albums followed for the Columbia Records company.

ROSEMARIE PATRONETTE: I was working at Sight and Sound in the Valley, on Van Nuys and Victory. I managed the classical department. Getting there from our house in Tarzana was frightening as well, seeing all the damage in real life as opposed to TV. All the cassettes were on the floor when I got to work. The wall of cassettes was huge, and ran the length of the store behind the counter and nearly up to the ceiling. Everything was alphabetized, so of course it was a nightmare to start over and reorganize it. Some of our dear friends were completely terrorized by that quake, and I don't think they ever recovered, psychologically!

In 1969, there had been warnings in the form of song— Mama Cass Elliot's "California Earthquake" and Shango's "Day After Day (It's Slippin' Away)." Carole King's "I Feel the Earth Move" could be perceived as a commentary on romantic or seismic activities from her Laurel Canyon abode.

During that Mother-Nature-induced rumbler in 1971, the brick chimney on top of our house crashed into my upstairs bedroom. I immediately fled to Fifth Street, clutching all my Rolling Stones Rubber Dubber

Samantha, Ami, and Micky Dolenz sitting in their Bentley outside their Laurel Canyon home in Los Angeles, 1969.

and TMQ bootleg albums, while UK TV host and model Samantha Dolenz, wife of Monkee Micky, first had to make a stop into her closet and have a think about her wardrobe before running out of their Laurel Canyon home.

JAN ALAN HENDERSON: My mother came in my bedroom and said, "Earthquake!" I said, "No. The Russians have finally done it." And I went back to sleep. It cracked the foundation of our house, but I slept through the geological holocaust. In Laurel Canyon, the white man violated the Native American's sacred burial space, and the karma is irreversable.

LONN FRIEND: Wasn't conscious of the seismic irony until years later, but the earth shook under my born and bred San Fernando Valley seven years to the day that the Beatles debuted on *Ed Sullivan*. Both events rocked all sentient songful beings on terra firma to the roots. I was a senior at Milliken Junior High. We lived in a small apartment—me, my brother, Rick, and Mom, who slept on a pullout sofa in the living room so we could have the bedroom.

I was reading Ray Bradbury's *R Is for Rocket*, particularly tweaked by the short story, "A Sound of Thunder." Theme is shaking out here. Then, during dream state, before dawn or morning whiz, I am thrown—no, *throttled*—out of bed. *Boom!* But it doesn't stop. Oh, no. Our whole place starts rippling and rolling like a canoe at sea in a hurricane. Mom's screaming, "Get in the hallway! We're having an earthquake!" The Friend brothers are surfing, not freaking, but definitely rattled.

Took hours for the building to stop quivering. Our Buffalo Avenue apartment faced Mr. Ito's garden, where I

WAKE ME, SHAKE ME

Don Peake, a Laurel Canyon resident, was present for a new sort of L.A. rock 'n' roll that occurred on the morning of February 9, 1971, at 6:41 AM—a sixty-second, 6.7 magnitude earthquake centered in nearby San Fernando Valley. Countless properties, buildings, concrete dwellings, and apartments, as well as several Los Angeles schools, were damaged. L.A. High School was destroyed, and their students were bused over to Fairfax High.

A traumatized Southland had witnessed sixty-two people killed, two hospitals wrecked, and 80,000 people evacuated. In Van Nuys, the popular Sight and Sound record store had its entire cassette section—tapes and cases—shattered all over the aisles.

planted cabbages. I came out in the morning to assess the damage. Couple windows in our courtyard were cracked, but thankfully, no one was hurt. They cancelled school, so I stayed in and listened to *Let It Be*, the Beatles vinyl finale, released a few months prior. And across the universe I went.

This earthquake had a much larger impact on SoCal culture than anyone would like to admit. This earthquake was not a subject for debate; it was an emergency message in a language of its own. Forget lifestyles—the very earth below you was in a state of flux!

The ramifications of this 1971 Sylmar-based shocker led to many affluent Laurel Canyon homeowners—a slew of hit-making songwriters, musicians, and record label executives housed in Mt. Olympus, plus a handful of record producers, sound engineers, entertainment studio managers, and AM and FM DJs—putting their houses up for sale.

Those who remained in Laurel Canyon would soon experience the blight of another Old Testament pestilence; cocaine and quaaludes began to march through the hillsides like marauding ants, eating away at the roots of community. The horrors of Wonderland Avenue were just a shot away.

In 1971, host and producer Don Cornelius took his Chicago-based dance show, Soul Train, *to Los Angeles and national.* Soul Train *shined an Afro-sized light on the inner workings of black youth—their outrageous fashion sense, the high-gloss dance routines, and the pervasive aura of smooth that young white America could only gawk at.*

On August 20, 1972, over 110,000 people witnessed a seven-hour concert in the Los Angeles Memorial Coliseum. The epochal Wattstax music festival celebrated a new direction in soul and R & B for 1972. Isaac Hayes, the Staple Singers, Luther Ingram, Albert King, Little Milton, Johnnie Taylor, and Rufus Thomas contributed to this event recognizing the increasing cultural and financial strength of the downtown and South Central L.A. communities. The entertainers' expenses, the equipment, the promotion, and the advertising were all paid for by the Stax organization, in conjunction with the Schlitz Brewing Company. Ticket sales benefited the Sickle Cell Anemia Foundation, the Martin Luther King Jr. Hospital in Watts, and the Watts Summer Festival. In 1973, the documentary film Wattstax, *directed by Mel Stuart, enjoyed a national theatrical release.*

MEL STUART: They asked me to do the show. I knew a lot about music, but I had never done a show like this. What I did was meet with the Stax people, and basically, the way I wanted to work was to be the only white person. Everybody else would be black. Everybody who would advise me, be around me, and guide me would be black, because they would understand that what we were trying to do was create some kind of personification of the way black people feel at a particular time. I made sure that we hired all-black crews because, at the time, they didn't get a chance to get jobs. I don't do storyboards. I've done too many documentaries, and just follow my brain.

We had Melvin Van Peebles to help with the crowd control. The Stax people lined up all their talent that was available. I was also fortunate, because three or four acts couldn't make it, so I had the Emotions on location in a church, both Johnnie Taylor and Richard Pryor in a funky club, and Little Milton out by the railroad tracks.

The Staple Singers at the Wattstax music festival at the Los Angeles Memorial Coliseum, 1972.

In September of 1972, another collection of regional musical voices was heard on the campus of Cal State Los Angeles, organized by Art Brambila's Brown Bag Productions. There was an emerging world with an emphasis on Chicano culture and self-identity.

Mark Guerrero and Lalo Guerrero at the 1972 dedication of the Robert F. Kennedy Elementary School in East Los Angeles. Lalo performed at the event.

MARK GUERRERO: On September 17, 1972, there was a historic concert in the stadium at Cal State L.A., in East Los Angeles. The artists included El Chicano, Tierra, Mark Guerrero with the Mudd Brothers, Elijah, and Carmen Moreno. The concert was organized by Art Brambila, who was the manager of Tierra and myself.

The concert was the culmination of a two-day, student-sponsored cultural event called Feria de la Raza ("Fair of the People"). Featured was the cream of the crop of L.A. Chicano artists of the time. El Chicano had become nationally known with their hit "Viva Tirado." Tierra had just finished their first album on Twentieth Century Records. I had two singles released by Capitol Records that year as a solo artist backed by the members of the Mudd Brothers. Elijah had just released a great album on United Artists Records. Carmen Moreno was a world-class vocalist with Epic Records. The lineup reflected the diversity in L.A. Chicano music. El Chicano's style contained elements of Latin, R & B, and jazz. Tierra combined elements of Latin, R & B, and rock. My band and music could be described as rock and country rock. Elijah was a funky horn band. Carmen Moreno was a folk singer, both in English and Spanish. The musical event was free to the public, so there

Flier for the 1972 Chicano Rock Concert.

were never any attendance figures. However, the football field and stands were virtually filled.

The Feria de la Raza concert is now considered historic because, as it says on the event's flyer itself, it was the first Chicano rock concert. There had been many shows with multiple Chicano artists, but they were shows in theaters or dance halls. This was a post-Woodstock-style outdoor gathering with festival seating and the scent of cannabis wafting through the air.

The quality of the music and the future accomplishments of the artists make it a significant event in Chicano rock history. El Chicano went on to have another major hit with "Tell Her She's Lovely" in 1973. Tierra had a major hit with "Together" in 1980, and played Carnegie Hall. I went back to school at Cal State L.A., earned a bachelor's degree in Chicano studies, and continued my musical career. My bass player, Rick Rosas, went on to play extensively with Joe Walsh and Neil Young. Elijah went on to record another album produced by rock legend Al Kooper. Elijah's horn section played with Neil Young on his *This Note's for You* album in 1988. Carmen Moreno won a National Endowment for the Arts award and performed at the Kennedy Center in Washington, DC in 2003. All the artists continue to perform to the present day.

I wrote and recorded "I'm Brown" for Capitol Records in 1972. The single, with the original lyric manuscript and picture of the band, was in the Grammy Museum in 2009, in an exhibit called *Songs of Conscience, Sounds of Freedom.*

CHAPTER 28

THE SOUL SURVIVOR AND THE MAESTRO ARRIVE

Pianist, composer, and producer Barry White was a symphony of vibrant contrasts: a great ebony hulk who moved with a sumo's grace; a basso profundo who uttered sweet nothings; a hugely popular and critical success who has been, if not lost, certainly misplaced over the years in the hearts and minds of his countrymen. With apologies to Clarence Clemons, Barry White was the original "big man."

He was born Barry Eugene Carter in Galveston, Texas on September 12, 1944. His family relocated to the Watts area of Los Angeles when he was six months old. He displayed an aptitude for music at an early age, picking melodies at the piano while listening to his mother's favorite classical composers. Hunter Hancock's Harlematinee show on radio stations KFVD and KPOP were part of his ear training. In 1956, the eleven-year-old White reportedly attended and played piano on the Jesse Belvin recording session that yielded the hit "Goodnight My Love."

White's teenage years were cast in iron; he ran with street gangs like the Slausens and the Businessmen, culminating with six months of jail time for car theft in 1960. The experience only hardened his resolve to find salvation through his love of songwriting. At sixteen, he made his first record, "Little Girl," singing harmony with the Upfronts for Lummtone Records. He was a member of two groups simultaneously, the Atlantics and the Majestics.

White played piano on Bob and Earl's 1963 hit single, "Harlem Shuffle," which he also co-arranged with Gene Page. In 1965, he went on the road as the drummer for Jackie "The Duck" Lee. White made his own recording debut in '65 with "I Don't Need It" for the local Los Angeles Downey label. Two years later, he was cutting sides for the Del-Fi, Bronco, and Mustang labels.

In the summer of 1966, Del-Fi owner Bob Keane hired White as an A&R man. White helped Keane produce the Bobby Fuller Four's "The Magic Touch" and "I'm a Lucky Guy" at their Hollywood studio. White also worked on a single with the Versatiles, who later became the 5th Dimension. He then produced "Lost Without the Love of My Guy" for Viola Willis White. Bob Keane and Gene Page then produced a soul album for Danny Wagner on the Imperial label. White recorded his own version of the Mac Davis-written Elvis Presley standard, "In the Ghetto," under the name Gene West on Art Laboe's Original Sound. White also was a recording artist on Eddie Davis's Faro label, receiving local airplay with "Tracy."

It was arranger Gene Page who helped White's musical education the most, letting him hang around and sit in on Motown sessions. Some of those mixing and orchestral techniques that White observed evolved into his seventies-era musical persona. With Keane and White's spiritual advisor/friend, Larry Nunes, White then cut three singles on the Mustang label with a female trio. One of them, "It May Be Winter Outside (But in My Heart It's Spring)," co-written with Paul Politi, featured Felice Taylor's vocals, and was a crossover hit in the U.S. and on the Billboard Top 50.

Another White and Politi composition for Taylor, "I Feel Love Comin' On," with an arrangement from Page, was nearly a Top 10 UK singles chart entry and spun in rotation on John Peel's BBC Radio One Top Gear program in October 1967. In September 1968, White appeared as a background vocalist on Jackie DeShannon's Laurel Canyon album on Liberty Records, and also wrote "I Got My Reason," which

Opposite: **Barry White in his office, Los Angeles, mid-1970s.**

he later sang with DeShannon on the 1969 television show Playboy After Dark.

Larry Nunes was a major player in L.A.'s record distribution business. A key rack jobber, Nunes started the Tip Top company in 1949, then partnered with Monroe Goodman. In 1969, he sold the operation to Transcontinental Music Corporation. Nunes formed Soul Unlimited, Inc., which worked closely with White to guide his career.

It was Nunes who made the fateful introduction of White to veteran record label executive Russ Regan, who was heading Uni/MCA Records at the time. Along with Gene Page, they collectively scored the million-selling "Walkin' in the Rain (With the One I Love)" with Love Unlimited (Glodean James, Linda James, and Diane Taylor) for the Uni label.

RUSS REGAN: Rick Frio at Uni/MCA was my sales manager, and Larry Nunes was a big rack jobber. Larry knew me, but he called Rick because he felt he couldn't get to me for some crazy reason. Larry brought "Walkin' in the Rain" to Rick, and he buzzed me on the intercom. "I've got a record over here you ought to hear." So he came to my office, and I bought it in four minutes flat. I had never heard a record like that in my life. His voice blew my mind, and the girls were great on it. It came out on Uni and went to number one on the R & B charts. Top 10 pop. Number fourteen in the UK in July of 1972. We sold a million records.

I left Uni Records on July 6, 1972, because I wasn't being treated right. I was then asked to run the new Twentieth Century Fox record label. I got a phone call from Barry. I said, "Barry, I didn't even know you could sing." So he came over to see me and said, "Russ. I can sing, and I want to make an album." "Okay. I'm the president of the company. What's it gonna cost to make this album?" He said, "Forty-seven thousand dollars." So I said, "You got it. No problem. Go make me an album." So the first record he brought me out of the studio was "I'm Gonna Love You Just a Little More Baby." His album, *I've Got So Much to Give*, went platinum.

Barry White is one of a kind. Have you ever heard a voice like that? The other thing I told him when we did the deal [was], "When you go platinum, Barry, I'm going to tear this agreement up and we will sign the agreement your lawyer wanted." That's exactly what happened. I

Barry White and his backing group, Love Unlimited, which included his second wife, Glodean James (*center*), Los Angeles, circa 1970s.

had support at the label. I saw the impact when he played live. I gave him everything. He had self-confidence.

The magic elements to Barry White's songs are great melodies and simple lyrics. They are not complicated songs.

DON PEAKE: I first met Barry at Gold Star, and he asked me to play on a song—"Until You Were Gone" by Brendetta Davis. Barry then said, "Don. I want you on all my records." Maybe 1967, '68. I knew he was a monster back then.

Barry White learned a lot watching Motown sessions and arranger Gene Page. Some of us on the Jackson 5 sessions became part of the nucleus on the early and mid-seventies Barry sessions. He knew what he wanted. Then he got his Love Unlimited thing happening, and I played on all those. He was really good about talking to us. We just played well together, and we knew each other well. Me, guitarists Dean Parks, Ray Parker Jr., David T. Walker, Wah-Wah Watson, Wilton Felder of the Crusaders, drummer Ed Greene, Gary Coleman on percussion . . . Barry would play keys, or someone else, but he would come in and Gene Page would have done some sort of rhythm chart at the Whitney studio in Glendale or ABC Studios.

These are different guys, because it's an R & B date. Barry would say something, give a direction to someone like Wah-Wah Watson—then over to David Walker, say something and David would do it, and then over to me. "Don, give me the gallop. *Bump. Bump.*" The dancing would fit. Barry was a very hands-on—come right up to your music stand and sing to you, or bring us over to the piano. They were longer recordings than the session guys on the Spector, Bono, and Wilson sessions. I can't explain why it worked on the radio and sold millions of records, except the grooves we were laying down were incredible. You can't help but tap your toe to those things.

On Barry's records and the Jackson 5 sessions, the guitarists were up front. We were not buried in the mix. There were hard grooves. That was Barry talkin' to us. Barry knew in his head what he wanted. He'd usually start with the drums, and he helped the rhythm section all the time. He also would walk in the studio with one-hundred-dollar bills, and walk around and put a hundred bucks on each music stand as he was going around the room. I never thought of his music as sexual. I thought it was love music.

From 1972 to 1978, White's aural odyssey dominated the charts, the clubs, the dance floor, and the bedroom. "Love's Theme" went number one on the Billboard Hot

100. It was also used as the interstitial music to introduce Million Dollar Movie, *an afternoon daily film program hosted by Ted Meyers on Channel 9—a childhood dream of White's fulfilled.*

DAVID RITZ: I love BW. In 1959, he helped pour the cement to build the Los Angeles Sports Arena. But you kind of have to understand him in the context of Isaac Hayes and Curtis Mayfield and Marvin [Gaye] and the orchestration of soul music, when Motown finally had the money to hire fiddlers. His genes were really Holland-Dozier-Holland, who really upped the ante by getting the little Jewish violin player from the Detroit orchestra into Motown. BW heard all that, loved it, and he hooked up with Gene Page.

Page is the key to Barry White orchestrations. He could read and write music, and BW couldn't. BW heard it all—he heard all the lines, he heard four different guitar parts, and he called it out to Gene Page, and Gene wrote it down. In a nutshell, it's Hollywood R & B, beautifully extravagant strings and ornate charts unafraid to be adorned. He was the king of beautiful schmaltz.

In a 1976 interview with me at his spacious home in Encino, White and I talked for a few hours. His favorite record was "Earth Angel" by the Penguins. Around the August 1965 Watts Riots, he had witnessed his friend, Charles Fizer of the Olympics, get his head shot off on the way to a group rehearsal. A decade later, Barry specifically explained why, since 1972, his music and disco in general had been so popular. "Let me tell you something," he said. "In the disco world, the audience is the star."

By 1967, Bobby Womack was living in Memphis and working as a session guitarist on recordings by Joe Tex and the Box Tops at Chips Moman's American Sound Studio. Wilson Pickett recorded his tunes "I'm in Love" and "I'm a Midnight Mover." Womack can also be heard on Aretha Franklin's "Chain of Fools." In Muscle Shoals, he plied his trade at Rick Hall's FAME Studio. Womack is on Dusty Springfield's "Son of a Preacher Man."

In 1969, Womack released his debut solo album, Fly Me to the Moon, *on the Minit label and achieved national airplay with a cover of the Mamas and the Papas' "California Dreamin'." In '69, he penned the instrumental "Breezin'" while working with jazz guitarist Gabor Szabo. The*

Bobby Womack, Hollywood, 1964.

song later became a staple in George Benson's repertoire.

Janis Joplin cut Womack's tune "Trust Me" for her Paul Rothchild-produced Pearl *LP in 1970. Womack was a guitarist on that session in Hollywood. Joplin's song with Michael McClure, "Mercedes-Benz," was inspired by her ride in Womack's car.*

BOBBY WOMACK: Janis called me. "Why don't you come to the studio? It's on Sunset. Come to the studio, and bring me some songs." Her producer [Paul Rothchild] was there.

The thing that blew me away about Janis was when she asked, "What bothers you the most in this business as far as the black and white thing?" And I told her, "Every time I cut a record, I try and cut a record so I can cross

over to appeal. I just don't cut the record. I just want to be able to cut a record, and that's it." And I said, "What about you?" She said, "Everybody keeps saying I'm trying to be Tina Turner." That blew me away. "You don't sound nothin' like her." Jokingly, I added, "You don't look anything like Tina. Well, we both got this problem. So why don't we do something together like a tour? You go out there and let them know."

I hadn't heard this Tina thing, and told her it was in her head. She was very serious. Janis loved Tina Turner. And she ran down how she went to [high] school and she had to blow the school that used to think she was ugly. Janis was talking about the problems she had.

So she told me to come by the Landmark Hotel in Hollywood. Night before she died. I go there, and she was very respectful. I found out a lot about her in a short time. Rothchild called the next day and told me Janis had OD'd.

Womack gained additional studio credits on Sly and the Family Stone's There's a Riot Goin' On, *which shipped in November 1971. That's Womack's wah-wah work on "Family Affair."*

In 1972, Womack signed with the United Artists label, where his album, Communication, *had two R & B hits—"That's the Way I Feel About Cha" and a number-one R & B smash, "Woman's Gotta Have It." The following year he would really arrive, with the Jim Ford-penned "Harry Hippie," which generated platinum sales.*

BOBBY WOMACK: Me and the songwriter Jim Ford became brothers and went to each other's houses all the time. Not just to write, but to hang out and eat. I spent a lot of time with Jimmy, but that's when I knew that drugs was a serious bad thing for a serious creative person.

Jimmy introduced me to Sly Stone. Another Pisces. I was just going through a divorce at the time, and Jimmy said we should meet each other. "You're both Pisces, and you-all gonna relate." But he would always say, "Never go over there without me."

Sly was in the hills. The thing I understood about him was that Sly was one of the sweetest guys in the world, but he's let the negative side of this business turn him into another person that he's not. I noticed it when he was the biggest thing that came along, before Earth, Wind and Fire.

In 1972, Womack was asked to do the soundtrack for the blaxploitation movie Across 110th Street, *which was released in 1973. All the songs were written and performed by Womack, and the musical score was composed and conducted by J. J. Johnson. The recording was subsequently utilized in such films as Quentin Tarantino's* Jackie Brown *and Ridley Scott's* American Gangster.

BOBBY WOMACK: I used to live in Westwood, and wrote *Across 110th Street* in an apartment there. That was very spiritual to me. When I was going through my divorce, [football player] Roosevelt Grier said, "Come on out here. Man, it's cool. There is an available apartment." I felt comfortable, because he was a very levelheaded guy. He wasn't crazy at all. Rosy introduced me to Pam Grier. She sings on the background of *Across 110th Street.*

I remember, when I was about to start *Across 110th Street,* United Artists would always go outside the label to get things for their movies. I approached them one day—the A&R man, Nik Venet—and told him, "The next movie, I want to do." He was definitely involved, because I told him, "If they don't do this, they are definitely gonna have problems with me."

So they brought me this movie. I saw it one time, and I was getting ready to go on tour three or four days later. They said, "You got to have it done and finished in two weeks." "Two weeks?" I stayed up twenty-four hours a day, and when I brought it back with "If You Don't Want My Love" and all the songs I had written, it fit. Man, it was easy to write those songs. I was born in the ghetto. That's what this whole story was about. Nik was the soundtrack co-producer on *Across 110th Street.* Decades later, I got the opening and closing track with it on the film, *Jackie Brown,* and Pam Grier is on-screen in front of my tune.

I got to know Bill Withers. I loved him because he reminded me of a deacon right out of the church. "Grandma's Hands" was done out here. His band had some guys from the Watts 103rd Street Rhythm Band, including drummer James Gadson. They had "Express Yourself" and "Love Land." That boy [Stephen] Stills is the lead guitarist on Bill's "Ain't No Sunshine," which Booker T. [Jones] produced. I did *The Midnight Special* TV show with Bill and Buddy Miles. Bill was real clean-cut, and very serious. In the mid-seventies, we made a record together, a remake of "It's All Over Now" that he sings on. I carry respect for him.

Later in the seventies, I sang on the version of "Harlem Shuffle" by the Rolling Stones. I knew Bob and Earl, who did the original, but when I was doing the vocal with the Stones, I never thought about them. Never thought, "Why did they pick that song?" I think it was Keith [Richards]. After that, I realized, "Man, music is a universal language." That song was cut fifteen years before. What happened to Bob and Earl? Barry White was involved with the original recording in 1963, but I had never met Barry. Then I went over to the A&M studio to put something on a record, and Barry came in. "Man, I love your music." We'd be complimenting each other.

BOSS HIT BOUNDS

FLAMINGO
Herb Alpert & The Tijuana Brass A & M

LAST TRAIN TO CLARKSVILLE
The Monkees Colgems

I CHOSE TO SING THE BLUES
Ray Charles ABC

WIN CASH!
play
TIME BOMB
on

93/KHJ
BOSS RADIO
IN LOS ANGELES

BOSS 30
FROM 93/KHJ

Hear THE REAL DON STEELE on 93/KHJ 3-6 p m

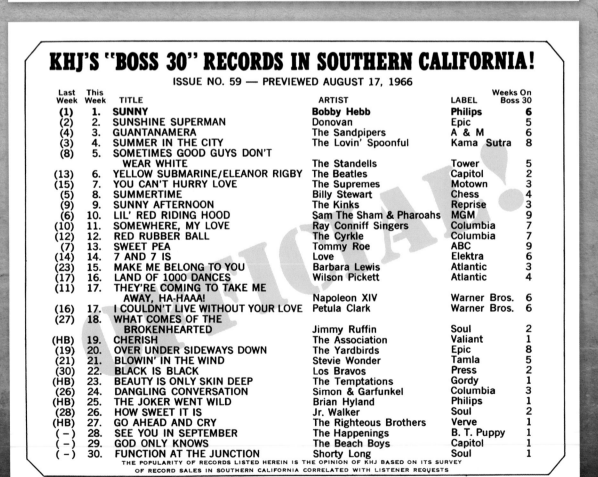

KHJ'S "BOSS 30" RECORDS IN SOUTHERN CALIFORNIA!

ISSUE NO. 59 — PREVIEWED AUGUST 17, 1966

Last Week	This Week	TITLE	ARTIST	LABEL	Weeks On Boss 30
(1)	1.	SUNNY	**Bobby Hebb**	**Philips**	**6**
(2)	2.	SUNSHINE SUPERMAN	Donovan	Epic	5
(4)	3.	GUANTANAMERA	The Sandpipers	A & M	6
(3)	4.	SUMMER IN THE CITY	The Lovin' Spoonful	Kama Sutra	8
(8)	5.	SOMETIMES GOOD GUYS DON'T WEAR WHITE	The Standells	Tower	5
(13)	6.	YELLOW SUBMARINE/ELEANOR RIGBY	The Beatles	Capitol	2
(15)	7.	YOU CAN'T HURRY LOVE	The Supremes	Motown	3
(5)	8.	SUMMERTIME	Billy Stewart	Chess	4
(9)	9.	SUNNY AFTERNOON	The Kinks	Reprise	3
(6)	10.	LIL' RED RIDING HOOD	Sam The Sham & Pharoahs	MGM	9
(10)	11.	SOMEWHERE, MY LOVE	Ray Conniff Singers	Columbia	7
(12)	12.	RED RUBBER BALL	The Cyrkle	Columbia	7
(7)	13.	SWEET PEA	Tommy Roe	ABC	9
(14)	14.	7 AND 7 IS	Love	Elektra	6
(23)	15.	MAKE ME BELONG TO YOU	Barbara Lewis	Atlantic	3
(17)	16.	LAND OF 1000 DANCES	Wilson Pickett	Atlantic	4
(11)	17.	THEY'RE COMING TO TAKE ME AWAY, HA-HAAA!	Napoleon XIV	Warner Bros.	6
(16)	17.	I COULDN'T LIVE WITHOUT YOUR LOVE	Petula Clark	Warner Bros.	6
(27)	18.	WHAT COMES OF THE BROKENHEARTED	Jimmy Ruffin	Soul	2
(HB)	19.	CHERISH	The Association	Valiant	1
(19)	20.	OVER UNDER SIDEWAYS DOWN	The Yardbirds	Epic	8
(21)	21.	BLOWIN' IN THE WIND	Stevie Wonder	Tamla	5
(30)	22.	BLACK IS BLACK	Los Bravos	Press	2
(HB)	23.	BEAUTY IS ONLY SKIN DEEP	The Temptations	Gordy	1
(26)	24.	DANGLING CONVERSATION	Simon & Garfunkel	Columbia	3
(HB)	25.	THE JOKER WENT WILD	Brian Hyland	Philips	1
(28)	26.	HOW SWEET IT IS	Jr. Walker	Soul	2
(HB)	27.	GO AHEAD AND CRY	The Righteous Brothers	Verve	1
(–)	28.	SEE YOU IN SEPTEMBER	The Happenings	B. T. Puppy	1
(–)	29.	GOD ONLY KNOWS	The Beach Boys	Capitol	1
(–)	30.	FUNCTION AT THE JUNCTION	Shorty Long	Soul	1

THE POPULARITY OF RECORDS LISTED HEREIN IS THE OPINION OF KHJ BASED ON ITS SURVEY
OF RECORD SALES IN SOUTHERN CALIFORNIA CORRELATED WITH LISTENER REQUESTS

CHAPTER 29

MAKE IT A LITTLE LOUDER

Technology is such a harsh mistress. We are living in an age when innovation, application, and integration is happening at a perplexing speed. It is somehow reassuring that a near-century-old device continues to engage our restless attention. The radio, born of vacuum tubes, enabled by transistors, and sustained by orbiting satellites, delivers its unique theater of the mind to the accompaniment of a soundtrack that, for this book's purposes, resides somewhere between Father Knows Best *and* The Twilight Zone. *Between 1956 and 1972, America may have been watching the world in black and white; in Southern California, however, we were listening to the splashiest summer colors. We could taste the music and smell the sounds—a kind of mass synaesthesia. You could experience it all through the turn of a dial. Thank you, James Clerk Maxwell!*

In 1972, KRTH was re-imagined with the new call letters K-EARTH, named after the first Earth Day, and even incorporated the influence of KHJ in its own station jingles. Golden oldies were their forum—the antithesis of what their local competitors were dishing out. Nostalgia was about to become big business.

A new retail world sprung up around musical sounds from previous decades that record labels and other conglomerates were now ignoring or not stocking in the bins anymore. Rhino Records was the great beneficiary of this corporate shortsightedness, gathering up the iconic rosters from Atlantic, Warner Bros., and Elektra Records, among many others. Rhino spearheaded a movement to restore the luster of these neglected gems, positioning the "box set" as an essential accoutrement of any self-respecting music geek. Inevitably, the labels came to recognize that, as with publishing, their catalogs were critical cogs in sustaining a business gutted by the onslaught of free downloads, file sharing, and a listenership seemingly indifferent to supporting the artists they claimed to love.*

GARY STEWART: My mission at Rhino Records was to turn people on to artists that they didn't know, songs they didn't know in general, or to artists that people knew only for the three to five songs they had heard from oldies radio or wherever they got exposure. It was to give people a deeper experience, and make a case for that. I was going on instinct. Once we started to grow and get a brand, we found ourselves competing with ourselves. When box sets came out, the major labels started to take catalogs more seriously and develop these elaborate packages, trying to beat us.

Today, the classic FM rock radio format soldiers on. Oldies-driven radio stations compete with college radio specialty shows and Sirius XM satellite radio, while National Public Radio programmers continue to examine the music and recording artists of 1956–1972 to satisfy their base of boomers and beyond.

DANIEL WEIZMANN: The pop radio phenomenon in Southern California is the lynchpin on which the old world turned into the new world. The East Coast, even at its most thriving, had deep roots in European strictures, and the weight of that history. But the West Coast was all about pioneering, and the early sixties were its blossoming.

Opposite: **KHJ Survey featuring the Real Don Steele and Mick Jagger, 1966.**

WHERE'S BARNEY'S BOY?

DAVID KESSEL: L.A. has always been one of the premier cities for recording music and influencing musical tastes around the world. Part of the history of recording and mixing records, not just sound recordings, revolves around the advent of the transistor radio and the capturing of amplitude modulation frequency integration, also referred to as AM radio. Introduced on a commercially viable basis in 1954, this genesis of hand-held entertainment became a staple for music listeners up until the late sixties. Producers and engineers who were trying to make hit records knew they had to sound great through those little three- and four-inch speakers and the home Hi-Fi, simultaneously. As a result, several of the L.A. studios would have a small mini-transmitter in the studio in order to play back mixes through a transistor radio right outside the playback room, tuned to an "in-house" frequency.

While the main goal of recording was to get a hit record and some filler for an album, recording jingles was a science of its own. The technique of playing back mixes through the transistor radio was elevated to mixing jingles directly through the transistor radio. The jingles were extra EQ-ed and compressed to be louder than the records being played on the radio, in order to jump into your ear. You can hear that at work today, with the TV commercials that are way louder than the TV shows.

Bill Bell's Bell Sound Studios in Hollywood was dedicated to only recording jingles and voice-overs. It was the premier jingle studio in Hollywood during the sixties and early seventies, utilizing very sophisticated recording and mixing techniques specifically designed for maximum sonic output. My brother, Dan, and I attended many jingle sessions there with our stepmother, B. J. Baker, a major vocal contractor and background singer. You can hear variations of sonic manipulation on rap records, where, for example, the bass in a car next to you at a stoplight is exploding in your car.

Records played on the AM radio were primarily in mono, from the origin of recorded music up until the late sixties. It was very important to get as big a sound as possible through the small transistor radio speakers, the home Hi-Fi, jukeboxes, and both standard radios and car radios, and have it all sound good. When you hear Phil Spector records, you're hearing mono at its peak. The AM transmitters were not set up to blend the two tracks of stereo into one signal, hence the emergence of FM radio. Not only was this a platform for stereo radio, but it also spawned an entire culture not concerned with playing hits, or the Top 40. These combined influences impacted the cultural growth pattern of the music being produced and recorded in L.A. studios.

David Kessel in the mid-1970s.

A revolution occurred in 1962, when Earl "Madman" Muntz introduced the Stereo-Pak four-track tape player in L.A. [and in parts of Florida] that you could install in your car and play the music you wanted and not have to listen to the radio. This opened up a whole new world for both the record industry and the music consumer/listener. The game-changer was that we were all not listening to the same radio stations anymore, and we had our own mobile music on demand. As L.A. is a car-driven town, millions of people, for the first time in history, got to be in their own music world simultaneously. This further stretched the influences of what songwriters, producers, and performers were recording.

DICK CLARK: In the old days, our interviews with the artists were short. Two to three minutes, max. I've done ten thousand of them—ten thousand individual interviews. I had what I hoped was a beginning, middle, and end. I tried to get something out of it other than, "Where do you go next?" I always tried to get something you could hang on to. Sometimes totally frivolous. Sometimes very stupid. Sometimes not memorable. Maybe just show the humanity.

I think radio is the most intimate medium there is, because it goes with you wherever. On the radio, I get background information, so I know what I'm walking into. On the flipside, what is this guy or woman on the radio for? To plug a record or a television show? Give them the courtesy of allowing them to get their plug in, and then get what you want out of it. It's a very symbiotic relationship. We are using one another.

I'm really not sure where the music business is headed, or what the role of the retailer will be. Some of the technology may have taken over, and may have outstripped the appetite of the general public. I'm not against progress. I don't want to sound like some old fogey hanging onto the past, but I don't know what we're going to do with all of these improvements. I don't know if we really need direct-to-automobile transmission of non-commercial radio, for which you'll have to pay.

But again, I can talk to more people, and communicate better, through radio than I can on the internet—for my purposes. I've been asked to spend time on the internet. I don't want to demean it, but who am I talking to? A handful of people. Give me the same twenty minutes and let me talk to three radio stations, and I'll reach more people than you'll reach in a whole year that have hit on that website.

ELLIOT MINTZ: I feel that the FM experience was almost ecumenical. It was religious in concept. See if you can buy this one—the real rock 'n' roll stars were gods and goddesses. We had elevated them to mythological level. In so doing, we brought about their own sacrifice. We killed a number of them by placing them on a pedestal, from which they could only fall. We demanded so

much of people like Jimi Hendrix, or Otis Redding, or Janis Joplin, or Jim Morrison. We placed them on the precipice. Whatever it was they took to fall off is socially irrelevant.

So, let us view the rock 'n' roll performers for a moment, the select few, as gods and goddesses in our mythology. They had the legions of followers. The radio station was the church, and the disc jockey was the priest. Why was he the priest or the high priestess? Because he had direct contact and communication with the gods. He was the liaison between his congregation and the mythological figure that the congregation demanded he reveal.

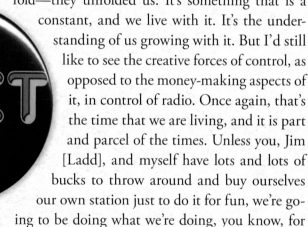

KMET button.

B. MITCHELL REED: The thing I miss is the fact that, when the money people saw there was a money-maker—in other words, instead of us taking them into our fold—they unfolded us. It's something that is a constant, and we live with it. It's the understanding of us growing with it. But I'd still like to see the creative forces of control, as opposed to the money-making aspects of it, in control of radio. Once again, that's the time that we are living, and it is part and parcel of the times. Unless you, Jim [Ladd], and myself have lots and lots of bucks to throw around and buy ourselves our own station just to do it for fun, we're going to be doing what we're doing, you know, for someone else, and will be living within the restrictions placed upon us. Luckily, we work for a station [KMET] that doesn't place that many on us.

ELLIOT MINTZ: When I reflect upon my years on the air, almost all of my memories are wonderful. Radio was such a powerful, personal healing force. I was able to have conversations with people I most likely never would have met, had I not been on radio and television. I estimate that I took more than twenty thousand phone calls over the radio waves, giving people the opportunity to share their thoughts with more people than they would have in their entire lifetime. I learned as much from them as I did from any single soul. It was the collective mind, with a voice. It was different than Facebook or Twitter. You could hear laughter, or sense alienation with your ears and your heart. That's not the same as reading text.

RAM DASS: Back in the sixties and early seventies, I spent a lot of time at the Fillmore, the Avalon, and the Family Dog in the San Francisco area. I went to the Monterey International Pop Festival.

Then the issue was AM or FM, and FM, to me, is like preaching to a choir. It doesn't have the challenge of broadening the audience like an AM station.

A lot of things have happened, and it's been fascinating because the AM experience has been entirely different from the FM experience. Radio is very intimate. It's interesting, because it is like pillow talk. It's a form of making love, actually. It's very intimate, because we get into shared psychic experiences, shared spaces of awareness. The predicament with AM is that you are locked into time frames, so you are constantly dealing with "two more minutes" or "three more minutes," hard cut, ads coming up, read this, do this, and it's very hard to stay in a deep enough telephone conversation. It's a whole new skill for me.

Later, the FM experience . . . I was doing a midnight show on a program, *Something's Happening*, that [KPFK personality] Roy Tuckman has been running for fifteen years with my tapes and Alan Watts's tapes being played regularly. My audience is gathered already, so I am inundated with phone calls. Eleven call lines are busy the entire shift. When I stop, they are still busy. It's a very loving and warm hangout.

HARVEY KUBERNIK AND JIM LADD INTERVIEW

HK: How has FM radio changed in the last forty-five years?

JL: That's a big question. The answer is it began in April of 1967, when Tom and Raechel Donahue walked into a radio station in San Francisco that was so poor, it could not pay its phone bill. They had an idea, not only to play the new music that was revolutionizing rock 'n' roll, but to present it in a completely new and different way. So they simply brought in their own albums from home, and freeform radio was born.

From those humble beginnings, a multi-billion-dollar industry grew out of it. It [came] from people who did it strictly for the love of music, but who were also involved in the social issues of the day—people who saw that we needed to make a connection between the activists in the streets and the musicians who were singing songs about those issues. We needed a way to combine those two things and broadcast it to the audience, and that is where the art form of FM rock radio came from.

The nice thing about rock 'n' roll is that you can give me any subject you can think of that has to do with life, and I'll play you a set about that, because rock 'n' roll has talked about it. Unlike swing or country music, rock 'n' roll deals with life, religion, sex, drugs . . . everything you can think of. That's why I'm able to take a subject that's in the news, come on the air and talk about it, and then play four or five songs that further expand the discussion.

HK: In 1980, the government voted to deregulate the airwaves.

JL: We were the canary in the coal mine. That was the worst thing that ever happened to FM radio and American media in general. Prior to President Ronald Reagan, the Federal Communications Commission had what was called the Seven and Seven Rule. That meant that one person or corporation could not own more than seven radio and seven TV stations. That's all you could own in the country. Then Ronald Reagan comes along and has the brilliant idea of deregulating radio. This came, obviously, from the lobbyists who got to the legislators.

After Reagan—and, by the way, also President Clinton, who is to be held accountable for this—where we once had thousands of independent broadcasters and a highly competitive marketplace, it now became all right for large corporations to buy up as many radio and TV stations as they could get their hands on, which forced out the small station owners and killed the free marketplace. That is where the threat to the first amendment comes in, because fewer and fewer people own more and more information outlets. It also took the choice of

You can't trace the history of FM rock radio in Los Angeles without encountering Jim Ladd, one of its most energetic and passionate advocates. Born in Lynwood, California, Ladd's path to the nascent world of FM began in May of 1968.

JIM LADD: I went to Long Beach Community College and took a class in radio and television communications. I immediately fell in love with it. I liked doing it, and seemed to have some sort of aptitude to do it.

In 1969, I'm living in a commune in Long Beach, directly across from the ocean in Crab Hollow. Right down the street was KNAC. So I started to go there. A guy, the late Don Bunch, was kind enough to sort of let me come in, empty the ashtrays, file records, and hang out. It was a MOR station. But at night, they let him do rock. The station told him, "They are gonna do this underground radio thing. So get me an audition tape." I said, "What's an audition tape?" He explained to me what it was. I cut the audition tape, and I'm sure, based on the fact that I had long hair, I was hired. Because they were gonna take the station to twenty-four hours of underground music. I got $1.65 an hour.

I got the idea, from listening to other people, that I could take these songs and combine them in a way that would tell a story that would be a narrative. That's what I started to do, almost from the very first night.

music out of the hands of the local DJs and replaced it with the radio consultant, who gave you the homogenized lists that you hear today.

Because I still do freeform radio and I still pick my own music, I am very aware that I'm the one carrying the torch. Now, I didn't ask the carry the torch. I just looked up one day, and I was the last guy standing. So I'm really aware of that.

One of the worst things that happened because of deregulation was that, initially, they didn't give a shit about us. But once we started making money, that's when it got serious for the owners. They brought in consultants and people who didn't care about the music.

HK: Who has your audience been the last five decades?

JL: Five years ago, a guy in a car called up with a request. He said, "I've got my son, who is sixteen. He wants to hear some Jimi Hendrix." I still have many people that call me who have been listening since [it was] KNAC in 1969, and then KLOS through 2011. Now, that's extraordinary. I also have kids who are sixteen, seventeen, and eighteen requesting Bob Dylan. That's even more extraordinary. They know who the Beatles are, and know their music inside and out. They love the Doors.

Because the music is that good. They wrote extraordinary songs that speak to people in a way that pop music does not. The Doors get inside of you. The difference with these guys is that they have a way of writing a song that became popular, but at the same time, it's talking about breaking on through to the other side. "Not to Touch the Earth"; "Ship of Fools" from *Morrison Hotel*, which talks about the human race dying out. This is stuff that is still applicable today.

A kid hearing the Doors' "Peace Frog" in 2012 for the first time is going to hear it different than I did, because the Vietnam War is not raging. Or the 1968 Democratic Convention, with people being beaten up in the streets. However, they are going to hear it in the context of their world.

The only thing today's kids are missing is context. I have to keep in mind that the songs say something to me, but they may say something completely different to someone else in the audience. So all I can do is play it in a way that says something to me, and then how it is interpreted by them in the context of the set may be different. If I put the songs together correctly, people should recognize that you have to listen to the lyrics when you listen to my show to really understand what's going on.

The particular issues that may have inspired a song like "Unknown Soldier" will change, but the human condition that causes them is the same. For example, the issues that triggered the war in Vietnam or war in Iraq may change, but war is still war.

In 2012, I still continue to do freeform radio and have even more autonomy and freedom than I've ever had, since I joined Sirius XM. Thank God for satellite radio!

EPILOGUE

The music celebrated in this book defined not only a time but a place; a supple, sun-splashed oasis free from the chokehold of New York's cultural hegemony. Many of the greatest innovators in Los Angeles were immigrants who brought with them the rich musical and social legacies of "their people," whether African American, Latino, or the blue-jeaned rectitude of the Protestant Midwest. Once settled in this vast, smoggy basin, a uniformity of purpose began to emerge—the liberation from teenage torment in three joyful minutes. From South Bay garages to the recording palaces of Elysian Hollywood, there emerged a new, intemperate sound married to an equally impertinent sensibility. It was four beats to the bar and no cheating; it was the clarion command of a Fender Twin Reverb. It was a time to turn up that radio!

JAMES CUSHING: One reason the music of the "sweet sixteen" years could only have happened in L.A. is the city's climate and proximity to the Pacific Ocean, hence to Asia—a place much less well-known and well-understood in the West during that period than it is today. If you're already close to something not yet fully familiar, it seems to me you have a better-than-average chance to be more aware of your surroundings, hence more appreciative of them and the human events that occur in them.

We have to remember that all the popular music of the time happened in the shadow of the draft and the Vietnam War, a fact that makes the appreciation of it morally complicated. A big part of the complication is that we can only artificially separate the music from that context—but then, the context comes right back. In order to understand the music, you have to understand the context. If you value the music, then you have to value the context.

Well, do you want those great sounds back again? Here's the rub. The price is having the context of those great sounds back. Do you want the Beatles back? Do you want Jimi and Janis and Buffalo Springfield, too? Good. So do I. But do you want the Vietnam War back? Do you want to see Robert F. Kennedy get shot to death in the Ambassador Hotel again? I'm sorry, but that comes with the package. The restaurant of history does not ask us what we want. It just serves us, and we have to eat.

The plate history used was that mono AM radio, which gave us the hippest music and the darkest assassinations. Around-the-clock, sixties AM radio gave us two kinds of news: the kind happening outside of Washington, Saigon, and New York, and the kind happening inside people's hearts and minds and spirits. Of course, when you have stereo, you have headphones, which assume that every important event happens only inside the mind.

GARY STEWART: I do think a lot of the 1956–1972 music remains popular throughout the work of new artists like the Fleet Foxes, White Stripes, My Morning Jacket, Wilco, the Strokes, Amy Winehouse, Adele. There's a lot of harkening back to earlier forms. In the nineties, there wasn't so much drawing from that previous period.

There is another thing about the popularity of this period—they got there first, just as in the early days of rap and that sort of second period. The possibilities for experimentation become narrower. They aren't gone, but

Opposite: Bones Howe at the KHJ Big Kahuna Royal Beach Luau in Malibu, 1966.

a lot of the stretching has been done. That period usually comes, not during a birth of a form—that's there—but comes right after the birth of a form, when there's money in it and enough support for taking risk. Then the money often takes over as record companies become profit centers. You've created this machinery you can't get out from under. If you look at the sixties, there were so many great records, because there was enough money for them. Part of the reason was that there were enough people who had grown up with rock 'n' roll for the previous ten years, so you had teenagers or early twenty-somethings to support it.

BILL INGLOT: A lot of the recordings of the fifties and the sixties were on two-track, four-track, and, late in the decade, eight-track machines. The truth is, everything was more direct because it was more immediate, and they weren't looking to beat stuff to death. The Wrecking Crew were doing three sessions a day—an orange juice commercial, a film score, and a rock date. So no one was overthinking it.

When multi-track recording came about, they were like, "Wow. We're gonna have more tracks, and get it done faster." Well, it got slower once it got to eight-tracks. The thing is, also, there is the three-track in the equation, because a lot of studios hung with three-track when four-track was around, and also went back and forth. Especially on three-track pop sessions, because they were thinking of a concept of "left, center, right, and we're done." The four-track was "left, center, right, and we have a spare."

You can hear certain artifacts of each regional studio. When you put up a tape from the engineers of the fifties and sixties, early seventies—like Lee Hirschberg, Thorne Nogar, Bones Howe—when you get into the post-production or mastering world or reissue world forty years hence, they tend to be the things you have to do the least, too. It wasn't like, "I've gotta mix this stuff so it sounds good in forty years." It was sounding good then, or it was doing what it needed to do. Those things usually require the least work in restoration or reissue.

What is very interesting about the 1956–1972 era is that it is basically the era of what I call "boutique mastering." Until 1972, it was basically, "Get it out." That is before the rise of the Mastering Lab versus Sterling

Sound in New York versus Capitol in Hollywood. I mean, everyone was trying to do good work, but at the same time, you were trying to get the work out. Mastering is the ninth inning of the game, but you can say that about the pressing, at least in the vinyl world. The thing is, I think it's easier to lose the game in the ninth inning than it is to win it. It always comes down to, "Is it a good source?"

As far as the music recorded from 1956 to 1972, it was always someone trying to do a better job with tape stock. In approximately 1973—and I'm speaking in very broad terms—the emulsions and formulas for tapes changed. There are a bunch of theories about it, like they couldn't get whale oil anymore.

Vinyl will always have a romantic appeal. The reality is that, in laying the signal to vinyl and playing it back with a stylus, you are kind of dragging a rock down a dirt road, creating an effect that roughs out the edges and smooths in the edges at the same time. Arguably, you're adding a level of distortion at the same time, too.

It shouldn't come as a surprise that the music industry itself, throughout the eighties and nineties, was disinclined to service its storied past. As the major labels were gobbled up by media conglomerates, the pressure was on to produce robust quarterly statements, amp shareholder returns, and bump up executive bonuses. As a consequence, the music was mostly stripped clean of anything authentically singular or soul-stirring, let alone subversive, so desperate was the need to reach the widest possible audience. As "product managers," the labels were driven by the tyranny of the next new thing—a sure-fire invitation to energetic mediocrity. Catalogs were either dispensed with altogether, or shunted off to small, specialty reissue houses.

DON RANDI: I like mono, but not quite a "back to mono" guy. I still like the old LPs and I still play them, for the simple reason that, unfortunately, when they do these things they have a tendency to digitize everything, where they clean it up so much that you lose the character of the song itself. You lose the room ambience. My God, if a guitar player squeaks on a note, leave it! But they can get it out today, so they choose to do that. If a singer took a breath before he or she sang a note, I used to love to hear that. It was part of the record. They don't do that anymore.

Look, we all like to hear how our music is being used after we cut it, in television shows, movie soundtracks, and reissues. Like with Elvis Presley and "A Little Less Conversation." I might have made, initially, $160. Local 47 contract. Over the years, with all the scales changing and everything being redone and remixed, I've made close to ten grand in residuals.

Let me tell you why. It's a very simple reason, and most people don't have any clue. There were a number of people. It started with Phil Spector, then Brian Wilson, and caught on with everybody else that when you hired us, there was a union contract. So, there was a Local 47

PIZZA, PUGILISM, AND REALITY

JOHN WOOD: What used to be boxing became professional wrestling. What used to be real became unreal.

From the time Thomas Edison invented the phonograph to the middle and late sixties, all recorded music came from a disciplined group of musicians going for a take. That's what made it great. It was an art form. Three-hour session, four finished songs. That's how records were made. At every level of the process, professionals were involved. They had to be. Songwriters, lyricists, musicians, singers, arrangers, the producer, the engineer. When the bell rang, they were all there together. Just like a baseball game. They all relied on each other to succeed. That's what brought out the best in everyone. It took more than money to make records. It took discipline, knowledge, talent, and a respect for what went before.

It was monaural first—that's one channel. Then it was two channels, and that was stereo. When they did introduce three-track, I'm guessing in the early sixties, that was merely an auxiliary thing. This is important to understand. Three tracks were okay, and they didn't call it overdubbing. They didn't use it as a way of life. But it was available, if they wanted to do a harmony part. They called it "sweetening." It wasn't overdubbing. So it was very simple. Of course, there was no remixing.

Rampaging technology empowers the unqualified and disempowers the qualified. Look, I like boxing, not professional wrestling.

The first bumper sticker I made was "BACK TO 2 TRACK" in 1980. Why did I make it? Because I had a ringside seat to watch American popular music over a half century. I was there in the great years and the garbage

years. I knew Elvis before he had a recording contract, and I'm sixty-one years old. In 1954, Elvis and Colonel Parker gave my brother and I a covered wagon in Gallatin, Tennessee.

I was in recording studios ten years before Paul McCartney or the Beatles ever set foot in a recording studio, and I'm nearly a decade younger. So, consequently, I have an overview that virtually no one else alive has.

Like boxing, it was real. That made it succeed, and that made it an art form and made it have value. Once you brought in the multi-track tape machines, you instantly devalued time. You see, the clock was everything. It was paramount in recording. If you went one second into overtime, that was a huge deal. Recording sessions were three hours, but when you brought in multi-track tape machines, now time meant nothing.

I was born in a recording studio session in 1950. I observed that it was accomplished by a disciplined group of musicians going for a take. That is why football, baseball, and basketball still have their immense appeal to the public, because what you are seeing is happening in front of you—a world where the participants and viewers alike are experiencing self-discovery and the adventure of the excitement of the unknown.

"BACK TO 2 TRACK" bumper sticker.

BACK TO 2 TRACK™

SOCIETY FOR THE REHUMANIZATION OF AMERICAN MUSIC – (323) 732-6160

on a contract. If that contract is there, they can trace it back to who was on the original track. Because of that, we get our residuals. Phil, Brian, and Jack Nitzsche made it possible, because if they could avoid it, they would. But these guys insisted on having these contracts. Because of this, we all have residuals and I'm talking to you.

It's nice, at age seventy-four, to get paid and hear these things again. Kim Fowley calls it "mailbox money." It's wonderful. There's a guy that's been logging everything and getting everything in order for years, 'cause it's an unthankful job. [Contracts investigator] Russ Wapensky—you might never hear his name except from me or Hal [Blaine]—he logged everything so nobody can fuck with us.

BONES HOWE: I went from a world where artists would cover songs from songwriters to a world where artists sang their own material. The 1956–1972 period is popular today because of the songs. The songs were great. They communicated with a wide audience of younger people, but as they got older, they got older. At an Association reunion concert, this woman walks up to me and says, "Somebody told me you're Bones Howe." "Yes, I am." "I've got to tell you something. I got pregnant my first time to 'Never My Love.'"

It's not, "Here it is, you dance to it." It's not, "Just put a metronome up and people can dance to it." You know what I'm saying? It's about communication, and what artists bring to the people.

Why does it still work—getting released and issued in many formats? Because nothing better came along. That's part of the reason. Music publishers initiated songs and placement more then. I saw Elvis pick tunes from the Hill and Range music publishing company. Then it goes to Tom Waits, writing his own stuff. In the middle is Louie [Adler] at Aldon Music and Lester Sill and the music publishers at Screen Gems. I did some work with the Monkees. I did a Screen Gems song with Davy Jones. I tried to stay with the plan, as they were involved with Screen Gems.

I don't think that music publishers get enough credit. Like Chuck Kaye at Almo, who started at Screen Gems Aldon Music with Lou Adler.

You can also do a genesis of that, with song guys that weren't musicians that wanted to produce or plug songs

COAST WITH THE MOST

The success of the Beatles might, in retrospect, seem obvious to anyone with a pair of functioning ears, but their earliest encounters with the music industry were less than admiring. It is even possible to suggest that, had it not been for a fateful alignment with Dick James and his music publishing company, suggested by producer George Martin, their career may well have stalled or been derailed altogether. Time and again, one discovers that the lowly music publisher, hidden in plain sight from the more glamorous sides of the record business, has played the pivotal role in providing the breakthrough for some of music's most exhalted artists. It was never more true than in that hula-hooped period of the late fifties on, before groups started writing their own material, that so many aspirants turned to publishers for a gig.

or wanted to be in the music business and be around artists. Lou at Aldon Music, with Carole King and Gerry Goffin, and all those great songs that came out of there—those people were saying yes. They were sitting at a piano, saying, "I wonder if anybody will like this song?" Writing these great songs and then taking them in, and somebody was there applauding for them. That's what they needed. There was that kind of support of the artist.

I found great tunes from music publishers. I would listen to everything and ideas to try to figure out if it made any sense for the recording artists that I was working with.

What am I gonna tell you? The business ain't what it used to be [*laughs*]. Nobody loves what they're doing anymore. They're all worried about the bottom line, and if they're gonna keep their jobs.

JAMES CUSHING: Engineer and producer Bones Howe applied his awareness, experience, and common sense, which told him that the music was better if the musicians were physically closer to one another when playing. The engineering emphasized correctness of microphone choice and microphone placement in order to serve the music, which was fundamentally understood as coming from a live organic sound source: several people in a room. In other words, Bones Howe's essentially offering a jazz/chamber music concept of pop. I think the jazz/chamber music concept gives the music an organic sense of it being a *human event.* Contrast that with the kind of popular music made of tracks and people overdubbing the guitar two weeks after the drums. They aren't even in the same building at the same time.

What Bones Howe advocates, and I hope more and more people hear, is that a brilliantly produced record is a document of an organic moment, or a sequence of organic moments. As we live in an increasingly inorganic world, we grow to cherish organic moments more and more. I think that's one of the biggest reasons we like music in the first place. Bones Howe was talking about people working together and making something beautiful, and technology as a way to serve that beauty by bringing it to as many people as possible.

Bones Howe at Wally Heider Studios, Hollywood, 1968.

ROGER STEFFENS: My favorite song of all time is "Earth Angel." There is something about the duel harmonic leads, which was unique, that got to me. Plus, best of all, it was a great make-out record. The music of the "Golden Age," 1956 to 1972, endures to this day because it had passion. It tapped the zeitgeist; it was about the underside of the sixties. It was in contradistinction to the mellow yellowness of San Francisco music, love, and peace. It had more of an edge. I don't know why. Maybe 'cause the cops were worse in L.A. But there was an otherness to it, and a poetry, and a social consciousness—an awareness of historic trends. A lot of different things that the other pockets of the time did not have.

As we examine Frank Zappa now, and the entire shape of the 1956–1972 period, we see who the standout figures really are and whose work has lasted longer than anybody else. I mean, Zappa was part John Cage, Edgar Varese, Pierre Henry, and the Penguins. Zappa was a hipster's dream, with the Straight and Bizarre record labels that reissued Lenny Bruce and Lord Buckley.

You could hear Buckley's "The Nazz" on KMET. Zappa resurrected the multi-voiced master of the "vernacular of the hip" for the hippie generation and made him a stylistic influence on everyone from Robin Williams to Richard Pryor.

KIRK SILSBEE: The bassist Roberto Miranda said something really interesting to me about the musicians in Los Angeles who were either born here or became acclimated to L.A.: "There is something that I hear in all of their sounds, and that is the only way I can describe it, as the 'open sky effect.' That is, there are no boundaries. There are no restrictions. If I feel I can take a chance on something, I can do it." It's similar to when folk musician Roger McGuinn left the Chad Mitchell Trio to come to L.A., before he helped form the Byrds. He left New York because the business opportunities here were much greater, and much looser.

The music of 1956 to 1972 endures because there was still a frontier that could be carved out. There was still new land to be cleared. People could come out here with a vision and an idea—or maybe no idea. Maybe they didn't have any money, but they could come out here, look around, reinvent themselves, come up with an idea, and make something of themselves and their ideas. You could still do that during this period. It's not like that now. California is now a different state, full of restrictions and boundaries and ever-higher taxes.

The DJs were Pied Pipers and heralds. Even if a record they played didn't become a hit, I got a taste of it. The program directors had taste, and they would take chances; the DJs still had some level of autonomy back then. They would bring in acetates from sessions, tell about music they heard in the clubs, and occasionally interview the artists on their shows. KRLA was a favorite stop with promo men—they could drive a band or an artist up to the station in Pasadena, the DJ would put the word out over the air that, say, Ian Whitcomb was answering phones at the station, and you could call in and speak to them for a minute.

There was one thread running through many of the musicians of that period: rhythm and blues. Leiber and Stoller studied it, and they came to define a certain portion of R & B. Phil Spector loved it, digested it, and incorporated it into his vision. Brian Wilson loved it, and he had an entirely different vision, but that doesn't mean it didn't come out in his music. You best believe R & B was a big part of Arthur Lee's musical vision. Frank Zappa came from deep R & B and doo-wop roots. Ray Manzarek brought the Chicago South Side blues to the Doors' music, and Jim Morrison had his own take on it, man. You can hear it on "Texas Radio and the Big Beat"—you know that he heard some of the great R & B DJs when he lived in Florida. The alchemy that happened between the colorful DJs and the music they programmed obviously made an impression on him. You can hear it in the authority he sang on "Back Door Man." George Lucas directed his USC student film on the local DJ, Bob Hudson—"the Emperor." You can bet he also heard Wolfman Jack up there in Modesto, or in L.A. when he was going to school, before he cast him in *American Graffiti.*

Left: Ian Whitcomb on *The Lloyd Thaxton Show,* Hollywood, 1965.
Right: Robert W. Morgan with co-host Kam Nelson (*left*) and dancers on the set of *The Groovy Show,* Hollywood, 1969.

There's another reason this 1956–1972 music struck people and made an impact. The L.A. market had a lot of dance programs, daily afternoon music shows that began in 1959 with *Lloyd Thaxton's Record Shop* on KCOP-TV, later *The Lloyd Thaxton Show* in 1961. Sam Riddle hosting *The Cinnamon Cinder* and then *9th Street West* and *Hollywood a Go Go*; Casey Kasem on *Shebang!*; Jimmy O'Neill introducing *Shindig!* for a couple of years; *Shivaree* with Gene Weed. Then Dick Clark moved *American Bandstand* out to Hollywood in the mid-sixties, and it was in color. He also had his daily *Where the Action Is* series, and another spin-off afternoon show, *Happening '68*. There was also *Groovy*, from the summer of 1967 to 1969, with Michael Blodgett and later Robert W. Morgan. Then toss in the Real Don Steele and his energetic TV dance program that went right into the early seventies. Until 1971, *The Ed Sullivan Show* booked L.A. bands all through the sixties.

ANDREW SOLT: Sullivan knew how to give a show that was for every generation that might be watching. He knew how to bottle lightning. He also knew, because he had great instincts, not only how to produce a show but who to put on and in what order. He really was the arbiter of taste for a period of time, which was that post-war era. The birth of television until the birth of the seventies. It is a remarkable reflection of American history.

Newspaper advertisement for *Shivaree*, 1965.

MIKE MELVOIN: I love that *Jazz Scene USA* 1963 show where I'm playing everything I know with Frank Rosolino. What would I now tell that guy on the piano bench in that show? Ooh . . . I have to think about that. I'd tell him to be more aware of the treasure that you're participating in. Try to have an understanding

of how privileged you are and the history that you're taking part in. Have a good time, but know the treasure of what you're doing. So often, what goes through your head when you're on the stand is thinking about what I call "the set after the set"—sticking your nose in some pussy. Time goes by, and the jobs you play and the music you make pile up, and you lose sight of the important thing that you're a part of.

JIM KELTNER: To me, music from that era, from everywhere, was special. Don't forget, it was very early on. The Beatles had just changed everything, the Rolling Stones were starting to change things, and English rock started to have a big effect on American rock 'n' roll, even though they were taking cues from our roots music. And it was right at the beginning of the FM thing.

FM became very popular, and there were albums to be played instead of just singles. So a whole lot of things started changing. The music, which was now being written more by the artists instead of outside writers, really began to resonate with the people. That period is generally thought of as an unusually fertile time for great songwriting.

BILL MUMY: From 1959 through 1969 I spent quite a lot of time traveling from studio to studio in the back seat of my mother's 1959 pink Cadillac. I didn't dig her car at all. I was embarrassed to be seen in it. Now I sure wish we'd kept it! But she turned it in for a new chocolate-brown Caddy in '69, and that was that. Poof. It was gone. And now it's missed. Just like the radio from those days.

I was born and raised in West Los Angeles, and popular music gripped me tightly from an early age. Indigenous artists like Ricky Nelson, Jan and Dean, the mighty

Brian Wilson and his Beach Boys, and later bands like the Byrds, Buffalo Springfield, and the Doors made the schleps from our home on a cul-de-sac in Beverlywood to Disney or Warner Bros., Universal, Columbia, or Paramount bearable and, at times, downright boss. DJs like Sam Riddle and Wink Martindale were our friends. On these drives to and from auditions and work, one thing was consistent—the radio was on, it was on loud, and it was tuned in to KHJ, KRLA, or KFWB. I can't even write or mention the call letters without hearing the jingle in my head—"Channel 98."

The radio was spontaneous in those days. The speakers crackled with an immediacy now long-lost. If the DJ dug the song they just spun enough, they'd spin it again! Brian Wilson might pop into a radio station with a new acetate rough mix, and they'd play it to gauge the audience's reaction. Nowadays, with the exception of Rodney Bingenheimer, who's only on the air three hours a week on KROQ, disc jockeys are powerless. They have no say in what gets played. It's a bummer. But back in the day, it was fun, fun, fun.

Pop music meant popular music, period. Whether that was rock 'n' roll, R & B, surf music, Motown, folk, or psychedelic heavy rock, it was all popular, and it was all good. It wasn't the slightest bit weird to hear a set coming out of the radio including the Beatles, Otis Redding, the Beach Boys, the Supremes, the Byrds, the Monkees, and Petula Clark. Nowadays? Forget about it. It's all categorized and compartmentalized into tiny little labels of style, and never shall they meld on the air together. Is that progress? Not in my book.

But here we are, half a century or so later, and happy days are here again. We can close our eyes, relax, and float downstream on good vibrations of memory, back to a time when music was fresh, when artists released two or three albums a year and gigged constantly without click tracks or Auto-Tune, when it was all about talent, energy, fun, and passion, when the music coming out of Southern California was created by genuinely inspired young artists. That was a good thing. A real good thing.

CHRIS HILLMAN: The sixties were wonderful. What does hold up from that era were melodies and lyrics. In the Byrds, our manager, Jim Dickson, drilled into our heads the greatest advice we ever got. He said, "Go for substance

in the songs, and go for depth. You want to make records you can listen to in forty years that you will be proud to listen to." He was right.

I think that's a big part of it. It was real, and so honest. The record companies were run by music people—people who loved music. It was not a corporate monster. They'd sign you, and you'd be on the label for three or four albums, you know.

Now when I do occasional shows, I have people who come to see me play. Either they're my age, or they're young kids—twenty to twenty-five or twenty-six, who are enamored by the Beach Boys, the Beatles, the Byrds, and the Flying Burrito Brothers.

In the Byrds, I was both a participant and a consumer, as well. I would buy a record and go home and play it. During that initial listening to the album, you are looking at the cover photo and reading the liner notes. That was the package. The whole deal. An audio and visual experience. This includes picture sleeve singles, which have never been duplicated with downloads and all that stuff. To some degree, CDs, but by the time those came out it was harder to read the information. The seventies were the highlight of packaging.

KIM FOWLEY: The 1956–1972 period—even dipping into 1973—was, and still is, a world that continues. This music keeps going because it's good. There's nothing sacred about it. It has a mythological validation to pop music that was supposed to be disposable. You think it's great, but it's just catchy, well-crafted.

Then Elvis showed up with a developed identity, and then Dick Clark showed up playing one-hit wonders, and the black music crossed into whitey's neighborhood. Suddenly, we had a teenage revolution.

By the early seventies, everyone at all the record labels wanted to control and own everything from the first step. Like the three hundred and sixty deals promoters with record companies offered earlier this century. Control became anti-artistic and interactive and against the very reason of improvisational, motivational, and inspired anything. So the inspiration got castrated. It became politically incorrect.

Now, take an LLC, or an attorney and his digital marketing plan. These specialists don't know how to write a song that will make you cry, kill somebody, fuck somebody, or change the world. There's no earth-shaking scope in any of the motivation or any result. The guys from my time wrote four hundred songs and one hundred and forty incomplete songs, and could entertain you with their band for long hours somewhere. Everybody apprenticed and put in a lot of work to learn the craft.

Then the synthesizer keyboard, and then the computer showed up. Each decade has its own drugs, haircuts, and diseases. It shapes the music.

JIM DAWSON: I think the popularity of some of many of the hit records coming out of L.A. in the late fifties

GOODBYE TO ALL THAT

by KENNETH KUBERNIK

In an article in the *Los Angeles Times* previewing the 2012 Grammy Awards, their music critic drew attention to the diminished role rock music occupied in the contemporary music landscape, subsumed, as it were, by the logorrheic riptide of rap and the numbing catharsis of electronic dance music. Rock 'n' roll, he opined, was being "junked for its parts," its rhythmic verve, its strut, its swagger put to greater effect by artists more fluent in Pro Tools and Auto-Tune than the ancient adepts of musty guitars, bass, and drums. "The guitar's got absolutely nothing on the computer as a sound maker as far as adaptability and ability to create the kind of dissonance that once was rock's monopolistic domain." He concluded by anointing the electronica producer, Skrillex, with his "insane bass-drop," as the evolutionary step forward in the "Jobsian" new world of pop music production. The Spectorian Wall of Sound was but a tinkling triangle compared to the micro-compressed rage of a laptop at full throttle.

It is axiomatic that every generation falls in love with itself, its playthings, its towering sense of entitlement. In a society preoccupied with commodity and acquisition, it follows that the cult of the new, like time's arrow, points only in one direction. The question then arises: Is this the true face of progress?

Many great minds have parsed this question since Pythagoras charted with his "music of the spheres" in the sixth century BCE. Has there been any point to composing in the aftermath of Bach's *St. Matthew Passion*, Beethoven's Ninth Symphony, or Wagner's *Ring* trilogy? On a less exhalted scale, consider the ineffable beauty of a Gershwin melody, the panache of Cole

Porter's lyric, the guileless grace of Johnny Mercer's pen, and imagine how they could be equaled. What is there left to say after hearing "I Thought About You"? Each of these artists spoke to their generation in terms that were both breathlessly intimate, yet written for the ages. And, praise the lord, so it was for Ike Turner, when he began the world anew with "Rocket 88."

British author Nick Hornby did us all a favor with his book, *High Fidelity,* once and for all exposing the locus-like avidity with which music fanatics eat their own. The worship of music is, really, pretty much a guy thing, a passion run rampant, a neediness bordering on pathology. "Listen up, you little git, our music's better than yours," has been the rallying cry since early man banged the first gong. And so it goes . . .

There's no gainsaying the fact that this book picks a side. A lot of the voices heard here are, with affection, welded to a past that precludes the opportunity to engage with a present, however flawed, which can only benefit from that variegated and nuanced historical perspective.

The music that emerged from Los Angeles during those halcyon days was not some sabertoothed relic excavated from a bubbly black pit. It was, and is, rather, a golden seam mined again and again for its timeless virtues: the command of song-writing craft; the convergence of community to realize a personal vision; an inextinguishable beacon to anyone who had a heart. "California Girls" has become "California Gurls," reimagined by a vivacious pop princess who entered a fabled world imagined by Pendleton-clad boys mind-surfing along the Pacific Coast Highway. Can Skrillex's bass-drop open that door?

and through the sixties owes a lot to the skills of the arrangers, and that goes back to the older records made at Modern with Maxwell Davis, Jake Porter, Johnny Otis, and Lloyd Glen.

Kids who were talented—might sing, or play guitar—needed help when they went into the studio. One of the things that is very special about some of these people, like Carol Kaye or Plas Johnson, was that they all thought of themselves as jazz players; when they went into the rock and pop sessions, they may have looked down their noses at this stuff, since they didn't really care about it, paradoxically. It allowed their talents to come through. Sometimes we excel at things that we feel half-assed about. If you are really serious about it, there is something curdled about it. When Raymond Chandler tried to write serious stuff, it was crap. When he wrote those throwaway detective stories, his real talent came out. Plas Johnson and all these other guys had all this talent and knowledge, and with these sessions it allowed them to be playful. The music was catchy and exciting, and it hadn't been overproduced yet.

LITTLE WILLIE G.: The newspaper media didn't quite know what to do with Thee Midniters and the music born and developed in East L.A. I think a lot of the early prejudices kind of contributed to that. They just saw us as second-class citizens.

I have no idea why the history of rock 'n' roll, especially in L.A., is always a black-and-white story. East L.A. became another land in terms of history and pop documentation.

This century, the media, museums, and academia are seriously examining Thee Midniters and Chicano music culture. In December 2011, I was in a musical conversation as part of the Getty initiative for *Pacific Standard Time: Art in L.A. 1945–1980*, presented by the Grammy Museum and the Museum of Latin American Art. I took questions and performed songs.

I really don't have an answer why, after forty-five years, this sort of thing is happening, other than perhaps we're so distracted by other things going on in the world that we kind of put things on a shelf, you know, until history begins to catch up with us. To be at the Grammy Museum was really gratifying, to hear the people who actually grew up in that era, that went to the Roger Young

Auditorium or the 5/4 Ballroom and remember the band when it was in its glory, so to speak. And, finally, then being a part of this acknowledgement, that they could co-sign that this was really happening.

GARY PIG GOLD: It's a psychological given for one, but we all know that to head west—to "follow the sun"—is in fact to bravely, courageously, utterly recklessly follow one's heart and imagination as far as it may ever physically, geographically, and psychologically lead. At that journey's only end, those who duly found themselves upon the Pacific's shore, or those who were lucky enough to have already arrived there natally during the mid-twentieth century, immediately found their sunlit joy best expressed via their art. Music, perhaps even above and beyond the moving picture, was L.A.'s most treasured and indelible gift to the rest of the world east of that basin.

Brian Wilson's particular California mythologizing was, and remains, a most potent and powerful force, of course. But right there, as well, sat and sang Phil Spector, Jan Berry, Frank Zappa, and a host of other Wild Westerners who made the rules and then ruled the airwaves. Theirs is a sound as hot and arid as only Stan Kenton or Dick Dale could make it, yet also as sweet and cool as a young Michelle Phillips coming to the canyon. Yet L.A. also can sound as happy as the Turtles, slick as Herb Alpert, sick as Lenny Bruce, or as flawlessly custom-built for the freeway as the Monkees.

Whatever and however the cases may be, though, there's no denying whatsoever that the L.A. sound runs far and wide, deep and bright, and, as such, will be playing forever, propelling all who continue to head, one way or another, their own way out west.

MICHELLE PHILLIPS: I think the Mamas and the Papas were kind of like a bubble. It was wonderful when that bubble was floating. Then the bubble popped, and that was the Mamas and the Papas. When you think about it, we were only together for two and a half years.

There are still millions of people that hear our music and the music of Los Angeles, which represents their youth, that was so tumultuous and so frightening to so many of their friends and relatives.

In a way, the Mamas and the Papas' music is comforting to them. You know what I mean? They can go

NOW THIS IS A RECORD MAN

RUSS REGAN: I know the durability of good songs and good records, and how rock music could work in a soundtrack. In 1972, I was in the original meeting at MCA Records in Universal City with George Lucas, Wolfman Jack, and Ned Tanen on *American Graffiti.* George was there, looking to assemble the soundtrack. I knew *American Graffiti,* 'cause I'm from Modesto, California, myself—where George was from. I cruised Tenth Street myself, so I knew that story.

One of the keys to a great soundtrack is people wanting to experience the movie at home or in their car. That's why soundtracks sell.

I approved every song on *Flashdance* and *The Morning After,* from *The Poseidon Adventure.* That movie premiered at the Egyptian Theatre in December of 1972. Both won Academy Awards. I approved the songs for *Chariots of Fire.*

Russ Regan and Ned Tanen at Uni/MCA Records, Universal City, 1971.

A song is like a movie. But a movie without a great script . . . you can't get a great movie. I don't give a damn how good your actors are. It's the same thing with a singer, if the singer doesn't have a great song. It's always about the song.

It goes back to Brian Wilson, when I named the Beach Boys. I met him and said, "This kid is unreal for age nineteen." Bernie Taupin is a great storyteller/ lyricist. Bernie Taupin's lyrics, if you analyze them, were incredible. He was ahead of everybody. For a twenty-one-year-old kid, at the time, he was amazingly talented. All these guys wrote great lyrics and great songs. Some extremely amazing writers have come into my life.

Sometimes I fill a void out there. When I signed Elton John, or Olivia Newton-John, or Barry White, or the Alan Parsons Project, my basic and number-one philosophy in A&R, then and now, is that I look for something that no one else is doing at the moment.

I heard a song by Olivia Newton-John, "If Not For You," in 1971 that was written by Bob Dylan. George Harrison previously recorded it in 1970 on his *All Things Must Pass* album that Phil Spector co-produced with him. I heard her version on an acetate. Somebody brought it to me. I then made the deal. I paid $25,000 for that record and was second-guessed. That's a whole other story. I loved it. I was put down for buying it. "She's too plastic, too beautiful, and will never happen." So I replied, "She's beautiful, she's not plastic, and it's gonna happen big time."

Success has many cousins, and failure is an orphan. I've had a lot of success, and a lot of people sort of jump on my bandwagon and take credit. I told a music industry conference in 1983, "Someday you'll go to a concert, and by the time you leave, you'll be able to buy the recording of that night's show."

back into their childhood and say, "That was the music of my era.'" "California Dreamin'" has surpassed any kind of era, and I think "Dream a Little Dream of Me" has done the same thing. I wish Fabian Andre was here to see what happened to his song. It was just licensed for a Marc Jacobs commercial.

In 2011, I got a phone call from a political activist who asked if I would agree to let "California Dreamin'" be the theme song for the Dream Act. "We want to call it the 'California Dream Act.'" I said, "Yeah, but are you going to license it?" "But we don't have the money to license it." So I said, "I'll call Universal and see if I can get them to waive the licensing on it."

So I called the president of licensing at Universal. "You know, I think we ought to give them this. I feel very strongly about this, and I would like to just give it to them." The John Phillips estate was called.

It's so much fun for me to see and hear "California Dreamin'" being played behind these political ads—the Dream Act, that enables children of Latinos who came here. I was so happy to be a part of it.

Why does our music still resonate? I don't know, but I am very lucky it does.

DANIEL WEIZMANN: It's only now that it's over that we've really started to understand the power of the little 45 rpm record, the way it fortified pleasure and prosperity in the America nestled between Hiroshima and Saigon. What would those years have been without a stack of small black discs with removable yellow or orange centers? The 45 was a contract guaranteeing joyous connection. Two songs, for pocket change, first heard on your car radio or your transistor. It was all the ID card you needed; it proved you were a citizen, proved that you pledged allegiance to the new age. But the 45 presented a Zen koan, too, because it was humble in its way—two lousy, three-minute tunes!—and yet, in the hands of visionaries like Spector and Wilson, the 45 could be a Trojan Horse that snuck into the square world and unleashed a whole army of energies that literally changed *everything*.

Jackie DeShannon in Laurel Canyon, 1968.

BOBBY WOMACK: You know, James Brown and guys like Sam Cooke taught me the ropes. Like, I just saw Jackie DeShannon on TV, singing one of her tunes. She looked great. That's a blessing in itself. We did some work together in 1969.

So you got to have passion for this business, and love it. Because anything can disappoint you, and the strongest thing can take you out. But if you have a passion for the music . . . when I look at new generations makin' it, I join them. "Mr. Womack. I love your music and what you do." I've been sampled [by Mariah Carey].

Damn, man, I never thought about, what am I gonna eat tomorrow? Will I live tomorrow and write a song? Or hang out with somebody? But what separates everything is the music that reached people's hearts, and the stories that will live on forever. They're bein' told over and over again.

MIKE STOLLER: Back in the early fifties—like '52 or '53 or whatever—those disc jockeys were banning records and saying rock 'n' roll is over. In fact, around '53, or maybe 1954, *Billboard* magazine, which was on newsprint at the time, came out in the year-end issue saying, "Rock 'n' roll is over.' And I remember Lester Sill saying, "No way, man. This music is here. This is going to last. This is going to be here for a long, long time." He was right.

MARIO ROCCUZZO: In 1965, I was working as an actor. I had a Tony Curtis split curl with a ducktail—a switchblade-knife punk kid. I was always in a leather jacket. I was also writing. I wanted to be a songwriter in the worst way. That was my dream, to be a songwriter. In 1957, when I was seventeen years old, I was working in a record store called Wallichs Music City in Hollywood, which at that time was the number-one store. I started work there when I was fourteen. Three years later, I was in charge of what we called the Top 40 records. Whatever I said sold in the Top 40 was played on the radio station KFWB.

At that time, KFWB was the Top 40 rock station. Now it's all news. Those were the days of payola. Guys used to come in and give me fifty bucks and say, "Mario, say my record sold more than it sold." Then it would make KFWB. Then, with thirty-eight that week, they would play it on KFWB. If it got played, it started selling automatically.

This young kid came in, and he said, "I hear you want to be a songwriter." I said, "Yeah." He said, "Have you written anything?" I said, "Yeah. I write love songs, ballads, sad things." He said, "Well, I got a couple of hit records out right now. Why don't you write something for me? But I don't sing sad songs. You got to write rock 'n' roll for me." I said, "Okay. Let me give it some thought." He said, "What are you doing tonight?" I said, "Nothing." He said, "Let's get together. I'll bring my guitar over. We'll write something." I said, "All right." I had my first my beer at the age of seventeen. I never drank in my life. I got smashed on one beer. We were sitting on the floor. There were a couple of other guys that we knew around there. On a napkin, I wrote a song in about five minutes called "Nervous Breakdown." The kid was named Eddie Cochran. He had this big electric guitar. I said, "Okay, Eddie. I'm having a nervous breakdown." He can play it and have a nervous breakdown.

A week later, I'm at Music City, working. I get this call. "What are you doing on your lunch hour?" "Nothing." "Come on down to Gold Star Studios. I'm recording your song." I go down, and there's Eddie Cochran recording my song. I couldn't get over it.

Eddie sang and recorded the song, and then he got killed in a car crash [in England on April 17, 1960]. He was in a car with Gene Vincent "Be-Bop-A-Lula." Eddie got killed, and Gene was hurt but didn't die. The song came out on Eddie's very last album. It only sold a few copies, so I didn't make anything off the song. Fade out and fade up. It's now twenty-three years later.

In 1982, my agent calls and says I have to do a show at CBS in the Valley. So I go, and I'm like forty-five minutes early. I'm walking on Ventura Boulevard to kill some time. I pass by this music store. I say, "Jesus, I haven't been in a record store in years. Let me go in and see what's selling." I walk in, and there's this whole punk rock section. Guys with orange and yellow hair. There's this punk rock album out by some guy I've never heard of. But there's a sticker on the front of the album that says, "Featuring the hit single 'Nervous Breakdown.'" I look. I say, "Hit single? I wrote a song once called 'Nervous Breakdown.'"

When the guy at the counter isn't looking, I slit the cellophane. I pull the record out. Words and music by Mario Roccuzzo. What do you mean, hit single? What hit single? Where's my bread? I couldn't believe it.

The next morning, I called BMI right down here on Sunset and Vine. I made an appointment. I went down that afternoon. I brought a copy of the album I bought. I told them the story. They said, "Hey, Mario. When you wrote this song for Eddie, you weren't a member of AS-CAP or BMI. You just gave it to Eddie. Somebody published it. But, who the hell knows who Mario Roccuzzo is? Do you live in Italy, Russia, Japan, America? Who is he? There's no way to pay you any money. What you have to do is now join ASCAP or BMI and then you have to get in touch with the publisher of 'Nervous Breakdown.'" I said, "Well, what do I do?" "Join us or them." I said, "I'll join you."

So, I filled out the application. I got it notarized that afternoon, and went back. The lady explained to me that BMI would pay me only for airplays, jukebox plays, where it's performed . . . and "Nervous Breakdown" hadn't been performed too much. You got maybe a hundred dollars coming for all the performances. I said, "Okay." The lady said, "Where you'll make some money is if you go to the people who published your record. They can pay for the sales." I said, "Well, on the album it says it's published by Elvis Presley Music." I knew that Elvis was in Nashville. I couldn't go to Elvis. She said, "No, Elvis was bought out by Chappell Music." I said, "Oh, where are they?" "On the nineteenth floor." I was in BMI's penthouse. I walked down to the nineteenth floor. All these executives were having their coffee break. I had the album. I held it up. I said, "Excuse me, did you people publish this hit record, 'Nervous Breakdown?'" Silence. They looked at it. I said, "I wrote it. Where's my bread?" They called me into the office. Within forty-eight hours, I had a check for $7,500 dollars. It sold 250,000 copies by this punk rocker, whoever he was. Terrible version of it. But, to this day, I still get royalty checks on that song. Eddie's was pure rock 'n' roll. It was beautiful. The punk rocker's version is an abortion . . . all synthesized stuff.

The only reason I got to tell you the story was this. In 1965, I ran into a couple, Sonny and Cher. Sonny said, "Write a song describing Cher and me. We're going to record our first album." I said, "Okay." He liked the words I wrote. So, I wrote this song describing him and Cher, the clothes they wear, the long hair. They had the hit record "I Got You Babe" out. Sonny said, "We're going to do our first album. Write a song." So I wrote this song called "Look At Us." I wrote the lyric, and I gave it to Sonny. It was too late. He had recorded all twelve tracks to their album. He said, "But I love your song so much. Can we call our album *Look At Us*? And can we use the lyric? Instead of liner notes on the back, just print your lyric and put your name—'written by Mario Roccuzzo'?" I said, "Sure." So, they put out their first album. It's called *Look At Us*, and on the back is my song. It sold three million copies. He gives me fifty dollars. That's what I learned about contracts. That's the end of my songwriting stories.

DAVE HULL: The recording artists I played during my radio career, which began in 1955, and then locally on KRLA during 1963–1969, and the bands I presented at Dave Hull's Hullabaloo in 1965 and '66 still endure. Can I give you my honest opinion why? This time period—even though the Vietnam War was on, and there was a lot of interaction politically—the 1956–1972 years were innocent times.

People were more innocent in their reaction to one another, through love affairs and anything that happened in that period. These times changed. And when they did, they brought places the innocent people and myself came from who either didn't understand it or didn't want to be part of it. So the people who go back to talk about this time period, or play the music from a more innocent time in their lives, are now beginning to feature it over and over again.

Myself and KRLA had a special connection with the listeners. It went beyond an autograph request or someone calling the station, asking for a record to be played. John Barrett used to tell us in one word how to approach our audience. *Care.* Listen to what they say and what they are saying to you. Care about them, about what you say on the air and what you do in your personal appearances. It may seem corny now to a lot of people. Yes, we were told to. We went to schools. That's all part of the caring. Myself, Casey, Reb Foster, and Dick Moreland at the station went into the community. It was a mission to bring the music out there.

The emergence of talk radio in the very late sixties impacted rock and pop music stations in town. Joe Pyne at KLAC—you can credit him with that. Nobody else. I had some moments at KFI between 1969 and 1971 that were ahead of everybody else, but in the case of talk radio, Joe Pyne was a pioneer. Talk radio and news started replacing rock and pop radio formats in town, because the radio stations didn't want the personalities making money, so they decided, "Let's get rid of music and go to talk."

In the 1970s world of music insiders, change was coming, and it could be staring you right in the face. I know—I saw it happen one night.

In October 1975, a young rock 'n' roller raised on the big beat of fifties and early sixties radio exploded into the consciousness of the American public. His face adorned the covers of TIME *and* Newsweek *magazines; he was Davy Crockett armed with a '53 blond Telecaster instead of Old Betsy, and he quickly became equally mythic. The week the magazines came out, Bruce Springsteen and the E Street Band headlined the Roxy Theater in West Hollywood, to an avalanche of fan and media interest. Opening night on October 17, 1975, was aired on KWST.*

I'd seen Bruce and the group on July 30, 1974, in a Columbia Records industry showcase at the Troubadour. He came on at around midnight and played until 3:00 AM to

Dave Hull at the microphone at KRLA in Pasadena, 1965.

the consternation of the staff but to the delirious delight of about thirty wild and innocent devotees.

In the wacky world of pop culture, things can blow up overnight, and now Bruce was the golden child. I was writing for England's Melody Maker in 1975, and was covering him for the weekly music periodical. At his sound check, I introduced myself to his right-hand man, guitarist "Miami Steve" Van Zandt. I mentioned that I'd been interviewing Phil Spector and singer Dion, who he knew from a summer 1974 job at the Hilton Hotel in Las Vegas, where Steve was the Dovells' musical director and guitarist. A Dick Clark-produced lounge show that also starred Dion, Jackie Wilson, Freddie Cannon, and the Coasters with a house band including keyboardist Joel Warren. Dion was now recording at Gold Star Studios on Santa Monica Boulevard and Vine Street, with Spector working his Merlinesque magic behind the board. I then invited Steve and Bruce to go to Dion's

session. Phil was always very kind to let me attend his recording activities.

A couple of nights later, we arrived. The temperature in the control room was about fifty-two degrees (we were freezing our asses off) and in the main studio, around twenty players—two acoustic guitarists, two bassists, two keyboardists, etc.—gathered in pairs that suggested not so much a symphony as Noah's Ark. Bruce was clearly basking in the proximity to a personal hero. Here was the old lion, coming face-to-face with the new guard. Babe Ruth meeting Henry Aaron; a sea change staring all of us right in the face, both figuratively and literally. This went on till the wee hours.

It was an inspiring time inside Gold Star. We watched Phil direct some Wrecking Crew veterans and Dion on "Baby, Let's Stick Together." I was definitely with some folks who loved the music that was made in L.A. Van Zandt

KINKY REGGAE IN ECHO PARK

ROGER STEFFENS: In 1969, Jimmy Cliff's "Wonderful World, Beautiful People," "Israelites," by Desmond Dekker and the Aces, and earlier in the sixties, Johnny Nash's "Hold Me Tight," received lots of radio airplay and sold records in the Los Angeles market.

Nash had hired Bob Marley as a songwriter and performer for his JAD label in 1968. So a lot of Marley songs had come out without anyone knowing who Bob Marley was. Nash struck later with "I Can See Clearly Now," a reggae perennial, alongside Marley compositions like "Stir It Up" and "Guava Jelly."

The landscape and musical climate was forever altered by the December 26–31, 1972, local premiere of Jimmy Cliff's movie *The Harder They Come.* It screened in Westwood, at the Nuart Theatre. With the attendant success of its soundtrack album from Chris Blackwell's Island Records label, distributed by Capitol Records, reggae arrived with its booming bass propulsion.

During the summer of 1973, Bob Marley lived with Lee Jaffe, a white harmonica player, and Yvette Anderson in an apartment on Hayvenhurst. They would shop for Ital food at the Chalet Gourmet on

Sunset Boulevard, and visit with music business friends in Malibu. The Island Records office was a short walk away on Sunset Boulevard.

In November of 1973, the Wailers came to Hollywood and rehearsed at Capitol Records, an event that was filmed and appears in many of the ongoing documentaries about the reggae king.

RAM DASS: Reggae—I loved that stuff. Bob Marley blew my mind. It was his thing, his message; the quality of his being. His quality of being touched me deeply. I felt that the deeper places I would get to in my own inner work . . . there would be people who were resonant like that. Those were people who were resonant in that place, in myself.

You meet somebody who knows your deeper truth. You're connecting sort of behind the kind of form and facade, and even though it's through the forms, you can feel you are meeting another mensch, another spiritual being. Reggae music fascinated me, and also because of Jamaica and all the grass. All of that. The records were always around, because everyone else around me had lots of records.

THE MAN WHO FELL TO SANTA MONICA

DAVID BOWIE: I can tell that I'm totally into being Ziggy by this stage of our touring. It's no longer an act; I am him. This would be around the tenth American show for us, and you can hear that we are all pretty high on ourselves. We train-wreck a couple of things—I miss some words, and sometimes you wouldn't know that pianist Mike Garson was onstage with us, but overall I really treasure this bootleg. Mick Ronson is at his blistering best.

RODNEY BINGENHEIMER: I'd seen a lot of shows, and it was the most amazing concert I had ever seen. The concept, performed and recorded, was another step from the *Ziggy* studio album. My mind was blown. Afterwards, there was a record company party at DJ Wolfman Jack's house in the Hollywood Hills. He was on KDAY at the time.

Only a year and a half before, I was walking on Hollywood Boulevard with David. I was working for Mercury Records at the time and doing West Coast promotion for the label around his *The Man Who Sold the World*. We drove to radio stations KMET and KYMS, out in Orange County. I took him around to see the sights of Hollywood—Dino's Lodge on the Sunset Strip, Lewin Record Paradise on Hollywood Boulevard, and restaurants like Ollie Hammond's on La Cienega. At Tom Ayres's home recording studio in the hills over West Hollywood, I watched David and Gene Vincent record a version of Bowie's "Hang On To Yourself." In 1971, David invited me to his *Hunky Dory* recording sessions in England.

KIM FOWLEY: Grelun Landon from RCA invited me to the Wolfman Jack party. I was an artist on the label. Bowie stood in the center of the room with me and Rodney. He said, "I'd really like to meet everybody, but they're afraid to come up and say hello. Yet, tomorrow at school and in work, they'll tell everybody they were hanging out with me tonight."

David copped to me that he politely lifted a line from my co-production of the Hollywood Argyles' "Alley-Oop" for his "Life on Mars?" In 2012, Ken Scott, who engineered and co-produced *Ziggy Stardust*, told me that the B-side of "Alley-Oop," "Sho Know a Lot About Love," influenced Bowie for the horn techniques in "Moonage Daydream."

and Springsteen were fans of Spector, the Ronettes, and the Crystals. The previous August, at the Bottom Line club in New York City, Bruce and his group included "Then He Kissed Me" in their repertoire, which I heard on an FM radio broadcast.

Steve, Bruce, and the E Street Band had recently done Jackie DeShannon's "When You Walk in the Room" onstage, and she was in the audience at their Roxy opening. So was Cher. Bruce praised the Topanga Canyon-based Spirit. In 1973 or '74, Bruce had met and talked at length with their keyboardist, John Locke. Steve and Bruce also cited the Byrds; Springsteen had gone to Tower Records on Sunset, purchased a Byrds LP, and then encored with "Goin' Back" at one of his Roxy shows.

Later, Bruce and Steve would also record and perform live with Ronnie Spector and Darlene Love. I eventually participated on a handful of Spector sessions as a percussionist and hand-clapper on tracks by the Ramones, Dion, Leonard Cohen, and the Paley Brothers, including their version of "Baby, Let's Stick Together," for which I shared a microphone with Phil Seymour and Rodney Bingenheimer. Being on that hallowed Gold Star floor again and banging a tambourine between Hal Blaine, Jim Keltner, Ray Pohlman, Dan and David Kessel, Don Randi, Steve Douglas, and Terry Gibbs provided a sense of security and identity to me. I never felt like a stepchild in the mix, either . . . although David Kessel taught me how to hide under a desk when the reps for the musicians union, Local 47, came by to monitor delinquent dues-paying members.

I hope the spirit of that 1975 Spector and Dion recording session is captured in these pages. It's about being present at the creation of something so special that no words can completely capture the magic. As Frank Zappa said, writing about music is like dancing about architecture, or something to that effect. Since I can't play guitar or piano just yet, or cast a lyric to a memorable melody, I'll just stick with what I really know—that if you hear a Rolling Stones record done at RCA in Hollywood in 1965, it'll change your life. Why? Because, within the confines of those two minutes and forty-eight seconds, you will hear the rhythmic drawl of Earl Palmer; the precise beats of Hal Blaine; the soulful croon of Sam Cooke, Bobby Womack, and Lou Rawls; the evil genius of Jack Nitzsche's arrangements; and the hustle and bustle of Sonny Bono working tunes from a publisher's hit list.

In 1972, I turned 21. I purchased my first alcoholic beverage at a Mose Allison gig. That year, the music changed, the radio changed, and my world changed. I found out that I was the only person in Hollywood who didn't have a phony ID. I could now legally enter the Whisky a Go Go. Mario Maglieri gave me a booth for the night, and all the French fries I could eat. I needed the nourishment to sustain me through the Mahavishnu Orchestra's epic assault there one school night in March. Their drummer came onstage in an Adidas tracksuit—a far cry from the au courant androgynous look that all the guys were striving for.

In June, I saw five Southern California-area Rolling Stones concerts promoting their Exile on Main St. album, overdubbed, mixed, and mastered in Hollywood at the Sunset Sound studio. Stevie Wonder opened for them every

Bruce Springsteen at the CBS Records Convention at the Fairmont Hotel, San Francisco, 1973.

night; he had dropped the "Little Stevie" act, and was now on the cusp of genius. Innervisions was a year away, and with it, a paradigm shift in pop music.

In September 1972, Los Angeles saw the arrival of KROQ, a new Top 40 AM radio station broadcasting from Pasadena, formerly country music outlet KBBQ. I went to the first KROQ-sponsored Los Angeles Coliseum show in November, hosted by Keith Moon of the Who. Admission was $1.06. Yoko Ono and John Lennon offered a prerecorded taped message of peace to the enthusiastic throng. Filling out the batting order were Arthur Lee and Love, Chuck Berry, the Bee Gees with an orchestra, Four Seasons, Raspberries, Eagles, Sly and the Family Stone, Mott the

Outtake from an Eagles photo session in Joshua Tree for their first album, 1972.

ANDY JOHNS ON ENGINEERING THE ROLLING STONES' EXILE ON MAIN ST.

ANDY JOHNS: I was still learning on *Exile*. So I wasn't influential, really, at all about anything except for perhaps choice of song, once or twice. "This shouldn't be a single." They had been making records for quite some time. Mick saw himself as sort of the producer. Jimmy Miller was on his way out. So Mick would be around for everything. "Let's put the chicks here." "Let's have Jim [Price] come up with something for this."

"All Down the Line" was the first one that was finished, because we'd been working for months and months. Mick got very enamored. "It's finished! It's going to be the single!" I thought, "This isn't really a single, you know." I remember going out and talking to him, and he was playing the piano. "Mick, this isn't a single. It doesn't compare to 'Jumpin' Jack Flash' or 'Street Fighting Man.' Come on, man." He went, "Really? Do you think so?" I thought, "My God. He's actually listening to me." [*Laughs.*] Then I was having a struggle with with the mix that I thought was gonna be it. Ahmet Ertegun then barged in with a bunch of hookers and ruined the one mix. He stood right in front of the left speaker, with two birds on each arm.

I told Mick, "I can't hear it here. If I could hear it on the radio, that would be nice." It was just a fantasy.

"Oh, we can do that. Stew [road manager Ian Stewart], go to the nearest FM radio station with the tape and say we'd like to hear it over the radio. We'll get a limo, and Andy can listen to it in the car." I went, "Bloody hell . . . well, it's the Stones. Okay."

So sure enough, we're touring down Sunset Strip and Keith is in one seat, and I'm in the back where the speakers are with Mick. Charlie [Watts] is in there, too. Just because he was bored. [*Laughs.*] Mick's got the radio on, and the DJ comes on the air: "We're so lucky tonight. We're the first people to play the new Stones record." It came on the radio, and the speakers in this car were kind of shot. I still couldn't tell. It finishes, and Mick turns around. "So?" "I'm still not sure, man. I'm still not used to these speakers." "Oh. We'll have him play it again, then."

Poor Stew. "Have them play it again," like they were some sort of radio service. It was surreal. Up and down Sunset Strip at nine o'clock on a Saturday night. The street was jumpin', and I'm in the car with those guys, listening to my mixes. It sounded okay. "I think we're down with that." So then we moved on.

When I finished the album, I made a seven-and-a-half-inch IPS copy for the band and left it out front at Sunset Sound, in the traffic office. Then a guy shows up like a messenger, and picks up the copy. "That's for me. I'm delivering it to the boys." Some stranger. It never got bootlegged. He kept it for himself. I was a bit freaked out about it, because I would be the one who got it in the neck.

You know, a lot of people like that record. I think they were at the height of their powers, in a way, as far as rock 'n' roll goes.

The Rolling Stones at the Inglewood Forum, 1972.

The Whisky a Go Go, West Hollywood, 1973.

Hoople, and Stevie Wonder. It was a trip to be cavorting on the same field the Los Angeles Rams football team called home.

In 1973, the KROQ owners bought the struggling KPPC and changed the call letters to KROQ. They then hired Shadoe Stevens, a former KHJ DJ from 1970 to '72, to launch a new rock format.

By 1973, the local and national climate had changed. Music and politics became scrambled in my mind; TIME magazine picked Richard Nixon and Henry Kissinger as their "Men of the Year" as Bruce Springsteen's debut LP, Greetings from Asbury Park, N.J., was released by Columbia Records in the first week of January (I was given a white-label promotional LP copy of it). The Hollywood Palladium hosted the first Surfer Stomp, where the beach crowd met for a mash-up with the new glitter-glam rockers on Sunset Boulevard. The Watergate burglars' trial began in Washington, DC, as the Vietnam cease-fire was announced in Paris. The Supreme Court addressed abortion in the Roe v. Wade decision. LBJ died at 64. Nixon announced the Vietnam Peace Accord, and a treaty was signed in Paris. It was the end of the U.S. draft. I no longer had to write the words "student deferment" anywhere. This began for

me at West Los Angeles College, and continued at Los Angeles City College and then San Diego State. This war is over—reminding me of what Jim Morrison sang in a Doors song back in 1968.

G. Gordon Liddy and James W. McCord Jr. were found guilty for their role in the Watergate burglary. Samuel James Ervin Jr., a Democratic U.S. Senator from North Carolina who chaired the investigation of the Watergate scandal that led to the resignation of President Nixon in 1974, got his own record deal on Columbia Records. Senator Sam at Home was a spoken-word LP mixed with tracks of him singing popular songs, including "Bridge Over Troubled Water."

In 1973, my family was living on Wetherly Drive, up behind the Roxy Theater, overlooking Sunset Boulevard. Neil Young was the first musician to play the room that year—the former site of the Largo Club. Igor Stravinsky once lived a few houses down from us. Sam Peckinpah was a neighbor up the street. Blue Jay Way was less than a mile away. The "Last Supper" photo inside the sleeve of George Harrison's 1973 Living in the Material World LP was shot at a Doheny estate right around the corner. I now had better AM and FM radio reception, in the hills of West Hollywood.

I've been chasing the music for decades now. You try to stay current, not lose sight of the fact that it's a flow, never-ending. To be honest, though, I'm still parsing my way through those early years, still trying to make sense of the bug that took hold. You gotta be patient if you want to see how all the pieces fit. The Chinese premier Chou En-lai was once asked about the role of the French Revolution in determining world events. "Too early to tell," he counseled. Now that's a time frame I can live with.

This is where the future was created.

du 2 au 28 mars 1971
maximy
MUSÉE D'ART MODERNE DE LA VILLE DE PARIS

AFTERWORD

BY ROGER STEFFENS

Harvey Kubernik is a national treasure. He's one of the very few people who can assemble so many different strains of music history together in such a compelling weave, because he was not only *in* it, but *of* it. He knew everybody! In this remarkable compendium, he has solidified the commanding position in popular music that L.A. held—particularly in the sixties, a decade much over-praised for its alleged "San Francisco sound." You may question, as I did after reading this book, the validity of that appellation.

Many years ago, a friend who worked in a Santa Monica Boulevard pawn shop turned me on to an amazing autograph book kept by a local high school student in the late fifties. It contained signatures not only from Elvis Presley, Jackie Wilson, Eddie Cochran, Phil Spector, and Alan Freed, but also from the cream of L.A.'s greatest disc jockeys of the time, as well as many of the local groups that might have disappeared beyond the pale, had it not been for Kubernik's constant reinvigoration of their accomplishments. Scrawled across the yellowing pages of this marvelous time capsule are the signatures of on-air personalities Hunter Hancock, Art Laboe, and Al Jarvis alongside artists like Spade Cooley, the Meadowlarks, the Robins, the Hollywood Flames, and Chuck Higgins, as well as quintessential writers Leiber and Stoller.

To this New York-raised radio freak, most of these names were part of a continent-separated world parallel to my own, but almost unknown. My heroes were the self-proclaimed King of Rock 'n' Roll and coiner of the term, Alan Freed, and Jocko Henderson, the rhyming jock whose show followed Freed's from way down the low-fi right end of the AM dial. They both threw huge live shows during the holidays each year and their playlists were all-encompassing, though Jocko's was much more blackly raw.

I saw Buddy Holly during Freed's massive Christmas '57 review at the Paramount Theater in Times Square. Also on that show were Fats Domino, Little Richard, Frankie Lymon's Teenagers, Jerry Lee Lewis, Lee Andrews and the Hearts, and a dozen others—all for $2.50! The revolution was afoot and we pioneering "teenagers"—a new classification then—knew that rock 'n' roll was no passing fad, as cluelessly vicious critics like Walter Winchell and Frank Sinatra were claiming.

I was delighted to read of Kim Fowley's swift, youthful progression through the ranks, starting with his gofer duties for my idol, Alan Freed, during his exile in L.A. As enamored of him as Fowley was, it was me who once told Freed that I wanted to be him when I grew up. He laughed and signed an autograph that I've kept ever since.

The "smooth vocal stylings" of Patti Page and Pat Boone (who is to rock 'n' roll what imitation margarine is to fine French cuisine) were being replaced on the charts by black artists. Their impact on a white audience unquestionably influenced the momentum of the black power movement. (I never heard my mother swear until the first time she heard me playing a 78 of Little Richard's "Tutti Frutti" over and over. She banged on my bedroom

Opposite: **Roger Steffens in Marrakesh, 1971.**

door, screaming, "Turn off that goddamn booga-wooga jungle music!")

West Coast artists like the ethereal Penguins, Ritchie Valens, Eddie Cochran, and others found a home on New York radio. I must give huge credit here to the deeply influential *Oldies But Goodies* albums curated by Art Laboe, which really brought home the fact that there was another world of rock bubbling on the West Coast. I began to learn new words like "pachuco," and wondered what it would be like to be among the raving teens at El Monte Legion Stadium.

When I began my first radio program in 1961 on WVOX in New Rochelle, New York, my first guest was Babatunde Olatunji, the great Nigerian musician whose groundbreaking album *Drums of Passion* has never been out of print since 1959. I learned of him from Symphony Sid, whose midnight show followed Jocko on "W-A-D-O rad-i-o," as their jingle had it. Later, Murray the K would use parts of Tunji's disc daily on his radio program, and its songs would be covered by Santana and others. I saw Miriam Makeba in 1961 at the Village Gate, and eventually made an interview album with her in the eighties. I'm also the guy who turned Paul Simon on to Ladysmith Black Mambazo for the *Graceland* album. I can draw a direct line linking all these things to my early exposure to African music on the radio.

Harvey's book once again brings attention to the regional and historic contributions of Jerry Leiber and Mike Stoller, two of the greatest songwriters for hire who ever lived: a witty lyricist and a master of the pop genre joining forces in the early regional birth of rock 'n' roll. They brought a street sensibility to the music. We feel it sizzle throughout these pages.

Harvey's expedition also reminds me of events that occurred over a half a century ago. Once the payola scandal hit in 1959 and 1960 and rock 'n' roll had been decimated, the only forces in music that kept my head alive were Phil Spector and Motown. Other than that, it turned real crappy, real fast. People were afraid. Black music became Motown, which was very slick and polished; they were aiming to have their acts groomed to be able to play the Copacabana for rich white people. There was huge power in the Spector music. You cannot believe the impact of those records. He was mining veins and adding dimensions to pop music that had never been heard before, especially with the symphonic Wall of Sound. Jack Nitzsche and Spector's session musicians are some of the essential people in the history of pop music, the most creative and inspired and, reputedly, the most fun to be around of anyone. Harvey brings them

Autographs by (*clockwise from top left*) Alan Freed, Eddie Cochran, Elvis Presley, Lloyd Thaxton, Art Laboe, and Johnny Otis.

vividly alive herein, and gives them their well-deserved pride of place.

When I got drafted in 1967 and shipped off to 'Nam, the Armed Forces Vietnam Network kept us supplied with most of the latest hits. But the real world of underground rock was kept vital by private shipments of records and, for me especially, weekly, up-to-the-moment tapes of Tom Donahue's mind-bending KSAN broadcasts from San Francisco. These featured Scoop Nisker's zany news-collages, and a mix of music from every corner of the globe combined with the finest of American forms.

From Harvey, I learned that Tom had been listening to Dave Diamond in Hollywood, and had brought that innovative format to the Bay Area. For me, the two greatest periods in radio were from 1954 to 1959 and 1964 to 1972, by which time the lawyers, accountants, and soulless corporations had taken over the music business and emasculated it.

KSAN, like KMET, had an "everything goes" format, so we could listen for hours as the Grateful Dead brought tapes of their previous evening's Fillmore concert to the station and played them uncut. It was through these tapes that I heard San Francisco's great sixties groups—Jefferson Airplane, Quicksilver Messenger Service, Santana, Janis Joplin and Big Brother—alongside the best of SoCal bands like the ineffable Buffalo Springfield, Love, the Byrds, the Mothers, and the Mamas and the Papas.

One of the great nights of my life came a few years ago, when Harvey introduced me to Michelle Phillips. I got to extend my gratitude to her for the life-enhancing power of her group's music for us GIs in the midst of such ongoing terror. She gave me a tight and lingering hug I'll never forget. With misty eyes, she thanked me for telling her this, because she had been led to believe it was only the fraught frenzy of Hendrix and others of that ilk that had been important to the troops.

Another record which had a major influence on us was Crosby, Stills and Nash's 1969 debut, one of the greatest albums in the history of rock. It's still in my all-time top ten. Those exquisite harmonies and lilting lyrics—that was what we played in Saigon, when attacks were taking place around us. It just cooled everyone out. "Lady of the Island" and "Guinevere" were so hauntingly soothing, yet edgy. Their music, for many of us, was like medicine. When you were out in the field with a little cassette recorder, whatever you played ran down your batteries, so it had to be crucial. L.A., in fact, did provide much of the soundtrack to that misbegotten war, heard in hooches and trenches from the DMZ to the Delta.

In November of 1967, the week before I shipped out to Nam, I heard the absurdist-surrealist, psychedelic comedy troupe the Firesign Theatre, and brought a copy of their brain-candy debut, *Waiting for the Electrician or Someone Like Him*, with me to Saigon. I must have made a hundred copies of it for guys in the field. When I finally moved to L.A. in 1975, I became friends with Firesign members Phil Proctor and Peter Bergman. A few years later, I was invited to be part of the briefly revived *Oz* show on KPFK, just prior to beginning my own program, *Reggae Beat*, on KCRW with Hank Holmes. There, I also hosted a show called *Sound of the Sixties*, and rebroadcast many excerpts from my two hundred hours of KSAN tapes, clueing a new generation in to what a treasure those years were.

Shortly after our reggae show began, I received a fan letter that opened with: "My name is John Densmore. I used to be in a group called the Doors." He said he was a regular listener and offered to come on *Reggae Beat* and play an unreleased track he and Robby Krieger had cut in Jamaica.

In this book, Harvey masterfully deconstructs the recording of "Light My Fire," nailing the crucial importance of Rothchild and Botnick as unofficial fifth and sixth members of that group. He does the same for Love's *Forever Changes*. I was reminded that Andrew Loog Oldham produced the Rolling Stones' albums from 1964 to 1967 in Hollywood, and then later, the Stones' *Beggars Banquet* and *Exile on Main St.* were mixed locally.

It was the openness of L.A.'s airwaves to so much of the experiments in sound that were being made in jazz, rock, blues, and R & B, that helped spearhead the Sixties Revolution.

With any justice, Harvey's book will be one of the definitive histories of that era, filled with fun facts and deep reconnaissance, elevating the behind-the-scenes workers to a new level of respect and celebrating the greats whose works have proven immortal. Every city should be blessed with a chronicler of such omnivorous tenaciousness and impeccable taste.

GLOSSARY

LOU ADLER: A songwriter, record producer, music publisher, record label owner, and still-active seismic force in the music and entertainment business since 1957, Adler guided the careers of Jan and Dean, Johnny Rivers, the Mamas and the Papas, Spirit, Carole King, and Cheech and Chong. Adler also produced the 1967 Monterey International Pop Festival with John Phillips. In 2013, he was inducted into the Rock and Roll Hall of Fame in the non-performer category.

GENE AGUILERA: Hailing from East Los Angeles, Aguilera listened to Thee Midniters on his small transistor radio and caught the Stones/Byrds/Beatles live during the mid-sixties. A USC grad, bank vice president, and East L.A. music historian, he guided the careers of both Little Willie G. and the Blazers. A songwriter and lyricist, he co-penned the opening track of Ry Cooder's Grammy-nominated *Chávez Ravine* album.

HERB ALPERT: As the leader of a faux mariachi band called the Tijuana Brass, Alpert parlayed a series of chirpy pop instrumental hits into the foundation of what would become the music industry's premier independent record label, A&M Records.

BURT BACHARACH: Burt Bacharach is a classically trained pianist who has had over 500 songs recorded by the most influential artists of the twentieth century: Frank Sinatra, the Beatles, Jackie DeShannon, the Carpenters, Barbra Streisand, Neil Diamond, Dionne Warwick, and Aretha Franklin. He has received three Academy Awards and eight Grammy Awards (including the 2008 Lifetime Achievement Award and 1997 Trustees Award with collaborator Hal David). In 2008, the Recording Academy awarded Bacharach the Lifetime Achievement Award, naming him music's "Greatest Living Composer."

WALTER BECKER: Part autodidact, part Maynard G. Krebs, Walter Becker was a dropout from the prestigious Bard College, content to take his love of literature and jazz with him to New York City and pursue a career as a songwriter with a bad attitude. With his college buddy (and Bard graduate) Donald Fagen, they crafted an unprecedented body of work that transformed white hipster jazzboes into Top Forty demigods. Becker was last spotted walking past Radio City holding a transistor radio with a large sum of money to spend.

MARSHALL BERLE: A music industry veteran from Hollywood, Berle is the nephew of comedian/actor Milton Berle. He became an agent trainee at the William Morris Agency in 1960, and helped create the music department there. His first signing was the Beach Boys. Over the next thirty years, Berle would serve as an agent for Ike and Tina Turner, Spirit, and Canned Heat, later managing Spirit in the sev-enties and eighties. In the mid-seventies, Berle managed Van Halen and brought them to Warner Bros. Records.

TOSH BERMAN: The son of assemblage artist Wallace Berman (who appeared on the cover of the Beatles' *Sgt. Pepper's Lonely Hearts Club Band*), Berman is a writer and the publisher of Tam Tam Books.

JELLO BIAFRA: Born Eric Boucher, Biafra is the former lead singer and songwriter of the San Francisco band the Dead Kennedys. Now a spoken-word artist and performer, Biafra oversees the Alternative Tentacles record label. In 2009, he formed a new band, the Guantanamo School of Medicine. Biafra and the outfit continue to tour today.

STEVE BINDER: A groundbreaking television director who helped invent the music video model and the modern rock concert film, Binder directed *Jazz Scene U.S.A.*, *The Steve Allen Show*, and the memorable *T.A.M.I. Show*, a rock 'n' roll theatrical extravaganza hosted by Jan and Dean starring James Brown, the Rolling Stones, Leslie Gore, the Miracles, the Supremes, and Chuck Berry. Binder then directed the NBC weekly pop music series *Hullabaloo*, now a weekly staple on KCET. Binder directed NBC TV specials on Leslie Uggums, Harry Belafonte, and Petula Clark before partnering with sound engineer and record producer Bones Howe to create Binder/Howe Productions. Binder also directed the heralded *Elvis '68 Comeback Special*.

RODNEY BINGENHEIMER: In 1970, Bingenheimer worked for Mercury Records at their Hollywood Boulevard office, overseeing FM radio promotions for their label artists, including Rod Stewart, David Bowie, Doug Sahm, and Uriah Heep. He was the former proprietor of Rodney Bingenheimer's English Disco from 1972 to 1975. He has been a longtime fixture on the L.A. radio station KROQ, hosting his weekly *Rodney on the ROQ* show.

HAL BLAINE: Born Harold Belsky, drummer Blaine is primarily known for the thousands of recording sessions he has played on over the last fifty years. A member of the Wrecking Crew, his work can be heard on dates with Elvis Presley, the Ronettes, the Beach Boys, Jan and Dean, Simon and Garfunkel, Nancy Sinatra, the 5th Dimension, Herb Alpert and the Tijuana Brass, the Carpenters, Frank Sinatra, Sonny and Cher, Henry Mancini, Tommy Roe, the Mamas and the Papas, and the Byrds. He is a member of the Rock and Roll Hall of Fame and the Percussive Arts Society Hall of Fame.

PAUL BODY: A player of the pagan skins and the accordion, Body recorded with his band, the Sheiks of Shake, in the seventies. Today, he dabbles in spoken word.

BRUCE BOTNICK: At age eighteen, sound engineer and record producer Botnick talked his way into a job at Liberty Records. There, he recorded Bud Shank, Bobby Vee, Johnny Burnette, Jackie DeShannon, Leon Russell, David Gates, and Jack Nitzsche. He then moved to Sunset Sound, where he engineered the Doors' albums and the first two Love albums. From his mixing desk at Sunset Sound, Botnick also documented the brave new world recordings of the Turtles, Buffalo Springfield, and the Beach Boys.

DAVID BOWIE: After playing sax with the Kon-Rads, the King Bees, the Mannish Boys, and the Lower Third, David Robert Jones changed his name to David Bowie and released "Space Oddity," an album that landed him on the UK record charts. Bowie went on to produce such landmark discs as "The Man Who Sold the World," "Hunky Dory," and "The Rise and Fall of Ziggy Stardust."

TOMMY BOYCE: Half of a songwriting duo with Bobby Hart, Boyce co-wrote "Be My Guest," recorded by Fats Domino. Boyce and Hart penned songs for Jay and the Americans and Paul Revere and the Raiders before Boyce wrote, produced, and played on the pilot of *The Monkees*. Boyce and Hart wrote nearly three dozen songs for the group.

LALA BROOKS: Born Dolores Brooks, La La was a member of the Crystals, the Phil Spector-produced and Jack Nitzsche-arranged uber girl group. Originally from Brooklyn, Brooks took the lead vocal duties on such hits as, "Then He Kissed Me" and "Da Doo Ron Ron." She left the Crystals in 1966 to marry jazz drummer Idris Muhammad. In 1968, Brooks was cast in the original Broadway production of the musical *Hair*, in which she sang "Aquarius." Brooks went on to tour and record with Bobby Womack and Isaac Hayes.

DENNY BRUCE: After a six-month stint drumming with Frank Zappa, who was in the process of forming the Mothers of Invention, Bruce held A&R jobs at the Vanguard and Blue Thumb record labels. He produced and managed guitarist Leo Kottke for a decade and later co-owned Takoma Records, where he signed and recorded Charles Bukowski and the Fabulous Thunderbirds.

RICHARD CARPENTER: In 1965, Carpenter started the Richard Carpenter Trio, with bassist Wes Jacobs and his sister, Karen Carpenter, on drums. Two years later, Richard and Karen branched off with students from Long Beach State to form Spectrum. Eventually, Richard and Karen did some demos, bringing them to the attention of Herb Alpert at A&M Records. The label head suggested a Burt Bacharach composition for the group, "(They Long to Be) Close to You," which went to number one on the *Billboard* charts.

ED CASSIDY: A drummer and co-founder of Spirit, Cassidy created jazz with Art Pepper, Gerry Mulligan, and Julian "Cannonball" Ad-

derly before joining the Rising Sons in 1964. He then formed the Red Roosters in 1965, later evolving into Spirit in 1967. Cassidy died in 2012.

MARSHALL CHESS: Chess's father, Leonard, and his uncle, Phil, co-founded the legendary Chess Records label. Marshall himself produced over a hundred recordings for the label while overseeing the recording careers of such blues icons as Muddy Waters, Willie Dixon, Howlin' Wolf, Bo Diddley, and Sonny Boy Williamson. In the late sixties, Marshall created his own record label, Cadet Concept, a division of Chess Records. He left Chess in 1969 to become the president of Rolling Stones Records for a seven-year period.

HANK CICALO: A sound engineer who began his career at Capitol Records in 1957 with artists Frank Sinatra, Dean Martin, and Nat King Cole, Cicalo moved up the ranks and engineered recording sessions for Peggy Lee and Lou Rawls. He then joined RCA and was behind the console for recordings with Duke Ellington and Wayne Newton. He later became affiliated with the Dot Records label, handling dates for Jimmie Rodgers and Harry James. It was at RCA that Cicalo recorded the Monkees albums for Colgems, even going on the road with them in 1967. Later, at A&M Records, he worked on Carole King's *Tapestry* and engineered George Harrison's *Thirty-Three and 1/3* LP.

DICK CLARK: One of the most recognized personalities in entertainment in America, Clark began his entertainment career at age seventeen at radio station WRUN in Utica, New York. Later, at WFIL Radio and Television, he became the host of the local television show *Bandstand*. Clark convinced the ABC network to carry the show nationwide, and shortly thereafter, *American Bandstand* became the country's highest-rated daytime show. Clark was also responsible for TV programs like *Where the Action Is, Happening '68*, and *It's Happening*. Over the last few decades, Clark spotlighted the sounds of Los Angeles on his two nationally syndicated radio shows (*Rock, Roll, and Remember* and *The U.S. Music Survey*), live shows (*Good Ol' Rock 'n' Roll*), and various rock 'n' roll video collections. He died in April 2012 in Santa Monica, California.

MERRY CLAYTON: An in-demand backing vocalist, Clayton worked with Ray Charles, Pearl Bailey, and Burt Bacharach. Jack Nitzsche enlisted her for Neil Young's debut solo album in 1968, and for his *Performance* soundtrack album. Clayton also sang the blistering counterpart to Mick Jagger on the Rolling Stones' "Gimme Shelter" session, and contributed vocals to Carole King's *Tapestry*. Clayton was married to the distinguished jazz saxophonist Curtis Amy, and her brother, Sam, played percussion in Little Feat.

CAROL CONNORS (formerly Annette Kleinbard): Initially known as the lead singer of the Teddy Bears, Kleinbard changed her name to Carol Connors and wrote the hit record "Hey Little Cobra" for the Terry Melcher-produced Rip Chords. In the seventies, she collaborated with Ayn Robbins and Bill Conti on "Gonna Fly Now," the

Academy Award-nominated theme to *Rocky*.

JAMES CUSHING: A poet and professor, Cushing began his radio career as a late-night DJ at KPFK in 1981. He has taught literature and creative writing at Cal Poly San Luis Obispo since 1989, and has continued to broadcast on the school's station, KCPR.

CHRIS DARROW: A member of the Nitty Gritty Dirt Band, the Corvettes, and Kaleidoscope, Darrow's multi-instrumental talents have been utilized on recordings by Leonard Cohen, James Taylor, Linda Ronstadt, John Stewart, Hoyt Axton, Kim Fowley, Helen Reddy, Gene Vincent, and John Fahey.

RAM DASS: The author of *Be Here Now*, now in its thirty-fourth printing, Dass is a former professor of psychology at Stanford, UC Berkeley, and Harvard. In 1961, he collaborated with Timothy Leary, Ralph Metzner, Aldous Huxley, and Allen Ginsberg researching psilocybin, LSD-25, and other psychedelic chemicals. Dass has been a regular voice on the radio dial since the inception of FM underground radio, appearing on stations such as KPFK.

EDDIE DAVIS: A former child actor and restaurant owner, Davis established his Rampart and Faro Records labels in 1960, both of which were devoted almost exclusively to the development of Mexican American musicians who forged the "East Side sound" on the West Coast. Davis issued records by the Premiers, Cannibal and the Headhunters, the Blendells, the Mixtures, and many others.

JIM DAWSON: The author of thirteen books, Dawson also wrote liner notes for Rhino Records' classic box set anthology of Los Angeles black music, *Central Avenue Sounds*.

FITO DE LA PARRA: After moving from Mexico City to Los Angeles in 1966, de la Parra had a short stint in Bluesberry Jam, backing Etta James, the Platters, and the Rivingtons. He was soon asked to replace Frank Cook as the drummer in Canned Heat, and debuted on their second album, *Boogie with Canned Heat*.

AL DE LORY: An award-winning record producer, arranger, and studio musician keyboardist, De Lory can be heard on records by the Four Preps, the Lettermen, Wayne Newton, and Dobie Gray and the Rip Chords. He was booked on Phil Spector's Gold Star studio dates and contributed to Brian Wilson's *Pet Sounds*. In 1967, famed Capitol Records executive Ken Nelson hired De Lory at the label, where he produced Glen Campbell's first million-selling singles.

ALEX DEL ZOPPO: Singer and keyboard player Del Zoppo was a co-founder and primary songwriter of Sweetwater. In 1967, the band attended the Monterey International Pop Festival, which inspired them to play increasingly larger outdoor festivals. Two years later, they were the first band to perform at the original Woodstock.

JOHN DENSMORE: In 1965, after meeting Ray Manzarek at the Transcendental Meditation Center in Los Angeles, Densmore became the drummer in Manzarek's band, which they renamed the Doors.

DAVE DIAMOND: A vital voice in the Los Angeles radio market from 1965 to 1968, Diamond was one of the original "Boss Jocks" at KHJ. His eighteen-month residency at KBLA from 1965 to 1967 established a new, adventurous format on the AM airwaves from exposing new regional bands and programming album tracks on his specialty show, *The Diamond Mine*.

JIM DICKSON: An engineer and former co-manager and co-record producer of the Byrds and Flying Burrito Brothers, Dickson was a pivotal force in the Hollywood folk and bluegrass-based musical community from 1960 to 1980. While at World-Pacific Studios, Dickson produced a slew of album sessions for Lord Buckley, most notably the LP *Hipsters, Flipsters, and Finger Poppin' Daddies*, as well as productions from Odetta, Hamilton Camp, the MFQ, the Dillards, and the Byrds.

HENRY DILTZ: In 1962, Diltz became a founding member of the Modern Folk Quartet. When the MFQ went on hiatus, Diltz embarked on his photographic career. His first shoots were for the Lovin' Spoonful. Along with art director Gary Burden, Diltz created over two hundred album covers for such stellar artists as the Doors, Crosby, Stills and Nash, the Eagles, James Taylor, and Cass Elliot.

MICKY DOLENZ: Best known as the drummer and lead vocalist of the Monkees, Dolenz sang lead on the band's "Last Train to Clarksville," "I'm a Believer," and "Pleasant Valley Sunday." He also helped write "Goin' Down," and sang lead on group member Peter Tork's "For Pete's Sake." Dolenz continues to act and participates in various Monkees projects and reunions, and even held a DJ stint in New York.

DONOVAN: Originally from Glasgow, Scotland, Donovan delivered such sonic gems as "Guinevere, " "The Trip," and "Season of the Witch," all recorded at Columbia Studios on Sunset Boulevard. In 1968, Donovan's "Hurdy Gurdy Man" became an anthem.

CHIP DOUGLAS: Musician, songwriter, and record producer Douglas changed the Hollywood musical landscape with his arrangements and studio dates with such recording artists as the Modern Folk Quartet, the Turtles, the Monkees, and Linda Ronstadt. As the Turtles' bassist, Douglas arranged their memorable "Happy Together." Invited into the Monkees' fold by Michael Nesmith, Douglas produced the hits "Daydream Believer" and "Pleasant Valley Sunday." In 1969, Douglas produced Ronstadt's debut solo album for Capitol Records, which broke new directions and established an alternative country audience.

DENNIS DRAGON: A drummer since age five, Dragon played in the Malibu Music Men Plus One, which featured a very young Natalie Cole as lead guitarist. Dragon went on to play professionally as a drummer and percussionist, touring with the Beach Boys, the

Byrds, and Neil Young, while also scoring and producing surf music soundtracks.

JOHNNY ECHOLS: In the fifties, Echols studied music with Adolph Jacobs, who backed the Coasters, and was soon jamming with local legends Billy Preston and Little Richard. Echols went on to co-found Love with Arthur Lee, a former Dorsey High School classmate. Their psychedelic spin on soul, R & B, and pop has earned them an impassioned cult status virtually unrivaled by any of their mid-sixties cohorts.

KIM FOWLEY: A record producer, music publisher, songwriter, recording artist, performer, and television and movie actor, Fowley wrote hundreds of songs and produced over a thousand recording sessions. His credits display the Hollywood Argyles, B. Bumble and the Stingers, the Paradons, the Murmaids, Manfred Mann, the Seeds, Gene Vincent, the Sir Douglas Quintet, Warren Zevon, and over a dozen co-writes for the Byrds.

LONN FRIEND: The editor of the iconic Larry Flynt publication *RIP* and host of the *Friend at Large* segment of MTV's *Headbangers Ball,* Friend chronicled the era of Guns N' Roses, Motley Crue, Metallic,a and countless other acts that ruled the charts during the decade of decadence.

RICHIE FURAY: After meeting Stephen Stills in New York, Furay joined Stills's band, the Au Go Go Singers. In California, they encountered Neil Young and linked up to form Buffalo Springfield, adding Bruce Palmer and Dewey Martin next. After three albums with the band, Furay co-founded Poco with Jim Messina. Alongside George Grantham, Randy Meisner, and Rusty Young, he created the template for the contemporary country-rock sound.

BILL GARDNER: The host of *Rhapsody in Black,* a two-hour weekly radio program on KPFK, Gardner was formerly heard on KPPC and KLON.

GARY PIG GOLD: Hailing from Toronto, Gold has led the Canadian band Endless Summer, produced and signed the first Western recording act exclusively to the former Soviet Melodiya label, and written here, there, and everywhere on all things rock and even roll for the MusicHound Essential Album Guides and the UK Mammoth Book series.

BILLY GOLDENBERG: The musical director of the *Elvis '68 Comeback Special,* Goldenberg also worked on the 1965 *Hullabaloo* television series with director Steve Binder. Goldenberg is a protégé of Broadway composer Frank Loesser and has had songs recorded by Barbra Streisand and Liza Minnelli.

BERRY GORDY, JR.: Motown Records founder Gordy shipped vinyl by the Supremes, Stevie Wonder, Marvin Gaye, the Temptations, the Four Tops, Martha Reeves and the Vandellas, the Marvelettes, Michael Jackson, the Jackson Five, Smokey Robinson and the Miracles, Brenda Holloway, Kim Weston, and Mary Wells.

MARK GUERRERO: A singer-songwriter, musician, and Chicano rock historian who grew up in East Los Angeles, Guerrero's teenage band, Mark and the Escorts, was part of the "East Side sound" of the sixties. He's recorded as an artist for labels such as Ode, Capitol, and A&M Records. His songs have been recorded by artists such as Herb Alpert, Trini Lopez, and his late father, Lalo Guerrero, the "Father of Chicano Music."

BILL HALVERSON: After working for engineer Wally Heider as a gofer and an assistant engineer on remote recording projects. Halverson went on to work on *Johnny Rivers At the Whisky A Go Go, Live in 3 and 2/3 4 Time* by Don Ellis, and the Beach Boys' *Wild Honey.* He also assisted Heider and Bones Howe in recording the Monterey International Pop Festival weekend in 1967.

BOBBY HART: Besides his collaborations with Tommy Boyce, Hart co-wrote Little Anthony and the Imperials' "Hurt So Bad" with Teddy Randazzo. During the Monkees' run of covering Boyce and Hart tunes, the duo carved out their own recording career in 1968 and had a hit record, "I Wonder What She's Doing Tonight." In 1975, Hart and Boyce toured with Monkees Micky Dolenz and Davy Jones.

JAN ALAN HENDERSON: An engineer, producer, and multi-instrumentalist, Henderson is also a published writer who has contributed to such periodicals as *FilmFax, American Cinematographer, Cult Movies* magazine, *Little Shop of Horrors,* and *Television Chronicles.* In the eighties, he was a founding member of Third Degree, the Haunted Garage, and Nyck Varoom's Tomb. In 2001, he formed a one-man band Guitarmageddon, which focused on movie soundtrack music.

CHRIS HILLMAN: Hillman was living with his parents in San Diego when a trip to L.A. to see the bluegrass band the Kentucky Colonels at the Ash Grove sent his life spiraling in a direction he could scarcely have imagined. He became a founding member and bassist for the Byrds, and his subsequent work with the Flying Burrito Brothers solidified his status as a pioneer in the country-rock movement. After the FBB disbanded, Hillman joined Stephen Stills's Manassas.

BONES HOWE: Dayton Burr "Bones" Howe arrived in Los Angeles with $200 in his pocket. His first job was as a recording engineer at Radio Recorders, working with Elvis Presley and Sam Cooke, before he became a staff engineer at Western Recorders, engineering all the Jan and Dean, Johnny Rivers, and Mamas and the Papas tracks for producer Lou Adler. Howe also did albums with the Turtles and Gary Lewis and the Playboys. He subsequently became a producer himself in 1967 and delivered memorable hit records by the Association and the 5th Dimension from a booth with a view. In 1968, he engineered and co-produced the *Elvis '68 Comeback Special* TV and soundtrack dates.

LORD TIM HUDSON: At the behest of B. Mitchell Reed, Who manager Pete Kameron, and actor James Coburn, Hudson came to America and landed a radio show on San Diego's KCBQ. As Lord Tim Hudson, he accompanied the Beatles on their '65 tour, before he landed at KFWB in Hollywood. Though his Channel 98 tenure was short (1965–1966), Lord Tim was a sensation with an avid SoCal following. He dove into artist representation next, managing the Seeds and other bands.

DAVE HULL: "The Hullabalooer" was hired at KRLA in Pasadena, California in 1963. He was one of the station's cheerleaders for Thee Midniters and heavily touted the Beatles and the Rolling Stones during his tenure at KRLA. To many, he was considered the fifth Beatle in Southern California and conducted over two dozen interviews with the group from 1964 to 1966.

IAN HUNTER: Born Ian Hunter Patterson, the English singer-songwriter was the lead singer of Mott the Hoople from 1969 to 1974, and headed a 2009 band reunion after a successful solo career that included the acclaimed records "Once Bitten, Twice Shy" and "Cleveland Rocks," the theme song for *The Drew Carey Show*.

ELLIOT INGBER: Ingber played guitar with the Moondogs and the Gamblers before becoming a founding member of the Mothers of Invention. After leaving the band, Ingber helped put together the Fraternity of Man. He then joined Captain Beefheart's Magic Band under the stage name "Winged Eel Fingerling." He later recorded on Little Feat's debut LP.

BILL INGLOT: A longtime audio producer and associate at Rhino Records.

MICHAEL JACKSON: After coming to America from England and holding radio stints at various stations, Jackson was asked to join KABC in 1966. He remained at the station for over thirty years, helping to develop the new arena of talk radio and parading songwriters, politicians, and actors as his in-studio guests. In 2003, Jackson was inducted into the Radio Hall of Fame.

ALAN JARDINE: A founding member of the Beach Boys, Jardine met Brian Wilson at Hawthorne High School and started a group that changed the direction of musical history.

ANDY JOHNS: A world class sound engineer and record producer, Johns's engineering credits include the debut Blind Faith effort, a handful of Led Zeppelin LPs, and Mott the Hoople's Brain Capers. His name can be found on the Rolling Stones albums *Sticky Fingers*, *Exile On Main St.*, *Goat's Head Soup*, and *It's Only Rock 'n' Roll*.

DAVY JONES: Born in Manchester, England, Jones became a member of the Monkees in 1966. In 1975, he joined the Dolenz, Jones, Boyce and Hart group. A popular entertainer, Jones died in February 2012 after completing a Monkees' forty-fifth anniversary tour.

LONNIE JORDAN: A vocalist and multi-instrumentalist, Jordan is a founding member of War.

HOWARD KAYLAN: Kaylan's first instrumental band, the Crossfires, evolved into the Turtles, for which Kaylan assumed lead vocalist duties. After recording a plethora of hit singles, Kaylan left the group with Turtles bandmate Mark Volman to become core members of Frank Zappa's Mothers of Invention, as the much respected duo Flo and Eddie. After their stint with Zappa, Kaylan and Volman went off on their own, now billed as the Phlorescent Leech and Eddie.

JIM KELTNER: After playing jazz with Albert Stinson, Gabor Zsabo, and other legends, Keltner joined Gary Lewis and the Playboys after their "This Diamond Ring" hit single. He then went on to record with the likes of Delaney, Bonnie and Friends, Leon Russell, and Dave Mason, and did session work with John Lennon, Ringo Starr, George Harrison, Steely Dan, Randy Newman, Bob Dylan, Elvis Costello, Warren Zevon, Willy De Ville, and Carly Simon. He toured with Dylan and Starr's All-Star Band, and was the drummer on the two albums by the Traveling Wilburys, playing under the pseudonym Buster Sidebury. In 2012, Keltner recorded with Dave Grohl at various sessions.

ELLIOT KENDALL: A musicologist and musician, Kendall has held executive positions at Del-Fi Records, Varèse Sarabande, and Universal Music Enterprises. He composed the score for the Showtime film *The Effects of Magic*, and was also responsible for casting the Wrecking Crew studio musicians portrayed in the ABC biopic *The Beach Boys: An American Family*. He has authored over twenty sets of liner notes, including those for Jan and Dean, Bruce Johnston, the Free Design, and the Hi-Lo's, and provided extensive session research for the Beach Boys' *The Pet Sounds Sessions* box set.

DAN KESSEL: Performed as a multi-instrumentalist and background vocalist, along with Hal Blaine and the Wrecking Crew, on records with John Lennon, Cher, Leonard Cohen, and Bob Dylan. He served as Phil Spector's production coordinator and co-produced recordings with Brian Wilson. While spearheading the original Hollywood punk rock scene, Dan also produced records with the Ramones and Blondie.

DAVID KESSEL: A production coordinator and guitarist with the Phil Spector Wall of Sound from 1973, Kessel worked on sessions with John Lennon, Leonard Cohen, Bob Dylan, Cher, and Celine Dion. Kessel is currently the president of Cave Hollywood Productions and a radio DJ, broadcasting *The Rockin' Surfer Show* as "Dave the K."

AL KOOPER: A Tin Pan Alley songwriter whose tunes have been covered by Gary Lewis, Lulu, Keely Smith, Lorraine Ellison, Carmen MacRae, and Donny Hathaway, Kooper was a member of the Blues Project and a session man on Bob Dylan's *Blonde on Blonde* after providing an organ part on Dylan's "Like a Rolling Stone" recording session. Kooper then assembled Blood, Sweat and Tears. He also produced the groundbreaking *Super Session* album, spotlighting Mike Bloomfield and Stephen Stills, before going on to record with the Rolling Stones, Taj Mahal, George Harrison, and B.B. King. Kooper later discovered Lynyrd Skynyrd and produced the band's first three albums.

ROBBY KRIEGER: After bonding with John Densmore and Ray Manzarek at the Transcendental Meditation Center in Los Angeles, Krieger joined Densmore and Manzarek to form the Doors with Ray's buddy, Jim Morrison.

KENNETH KUBERNIK: A writer mainly focused on the music and popular culture of the sixties, Kubernik has had work published in *Variety*, *The Hollywood Reporter*, the *Los Angeles Times*, and *Treats* magazine, among others. Kubernik is also the co-author of *A Perfect Haze*: *The Illustrated History of the Monterey International Pop Festival*.

ART LABOE: Born Arthur Egnoian, Laboe was the first DJ in town to play Elvis Presley records and was granted the only interview to promote Presley's debut area appearance. Laboe was a regular fixture on stage at the El Monte Legion Stadium in the late fifties and early sixties, hosting memorable shows at the venue. In 1957, he formed the Original Sound record label, which he continues to run today. Laboe was instrumental in the development and marketing of the licensed compilation album, and also copyrighted the phrase "Oldies But Goodies."

JIM LADD: A longtime fixture in the Southern California radio market and known throughout the world, Ladd began his DJ career on KNAC, soon followed by stints on KLOS and KMET. He subsequently returned to KLOS from 1985 to 1986, moved to KMPC on the AM dial from 1988 to 1989, had an audio residency at KLSX from 1991 to 1995, and finally rejoined KLOS again in 1998. Since 2012, Jim has hosted his own show on Sirius XM.

DAVID LEAF: An award-winning writer, director, and producer, Leaf is best known for his work in feature documentaries, live event specials, and a series of highly regarded music and comedy pop culture retrospectives.

JERRY LEIBER: Working with partner Mike Stoller for sixty years, Leiber helped produce the melodic and lyrical R & B, pop, and rock tunes that influenced three generations of tunesmiths, musicians, and record producers. He has been inducted into the Songwriters' Hall of Fame and the Rock and Roll Hall of Fame. He died in Los Angeles in 2011 of cardiopulmonary failure.

MALCOLM LEO: Among his various filmmaking credits, Leo is the producer, writer, and director of the one-hour Crosby, Stills and Nash television special, *Long Time Comin'*. Along with Andrew Solt, Leo also produced, wrote, and directed *This Is Elvis*, a feature film for Warner Bros.

LARRY LEVINE: Levine worked as a recording engineer at Gold Star Studios for his cousin, Stan Ross, the co-owner and founder of the company. Levine was the house engineer at the monumental facility and behind the board for sessions with Eddie Cochran, the Tijuana Brass, the Ronettes, Jewel Akens, MFQ, Phil Spector, the Righteous Brothers, Leonard Cohen, and the Ramones. He helped develop the sound that informed Spector's employment of Gold Star's echo chamber in his orchestral productions.

LITTLE WILLIE G.: An iconic figure and legendary singer and composer best known for his work fronting Thee Midniters, God's Children, and Malo, Willie is a native Angeleno and a product of the South Central and East Los Angeles music scene. He has worked with such Grammy Award-winning notables as Los Lobos, Ry Cooder, and Andraé Crouch.

DARLENE LOVE: Born Darlene Wright in South Central Los Angeles in 1941, Love was a member of the Blossoms, performing back-up singer duties for Sam Cooke, Elvis Presley, Aretha Franklin, and Frank Sinatra. She famously collaborated with Phil Spector, belting out vocals on his hit records, including "He's a Rebel" and "He's Sure the Boy I Love" by the Crystals. A sought-after session singer, Love can also be heard on the Spector-produced "Be My Baby" by the Ronettes and the Righteous Brothers' "You've Lost That Lovin' Feelin.'" In 1965 and '66, Love and the Blossoms were featured on the ABC series *Shindig!* and Presley's *'68 Comeback Special*. In 2011, Love was inducted into the Rock and Roll Hall of Fame.

MIKE LOVE: A co-founder of the Beach Boys, Love was the lead vocalist of the group and wrote many songs with Brian Wilson.

RAY MANZAREK: After transferring from law school to UCLA's film school, Manzarek met fellow film student Jim Morrison. Later on, the duo re-connected on the beach in Venice and jointly decided to form a band called the Doors.

ROBERT MARCHESE: The former manager of the Troubadour club in Hollywood, Marchese became a record producer and won a Grammy for producing the debut Richard Pryor album, recorded live at the Troubadour. He later did double duty as producer and manager of the Sheiks of Shake.

WINK MARTINDALE: Radio DJ, TV game show host, and musicologist Martindale began his career in 1956 as the host of WHBQ-TV's *Top Ten Dance Party*, which featured live performances and interviews with Elvis Presley and Roy Orbison. After relocating to the West Coast, he headlined *The Wink Martindale Dance Party* on KHJ-TV before a brief stint for Dot Records in an A&R capacity. Wink then returned to DJ work on KFWB, having been behind the microphone of both KHJ and KRLA radio outlets. Martindale has hosted nineteen TV game shows over multiple decades, including *Gambit*, *Tic-Tac-Dough*, *Shuffle*, *Trivial Pursuit*, *High Rollers*, *Debt*, *Words and Music*, and *What's This Song?*

ROGER MCGUINN: A Greenwich Village folkie bitten by the Beatle bug, McGuinn found musical salvation in the form of a Rickenbacker twelve-string and the cascading harmonies of his West Coast bandmates, the Byrds. McGuinn toured with the Limelighters, the Chad Mitchell Trio, and Bobby Darin, but it's his guitar and vocal on "Mr. Tambourine Man" that will forever endear him to generations of listeners, let alone the Rock and Roll Hall of Fame.

BRYAN MACLEAN: A former road manager for the Byrds, guitarist and songwriter MacLean joined up with Arthur Lee and Johnny Echols in the Grass Roots, soon to become Love. On their self-titled debut LP, MacLean co-wrote two numbers and solely penned and sang his inviting "Softly to Me."

MIKE MELVOIN: One of the most prolific and versatile session pianists during the golden age of Hollywood's recording studios, Melvoin could assume the styles of Wanda Landowska, Floyd Cramer, Walter Wanderly, Leon Russell, and Billy Preston. His organ can be heard on "Good Vibrations" and Sinatra's "That's Life," and his piano appears on "Then and Now" by Joe Williams, Tom Waits's "Nighthawks at the Diner," and Barbra Streisand's "Evergreen" album, among countless others. Melvoin also wrote and arranged three albums for Peggy Lee.

SERGIO MENDES: Mendes began his musical journey in Brazil as a pianist in the fifties, later playing with Antonio Carlos Jobim and recording with Herbie Mann and Cannonball Adderly before cutting a couple of LPs under the Brazil '65 moniker for the Capitol and Atlantic labels. Mendes helped pioneer a bossa nova jazz, funk and pop sound that has consequently resulted in over fifty album releases.

ELLIOT MINTZ: An internationally respected media consultant, Mintz has worked with Yoko Ono, Bob Dylan, Diana Ross, Crosby, Stills and Nash, and dozens of others. Prior to his public relations work, he hosted a radio and television show, interviewing more than two thousand people. He was the youngest talk show host in America.

BILL MUMY: An actor, musician, writer, and producer, Mumy started his career at the age of five and has worked on over four hundred television shows. As an actor, he's best known for his roles on *Lost in Space*, *Babylon 5*, and *The Twilight Zone*. As a musician and songwriter, Mumy has made twelve solo albums and is half of the novelty-rock band Barnes and Barnes.

GRAHAM NASH: While on tour in America with his band, the Hollies, Nash had a fateful encounter with David Crosby and Stephen Stills through Cass Elliot. Their informal collaboration on "You Don't Have to Cry," led to the formation of that quintessential sixties super group, Crosby, Stills and Nash. Neil Young, the poster boy for commitment issues, joined them when he felt it; and when they all felt it, some mighty great music followed.

JACK NITZSCHE: Nitzsche's collaborations with Phil Spector, Jackie DeShannon, the Rolling Stones, the Walker Brothers, and Buffalo Springfield, as well as his work on the *Performance* soundtrack, are just a handful of listings on the ultimate cool resume that is further peppered by a string of soundtrack work. In the late seventies and early eighties came production collaborations with Willy De Ville and Graham Parker. Nitzsche died in 2000, but his vast contributions to our record collections live in this century.

HARRY E. NORTHUP: An actor and poet who lives in East Hollywood, Northup has made a living as an actor for thirty-four years. He's acted in thirty-seven films, including *Mean Streets*, *Taxi Driver*, and *The Silence of the Lambs*.

ANDREW LOOG OLDHAM: Producer, recording artist, and Sirius XM DJ Oldham served as the Rolling Stones' record producer, manager, and publicist from 1963 to 1967. He is the co-writer of the Stones' "As Tears Go By."

JOE OSBORN: Originally a guitarist, Osborn switched to the bass and played in Ricky Nelson's band and on his recording activities. In 1965, Johnny Rivers nabbed Osborn for live dates and sessions. Osborn chose studio work in Hollywood as the "first-call" Fender Jazz bass player for producers Lou Adler, including Rivers's "Changes" LP and Bones Howe's 5th Dimension records.

JOHNNY OTIS: Born John Alexander Veliotes, Otis was a bandleader, songwriter, record producer, talent scout, and label executive whom many consider the "Godfather of Rhythm and Blues." He penned Etta James's first hit, "The Wallflower," in 1955 and produced Big Mama Thornton's "Hound Dog" in 1952, later made famous by Elvis Presley. A DJ on KFOX and KPFK and a television host on KTLA and KTTV, Otis was inducted into the Rock and Roll Hall of Fame in 1994. He died in 2012.

ROSEMARIE PATRONETTE: From classic rock to punk rock, Patronette has managed to witness the L.A. music scene as it unfolded, without losing her mojo. Over the past four decades, she has worked in public relations, as a fashion stylist, and as an interior designer. Patronette is currently living the dream in a rainforest on the island of Hawaii.

DON PEAKE: A guitarist who studied with Barney Kessel, Howard Roberts, and Joe Pass, Peake toured with the Everly Brothers from 1961 to 1963, headlining shows with the Beatles and the Rolling Stones. As a session musician with the famed Wrecking Crew, Peake can be heard on countless recordings produced by Lou Adler, Phil Spector, and Brian Wilson. He was also a guitarist with the Ray Charles Orchestra for over ten years.

JOHN PHILLIPS: Part poet and part drifter, Phillips was a street-savvy hustler with a portfolio. In the early sixties, he honed his songwriting craft around New York, where he encountered Denny Doherty and Cass Elliot. With the lithe ingenue Michelle Gilliam holstered at his waist, the ingredients were in place for sound that would not only dominate the charts, but also evoke a mythos worthy of Arthurian legend. Phillips was the principal songwriter and musical arranger of the Mamas and Papas, shaped into gold by producer Lou Adler. He died of heart failure in 2001.

MICHELLE PHILLIPS: Holly Michelle Gilliam met her future husband, musician and songwriter John Phillips, while he was touring with the Journeymen. The duo joined with Cass Elliot and Denny Doherty to form the group the Mamas and the Papas. Phillips is a working actress with scores of TV and movie credits. In 1998, she and the other band members were inducted into the Rock and Roll Hall of Fame.

PETER PIPER: A professional surfer and inveterate concert-goer, Piper has seen performances by Ritchie Valens, Peggy Lee, George Shearing, the Kingston Trio, Love, the Sons of Adam, the Doors, Mose Allison, and, most memorably, Jimi Hendrix in 1968 at the Hollywood Bowl.

PHIL PROCTOR: An award-winning actor, singer, writer, and producer, Proctor has been a member of the thrice-Grammy-nominated and nationally celebrated Firesign Theatre comedy group for forty-five years.

DON RANDI: After working in record distribution, Randi began to play recording sessions and was steered into Phil Spector's world by arranger Jack Nitzsche. Randi was on studio dates with Nancy Sinatra, the Beach Boys, Herb Alpert, and Frank Zappa.

B. MITCHELL REED: Born Burton Mitchel Goldberg, Reed was one of KFWB's original "Seven Swingin' Gentlemen," hosting the station's show, *The Wide Wide Weird World of BMR*. In 1967, Reed became the program director of KPPC in Pasadena. In 1968, Reed and Tom Donahue, now considered two FM radio pioneers, were supplying upstart station KMET with taped automated music while Reed also programmed the new "Underground Radio" sounds. In 1979, BMR moved to KLOS.

RUSS REGAN: Working in record distribution, Regan gave the Beach Boys their moniker and became a promotion man for Motown Records before being hired as general manager of Loma Records. He then ascended to the presidency of Uni/MCA Records, where he inked the Strawberry Alarm Clock and signed Elton John to the label for North America. Later, he brought Barry White to 20th Century Records when he was president there in 1972.

KEITH RICHARDS: Guitarist, songwriter, and co-founder of the Rolling Stones.

DAVID RITZ: An author with over two dozen books to his credit, Ritz has written biographies on Ray Charles, Marvin Gaye, Aretha Franklin, Smokey Robinson, B.B. King, Jerry Wexler, Mike Stoller, and Jerry Leiber. He also supplied the liner notes on Rick James's

compilation, *The Ultimate Collection*, and Linda Ronstadt's *The Very Best of Linda Ronstadt*.

JOHNNY RIVERS: Born John Henry Ramistella, Rivers is a rock 'n' roll singer, guitarist, songwriter, and record producer. Rivers and his record producer, Lou Adler, earned over a dozen hit singles, including "Secret Agent Man," "Poor Side of Town," and "Summer Rain."

SANDY ROBERTSON: After a decade spent championing L.A. music and interviewing everyone from Brian Wilson to Kim Fowley and plugging unjustly neglected musical talents at the legendary UK rock weekly *Sounds*, Robertson became an associate editor/film critic at *Penthouse* UK.

MARIO ROCCUZZO: After working as the manager of Wallichs Music City in the late fifties, Roccuzzo went on to write "Nervous Breakdown," recorded by Eddie Cochran in 1960 and then by Wanda Jackson with producer Jack White in 2011. Roccuzzo also supplied a song lyric printed on the back cover of Sonny and Cher's "Look at Us" album. Roccuzzo has worked as an actor for over sixty years, appearing in 250 television roles on such shows as *The Monkees* and *Baretta*.

RICK ROSAS: Affectionately known as Rick the Bass Player, Rosas has played with Joe Walsh, Dan Fogelberg, Neil Young, Buffalo Springfield, and Crosby, Stills, Nash and Young.

STAN ROSS: In the mid-fifties, Ross and Dave Gold founded Gold Star Studios, where they changed the recording landscape for the next third of a century. Ritchie Valens, Eddie Cochran, the Champs, the Righteous Brothers, Sonny and Cher, the Beach Boys, Buffalo Springfield, and Iron Butterfly all worked with Ross, who also mentored a young Phil Spector. He died in 2011.

AL SCHMITT: After working as an engineer at Radio Recorders, Schmitt joined RCA and engineered dates for Henry Mancini, Sam Cooke, Shorty Rogers, Elvis Presley, Lou Rawls, and all the Jesse Belvin bookings. He would subsequently produce Jefferson Airplane's "After Bathing at Baxter's."

RAVI SHANKAR: A sitar player from Benares, United Province, Shankar's body of work brought attention to the music and culture of India. He died in 2012.

LESTER SILL: A sales and promotion man for the Modern Records label, Sill encouraged Mike Stoller and Jerry Leiber to work with the Coasters. He went on to form Gregmark Records with Lee Hazelwood and hit with the Paris Sisters before teaming up with Phil Spector to launch Philles Records with the Crystals. At Colgems Records, he guided the recording activities of the Monkees.

KIRK SILSBEE: With a publishing career of over forty years under his belt, arts journalist Silsbee can be read most consistently in the *Los*

Angeles Times, *Downbeat*, and the *Jewish Journal*.

P. F. SLOAN: Before he turned fourteen, Sloan, a budding songwriter, landed a contract with Aladdin Records. He teamed up with Fairfax High School classmate Steve Lipkin (Steve Barri); together, they wrote a hit single for Round Robin, "Kick that Little Foot, Sally Ann." The Sloan and Barri songwriting partnership would go on to craft "Eve of Destruction" for Barry McGuire, "Secret Agent Man" by Johnny Rivers, and "Where Were You When I Needed You" by the Grass Roots.

ANDREW SOLT: A producer, director, writer, and documentary filmmaker, Solt has worked on *This Is Elvis* and *Imagine: John Lennon*, and owns the library of *The Ed Sullivan Show*.

PHIL SPECTOR: A record producer, songwriter, and label owner, Harvey Phillip Spector started out as a member of the Teddy Bears before embarking on a production career that yielded over two dozen Top 40 hits from 1960 to 1965. Spector worked with the Ronettes, the Crystals, the Righteous Brothers, the Beatles, and John Lennon. Spector and George Harrison are the producers of the Grammy-winning Concert for Bangladesh. In 1989, Spector was inducted into the Rock and Roll Hall of Fame in the non-performer category.

DON STEELE: "The Real Don Steele" became one of the most popular DJs in Boss Angeles from 1965 to 1987. He died in 1997.

ROGER STEFFENS: The co-host of L.A.'s most popular non-commercial radio show in the eighties, *Reggae Beat*, Steffens has written six books about Bob Marley and was an opening act for the Wailers' winter 2013 tour.

GARY STEWART: After a long run of jobs in sales, business affairs, artist picking, and record collecting at Rhino Records, Stewart became vice president of the company. He then went on to work in catalog and repertoire development at iTunes.

MIKE STOLLER: One half of a dynamic team with Jerry Leiber, pianist, songwriter, and record producer Stoller penned such monster hits as "Hound Dog" for Big Mama Thornton, later adapted by Elvis Presley.

MEL STUART: Stuart was the director and producer of dozens of documentaries, among them *Love from A to Z with Liza Minelli and Charles Aznavour* and the epochal *Wattstax* music documentary. He won four Emmy Awards and a Peabody Award, and also earned an Oscar nomination. He also served as the president of the International Documentary Association for a two year period. Stuart died in Los Angeles in 2012.

LARRY TAYLOR: Larry "The Mole" Taylor has expanded the blues-buying public for over half a century. A principal player in Canned Heat, Taylor has played with the Monkees, the Ventures, Tom Waits, John

Mayall, Harvey Mandel, Sunnyland Slim, Albert King, Shakey Jake Harris, Leo Kottke, and Don "Sugarcane" Harris in Pure Food and Drug Act.

RUSS TITELMAN: A former staff writer for Screen Gems-Columbia Music, Titelman is a three-time Grammy winner who co-wrote songs covered by the Hollies and the Monkees and produced Little Feat's debut LP.

PETE TOWNSHEND: Guitarist, vocalist, and principal songwriter for the Who.

TINA TURNER: Born Anna Mae Bullock, Turner met bandleader and multi-instrumentalist Ike Turner in 1958. The duo went on to form the Ike and Tina Turner Revue and had a number of R & B and pop chart records. In 1966, Tina sang "River Deep, Mountain High" inside the Phil Spector Wall of Sound; it was an epic performance that fell on deaf ears. Its failure to top the U.S. charts crippled Spector, but the Turners remained undaunted, continuing to tour and score hits over the years for a variety of labels.

NIK VENET: As a twenty-one-year old A&R executive for Capitol Records, Venet discovered and signed the Beach Boys. In his dazzling career, Venet went on to produce and compile three hundred albums by such artists as the Lettermen, Lou Rawls, Sam Cooke, Kim Fowley, Johnny Rivers, Glen Campbell, the Four Preps, the Stone Poneys, John Stewart, Dory Previn, and Bobby Womack.

MARK VOLMAN: A founding member and vocalist of the Turtles, Volman went on to record with Frank Zappa and the Mothers of Invention. He also contributed background harmonies for recordings by T-Rex, Bruce Springsteen, and Roger McGuinn.

TOM WALDMAN: Waldman is the author and co-author of four books, including *Land of a Thousand Dances: Chicano Rock and Roll from Southern California*. He also served as associate producer of the documentary *Chicano Rock! The Sounds of East Los Angeles*, broadcast nationally on PBS in 2008. Waldman is currently the director of media and communications for the Los Angeles Unified School District.

JOHN WARE: Ware has played drums for and recorded with Ed Sanders, Jesse Ed Davis, the West Coast Pop Art Experimental Band, Buck Owens, Chris Darrow and the Corvettes, George Jones, and the First National Band led by Michael Nesmith. He held a two-year stint with Linda Ronstadt, and spent over a decade touring and recording with Emmylou Harris and the Hot Band.

CHARLIE WATTS: The drummer of the Rolling Stones, who was also an avid supporter of jazz and the ongoing legacy of Charlie "Bird" Parker.

JIMMY WEBB: A member of the National Academy of Popular Music Songwriter's Hall of Fame, the Nashville Songwriter's Hall of Fame, and the Oklahoma Hall of Fame, Webb's has had his songs recorded by Johnny Rivers, Richard Harris, Glen Campbell, the 5th Dimension, Art Garfunkel, and Linda Ronstadt.

GUY WEBSTER: A California-based photographer known for his memorable musical images of the Mamas and the Papas, the Doors, Simon and Garfunkel, the Beach Boys, Tim Buckley, Judy Collins, the Byrds, Nico, Captain Beefheart, Lee Michaels, and Herb Alpert.

JULIUS WECHTER: A vibes, marimba, and percussion player, Wechter cut his teeth with the Martin Denny group, appeared on the Tijuana Brass's "The Lonely Bull" before composing "Spanish Flea" for Herb Alpert. Session gigs with Phil Spector, Sonny and Cher, and Brian Wilson set the stage for him to lead the Baja Marimba Band in 1964.

DANIEL WEIZMANN: A fiction and humor writer, Weizmann has had work published in the *L.A. Weekly*, *California* magazine, the *Jewish Journal*, *Buzz*, the *L.A. Reader*, and several anthologies.

JERRY WEXLER: As a writer and editor at *Billboard* magazine, Wexler birthed the term "rhythm and blues." He went on to become a partner at Atlantic Records, where he produced Ruth Brown, Ray Charles, the Drifters, Aretha Franklin, Wilson Pickett, and Dusty Springfield for the label, and also worked with Otis Redding. In 1968, he and Ahmet Ertegun signed Led Zeppelin to Atlantic. Wexler also produced Bob Dylan's "Slow Train Coming" at Warner Bros.

IAN WHITCOMB: Born in Surrey, England, Whitcomb hit the American Top 10 charts in 1965 with "You Turn Me On." Since then, he's released a slew of records and books, performed globally, and served as a KROQ DJ in Los Angeles. Whitcomb was also the original host of the rock television program *The Old Grey Whistle Test* in Britain.

BRIAN WILSON: As chief songwriter and producer of the Beach Boys, Wilson garnered more than two dozen Top 40 chart successes. In 1988, the group was inducted into the Rock and Roll Hall of Fame.

DON WILSON: Guitarists Wilson and Bob Bogle formed the Ventures in 1958. After their first hit in 1960, "Walk, Don't Run," the group became the best-selling instrumental rock band in history, with sales over the 100 million mark.

BOBBY WOMACK: A musical warrior who has navigated the treacherous road of the entertainment business, Womack has written and recorded dozens of songs, many of which became R & B hits. As the lead vocalist of the Valentinos, Womack wrote "It's All Over Now," later recorded by the Rolling Stones. He backed Sam Cooke on numerous sessions and toured with him as a member of the Soul Stirrers. Womack's world has spanned a repertoire of penned tunes that are the connective tissue of doo-wop, R & B, soul, gospel, country, jazz, and rock. He was inducted into the Rock and Roll Hall of Fame in 2009.

JOHN WOOD: A pianist who has recorded fifteen solo albums and the son of Dot Records founder Randy Wood, John is the creator of the "Drum Machines Have No Soul" bumper sticker and president of the Society for the Rehumanization of American Music.

BILL WYMAN: In 1962, Wyman answered an ad in a British pop weekly trade publication soliciting bass players for a rhythm and blues outfit calling themselves "the Rollin' Stones." After arriving at the audition with not one, but two highly coveted Vox amplifiers, the group hired him on the spot. Wyman was not particularly keen on the Chicago blues style the band was exploring, but was duly impressed by their passion and decided to throw in his lot with them. It worked out.

FRANK ZAPPA: A composer, songwriter, guitarist, lyricist, recording producer, engineer, conceptualist, artist activist, touring attraction, and record label owner, Zappa played guitar in the Mothers of Invention and produced nearly sixty of the band's albums. He died in 1993.

ACKNOWLEDGMENTS

KENNETH KUBERNIK: My editorial director. The Graham Greene of the lot. Thanks for your literary efforts, text contributions and revisions, and TOC collaboration, the slicing down attempt of my initial 204,000-word document, the occasional barking and once-in-a-while verbal accolade. You readily accepted the mission and my directive for the undertaking: "We're not a jazz band—no discussion or playing of prog music anywhere around this gig." A bottle of sparkling Martinelli's apple juice and a Fanta root beer are on the way for your services.

I also really appreciate your hands-on daily involvement to pressing family concerns so I could devote as much time as possible to this labor-intensive expedition. We are fortunate and very lucky. I enjoyed our chat with John Mayall about his *Bare Wires* album at that Rolling Stones' opening night show. But, as you of all people know well, for eighteen months I've been on my own "*Crusade*."

GARY STROBL: My visual editor and photo librarian, and so much more. Okay. So it's a Chicago Cubs baseball thing. I'm Ernie Banks, so you are definitely "Sweet-Swinging" Billy Williams. You even know his batting stance. Yes, sometimes we have to play a double-header starting after midnight. Your help and energy on the assembly and production aspects of this book are enormous. The readers and the musical community, even those we have not met yet, will relish our forensic navigation. There were times when your brother, Greg, just sort of showed up in metaphysical cheerleader capacity and pushed the winning run ahead in an extra inning slugfest. That was magic instead of tragic. And your spiritual link to Davy Jones is not lost on me or anyone who loves you. Ultimate team player. The only real difference between us is my Chicago world is Muddy Waters and yours is the Buckinghams. And Gary, not to forget Paul Surratt, and Tina from the yogurt place. "You Know What I Mean" on a Turtles level.

HENRY DILTZ: There would not be a book without your photos or slide library, or at least one not nearly as potent without your generosity and licensing of images at the "Paramahansa Yogananda discount" fee. Nice to know a real hippie still roams our earth. "Harvey. It's Henry. Hey. I've got a photo of . . . " Your studio was often my sanctuary this decade. Hope you do not miss the Trader Joe's pita chips constantly devoured from your kitchen.

JEFFREY GOLDMAN AND SANTA MONICA PRESS: A Taft High product who cherishes the melodic legacy and always-influential world of Los Angeles. Thank God you didn't grow up in New York and instead listened to KHJ on a transistor radio at Will Rogers beach. Your suggestions, guidance, and vision allowed me to stretch the court past our original contract requirement. In doing so, I was able to implement more of my three-point shots in the schedule that yielded the results I think we both wanted. And mutually desired for this saga.

From the first concept presented, your requests, not rigid demands, propelled additional aspects of the music of my life to be woven further into the triangle offense installed this season. Mr. Jerry West. Scoreboard.

KATE MURRAY: Thank you for all your manuscript review and editing prowess, grammar corrections, and some sentence re-workings that make me almost want to go back to college for a graduate degree in journalism. What was most important was that the information I delivered to the page was never doubted, and was only made better by your stream of well-intentioned questions that only benefited the reality examined and displayed.

AMY INOUYE: Most grateful for your understanding of photo selections, ephemera, and written language, as well as my custom-built sidebars incorporated in and around your awe-inspiring graphic design and layout. What a pleasure it is to have someone on my team who can take the ball and visualize the hoop. Jeffrey Goldman said, "She really knows what to do. And, remember, at age ten she and a girlfriend went to the Monterey International Pop Festival." Good enough for me.

KIRK SILSBEE: I lucked out with you on my squad. The radio connected us initially from downtown L.A. to Inglewood. Then the records from our city became signals of a shared bio-regional existence. Your available research and subject-specific writing tasks helped change the way history will view the musical heritage and printed word from our hometown that is firmly housed and portrayed in this volume.

CHRIS DARROW: Yet another righteous hippie in my orbit. I am blessed. Definitely the sixth man off the bench. Who else would phone at 3:30 AM and offer his brand of career advice: "You know, I've been vibing this radio and local music book deal. You should take it. Not just because the Jeffrey guy is a Pisces and from the San Fernando Valley, but also because you told me his mother is from Boyle Heights." That is so Nadine from Pasadena. As author Michael MacDonald has often stated, "All roads lead to Darrow." Believe it.

ANDREW LOOG OLDHAM: There are only a few people who are born to find and then hurl the music and recordings at us for a "Long Long While." You are one of them, prodding and steering me to the heart of the matter in emails and long distance calls, pointing to both the loyalty and betrayal that inherently exists near and within the favorite things we find and jointly chronicle. Your friendship and encouragement is deeply felt, and is also reflected in several chapters. When I needed an immediate quote for a passage or wanted to discuss the impact of the Rolling Stones on the Decca or London labels, Liberty Records, Eddie Cochran, or the Sunset Strip we both frequented, you were always accessible and replied.

Guv'nor, many decades ago you changed everyone's radio life and record shelves by your belief in rock 'n' roll. Then there was your satellite radio show, and a slew of exceptional memoirs. "I Am Waiting" for the first student in an American high school to do a term paper on *2Stoned*.

GARY PIG GOLD: Ninth inning bull pen relief beyond belief. Like Fremont High's Andre Dawson with the Montreal Expos. Somebody got hit by the CHUM radio station meatball in Canada, and I am the recipient of your educational and passionate praise of West Coast sounds that brought several choices and voices into this print mix.

COUSIN SHEILA KAYE: Thanks for driving Kenny and I to the Seeds concert at the Valley Music Center in 1967.

MARSHALL AND HILDA KUBERNIK: Always and forever. And still hanging on Pico, near Western.

DR. JAMES CUSHING: Ken and I never knew we had a gentile third brother in our family since 2002. Now I am no longer the person my mother constantly asks, "When are you getting a haircut?" You came to the Kubernik clan with 176 Miles Davis CDs, sixteen of his LPs, and twenty-one Grant Green solo albums, while worshiping the sonic lure and lore of L.A. Your support of my writing process—championing early manuscript drafts and consequently shaking your head in glee when discovering yet another submitted and unearthed fact—was all the positive feedback I ever needed around your own hectic 2012 and 2013 school semesters. I might consider enrolling at Cal Poly San Luis Obispo so you can be my English or literature instructor. However, is there a delicatessen in this area code 805 neighborhood?

GUY WEBSTER AND LISA GIZARA: True artists who know the game and the frame. I totally appreciate your various scanned Guy photos for my science fair-like project. Some impressions first seen on Webster-shot LP covers I purchased steered me into legendary West Coast grooves in the first place.

ROSEMARIE PATRONETTE: A present to you. "Strawberry Letter 22." Always in my corner and having my back. Velvet Vibes! You trusted the idea and the subsequent impulse of my book origins when so many others initially waffled. Wyline: I just hope you aren't bummed out by the inclusion of too many white people in the action.

DANIEL WEIZMANN: Your emails and communications are like Chick Hearn describing a Lakers basketball game on AM radio. I am very proud of your continued growth as a writer and lover of all things real L.A. Who else calls from Israel and inquires, "I hope you have a bunch of Monkees, Zappa, and Bobby Womack in this thing"? Child, please. Welcome back, kid.

LONN FRIEND: Who the fuck in the world would leave this voice mail message? "I know you are editing on a Saturday night, but listen to *The Twilight Zone* radio dramas on KFWB. If it all started on KFWB, then it should end there as well. As Ram Dass says, 'Honor the incarnation.'" Lonn, it is my obligation to remain in service even while putting this jigsaw puzzle together. When your daughter, Megan, asks questions about the Doors, that's a real good thing.

ROB HILL: Dude, you've seen it all the past two years. A magazine editor with a .350 batting average who operates on instinct and brings old school into the fold, when appropriate is rare. Especially in Hollywood. Ageism is not in your dictionary or Rolodex. Dug the assignments and the Vin Scully-autographed baseball from your dad.

HARRY E. NORTHUP: You reminded me that "the last man standing gets to tell the story, and you're the last man standing." When Doughboy or Mr. Bimmel talks on- or off-screen, I listen. I could write a movie script after that one Dodger game we attended, sitting upstairs in the top deck. What a bitchin' geographical method for me to construct and finalize the chapter lineups and photo captions and organize the concluding words, all during the ninth inning of a tight pitching duel.

NANCY ROSE RETCHIN: Your nutritional and health advice, streams of pictures, girl from Palisades High School diary, and those Whole Foods gift cards in the mail were most welcome. Critter, you and Lulu are always on the leaderboard. See you around the links after the eighteenth hole is in the books, darling.

DAVID CARR: You are sorely missed in the physical world as my copy editor and way more. But every time I hear a record by the Fortunes or the Ventures, I think of you.

BOBBY WOMACK: For being Bobby Womack.

DAN KESSEL: I really enjoyed enjoyed our dialogue. I did not get any acne this time from our exchanges, coupled with the usual stress of book-birth. I am so happy you kept an archive of Barney Kessel and the B. J. Baker-related music items. They truly underscore the remarkable BK and Betty studio lives which enhanced influential and groovy audio moments that helped define the aural environment of the Southland and the world.

BOB SHERMAN: The only person who ever thought I could put two words together in Ms. Cotter's English class at Fairfax High School, and then worked with me for eighteen months during 1969–1971 at the West L.A. College Library. Robert "Cig" Sherman, witness. "You know, you collect so many records, see so many concerts, maybe somebody will let you write a music article one day. But I guess you have to know the right people to get in." Tell me about it . . .

FRANK AND ANTHEA BURTLE ORLANDO: "Too many books," but really nice and smart people.

STEPHEN J. KALINICH: Of the universe and planet awareness. As we all should be.

KIM FOWLEY: So cool you schlepped out the scrapbooks and choice items to view and then land in the permanent furniture. A real yenta with a photographic memory.

S. TI MUNTARBHORN: Buddhist teacher and music lover. They certainly didn't make women or guitarists like you at my college—or I wasn't ready then for the lessons.

ROY TRAKIN: The way your ball club is going, we'll both end up in the Midget Mets again. Props to you for hiring me for some long form Q-and-A writing jobs in the nineties.

DR. DAVID B. WOLFE: A nice feeling to know that you and your mother Edith are still with me "fifty years on." "Keep writing deeper. Just pretend you're back in Culver City, and no one is looking."

BONES HOWE: For your phone calls, full anecdotal and technical recall. L.A. is indeed where the future really began.

DAVID KESSEL: I'm Engineer Bill on this trip, and you're one of the kids munching on DiMaggio carrots. Drink your glass of milk and send me the Gold Star studio paragraph by email this week, or I will tell Sheriff John and Skipper Frank you are delinquent.

RODNEY BINGENHEIMER: I was so embedded in the fifties and sixties era for this book's creation and penetration, always residing in that powerful time period. Your weekly KROQ radio show of current-century playlists was a respite from the world I happily explored. "You're staying home all weekend to write? Even after that English chick with bangs phoned you on her land line? Man, then it better be a totally happening book." It is.

JUSTIN PIERCE: Now that was the way to see a Rolling Stones concert. Once in a while, the good guys win.

To: Jim Keltner and Charlie Watts, and the memory of Freddie Gruber and Stan Levey.

ORAL HISTORY CREDITS

I conducted over two hundred interviews for this book over thirty-eight years, and transcribed them all. Along the way, I would like to cite numerous people and periodicals, including *Goldmine*, *MOJO*, *HITS*, the defunct *KFWB/98 Hitline*, and *Melody Maker*, that were sources of data utilized for research that informed the documentation.

Lee Joseph and Dionysus/Bacchus Archives Presents "The East Side Sound 1959–1968" for the usage of their Eddie Davis interview excerpts. Booklet permission.

Jimmy Webb and Burt Bacharach quotations from their appearances at the Herb Alpert UCLA School of Music with professor David Leaf in his landmark course, Songwriters on Songwriting: Killer Hooks, Essential Songs and Songwriters of the Rock Era.

For the "Circus Boyz" chapter, quotes were provided by Gary Strobl in coordination with Jim Monaghan, who interviewed Micky Dolenz, and Paris Stachtiaris, who interviewed Tommy Boyce and Bobby Hart.

Gary Strobl interviewed Davy Jones, Hank Cicalo, Lester Sill, and Mario Roccuzzo from his archive licensed for print exhibition.

Thanks to Alan Watts for his subject-specific Frank Zappa 1965–1966 research and words provided.

The Dave Hull interview was arranged by Bill Hayes and Jennifer Thomas, authors of *Hullabaloo!: The Life and (Mis)Adventures of L.A. Radio Legend Dave Hull*.

The Al De Lory, Mike Melvoin, and Hal Blaine quotes, as well as one of the Larry Levine quotes, are courtesy of David Leaf and *The Making of Pet Sounds*.

The Johnny Otis narrative was provided by Ian Whitcomb, who supplied me with his 1987 documentary film for the BBC on the history of rhythm and blues in Los Angeles, for the series *Repercussions: A Celebration of African-American Music—Legends of Rhythm and Blues*.

The Frank Zappa to Les Carter interview was heard on KPPC-FM on November, 28, 1968.

Quotes from B. Mitchell Reed and one of the Elliot Mintz's responses were taken from Jim Ladd's *History of FM Radio* series.

Lord Tim Hudson interview courtesy of Kirk Silsbee, July 8, 2009.

The Lonnie Jordan paragraph quote was culled from the December 23, 2010, issue of *Orange County Weekly* in an interview conducted by Gabriel San Roman.

Joe Osborn interview courtesy of Chris Campion.

The Mel Stuart citation is from a *Goldmine* article written by me.

Material utilized from Jack Nitzsche, Marshall Chess, Keith Richards, Merry Clayton, Bill Wyman, Andrew Loog Oldham, Al

Schmitt, and Andy Johns was previously published in *Goldmine* and *Discoveries*, as well as archives owned by Harvey Kubernik.

Select quotes by Phil Spector, John Phillips, Lou Adler, Julius Wechter, and Sergio Mendes are from the memorable and inspirational 1969 KRLA radio series, John Gilliland's *Pop Chronicles*.

The Lou Adler interviews were conducted by Harvey Kubernik, with additional attribution to Andrew Loog Oldham. The *Underground Garage* interview with Lou Adler was conducted in a June 2009 broadcast. Harvey Kubernik to Barney Hoskyns correspondence regarding Sam Cooke. Additional Lou Adler quotes taken from an interview on KLOS's *The Mark & Brian Show*.

Herb Alpert quotes from a 1966 aircheck with Jim Ameche on WHN-AM 1050, with Herb Alpert and the Tijuana Brass. Alpert bio information from www.herbalpert.com.

Keith Richards mini-paragraph on Don Peake from the now-defunct *Melody Maker*, 1963, and exhibited in 2013 on www.donpeakemusic.com.

Berry Gordy Jr. paragraph entry from an interview with Harvey Kubernik published in *HITS*, *Goldmine*, and *BAM*.

Richard Carpenter sidebar is from a 2012 *Daily Bruin* interview conducted by Manjot Singh and used by permission.

Respect to Art Kunkin for his images originally published in *The Los Angeles Free Press*, courtesy of www.lafreepressreunion.com.

Bryan MacLean and P. F. Sloan interview segments courtesy of Roger Steffens, who conducted the original interviews for his *Sound of the Sixties* radio program.

Cindy Bandula-Yates created the beautiful KPPC and XERB promotional posters for use in this book.

Thanks to Kent Crowley for the wonderful Gold Star photos you delivered.

Many record labels released and provided albums and CD reissues that aided my work during the building and remodeling stages of my own collection.

Thanks to Dionysus Records and its Bacchus Archives, as well as to Norton, Sony/Legacy, Hip-O Select, Poptones/Rev-Ola, Sundazed Music, Drag City, Audio Fidelity, MsMusic Productions, Audio Fidelity, Rhino Handmade, Shout! Factory, Ace, Del-Fi, and Now Sounds.

There were also a handful of radio stations, terrestrial and satellite, that were valuable companions during essential phases of the entire trek.

In the Southern California market, no one delivers a better Triple A radio roots-based Americana shift (since Rene Engel's *Citybilly* show last century on KPCC) than host Pat Baker on his KCSN *Tangled Roots* show, in the Sunday noon to 3:00 PM slot (www.kcsn.org).

A required stop on the dial, computer, or iPod is *Rhapsody in*

Black, hosted by Bill Gardner on Friday nights at 8:00 PM on KPFK (www.kpfk.org). I also recommend Mike Grant's *The California Music Show*, on Biggles FM (www.bigglesfm.co.uk).

Gary Schneider and his weekly *Open Mynd Excursion* is a must-hear internet radio experience (www.luxuriamusic.com). Schneider also operates www.openmyndcollectibles.com. His library radio air checks were extremely valuable in revisiting portions of my audio life from age six to twenty-one.

Steven Van Zandt of *Little Steven's Underground Garage* on Sirius XM curates his four-thousand-song digital jukebox playlist like religious scripture (www.undergroundgarage.com). Thank you, Steven, for your friendship and your constant commitment to rock 'n' roll. I have extra tickets for the Byrds at Ciro's on Sunset for you and Maureen at the box office. Go to the will call window under your true name.

Bob Say's Freakbeat Records, a retail outlet selling the sounds of yesterday and the reissue tissue product of today, was a viable addition to my preparation and is a required destination visit in Sherman Oaks, California (www.freakbeatrecords.com).

Many friends, publicists, record label folks, musicians, and talent managers provided crucial support and assistance in handcrafting this (ad)venture. I celebrate and recognize their roles in the collective journey: Izzy Chait, David Leaf, Eva Leaf, Michele Myer, Jim Kaplan, Richard Bosworth, Amanda Whiting, Universal Audio, Randy Haecker of Legacy Media Relations/Sony Music Entertainment, Grelun Landon, RCA Records, Tracey Jordan, ABKCO Music and Records, Inc., Rob Santos, Toby Silver, Sony Music Entertainment, Jason Elzy, Warner Music Group, Joanna L. Morones, Helen Ashford, Roger Armstrong, Ace Records, GNP Crescendo, Jennifer Ballantyne, Cap/EMI Records, Fran Curtis, Rogers and Cowan, Michael Jensen Communications, Carol Schofield, MsMusic Productions, Jeff Schwartz, Gary and Theresa Schneider, Josh Mills and It's Alive! Media and Management, the Los Angeles Free Press bookstore, Greg Franco and Rough Church, Howard Frank, Rick Williams, Jan Henderson, Linda Dixon, Michael MacDonald, Gore Vidal, Buddy Collette, Jackie Robinson, Coach John R. Wooden, Phil Spector, Kathe Scheyer, Sylvie Simmons, Howard Kaylan, Jon Voight, Hal Lifson, Jack Nitzsche, Dr. Cindy Summers, Dr. Robert Wolfe, Gene Aguilera, Art Aragon, Joel Lipman, Nik Venet, Tim Doherty, Holly Prado, Allen Ginsberg, Marisela Norte, Wanda Coleman, Kurt Ingham, Lanny Waggoner, John from next door, Amber and Sarah, Jim Roup, David Keeler, Karen Dusenberry, Laura Nyro, Roxanne Teti, Sherry Hendrick and Mick Vranich from Detroit, George Harrison, Marina Muhlfriedel, Nurit Wilde, Miles Ciletti, Robert Marchese, Louie Lista, Lil Paul Body and wife Nancy, Nine Antico, Suyen Mosley, Shredder, Michael Hartman, John and Randy Wood, Bruce Gold, Michael Hacker, Bobbi Marcus, Chris Hillman, Connie Hillman, Elliott Lefko, Larry Vallon, Bob Merlis, Jeff Jampol, Jim Ladd, Miss Pamela De Barres, Mark London, Kent Krowley, Phil Bunch, Graham Nash, Holly Roberts (extra garlic, please), Lauren and Jeanne, David M. Berger, Roger Steffens and his family, Bob Marley and the Wailers, Rod Serling, Bob "Deacon" Kushner, Heather and Mr. Twister, Matt King, Bruce

Gary, Dorothy and Pablo Manzarek, Laurette Taylor, Vivian, Jeremy, Gail, Fran, Neil Norman, Jill, David A. Barmack, Denny Bruce, Morley Bartnof, Elliott Kendall, Gary Stewart, Harold Sherrick, Tina Malave, Kara Wright, Kristian St. Clair, Larry Battson, Michael Simmons, Mark Nardone, Dean Dean, the Taping Machine, Scott Goddard, Steven Gaydos, Tony Funches, Andie Cox at the Grammy Museum, Stacy, Denny Tedesco and the Wrecking Crew, Lou Adler, UCLA Powell Library, Slash and Ola Hudson, Andy Johns, Chet Flippo, Robert Steven Silverstein, Ken Sharp, Bobby "Blue" Bland, Richard Matheson, Sarah El Ebiary, Linda Dixon, Craig Snyder, Mark Blake, Brian Wilson, Sandy Robertson, Kobe Bryant, Matt Barnes, Book Soup, Bryan Skryha, Richard from the Frigate, Kenny at Wallichs Music City, Dana at Moby Disc, Dave Diamond, Bryan Thomas, Robert Hilburn, Richard Kimble, Richard Cromelin, Steve Popovich, Bonnie Freeman, Waldo and the Psychedelic Supermarket in Hollywood, Eldon Taylor and Robert Roy Sherman at the Infinite Mind, Tom Gracyk and Bob Say from Freakbeat, Justin and Pam Pierce, Peter Piper, Candy and Taffy, Georgiann DiOrio, Dick Clark, O'Neil, Curtis Mayfield, Hal David, Cindy and Schelin Ireland in Hawaii, Ronald Lando at Clic Goggles, Inc. for your visual and musical services, Michael Lloyd, V.A. Hospital, Bill Mumy, Sue Michelson, Dennis Dragon, Tom Johnson, Pooch, Jeremy Gilien, Jeff Morrison, Robert Kory, Bill Sharman, Joseph McCombs, Zloz, Donald S. Revert, Tina Delgado, Randy Chenault, Dave Kephart, Ian Whitcomb Memorabilia Library, Alan Gasmer, Martin Banner, Ram Dass, Trevor Bolder, Gered Mankowitz, David "Deacon" Jones, Thunder Pigs, Mollie O'Neal, Peter Bergman, Jeff Gold at Record Mecca, Paul Williams, Jean Sievers at the Lippin Group, Peter Pasternak, Peter Stoller, Wayne Johnson, Mark Guerrero, Larry Taylor, Tower Records, Barry Smolin, Manny at Aaron's Records, Patrick Tovatt, Russ Titelman, Rafer Johnson, "To Ramona," Foothill Records, Billy Davis Jr. and Marilyn McCoo, Barbara Rochelle Friend, Mary Klauzer, Tony Dimitriades, Tom Petty, Jim Pierson, funny Jen, Anna, Tom Donahue, Moshe Weizmann, Mick Farren, Sal Castro, Sky Saxon, Steve Allen, Soupy Sales, Norman Winter, Jim and Helene Hodge-Ladd, Caroline, the Dark Horse, James Gadson, Murfield Elementary School, and Stanley and Lydia Pierce.

Television and radio relief: Sometimes I needed a rest break on the bench before every "Daily Nightly" fourth quarter: *Lakers All-Access*, *Chelsea Lately*, *GirlCode*, *The Twilight Zone*, *Alfred Hitchcock Presents*, *30 for 30*, *SportsCenter*, Vin Scully, *The Dan Patrick Show*, *Colin Cowherd*, John B. Wells hosting *Coast to Coast*, and *Roy of Hollywood* featuring Gary Null and Dave Emory.

Story Development: The Pantry, Pacific Dining Car, Manuel's Original El Tepeyac Café, Orange Julius, Andre's Italian Restaurant, Brent's Deli, Musso & Frank Grill, Paul's Kitchen, Carnation Company, the Hot Dog Show, the Gingham Dog, Man Fook Low, Barone's, the Soup Plantation, Ting Ho, Smokey Joe's on La Cienega, Martoni's, Kosher Puppy, Papa Christo, Leo's Ribs, Uncle Andre's BBQ, Flooky's, the Old World, Woody's Smorgasbord, Langer's Delicatessen-Restaurant, Hamburger Hamlet on Sunset, Dick Webster's, the Luau, Mr. Chow's, Pink's Hot Dogs, the Coffee Cup, Airport Village, Mr. Chow's, Bill White's Food for Health, El

Carmen, Ah Fong's, the La Brea Tar Pits, El Cholo, Ben Frank's, Follow Your Heart, Barney's Beanery, Ocean Way, Apple Pan, Eddie Blake's Tail o' the Pup, Pandora's Box, Clifton's, Philippe the Original, Ontra Cafeteria, the Wich Stand, the Valley Inn, the Source, Mastro's Steakhouse, Randy's Donuts, the Fifth Estate Coffee House, Denny's on Sunset, Twin Dragon, On the Thirty, Hop Li, India's Oven, Carnival Restaurant, the Good Earth, Porto's Bakery and Café, Baker's Tacos, Schwab's Drug Store, La Cabanita, Fish King, Henry's Tacos, Jerry's Deli, the Corkscrew, Aki, Nickodell, the Baked Potato, In-N-Out Burger, Johnny's Steakhouse, Johnny O's Donuts, Art's Chili Dogs, Sternberger's on Figueroa in Highland Park (where the cheeseburger was supposedly invented), Slim's Eat-A-Burger, Ernie's Taco House, North Woods Inn, Sportsmen's Lodge, the Castaways, Coffee Dan's on Vine Street, the Brown Derby, Aldo's on Hollywood Boulevard, Goldie's, John O'Groats, Starfish Sushi, Cassell's Hamburgers, La Barbera's, Wan-Q, Bob's Big Boy in Toluca Lake, the Smokehouse, Gaylord India Restaurant, the Hip Bagel, El Coyote, Farmers Market, Canter's, Dolores Restaurant and Bakery, Lance's Grill, Earlez Grille, the Copper Skillet, Tiny Naylor's, Chicken Delight, Piece O' Pizza, Du-Pars Restaurant and Bakery in Farmer's Market, Bob's Big Boy (Van Nuys Boulevard), Tick Tock Tea Room, Fish Shanty, Handy Burgers, Cupid's Hot Dogs, the Aware Inn, C.C. Brown's, Paco's Tacos Cantina, the Bengal Tiger, Duke's Tropicana Coffee Shop, Jinky's, Tail O' the Cock, H.E.L.P. Restaurant, the Samoa House, Ricksha Japanese Restaurant, the Hot Dog Show, Kelbo's, Chasen's, the Flying Saucer, Ho-Toys Chinese Restaurant, Taco Tah, Sompun on Santa Monica, O Sole Mio Pizza, the Candy Store, Will Wright's, Tracton's Exceptional Cuisine, Ships Coffee Shop, Morton's Steakhouse, Shakey's Pizza Parlor, Ole Solo Mia Pizza, Corky's, Tam O'Shanter, Joe's Little Italy, Lawry's the Prime Rib, Norm's Restaurant, Astro Burger, the Sizzler in Inglewood, Farrell's Ice Cream Parlor and Restaurant, A&W Root Beer in Culver City, Villa Capri, Paru's on Sunset and Normandie, Scot's Hamburgers, Curry's Ice Cream, the Climax Club, Harry's Open Pit BBQ, Chin Chin, Ruth's Chris Steakhouse, Veggiegrill, Bullocks Wilshire Tea Room, Gypsy Boots Health Hut, and Hollywood Ranch Market.

PHOTO CREDITS

Front cover: Henry Diltz
Back cover: Henry Diltz (top left, middle left, and bottom right); Guy Webster (top right); Bill Greensmith Collection/ Cache Agency (bottom left)
Author photo: Heather Harris
Page 3: Guy Webster
Page 6: Red Slater
Page 8: Henry Diltz
Page 9: Henry Diltz (top); Mark London (bottom)
Page 10: Jim Dawson (top); Henry Diltz (bottom)
Page 11: Neil Norman/GNP Crescendo (top left); Jim Dawson (top right); Alan Kleinfeld (bottom)
Page 12: Henry Diltz (left); Ian Whitcomb/George Sherlock (middle); Kirk Silsbee (right)
Page 13: Henry Diltz (middle, bottom left, bottom right)
Page 14: Henry Diltz (top, all); Gary Schneider/Open Mynd Collectibles (bottom, all)
Page 15: Mark London (button); Elliot Mintz (left)
Page 16: Daryl Stolper
Page 17: Harold Sherrick
Page 19: Jim Dawson (top); Kirk Silsbee (bottom)
Page 20: Jim Roup
Page 21: George Rodriguez/Cache Agency
Page 22: Kirk Silsbee
Page 23: Courtesy of Art Laboe
Page 24: Courtesy of Art Laboe
Page 25: Courtesy of Art Laboe
Page 26: Peter Stoller, Leiber & Stoller Music Publishing
Page 27: Peter Stoller, Leiber & Stoller Music Publishing
Page 28: Peter Stoller, Leiber & Stoller Music Publishing
Page 30: Peter Stoller, Leiber & Stoller Music Publishing
Page 31: Neil Norman/GNP Crescendo
Page 32: Peter Stoller, Leiber & Stoller Music Publishing
Page 34: Universal Audio
Page 36: Beth Changstrom/Chris Darrow
Page 37: Kim Fowley (all)
Page 38: Kim Fowley (top); Chris Darrow (bottom)
Page 39: Universal Audio
Page 40: Kirk Silsbee
Page 42: CEA/Cache Agency
Page 43: ABKCO Music & Records, Inc.
Page 44: Chuck Boyd Collection
Page 45: Harold Sherrick

Page 46: Carol Conners
Page 48: Consolidated Image Foundation/Cache Agency
Page 50: Pictorial Press/Cache Agency (top); Chuck Boyd Collection (bottom)
Page 51: CEA/Cache Agency
Page 52: Courtesy of the David S. and Mitzi Gold Collection
Page 53: Courtesy of the Stan and Vera Ross Collection
Page 54: Pictorial Press/Cache Agency
Page 56: Kim Fowley (all)
Page 58: Dan Kessel. Copyright Dan Kessel Productions. All rights reserved.
Page 59: Jack Nitzsche Jr.
Page 60: Jack Nitzsche Jr. (top); ©Ray Avery/CTSIMAGES (bottom)
Page 61: Jeff Allen/Cache Agency (left); Henry Diltz (middle, right)
Page 62: Ian Whitcomb/George Sherlock
Page 63: Debbie Schow (top left). Courtesy of Dan Kessel Productions Archive. All Rights Reserved; Maria Linda Martinez (top right). Copyright Dan Kessel Productions. All rights reserved; Jasper Dailey/David Leaf Productions Inc. (bottom)
Page 65: Kim Fowley (left); Jasper Dailey/David Leaf Productions Inc. (right)
Page 66: Wayne Johnson/Rockaway Records
Page 67: Wayne Johnson/Rockaway Records (all)
Page 69: Wayne Johnson/Rockaway Records (all)
Page 71: Jasper Dailey/David Leaf Productions Inc.
Page 73: Chuck Boyd Collection
Page 74: Jasper Dailey/David Leaf Productions Inc. (all)
Page 76: Carol Conners
Page 77: Chuck Boyd Collection
Page 78: Bones Howe
Page 80: George Rodriguez/Cache Agency
Page 82: Mark Guerrero
Page 83: Mark Guerrero (all)
Page 84: Guillermo Garcia
Page 86: Mark Guerrero
Page 87: Guillermo Garcia (top); Mark Guerrero (bottom left and right)
Page 88: Dave Hull Archive/Bill Hayes and Jennifer Thomas/Final Word Press

Page 89: Gene Aguilera (top); Dave Hull Archive/Bill Hayes and Jennifer Thomas/Final Word Press (bottom)

Page 90: Mickey Rooney Jr. Copyright Dan Kessel Productions. All rights reserved.

Page 93: Courtesy of Dan Kessel Productions Archive (top). All rights reserved; Tim Rooney (bottom). Copyright Dan Kessel Productions. All rights reserved.

Page 94: Courtesy of Dan Kessel Productions Archive. All rights reserved.

Page 95: Maria Linda Martinez. Copyright Dan Kessel Productions. All rights reserved.

Page 96: Gene Aguilera

Page 97: ©Ray Avery/CTSIMAGES

Page 99: ©Ray Avery/CTSIMAGES (top); Alan Kleinfeld (bottom)

Page 100: Chuck Boyd Collection

Page 101: Henry Diltz

Page 102: Craig R. Clemens (top); Mickey Rooney Jr. (bottom). Copyright Dan Kessel Productions. All rights reserved.

Page 103: Ray Randolph

Page 104: ©Ray Avery/CTSIMAGES

Page 105: Jim Roup (all)

Page 106: Guy Webster

Page 108: Gered Mankowitz

Page 109: ABKCO Music & Records, Inc.

Page 110: Gered Mankowitz

Page 111: Chuck Boyd Collection

Page 113: Dave Hull Archive/Bill Hayes and Jennifer Thomas/Final Word Press (all)

Page 114: Jim Dickson

Page 115: Jim Dickson

Page 116: Henry Diltz (top); Jim Dickson (bottom, all)

Page 117: Guy Webster (top); Jim Roup (bottom)

Page 118: Bill Mumy (top); Henry Diltz (bottom)

Page 119: Ian Whitcomb/George Sherlock

Page 120: Bill Greensmith Collection/Cache Agency

Page 121: Chuck Boyd Collection

Page 122: Courtesy of Peer Music

Page 123: ©Ray Avery/CTSIMAGES

Page 124: The Rudy Calvo Collection/Cache Agency

Page 125: Henry Diltz

Page 126: Neil Norman/GNP Crescendo

Page 128: Jim Roup

Page 129: Henry Diltz (all)

Page 131: Courtesy of Michael Jackson

Page 133: Chuck Boyd Collection

Page 134: Jasper Dailey/David Leaf Productions Inc.

Page 136: Guy Webster (top); Jasper Dailey/David Leaf Productions Inc. (bottom)

Page 137: Guy Webster

Page 138: Bones Howe (top); Guy Webster (bottom)

Page 139: Henry Diltz (all)

Page 140: Henry Diltz

Page 141: Henry Diltz (left); Chuck Boyd Collection (right)

Page 142: Henry Diltz

Page 143: Henry Diltz

Page 144: Henry Diltz

Page 145: Denny Bruce

Page 146: George Rodriguez/Cache Agency

Page 147: George Rodriguez/Cache Agency

Page 148: Harold Sherrick

Page 149: Jim Roup

Page 150: Chuck Boyd Collection

Page 151: Alice Ross/Courtesy of Paul Body

Page 152: Guy Webster

Page 156: Henry Diltz

Page 158: Henry Diltz

Page 159: Nurit Wilde (all)

Page 160: Nurit Wilde

Page 161: Nurit Wilde

Page 162: Henry Diltz

Page 163: Henry Diltz

Page 164: Henry Diltz

Page 165: Henry Diltz

Page 166: Henry Diltz (left); Jeff Gold/Record Mecca (right)

Page 167: Mark Guerrero

Page 168: Jim Dickson (top left); Gary Schneider/Open Mynd Collectibles (top right); Henry Diltz (bottom)

Page 169: Guy Webster (right); Gary Schneider/Open Mynd Collectibles (left)

Page 170: Henry Diltz

Page 171: Rick Klein

Page 172: Henry Diltz (all)

Page 173: Peter Stoller/Leiber & Stoller Music Publishing (top); Henry Diltz (bottom left, bottom right)

Page 174: Gary Strobl Archives (top); Henry Diltz (bottom)

Page 175: Henry Diltz (all)

Page 176: Henry Diltz

Page 177: Henry Diltz (top); Ray Randolph (bottom)

Page 178: Henry Diltz (top); Kirk Silsbee (bottom)

Page 179: Henry Diltz

Page 180: Henry Diltz

Page 181: Henry Diltz

Page 182: Henry Diltz

Page 183: Henry Diltz

Page 184: Henry Diltz

Page 188: Bones Howe

Page 190: Henry Diltz (all)

Page 191: George Rodriguez/Cache Agency (top); Henry Diltz (bottom)

Page 192: Dave Diamond (top); Neil Norman/GNP Crescendo (middle); Henry Diltz (bottom)

Page 194: Jim Roup

Page 195: Henry Diltz

Page 196: Sue Michelson/Soul Gallery Productions

Page 197: Henry Diltz

Page 198: Henry Diltz

Page 199: Matt King Archives

Page 200: Courtesy of Sony BMG Music Entertainment

Page 201: Kirk Silsbee

Page 202: Jim Dickson

Page 203: Jim Dickson

Page 204: Henry Diltz

Page 206: Alex Del Zoppo (top left); Henry Diltz (top right); Henry Diltz (middle); Jeff Gold/Record Mecca (bottom right)

Page 207: Henry Diltz (all)

Page 208: Henry Diltz (all)

Page 209: Chris Darrow (top left); Pat Baker Collection (top right); Chris Darrow (middle left); Heather Harris (middle right); Chris Darrow (bottom left)

Page 210: Kurt Ingham

Page 211: Kurt Ingham

Page 212: Guy Webster (top); Henry Diltz (bottom)

Page 213: Kirk Silsbee (top left); Kirk Silsbee (top right); Chris Darrow (bottom left); Kirk Silsbee (bottom right)

Page 214: Guy Webster (top); Chris Darrow (bottom)

Page 215: Pat Baker Collection

Page 216: Steve Binder

Page 217: Bob Say/Freakbeat Records

Page 218: Courtesy of Sony BMG Music Entertainment

Page 219: Dan Kessel. Copyright Dan Kessel Productions. All rights reserved.

Page 221: Henry Diltz (all)

Page 222: Heather Harris

Page 223: Guy Webster

Page 224: Andrew Solt/SOFA Entertainment

Page 225: Nurit Wilde

Page 226: Kurt Ingham (top); Neil Zlozower/Atlas Icons Agency (bottom)

Page 227: Neil Zlozower/Atlas Icons Agency (all)

Page 228: Henry Diltz

Page 229: Nurit Wilde (left); Henry Diltz (right)

Page 230: Henry Diltz (all)

Page 231: Henry Diltz (left); Nurit Wilde (right)

Page 232: S. Ti Muntarbhorn

Page 233: Guy Webster (top); Nurit Wilde (bottom)

Page 234: Henry Diltz

Page 235: Henry Diltz

Page 236: Henry Diltz

Page 237: Henry Diltz (all)

Page 238: Henry Diltz

Page 239: Henry Diltz

Page 240: Henry Diltz

Page 241: Henry Diltz

Page 242: Chris Darrow

Page 243: Nurit Wilde (top); Chris Darrow (bottom left); Steve Cahill (bottom right)

Page 245: Chris Darrow (top); Nurit Wilde (bottom)

Page 246: Henry Diltz

Page 247: Chuck Boyd Collection (top); Henry Diltz (bottom)

Page 248: Kurt Ingham

Page 249: Sue Michelson/Soul Gallery Productions

Page 250: Henry Diltz

Page 251: Kirk Silsbee

Page 252: Kurt Ingham (all)

Page 253: Courtesy of www.TGOPHOTO.com

Page 255: Henry Diltz (all)

Page 256: Neil Norman

Page 257: Henry Diltz (top); Chuck Boyd Collection (bottom)

Page 258: George Rodriguez/Cache Agency

Page 260: Henry Diltz

Page 262: Henry Diltz

Page 263: Henry Diltz

Page 264: The Rudy Calvo Collection/Cache Agency

Page 265: Mark Guerrero (all)

Page 266: CEA/Cache Agency

Page 268: Pictorial Press/Cache Agency

Page 270: John Reed/R.A. Andreas/Cache Agency

Page 272: Ray Randolph (all)

Page 274: David Kessel/Hans Mickelson

Page 275: Gary Schneider/Open Mynd Collectibles

Page 278: Henry Diltz

Page 281: John Wood/Society for the Rehumanization of American Music

Page 283: Bones Howe

Page 284: Ian Whitcomb/George Sherlock (left); Henry Diltz (right)

Page 285: Jim Roup

Page 289: Russ Regan

Page 290: Sue Cameron/Courtesy of Jackie DeShannon

Page 292: Dave Hull Archive/Bill Hayes and Jennifer Thomas/Final Word Press

Page 295: Henry Diltz (all)

Page 296: Kurt Ingham

Page 297: Henry Diltz

Page 298: Cynthia Copple Steffens/Roger Steffens Archives

Page 300: Roger Steffens Archives

INDEX

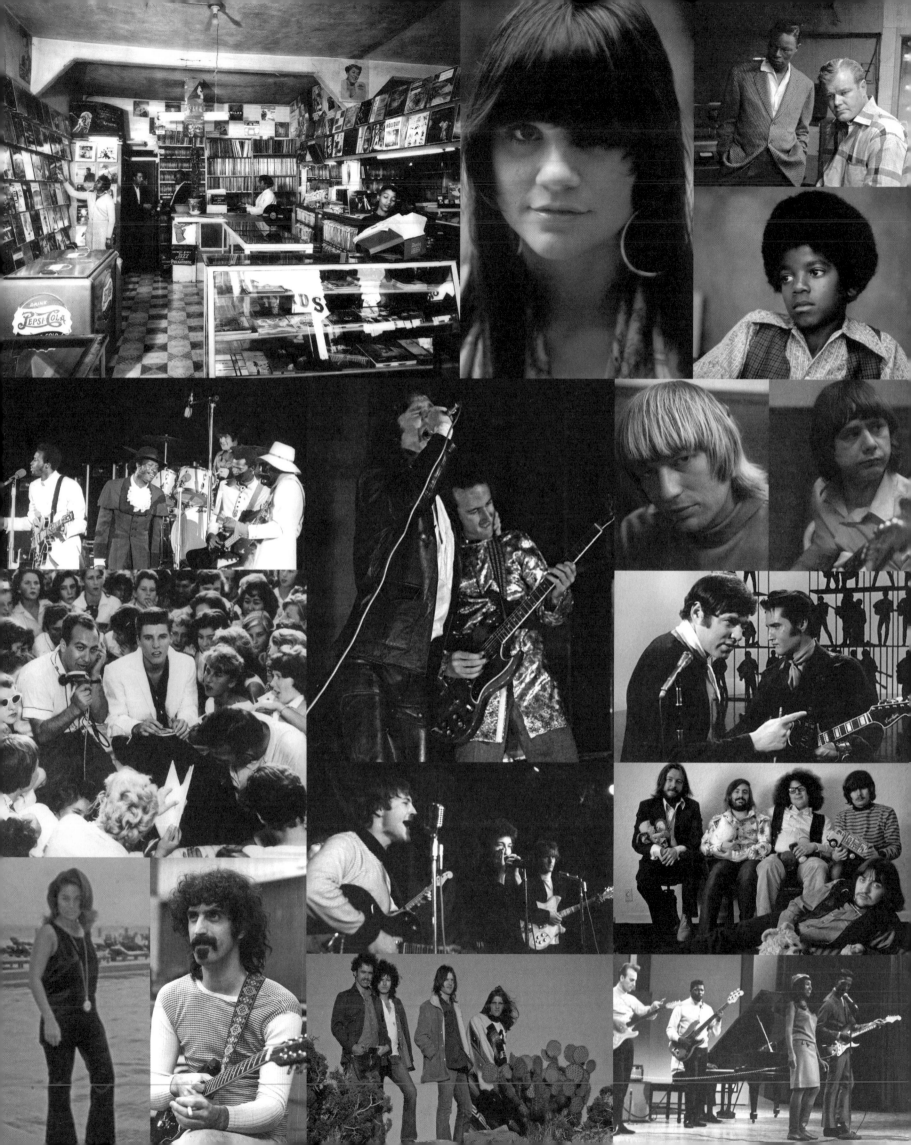